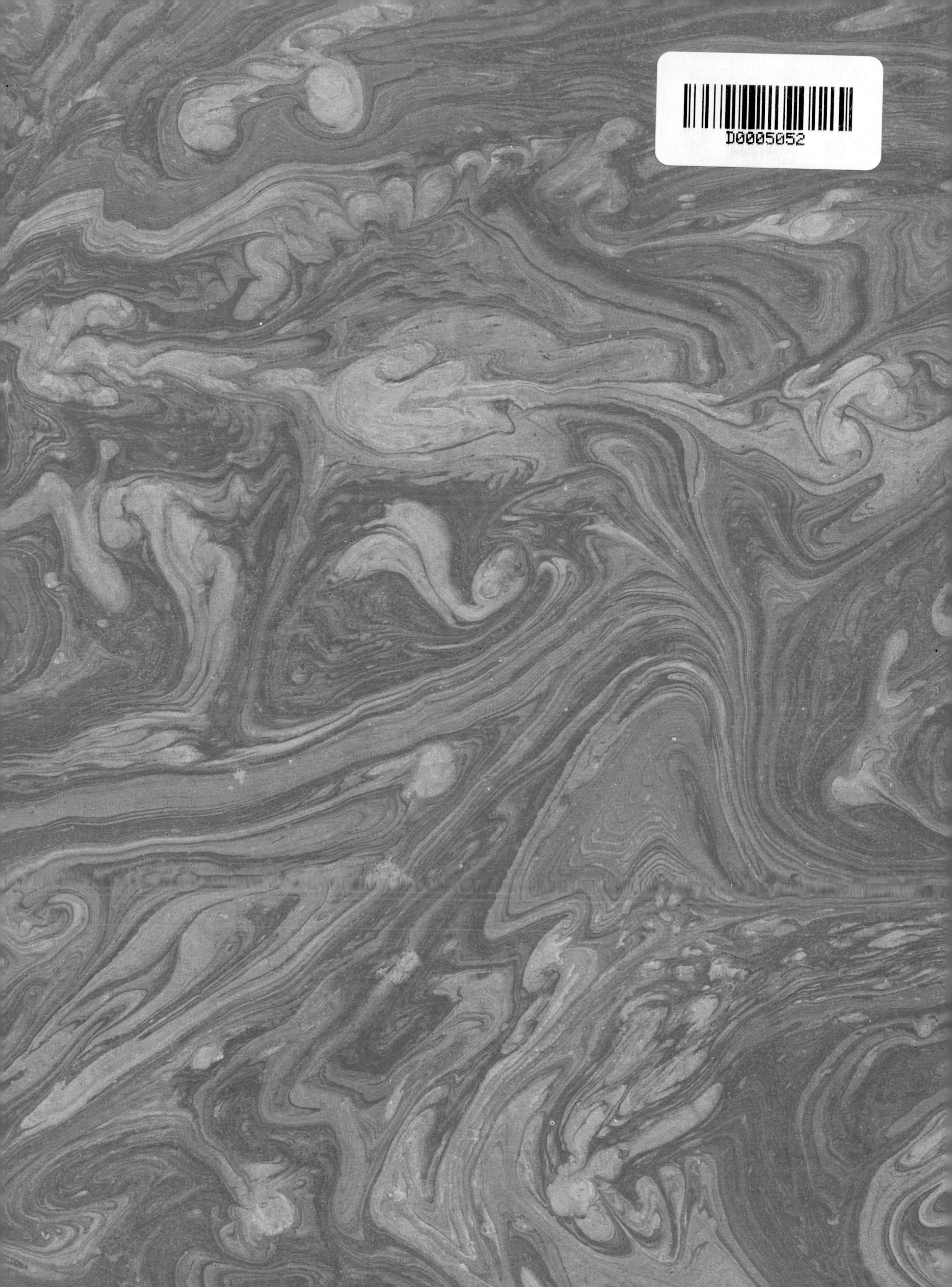
D0005052

To John,
my treasure,
on his 37th birthday!
Love,
Peggy

Treasures of the
BRITISH LIBRARY

TREASURES OF THE BRITISH LIBRARY

Compiled by

Nicolas Barker and the Curatorial Staff of The British Library

HARRY N. ABRAMS, INC., PUBLISHERS, NEW YORK

AA.C
AA.C
B

W
W
S
C
C

Designed by Roger Davies

Library of Congress Cataloging-in-Publication Data

Barker, Nicolas.
Treasures of the British Library/ Nicolas Barker. 272 p. 29 cm. Bibliography: p.
Includes index. ISBN 0-8109-1653-3 1. British Library. 2.
Libraries, National—Great Britain—Collection development. 3. Libraries,
National—Great Britain—History. 4. Library resources—England—London. I. Title
Z792.B85932B37 1989
027.541—dc19 88-176783

Published in 1989 by
Harry N. Abrams, Incorporated,
New York

A Times Mirror Company

Printed and bound in Italy

Half-title. A king. The Westminster Psalter (added drawing). English, *c*.1250.
Royal MS 2.A.XXII.

Previous page. The Reading Room in the British Library's Bloomsbury building.

This page. Girls learning the 'four virtues' through books. From *Jidō kyōkun iroha uta*, illustrated by Shimokōbe Shūsui. Kyoto, 1775.
Or.64.c.23/3.

Contents

+ Lucas uitulus 7

Incipit euangelium secundum lucam

QUONIAM QUIDEM MULTI CONATI SUNT ORDINARE NARRATIONEM

Foreword

THE BRITISH LIBRARY is not a museum, but its nucleus was, for many years and until just recently, part of a museum, indeed the major part of it. The great royal and private collections on which it was founded were preeminently made up of manuscripts and books that were old or, because of their beauty or their historical associations, interesting. In a national library which seeks to maintain a complete store of the nation's published output (as well as a comprehensive selection of the more important works produced in other countries) these stand out as the most glorious of its holdings, things to be looked at and enjoyed even by those who, for one reason or another, would not read them. Only the most grimly functional libraries do not have something of the character of a museum or treasure house.

The story told in this book is like that of some cruel and perilous expedition, an Odyssey or circumnavigation of the world in which many of the voyagers are lost or captured or allowed to desert. Through the ages dedicated lovers of books have built up magnificent accumulations only to have them scattered by maladministration, pilfering, precipitate sales, governmental indifference and delay, the ravages of fire and wartime bombing. Happily quite a number do make their way back, thanks to bequests and keen-eyed acquisitions on the part of curators.

The great thing about a book collection is that usually it is an end in itself, not just an investment, and it can indefinitely outlive its creator. Every lover of books benefits in the British Library from the collectors – of whom Cotton, the Harleys, Sloane, the less celebrated Cracherode and George III stand out – who took steps to make sure that their creations should survive them and be an enduring monument to them.

England – or Britain, since we are concerned with the original home of the English language – is above all a literary culture. Our achievement in literature surpasses both what we have done in the other arts and also the literature of any other nation. The British Library is the chief container of the products of this achievement and is thus an emblem of the nation's special cultural excellence. The wealth and variety of its holdings have never been more fully and accessibly presented to the general reader than in *Treasures of the British Library*.

LORD QUINTON
CHAIRMAN
THE BRITISH LIBRARY BOARD

Opening of St Luke's Gospel. The Lindisfarne Gospels
*c.*698
Cotton MS Nero D.IV, f.139

HEERE BIGYNNETH THE KNYGHTES TALE

JAMQUE DOMOS PATRIAS, SCITHICE POST ASPERA GENTIS PROELIA LAURIGERO, et cetera (Stat. Theb. xii. 519.)

WHILOM, AS OLDE STORIES TELLEN US,
Ther was a duc that highte Theseus;
Of Atthenes he was lord and governour,
And in his tyme swich a conquerour,
That gretter was ther noon under the sonne.
Ful many a riche contree hadde he wonne;
That with his wysdom and his chivalrye
He conquered al the regne of Femenye,
That whilom was ycleped Scithia;
And weddede the queene Ypolita,
And broghte hire hoom with hym in his contree
With muchel glorie and greet solempnytee,
And eek hir faire suster Emelye.
And thus with victorie and with melodye
Lete I this noble duc to Atthenes ryde,
And al his hoost, in armes hym bisyde.
And certes, if it nere to long to heere,
I wolde have toold yow fully the manere,
How wonnen was the regne of Femenye
By Theseus, and by his chivalrye;
And of the grete bataille for the nones
Bitwixen Atthenes and Amazones;
And how asseged was Ypolita,
The faire hardy queene of Scithia;
And of the feste that was at hir weddynge,
And of the tempest at hir hoom comynge;
But al that thyng I moot as now forbere.
I have, God woot, a large feeld to ere,
And wayke been the oxen in my plough.

Preface

UNLIKE THOSE OF a museum or gallery, the treasures of a great library are not easily defined. There are a number of reasons for this lack of focus. One is size: libraries count their contents by the thousand, where pictures and other artefacts are numbered singly. Another is their intrinsic nature: a picture turns its face towards you (though you may have to look elsewhere to penetrate its meaning), while a book remains hidden within its covers. Lastly, and most important, books, even the grandest, are only the means to an end. They gain, individually, from the company they keep: in a large library with a long history each book has an added value as part of a still greater whole. Beyond this again is the use made of books: their real existence is in what their readers make of them. The true treasure of a national library is the collective wisdom of the nation, and its history, its imaginative literature, its laws and commerce, its scientific and technical innovation.

All these considerations bear on the choice and framework that lie behind *Treasures of the British Library*. Just as the books themselves are the witnesses of a continuous cultural process (and also the tools that effected it), so the institutions and persons through whose hands the books reached their present home are part of the same process. The British Library itself is the result of a fusion of a whole series of initiatives, going back almost four centuries; its roots lie still further back. So, rather than view its treasures singly or in groups linked by common date or origin or subject matter, the reader is invited to consider these treasures not just for what they are individually, but as landmarks, among the many other books and documents with which they share space, in the history of the British national library, and, through it, in the history of the nation itself.

The treasures of the British Library today span almost three millennia, from the earliest documents of oriental civilization onwards. The oldest documents are, however, relatively recent additions to the national literary heritage, the outcome of British expansion overseas during the last two or three hundred years. Before this, antiquarians, Sir Robert Cotton in particular, were already engaged in preserving the country's own literary heritage, the manuscript treasures that stretch back to the time of St Columba and St Cuthbert. Cotton's successors, notably Robert and Edward Harley, 1st and 2nd Earls of Oxford, continued the task, while public pressure for a national repository grew. It was, however, the public spirit of one man, Sir Hans Sloane, that resolved the matter. The will that left his large and catholic collection of the works of nature and man to the nation effectively dictated terms for the creation of a British Museum that Parliament could not, and did not, ignore.

For two more centuries the history of the national library is indivisible from that of the British Museum, although elsewhere, notably at the East India Company's offices in the City of London, other initiatives led to the preservation of documents and books, oriental as well as British, a collection only recently joined to the mainstream of the national collection. The Herculean figures of the 19th century, Frederic Madden and Antonio Panizzi, built the great Departments of Manuscripts and Printed Books in the British Museum, to which was later added that of Oriental Manuscripts and Printed Books, with the specialist Map and Music Libraries and the reading rooms for State Papers and Newspapers. The growth and change of these administrative units is another element in the interaction between books and their users in more recent times.

A more significant and substantial change came with the establishment in 1973 of the British Library, created by the separation of the library departments from the British Museum, to which were added other government-funded libraries, including the Patent Office Library and the National Central Library, the nucleus of the country's public library system. Already, in the short space of 15 years, the new British Library has changed and evolved.

Opening of 'The Knight's Tale', from *The works of Geoffrey Chaucer*, ornamented with pictures designed by Edward Burne-Jones and engraved on wood by W.H. Hooper. Printed at the Kelmscott Press, Hammersmith, 1896.

The old British Museum departments and its other component parts have changed, in both structure and name (although their old names will be used here). The India Office Library and Records was added in 1982. The National Sound Archive followed in 1983. It is all part of a tradition of development and growth which can be seen stretching back a thousand years to the time of King Alfred and his Anglo-Saxon successors, and has, God willing, as long a future in a world complicated and stimulated by other forms of documentary record, in sound, in visual and in electronic form.

It only remains for the present writer to record the debt and thanks due to those who brought this book into being. It was Alexander Wilson, lately Director General of the Reference Division (now the Humanities and Social Sciences Division) of the British Library, who originally conceived the idea of a book that would describe and illustrate the treasures of the British Library as a whole. The execution of this plan in its present form is due to the present staff of the Library. Their names are too many to be recorded here – almost all the members of the curatorial staff have given generously of their knowledge and time, already fully engaged with other tasks – and the thanks of all the readers this book will reach, as well as the compiler who has put their work together, are due in large measure to them.

Three names must, however, be mentioned here. Professor T.A. Birrell, who has retired from the University of Nijmegen to devote himself to the history of the Old Royal Library (which forms the earliest part of this record), and two recently retired members of the Library's own staff, Alec Hyatt King, former Head of the Music Library, and Philip Harris, former Head of Acquisitions and the West European Branch, have all put their wide knowledge of the Library's history and contents to the benefit of an account which can only partially reflect all they know.

Thanks in equally full measure are due to the staff of the Photographic Section for the magnificent illustrations which make up a substantial – and the more vivid – part of this book, and to the Marketing and Publishing Office, who have seen it through the press with the utmost care. Finally, Roger Davies, whose abilities I have long had occasion to admire, has designed its pages with all his customary sensitivity and skill.

NICOLAS BARKER 1988

Opposite. Bust of Sir Hans Sloane.

Photograph by Lee Boltin. Reproduced by permission of the Trustees of the British Museum.

1
Sir Hans Sloane and the Foundation of the British Museum

PROPOSALS FOR THE establishment of a national library date back to the 16th century, but it is proper to begin any account of the treasures of what is now the British Library with a tribute to the man whose generosity turned these proposals into reality, Sir Hans Sloane. Born in Ireland in 1660, Sloane was to become the greatest collector of his time not only of books and manuscripts, but of pictures, prints and drawings, coins and medals, 'antiquities, viz, urns, instruments etc', seals, gems, specimens of minerals, insects, fish, shells, birds and animals, and (most of all) plants.

'I had from my youth been very much pleas'd with the study of plants, and other parts of nature, and had seen most of those kinds of curiosities, which were to be found either in the Fields, or in the Gardens or Cabinets of the Curious in these Parts'. So Sloane wrote in the Preface to his *Natural History of Jamaica* (1707). By then he was famous, famous enough already to have been invited to go with Christopher Monck, 2nd Duke of Albemarle, appointed Governor of Jamaica in 1687, as his personal physician. It was perhaps this journey, and the specimens that he brought back from the West Indies, that decided him to form a 'cabinet of curiosities'. But his interest in books went back still further. On 11 December 1696 he wrote to his friend John Locke about his 'pamphletts relating to travells, husbandry, trade and physick':

I have ventur'd to send those small books to Mr. Churchill to be sent to you that you may pick out anything you fancy & distribute the rest for making plum pyes, I confess I like to look over such tracts because most of them are used to such like purpose that deserve sometimes better usage for w[ch] reason I have turn'd over many thousands within this 10 years and have bound up many volumes.

It was thus in 1686 or earlier, when he was a young man newly returned to London from his medical studies at Orange and Montpellier, that Sloane had embarked on serious book-collecting. He may have caught the taste from his early friend (and perhaps patron) Robert Boyle, or John Evelyn who (like Sloane) frequented the Physick Garden established by the Society of Apothecaries at Chelsea, or from his grateful patient Samuel Pepys. He became a knowledgeable and professional bibliophile, as his biographer Sir Gavin de Beer makes clear:

Sloane's knowledge of books is seen in his letters to William Sherard. On 2nd September 1698 he wrote: 'you cannot err in buying any books of voyages, elogia, icones of learned men, lives or odd physick books.' Or again, to Richard Richardson, on 24th December 1702, he wrote: 'There is nothing new coming out of England or beyond sea that I know of, unless it be Strabo and Suetonius that are printing in Holland.' Similarly, to William Sherard on 5th September 1704, Sloane confided: 'The Geoponics are published at Cambridge by their press and Dr Bentley has almost finished his Horace wherein are a good many corrections as is pretended. Mr Halley talks very much of setting out Ptolemy with emendations from the copy of the Vienna MS. They are here taking pains abt the Septuagint & have gott out of the Cotton library the book of Genesis which is said to be 1400 years old to collate with the other edition.'

Sloane was extremely generous in lending the treasures of his library. For instance, Pepys wrote to him: 'I am mightly afraid you may want your Recueil Astronomique, which I have long expected back from Sir Christopher Wren, and will now send to him for, if he returns it not of himself in a few days.' A letter from Halley to Sloane begins: 'I must entreat you to putt into your Coach tomorrow Michael Maestlin's Observations of the Comet of 1580, which I want to compare with Tycho Brahe's Observations of the same.... I know you have the book, for I formerly borrowed it from you.' William Sherard wrote to Richard Richardson on 7th May 1723: 'I dined on Sunday at Sir Hans's (with Mr. Thoresby), who was very kind, and lent to me the two volumes of Dr Merret's Plants.' The correspondence of Richard Richardson has constant allusions to loans and gifts of books by Sloane. Through his friend Johann Jakob Scheuchzer, Sloane is seen lending a Welsh Bible to the Hungarian Koleseri, and the famous French philosopher Pierre Bayle had to rely on Sloane for a copy of the *Mystère des Actes des Apôtres*.

Sloane lived in Great Russell Street, occupying what is now 3 and 4 Bloomsbury Place, a stone's throw from where his collection came to rest. Among his neighbours were Sir Charles Sedley and Sir Richard Steele, his fellow doctors Dr John Radcliffe and Dr Richard Mead (also a book-collector), Sir Christopher Wren and Sir Godfrey Kneller, who painted his portrait. He attended Queen Anne's death-bed and was made a baronet by George I in 1716. He became President of the Royal College of Physicians and in 1727 succeeded Sir Isaac Newton as President of the Royal Society. As early as 1691, when Evelyn visited and described his collection, distinguished visitors came to see it. It grew rapidly: in 1702 he was bequeathed 'the most noble collection of natural and artificial curiosities, of ancient and modern coins and medals that any private person enjoys', that of William Charleton or Courten, grandson of the developer of the Barbadoes and, like Sloane, an enthusiastic botanist. He later acquired the collections of James Petiver and Christopher Merrett. He was visited by Voltaire, Linnaeus, Handel and Benjamin Franklin, who sold him 'a purse made of Stone Asbestus' made by North American Indians. In 1710 the pertinacious Zacharias von Uffenbach came and with his customary care noted what he saw:

In the afternoon Herr Campe took us to Dr Hans Sloane, who received us very politely and in a manner greatly different from that of the coxcomb Dr Woodward. He spoke to us at once in French, which, for an Englishman, is quite out of the ordinary, as they usually prefer to remain silent than to speak to a foreigner in any language other than their own, even if they are able to do so. He led us into four moderately large-sized rooms which were surrounded with filled cabinets. The tops were bookshelves arranged in three to four tiers, the cabinets below filled with natural history specimens. Here we found not only a great quantity of specimens but most of them are rare or unique. It contains the whole of the Charleton collection, and also a great many objects which were partly brought back from the West Indies by Sloane himself, and others which he continually adds at great cost. He assured me that the Venetian Ambassador had offered him £15,000 for the Collections but that he had declined the offer.

When we had seen as many of the things as time permitted, Dr Sloane invited us into another room where we sat down at a table and drank coffee, while he showed us all manner of curious books namely, various large volumes containing nothing but paintings from life of all sorts of exotic beasts, birds, herbs, flowers, shells, etc.; and a notable volume with the costumes of various nations. The paintings were done by the best artists and collected sheet by sheet from all parts of the world, often by Dr Sloane himself on his extensive travels, regardless of cost. The book with excellent paintings by Madame Merian of insects and plants was among them, but do not compare well with the illustrations. Lastly Dr Sloane showed us some manuscripts, mostly of medical interest which were of recent times. The most outstanding of these was a description of the West Indian coast, written in Portuguese, and accompanied with elegant paintings.

We were very sorry that this large and wonderful collection had to be seen in such a comparatively short time, but he had so very little leisure because of his medical practice. It is said that an hour of his time is worth a guinea. We thought, indeed, that he did us a very great honour by sparing us the time between half past two and seven o'clock. Being a much travelled man he is vastly amiable, especially to Germans and such people as have knowledge of his collections.

In 1712 Sloane had bought the Manor House in Chelsea, which he kept as a country house, adding to it in 1737 Beaufort House, once the home of Sir Thomas More, of whom Sloane once had a drawing by Holbein which seems to have disappeared. In 1742, now over 80, he decided to retire, and all his vast collection was moved from Bloomsbury to Chelsea. At the same time he sent Alexander Pope some basalt for his grotto at Twickenham, which Pope, thanking him, called 'two joints of the giant causeway'. Six years later, aged

88, he received still more distinguished visitors, the Prince and Princess of Wales, who were taken round by Cromwell Mortimer, Secretary of the Royal Society and Sloane's assistant. The *Gentleman's Magazine* gives a vivid picture of their visit and the collection, half-way between the *Wunderkammer* of an earlier age and a modern museum:

Dr Mortimer, Secretary to the Royal Society, conducted their Royal Highnesses into the room where Sir *Hans* was sitting, being antient and infirm. The Prince took a chair and sat down by the good old gentleman some time, when he expressed the great esteem and value he had for him personally, and how much the learned world was obliged to him for having collected such a vast library of curious books, and such immense treasures of the valuable and instructive productions of nature and art. Sir *Hans*'s house forms a square of above 100 feet each side, inclosing a court; and three front rooms had tables set along the middle, which were spread over with drawers fitted with all sorts of precious stones in their natural beds, or state as they are found in the earth, except the first, that contained stones formed in animals, which are so many diseases of the creature that bears them; as the most beautiful pearls, which are but warts in the shell fish; the *bezoars*, concretions in the stomach; and stones generated in the kidneys and bladder, of which man woefully knows the effects; but the earth in her bosom generates the verdant *emerald*, the purple *amethist*, the golden *topaz*, the azure *sapphire*, the crimson *garnet*, the scarlet *ruby*, the brilliant *diamond*, the glowing *opal*, and all the painted varieties that *Flora* herself might wish to be deck'd with; here the most magnificent vessels of cornelian, onyx, sardonyx and jasper, delighted the eye, and raised the mind to praise the great creator of all things.

When their Royal Highnesses had view'd one room, and went into another, the scene was shifted, for, when they returned, the same tables were covered for a second course with all sorts of *jewels*, polish'd and set after the modern fashion; or with *gems* carv'd or engraved; the stately and instructive remains of antiquity; for the third course the tables were spread with gold and *silver ores*, with the most precious and remarkable ornaments used in the *habits* of men. From Siberia to the Cape of Good Hope, from Japan to Peru; and with both ancient and modern *coins* and *medals* in gold and silver, the lasting monuments of historical facts; as those of a *Prusias* King of *Bithynia*, who, betray'd his allies; of an *Alexander*, who, mad with ambition, over-run and invaded his neighbours; of a *Caesar*, who inslaved his country to satisfy his own pride; of a *Titus*, the delight of mankind; of a Pope *Gregory* XIII, recording on a silver medal his blind zeal for *religion*, in perpetuating thereon the *massacre* of the protestants in France; as did Charles IX, the then reigning king in that country; here may be seen the coins of a *king of England*, crown'd at *Paris*; medals representing France and Spain, striving which should first pay their obeisance to Britannia; others shewing the effect of popular rage, when overmuch oppressed by their superiors, as in the case of the *De Witts* in *Holland*; the happy deliverance of *Britain*, by the arrival of King *William*; the glorious exploits of a Duke of *Marlborough*, and the happy arrival of the present illustrious royal family amongst us.

The gallery, 110 feet in length, presented a most surprising prospect; the most beautiful *corals*, *crystals*, and figured stones; the most brilliant *butterflies*, and other insects, *shells* painted with as great variety as the precious stones, and feathers of *birds* vying with gems; here the remains of the *Antediluvian* world excited the awful idea of that great catastrophe, so many evident testimonies of the truth of *Moses's* history; the variety of animals shews us the great beauty of all parts of the creation.

Then a noble vista presented itself thro' several rooms filled with books, among these many hundred volumes of dry'd plants; a room full of choice and valuable manuscripts; the noble present sent by the present *French* king to Sir *Hans*, of his collections of paintings, medals, statues, palaces, in 25 large atlas volumes; besides other things too many to mention here.

Below stairs some rooms are filled with the curious and venerable antiquities of *Egypt*, *Greece*, *Hetruria*, *Rome*, *Britain*, and even *America*; others with large animals preserved in the skin; the great saloon lined on every side with bottles filled with spirits, containing various animals. The halls are adorned with the horns of divers creatures, as the double-horn'd *Rhinoceros* of *Africa*, the fossil deer's horns from Ireland nine feet wide; and with weapons of different countries, among which it appears that the *Mayalese*, and not our most *Christian*

Depiction of Goa by P.B. de Resende, 1646.
Sloane MS 197, ff.247v–48.

> neighbours the *French*, had the honour of inventing that butcherly weapon the *bayonet*. Fifty volumes in folio would scarce suffice to contain a detail of this immense museum, consisting of above 200,000 articles.
>
> Their *Royal Highnesses* were not wanting in expressing their satisfaction and pleasure, at seeing a collection, which surpas'd all the notions or ideas they had formed from even the most favourable accounts of it. The Prince on this occasion shew'd his great reading and most happy memory; for in such a multiplicity, such a variety of the productions of nature and art; upon any thing being shewn him he had not seen before, he was ready in recollecting where he had read of it; and upon viewing the ancient and modern *medals*, he made so many judicious remarks, that he appear'd to be a perfect master of *history* and *chronology*; he express'd the great pleasure it gave him to see so magnificent a collection in *England*, esteeming it an ornament to the nation; and expressed his sentiments how much it must conduce to the benefit of learning, and how great an honour will redound to *Britain*, to have it established for publick use to the latest posterity.

So Prince Frederick, 'poor Fred, who was alive and is dead', who spent his life at loggerheads with his father, who none the less inherited connoisseurship in all the arts from his mother, Queen Caroline, and passed it on to his son, the future George III, may reasonably be claimed as the founder of the British Library. For Sloane, who was childless, had long wanted to see his collection pass into public possession. He had considered and rejected both the Royal Society and the Ashmolean Museum at Oxford (of which his friend Thomas Hearne was critical). So it was that in his will, first made in 1739 and modified by codicils in 1749 and 1751, he determined to create the institution that would best preserve what he had put together, appointing trustees to see that his purpose was achieved.

Sloane died on 11 January 1753 and on 27 January, 34 of the Trustees met. They appointed James Empson, for many years curator of the collection,

H. Hysing. Portrait of Arthur Onslow.
National Portrait Gallery London.

their secretary and requested him 'to take care of the museum – the same as he had done in Sir Hans Sloane's life time', and Lord Macclesfield agreed to present a petition to the King who 'doubted if there was money sufficient in the Exchequer'. Undaunted, the Trustees petitioned Parliament. The Chancellor of the Exchequer, Henry Pelham, took the same view as the King, but the House, inspired by the speaker, Arthur Onslow, who had long supported the cause of the national library, referred the petition to a committee of the whole House. The committee, which included several of the Trustees, debated the matter, taking note of the 'Fundamental principles from which the Trustees do not think they can in honor or conscience depart', that the collections should be preserved intact, open to 'free access' by the public and within 'the cities of London or Westminster or the suburbs thereof'.

Onslow and Pelham were determined that history should not repeat itself a third time, that the chance of establishing a national library, lost through inertia in 1700 when the Cottonian Library was given to a neglectful nation, and again in 1741 when the Harleian Library was dispersed, should not now be missed. Onslow left the chair, his place being taken by Philip Yorke, son of Lord Chancellor Hardwicke and also one of Sloane's Trustees, and addressed the Committee:

> The Speaker spoke a long while, gave history of the Cotton Library, said Dr. Castley had but about £70 a Year, spoke of his great merit that he was almost worn out thro' age. He then gave a history of removing the Cotton Library from Essex Street to Ashburnham House and the Fatal Accident which happen'd there by Fire that he was at the Fire and took what care was possible to save the MS. which Mr. Castley had prudently thrown into the Yard – that he got them removed to the New Dormitory being wanted they were removed to the Old Dormitory where they now lay. – that the public faith was pledged to erect a building proper to take care of them – that he wished to see them united with Sir Hans Sloane's Collection and also wished to see the Harleyian Collection added therto – He then mention'd that the late Major Edwards had left £7000 after the death of a Lady of 75 to build a room for the reception of the Cotton Library. that he apprehended by the aid of Parliament the £7000 might be had on pay[in]g the Lady her Annuity – that about £3000 added thereto would in his Opinion purchase the Harleyian Collection – to defray the whole expense would amount to £50,000, that he was against taking any money from the sinking fund. Therefore he recommended that the £50,000 might be raised by way of Lottery, that £400,000 at 12½% would raise the sum intended. That he was against Lotteries – but on this laudable occasion, this Debate lasted near 3 hours – after which Mr. York left the Chair being directed by the Committee that they may have leave to sit again & that it be instructed to the Committee they have power to consider of the estate and condition of the Cottonian Library. and of additions that may be made thereto.

On 6 April the Committee made its report, agreeing that the sum of £20,000 should be paid to Sloane's executors 'for the said Museum, to be kept intire, and maintained for the use and benefit of the publick'; that a 'proper Repository' should be provided for the Cottonian Library; that the bequest made in 1738 by Arthur Edwards of his library and £7000 (subject to the life interest of Mistress Elizabeth Milles) to erect a house for the Cottonian Library should be devoted to that purpose; and, finally, that the Harleian manuscripts, all that now remained undispersed of the greatest library hitherto made in England, should be purchased for £10,000.

The Act embodying these proposals received the Royal Assent on 7 June 1753. It established a body of Trustees, three Principal, the Archbishop of Canterbury, the Lord Chancellor or Lord Keeper, and the Speaker of the House of Commons, with other officers of state and representatives of the Sloane, Cotton and Harley families. They were directed to find a repository within the cities of London or Westminster, where the collections named and any additions to them 'shall remain and be preserved therein for publick use, to all posterity', with free access to 'all studious and curious persons'. A Principal Librarian was to be appointed who with the other officers and servants was forbidden to employ a deputy to do the work of his office (still a common practice then). The Act then went into considerable detail about the Public Lottery which should provide the funds to establish and endow the British Museum, as it was to be called. This remained the framework by which the foundation was governed until the British Museum Act of 1963, which altered the constitution of the Trustees and prepared the way for further change.

The lottery that followed, organised by an experienced operator, Peter Leheup, an odious character, was, despite the minute provisions of the Act, outstandingly corrupt even by 18th-century standards, so much so that it brought an end to the practice of holding parliamentary lotteries to finance public causes. It was, however, successful, and when all was settled the Trustees were left with £75,194 8*s* 2*d* with which to start work. First they visited their new charges, the Harleian, then Sloane's and finally the Cottonian Library. Then came the question of the building. Buckingham House (later sold to George III, and now Buckingham Palace) was rejected as too expensive and inconvenient. They chose instead Montagu House, built in 1686 for Ralph, then Lord Montagu and later Duke of Montagu; he had been ambassador in France, and the house was built and decorated by French artists. Once in the country between London and Westminster, it was now surrounded by newer houses, one of which Sloane had occupied, and had been empty for some time. But the structure was sound and, although the cost of renovation proved greater than expected, by the end of 1755 the house was cleaned, repaired and redecorated, the fine 17th-century painting of La Fosse, Rousseau and Monnoyer restored, and the collections installed, Sloane's on the first floor, the Harley manuscripts on the second, with a room each for the Edwards and Cotton collections and five for the Sloane residue.

Then came the first great gift. On 17 May 1757, the Trustees recorded in the minutes of their meetings that 'his Majesty had been graciously pleased to give orders . . . for a Donation to the Trustees of the British Museum of . . . his Royal Library'. The Old Royal Library had shared the sad state and neglected quarters of the Cottonian Library for half a century. For longer, plans had been canvassed for its establishment as a public library. Now, linked with the Cotton, Sloane and Harley collections, it gave the new British Museum a four-square foundation based on major historic collections of books and documents, reaching back to the Middle Ages.

The first appointments were now made. The king nominated a physician, Gowin Knight (1713–72), as Principal Librarian, with two other physicians, Matthew Maty (1718–76) and Charles Morton (1716–99) as Keepers of Printed Books and Manuscripts, who succeeded in turn to the Principal Librarianship. The first 'statutes and rules' were drafted in 1757 and after substantial revision, mainly by Lord Macclesfield, they were published in 1759. From the first, it was determined that the contents of the Museum should be open to the public at large, since, 'tho' chiefly designed for the use of learned and studious men, both natives and foreigners, in their researches into the several parts of knowledge, yet being a national establishment . . . it may be judged reasonable, that the advantages accruing from it should be rendered as general as possible'. This principle has been maintained ever since, although it was a notably enlightened gesture at the time, when (and the possibility occurred to the Trustees) the violence of mob riots was an all too present threat.

The museum was to be 'kept open . . . every day, except Saturday and Sunday in each week' (on holidays, and for a week after Easter and Whit Sunday) from nine in the morning till three in the afternoon, except in the summer, when on certain days it was to remain open from four until eight in the afternoon, for the benefit of those engaged in business. Admission was not easily obtained, none the less. Application for a ticket had to be made to the Porter, well in advance, with details of 'names, conditions and places of

The Felbrigge Psalter. Upper cover, English, 14th century.
Sloane MS 2400.

Stages in an operation to treat a fractured skull, described by Roger of Parma in his treatise on surgery. From a French medical manuscript, early 14th century.
Sloane MS 1977, f.2.

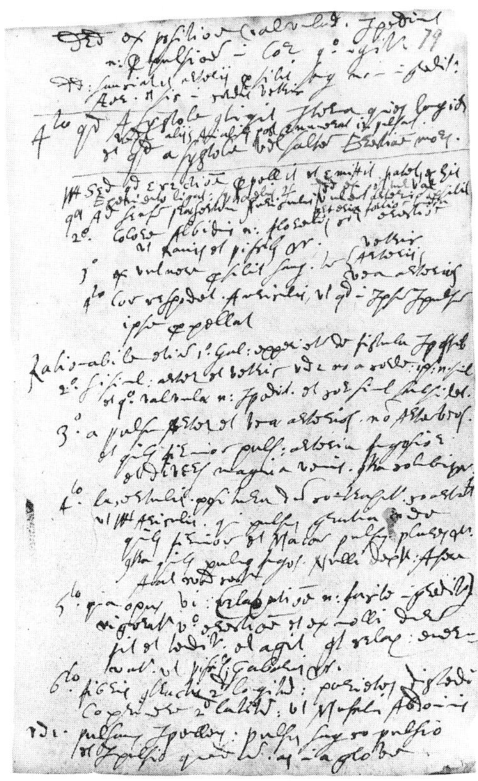

Autograph lecture notes of William Harvey, demonstrating that he had already completed his discovery of the circulation of the blood, 1616.
Sloane MS 230, f.79.

abode', and tickets were only issued after the application had been approved by the Principal Librarian. No more than ten tickets were to be issued for each hour, while parties of not more than five were conducted by one or other of the Under-Librarians or his assistant. Thus provided and fortified, and with these cautions, the British Museum opened its resources to 'studious and curious persons' on 15 January 1759.

The treasures that thus became the property of the nation were by no means unknown, and the three older collections will be considered in the next chapters. Here it remains to signal some of those that Sloane, the catalyst who had made all this possible, had himself collected. These are now not as well known as they might be, for a number of reasons. Sloane's printed books, like the rest of the 'Foundation Collections', were first maintained as a separate entity. But about 1790 Samuel Ayscough, who had become Assistant Keeper of Printed Books in 1787, re-shelved them following a 'synthetical arrangement', that is, by subject. This system, though more convenient and economic of space, destroyed the integrity of the Foundation Collections. To some degree this had already been broken by successive sales of duplicate books, in which the unfortunate principle of discarding the older in favour of the newest acquisition was adopted. Until recently, no way of distinguishing Sloane's books from the other collections existed. In 1782 the energetic Ayscough, before he joined the staff, compiled what is still the only published descriptive catalogue of Sloane's manuscripts. Adequate by the standards of its time, it is now the least satisfactory of the main catalogues, and this too has prevented Sloane's collection from being better known.

Sloane also had a strong interest in maps and cartography, proper in a man of his interests and time. Somehow, perhaps through his patron the Duke of Albemarle, he had acquired the great pictorial atlas of the west coast of India made in 1646 by Pedro Barretto de Resende, which may have reached England a generation later in response to an appeal for information about Bombay by the Committee for Plantations. This was the 'description of the West Indian Coast', that caught the attention of Zacharias von Uffenbach.

Sloane's own voyage to the West Indies must be responsible for the account of Sir William Penn's capture of Jamaica in 1654–55, the English charts of the Caribbean made in 1683–84 for the Duke, and the related charts made by the prolific cartographer William Hack. He also had Francis Fletcher's account of Drake's circumnavigation and the journals of Robert Dudley's 1594 voyage to the West Indies, and of John Jourdain's in the East Indies, as well as that of Richard Bell, gun-founder to Shah Jehan and Aurangzebe. Most important of all, he had the journal of William Dampier's South Sea voyages, the first of the series of British explorations of the Pacific.

Perhaps the best known of all his manuscripts are the lecture notes of the great anatomist William Harvey (1578–1657), the first public statement of his discovery of the circulation of the blood, scribbles whose importance Sloane realised with characteristic prescience. He was equally punctilious in preserving his own correspondence, and the letters that he received from Locke and Leibniz, both of whom admired and respected him, now adorn his collection. Another work of major historic importance is the sketches and notes on the proportions of the human body, architecture and fortification by Albrecht Dürer (1471–1528), the raw material from which his *Unterweysung der Messung* was drawn.

Besides these, which Sloane must have regarded as useful as well as historic, were books which would have been considered as of antiquarian interest in his lifetime, such as the minute early 16th-century French devotional book, used (as such books sometimes were then) as an autograph album by an early owner; it has inscriptions in it in the hands of Henry VIII and Cardinal Wolsey. Sloane's antiquarian taste is also apparent in the 13th-century English psalter that belonged in the 14th century to Sir Simon

A physician's folding calendar. English, 15th century.
Sloane MS 2250.

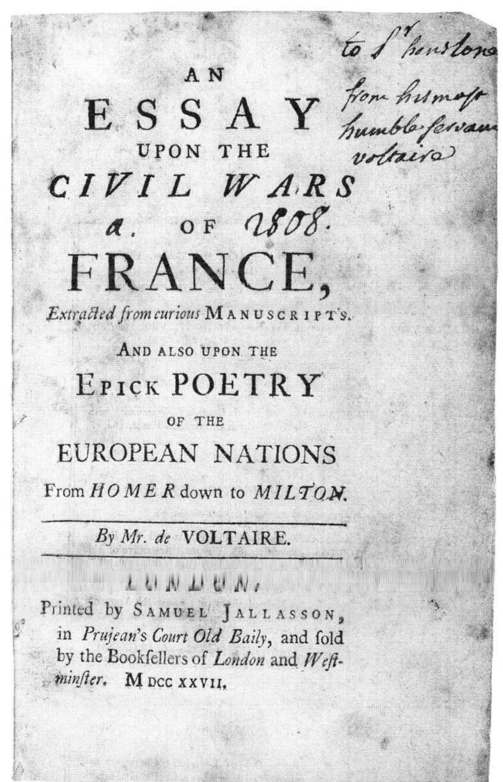
to Sr hanslone
from his most
humble servant
voltaire

AN
ESSAY
UPON THE
CIVIL WARS
OF
FRANCE,
Extracted from curious MANUSCRIPTS.
AND ALSO UPON THE
EPICK POETRY
OF THE
EUROPEAN NATIONS
From *HOMER* down to *MILTON*.

By Mr. de VOLTAIRE.

LONDON,
Printed by SAMUEL JALLASSON,
in *Prujean's Court Old Baily*, and fold
by the Bookfellers of *London* and *Weftminfter*. MDCCXXVII.

Title-page of Voltaire, *An Essay upon the Civil Wars of France*. London, 1727.
C.60.g.11.

Felbrigge and still retains two panels of a medieval embroidered binding. Another medieval manuscript, the illuminated 15th-century French legal code, had escaped from the collection of Sir Robert Cotton, to whom it was given by his friend, the French antiquary Nicolas Fabri de Peiresc.

But the most important of Sloane's medieval manuscripts are the substantial number on medicine, science, alchemy and natural history, subjects that interested him professionally, but which were less regarded then by his fellow antiquaries. Among these are the 14th-century French illuminated treatise on surgery, translated from the Latin of Roger of Parma, the original (and perhaps autograph) manuscript of one of the most popular English herbal texts, the *Agnus Castus* (so called from its first words), and illustrated herbals, such as the fine Italian medical picture book of *c.*1400. Other notable medieval manuscripts are the *Aviarium* of Hugh of Folieto, *Le Regime du Corps* by Aldobrandino of Siena, several of the much-copied John of Ardern *Fistula in ano* and a folding calendar, designed to be slung from a girdle.

Later in date are the autograph writings of John Dee and William Lilly, the most famous English astrologers of the 16th and 17th centuries, and Sir Walter Ralegh's notes on his chemical experiments. Nearer Sloane's own time are the papers of great botanists, notably those of his friend John Ray, Nehemiah Grew and Marcello Malpighi, as well as the beautiful watercolour drawings of insects by Maria Sibylla Merian, so admired by Uffenbach. Also in the collection are the works of Sloane's eminent contemporaries in the medical world, Hermann Boerhave, Reaumur, Richard Mead (an even greater book collector – Pope wrote that it was 'Books for Mead and butterflies for Sloane'), Sir Samuel Garth, and Francis Glisson's lectures at the Royal College of Physicians.

Sloane's printed books reveal the same tastes. One of his most important acquisitions was a substantial number of books (as well as manuscripts) from the library of Sir Thomas Browne (1605–82); some of these were identified by Jeremiah Finch in 1941, together with what was in fact Sloane's accession register, which could be connected with the 1711 sale catalogue of the libraries of Sir Thomas and his son, Dr Edward Browne. Among these are Browne's own copy of the Dutch translation of *Religio Medici* (1665), his Hippocrates (1625) and other books on medicine, numismatics and antiquities. The same source identified Sloane's copy of Edmund Waller's *Poems* (1664), inscribed 'William Courten 1664/5' by his old friend, whose collections were left to Sloane. Another more distinguished acquaintance is recorded by Voltaire *An Essay upon the Civil Wars of France* (1727), inscribed 'to Sr hanslone from his most humble servant Voltaire'.

The most important of Sloane's printed books are those on medicine and natural history, especially the engraved picture books of plants, animals and insects, some specially coloured for him. Among these are the copies of Maria Sibylla Merian's books on insects of which he also possessed the original drawings, and Goedart *Metamorphosis et historia naturalis insectorum*, one of the books discarded in the duplicate sales in favour of Sir Joseph Banks's copy but happily recovered at Graham Pollard's sale in 1977. Finally, and most evocative, there is Sloane's own heavily annotated copy of the results of his Jamaican expedition, *Catalogus plantarum que in insula Jamaica sponte proveniunt* (1696).

It is very much to be hoped that future research will reveal more of these books, now the principal memorial of the man whose energy, taste and imagination brought the national library into existence and gave it the character that it bears to this day. Sloane's long life and catholic tastes embraced a view of the function of collecting that changed in his lifetime from a 'cabinet of curiosities' to a body of information and material organised on scientific and historic principles; this legacy to his country is commemorated in the ever-increasing resources of the British Library and Museum which he inaugurated.

Dixit dominus do
mino meo: sede a
dextris meis
Donec ponam i

Beatus

2

Beginnings: the Old Royal Library

THE OLD ROYAL collection is of respectable, though not of extreme, antiquity', wrote the learned J.P. Gilson in his introduction to the *Catalogue of Western Manuscripts in the Old Royal and King's Collections* (1921), echoing, consciously or unconsciously, Dickens's characterisation of Sir Leicester Dedlock's family pride in *Bleak House*: 'the Dedlocks were a family as old as the hills and infinitely more respectable'.

Scholarly modesty and precision might regret that nothing survives from the royal collection of King Aethelstan's books at the court at Winchester in the 10th century, apart from the gospel book that (according to later tradition) he gave to St Augustine's, Canterbury. None the less, the Library does have King Edgar's charter for the foundation of New Minster in 966, a Psalter that may have been made for Archbishop Oswald, the Benedictional of St Aethelwold, and two other books among the Cottonian manuscripts connected with Aethelstan – the Coronation Gospels and the Aethelstan Psalter. It also has two gospel books of royal quality of the early 11th century, one, which later came to the royal library, with a contemporary record of the visit of King Cnut to Christ Church, Canterbury, and the contemporary biography, with 'presentation' portrait, of his Anglo-Saxon Queen Aethelgyfu, as well as the Tiberius Psalter, the Prayer Book of Aelfwine and 'Liber Vitae', all from the royal abbey of New Minster. Such a library can be proud of its share of the great books associated with the Anglo-Saxon monarchy that still survive today.

Among the books of possible earlier royal provenance that remained in the Old Royal Library is the grandest of all, the so-called Queen Mary's Psalter (for the story of which, see page 30). Richard II's Bible remains to testify to the new European influence on English book decoration in the late 14th century, of which the Carmelite Missal is also evidence. The astrological 'Iudicia', written *c.* 1390 at Richard's request, shows his interest in the subject, and the *Songe du Vergier* by Philippe de Mézières, who also addressed a plea for peace to Richard, may have come from Charles V of France, whose autograph note it bears. Charles V's own Coronation Service Book may have come through Henry V's brother John, Duke of Bedford, whose own famous Book of Hours was given by his wife to Henry VI. Henry VI's psalter, a present from his mother, Katherine of France, is now one of the Cotton Manuscripts. Still in the Old Royal Library is the Psalter of Henry V's other brother, Humphrey, Duke of Gloucester, whose gift of books was the foundation of the first University Library at Oxford. Another famous book which was part of the medieval royal library was the illuminated copy, probably made for Edward IV, of the poems of Charles d'Orléans, who wrote English poetry as well as French during his long imprisonment after the Battle of Agincourt in the Tower of London, the subject of the book's best-known miniature.

The real founder of the Old Royal Library in the form in which it has survived was Edward IV. Over 30 books still exist, all similar in appearance, which suggest the powerful impression made on Edward during his brief exile in Flanders by the impressive size and imposing decoration of the books commissioned by his brother-in-law, Charles the Bold, Duke of Burgundy, and Louis de Gruuthuyse, in whose house at Bruges he stayed in 1471. J.P. Gilson wrote:

> The Burgundian influence is apparent in the very narrow limits of the King's market for buying; the character of his interest in the books by the small range covered by their contents. The Ghent and Bruges illuminators evidently catered for a class that wished to be read to, rather than to read. Their productions give the impression of being bought by the pound, or rather by the hundredweight. These huge volumes are not to be handled. They are to be placed on a high desk and read aloud by a standing lector, over whose shoulder the noble master or mistress may occasionally take a glance at a miniature, without inspecting it too closely in detail; for these pictures look better at a little distance, and reproductions of them are most effective when executed on a smaller scale. The

Tower of London. Miniature of the White Tower. (Detail.) From a manuscript of the poems of Charles d'Orleans, possibly intended for King Edward IV. Flemish, late 15th century.
Royal MS 16.F.II, f.73.

Opposite. Christ's entry into Jerusalem. From Queen Mary's Psalter. English, early 14th century.
Royal MS 2.B.VII, f.233*v*.

language is almost exclusively French. As to the contents, it is equally clear that they tend to entertainment and edification rather than to study and the advancement of learning. History there is in plenty, but chiefly of the kind that is read for example of noble deeds, and shades off imperceptibly into historical romance.

History of a sort included Raoul le Fevre's *Recueil des histoires de Troie*, the first work that Caxton translated and printed, and the chronicles of Froissart and Wavrin, while sacred history was represented by the *Bible historiale*. There were Xenophon, Caesar, St Augustine's *City of God*, the English Friar Bartholomew's encyclopaedia *De proprietatibus rerum* and Boccaccio's *Decameron*, all in French translation. All these books are large and colourful, with some fine miniatures (although the lesser pictures are – not surprisingly, in view of their quantity – more commonplace).

With Edward IV's death, active royal interest in books ceased, although the lack was partially made good by New Year's gifts. Thus Petrus Carmelianus, an Italian who came to England in search of preferment about 1480, presented one of his works to the Prince of Wales, later Edward V, in 1482. He followed it in 1486 with his *Laus Angliae*, illuminated in contemporary English style, addressed to Henry VII, who made him his Latin secretary (this later escaped from the Royal Library and only returned with the bequest of Thomas Grenville's Library in 1847).

Antoine Vérard, the great French printer, publisher and bookseller, provided Henry VII with a vellum copy of one of the books printed for him, Boethius's *De consolatione philosophiae* (1494) in French. The name and style of the original dedicatee, Charles VIII of France, was carefully erased and Henry VII's substituted, with painted miniatures added, one of them showing Henry VII receiving the book. This is one of several of Vérard's books, including romances of chivalry, printed on vellum and illuminated in this style. Was the dedication copy a temptation to induce purchase, or a thank-offering for patronage received? In either event, we perhaps see the influence of the first Royal Librarian whose name is known, Quintin Poulet: in his youth he was recorded as an apprentice of the St John's Guild of Illuminators of Bruges, and may have redirected royal patronage from Flanders to France after the Peace of Brétigny. His name, in his own calligraphy, appears at the foot of the first page of another Old Royal Library book, Guillaume de Digulleville's *Pélerinage de l'âme* (1499), printed by Vérard, who certainly received payment for another of his books, the *Jardin de santé* (1501); the transaction (it cost £6) is entered in the Wardrobe Accounts.

The huge volumes of the *Chroniques de Saint Denis* were probably another present, given or commissioned by Sir Thomas Thwaytes, Treasurer of Calais, in Henry VII's time. The indefatigable Petrus Carmelianus contributed an account of the betrothal of Princess Mary to Charles of Castile in 1508, printed on vellum by Richard Pynson, while Geoffrey Chamber brought back from Italy the copy of the *Apologi* of Pandolfo Collenuccio which he had specially commissioned from the leading scribe in Rome, Ludovico degli Arrighi, and the most fashionable illuminator of the day, Attavante degli Attavanti. Quintin Poulet's successor as Royal Librarian was another Fleming, Gilles Duwes, who wrote a French grammar for Henry VIII's daughter Mary which reveals an entertaining character. He was Keeper of the King's Library at Richmond, the new palace built by Henry VII. The library there, of which a partial list made by an enterprising French visitor in 1535 (the year of Duwes's death) survives, contained Edward IV's manuscripts and some printed books. There was, however, another library in the King's Palace at Westminster (Wolsey's York Place, later Whitehall). Duwes's successor, one of the household officers, William Tyldesley, probably had charge of this under Sir Anthony Denny (1501–49), the King's remembrancer and groom of the stole, a scholar and perhaps a protégé of Thomas Cromwell whose religious views Tyldesley shared.

A page from the manuscript of Aelfric's first book of Homilies. 990.
Royal MS 7.C.XII, f.105.

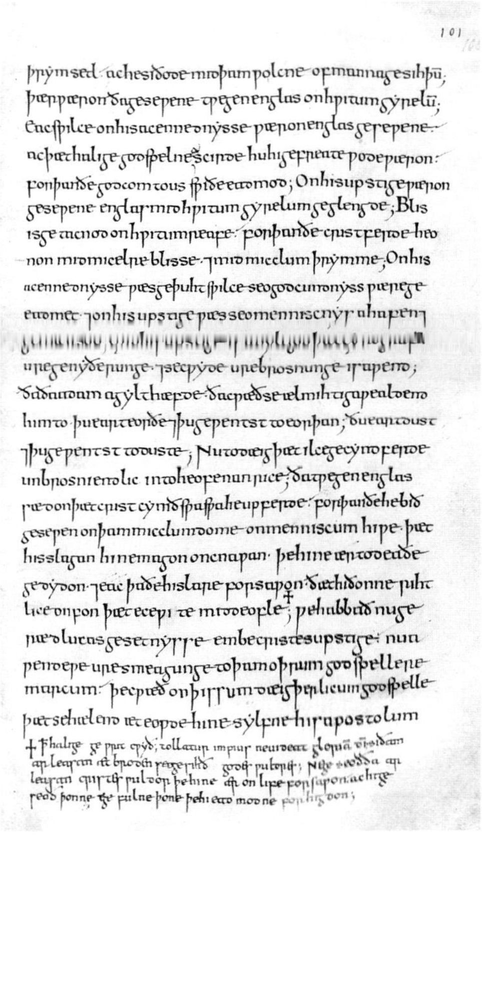

It is now that John Leland enters the scene, perhaps through Tyldesley – both were Lancashiremen, their families later related. It is through his eyes that we first see the idea of a national library growing, as it must have done in the minds of reformers, and of Thomas Cromwell and Henry VIII. It was to the King that Leland addressed in 1546 *The laboryouse journey and serche of Johan Leylande for Englandes antiquitees*, recalling that, in 1533–4,

> it pleasid yowr Highnes apon very juste considerations to encorage me, by the autorite of yowr moste gratius commission yn the xxv. yere of yowr prosperus regne, to peruse and diligently to serche al the libraries of monasteries and collegies of this yowr noble reaulme, to the intente that the monumentes of auncient writers as welle of other nations as of this yowr owne province mighte be brought owte of deadely darkenes to lyvely lighte, and to receyve like thankes of the posterite, as they hoped for at such tyme as they emploied their long and greate studies to the publique wealthe; yea and farthermore that the holy Scripture of God might bothe be sincerely taughte and lernid, al maner of superstition and craftely coloured doctrine of a rowte of the Romaine bishopes totally expellied oute of this your moste catholique reaulme.

This he had done with the set purpose of getting the books he found into the royal library, which, he wrote to Cromwell in 1536:

> would be a great profit to students, and honour to this realm; whereas now the Germans perceiving our desidiousness and negligence, do send daily young scholars hither, that spoileth them and cutteth them out of libraries returning home and putting them abroad as monuments of their own country.

When John Bale came to print *The laboryouse journey* in 1549, he was inclined to see Leland's work as too little, too late;

> Neuer had we bene offended for the losse of our lybraryes, beynge so many in nombre, and in so desolate places for the more parts, yf the chiefe monumentes and most notable workes of our excellent wryters, had been reserued. If there had bene in euery shyre of Englande, but one solempne lybrary, to the preseruacyon of these noble workes, and preferrement of good lernynges in oure posteryte, it had been yet sumwhat. Bot to destroye all without consyderacyon, is and wyll be vnto Englande for euer, a most horryble infamy amonge the graue senyours of other nacyons... A great nomber of them wych purchased those superstycyouse mansyons, reserued of those lybrarye bokes, some to serue theyr iakes, some to scoure theyre candelstyckes, and some to rubbe their bootes. Some they solde to the grossers and sope sellers, and some they sent ouer the sea to the bokebynders, not in small nombre, but at tymes whole shyppes full, to the wonderynge of the foren nacyons. Yea, the unyuersytees of thys realme, are not all clere in this detestable fact... yea, what maye bryng our realme to more shame and rebuke, than to haue it noysed abroade, that we are despysers of lernynge!

It is clear that he saw the dispersal as a tragedy that long pre-dated the Reformation (Poggio came to look for manuscripts in England early in the 15th century), but which had been heightened by the events of the last 13 years. What success Leland had can be measured, in a way, by the number of books in the inventory of the Royal Library at Westminster prepared for Denny in 1542. Of the 1450 books listed, many can be identified with books sequestered from suppressed monasteries; 500 manuscript books, plus one or two printed books, from English houses are to be found in the Old Royal Library today. Although Leland's lists for Lincolnshire marked by the King exist, it is unlikely that the choice was systematic. Some oddities – a hundred books were taken from Rochester, barely twelve from the far larger Library, much admired by Leland, at St Augustine's, Canterbury – may be explained by Leland's longing for 'but one solemn library' in every *shire*; the Royal Library was not the only repository he had in mind.

Among the treasures that came, now or later, to the Old Royal Library from older monastic libraries were the 8th/9th-century book of prayers and readings from Worcester and the 10th-century text of the homilies of Aelfric, 'the most accomplished writer of Old English prose', written in 990 at Cerne

Petri Carmeliani Brixiensis poetę Suasoria
Lętitię ad angliam pro sublatis bellis ci
uilibus et Arthuro pricipe nato epistola
Anglia post tatas clades tatas q; ruinas
Et tot cognata prelia facta manu
Post odiuz antiquum geminę de sanguię regu
Stirpis et innumeras gentis utriq; neces
Te superum rector tandem prospexit ab alto
Cum facies esset tam miseranda tibi
Vndiq; ciuili cum sanguine terra maderet
Inq; tuis populis luctus ubiq; foret
Cum genitrix natum natus fleretq; parete;
Et fratrem frater : nupta pudica uiruz
Filius et patrem fratrem quandoq; necaret
Frater ... furens iret in omne nefas

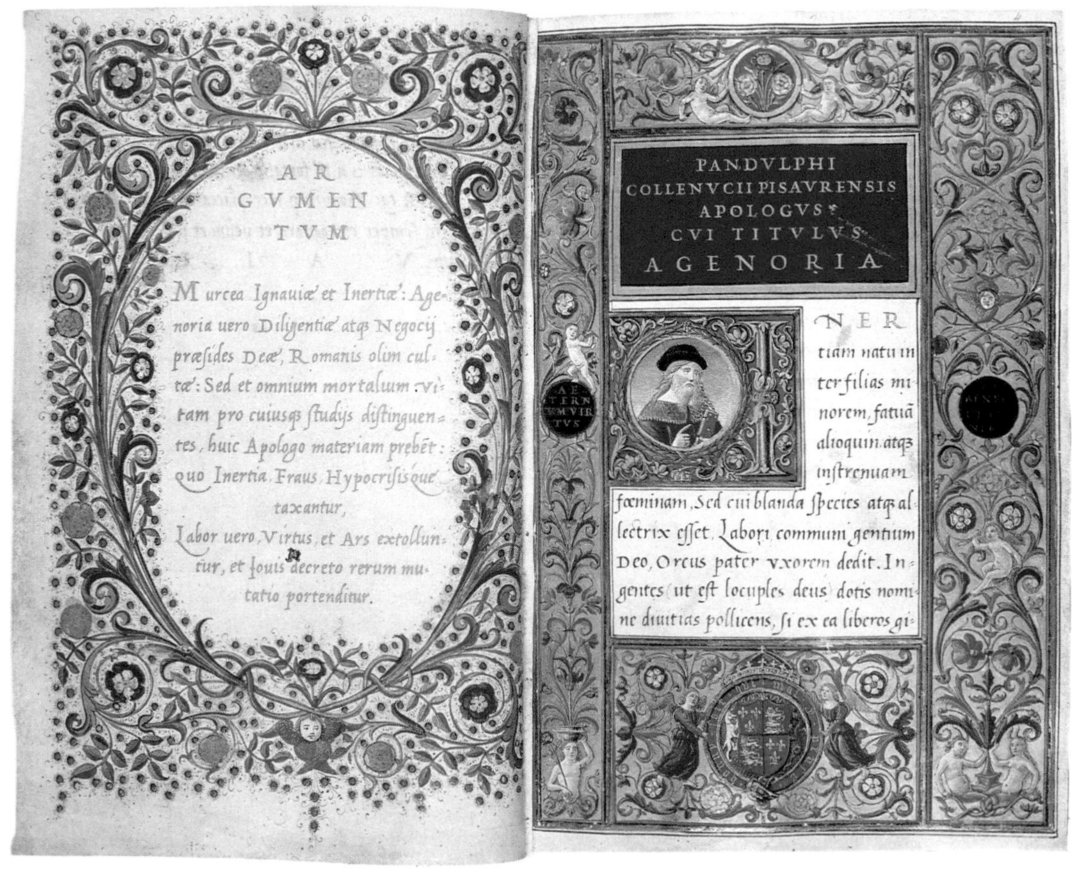

AR
GVMEN
TVM

Murcea Ignauiæ et Inertiæ: Agenoria uero Diligentiæ atq; Negocij præsides Deæ, Romanis olim cultæ: Sed et omnium mortalium vitam pro cuiusq; studijs distinguentes, huic Apologo materiam prebet: quo Inertia, Fraus, Hypocrisisque taxantur,
Labor uero, Virtus, et Ars extolluntur, et Iouis decreto rerum mutatio portenditur.

PANDVLPHI
COLLENVCII PISAVRENSIS
APOLOGVS
CVI TITVLVS
AGENORIA

INERtiam natu inter filias minorem, fatuā alioquin atq; instrenuam fœminam, Sed cui blanda species atq; allectrix esset, Labori commum gentium Deo, Orcus pater vxorem dedit. Ingentes (ut est locuples deus) dotis nomine diuitias pollicens, si ex ea liberos gi-

Matthew Paris, itinerary from London to Jerusalem. English, mid-13th century. Detail showing Acre in the Crusader Kingdom.
Royal MS 14.C.VII, f.4*v*.

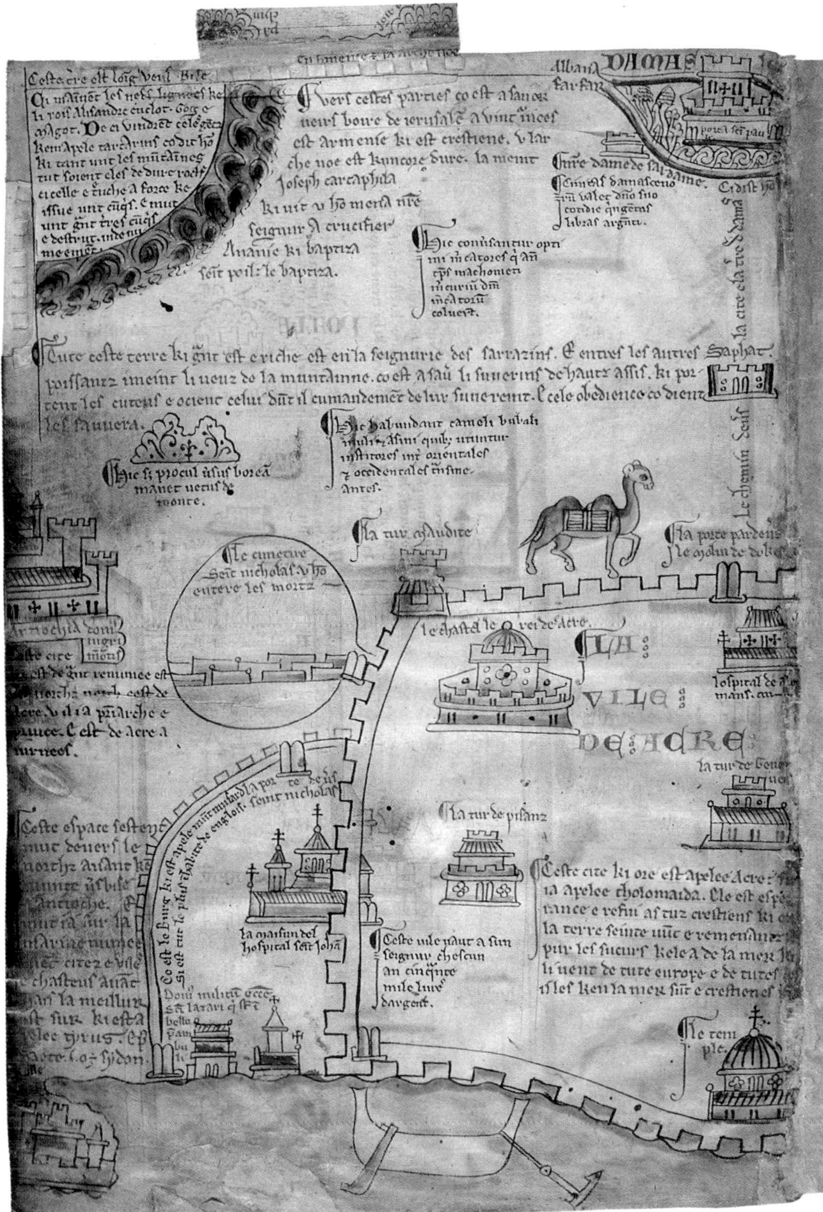

Opposite, above. Petrus Carmelianus, *Laus Angliae*, 1486. The greyhound and dragon devices belonged to Henry VII, to whom this volume was dedicated.
Add. MS 33736, V.1–2.

Abbas, and corrected by Aelfric himself; amongst the great 12th-century books were the Westminster Psalter, the Breviary and the encyclopaedia of Rabanus Maurus from St Albans, Bede's commentary on Ezra from Cirencester, St Augustine's *De Trinitate* from Rochester and the chronicle of William of Malmesbury from Margam; among 13th-century books the autograph chronicle by Matthew Paris from St Albans and the works of Ailred of Rievaulx from Christ Church, Canterbury; and, from the 14th century, the Smithfield Decretals, a repertory of canon law, written in Italy, but copiously decorated (the pictures make it an illustrated encyclopaedia of life in medieval England) for, and perhaps at, the priory of St Bartholomew's, Smithfield.

This great accession of the medieval library wealth of Britain completely changed the character of the Royal Library. It continued, more conventionally, to receive gifts. Thomas Linacre (1460–1524), Henry VIII's physician and a distinguished classical scholar, presented his edition of Galen (1519) and, later, grateful and hopeful German reformers gave their works too: Johannes Bugenhagen his translation from Melanchthon, *Instructio visitationis Saxonicae* (1538) and Heinrich Bullinger his *De scripturae sanctae auctoritate* (1538).

Neither work may have been lost on Henry VIII. He was himself a scholar and a patron of scholarship, the first reigning English sovereign to write a

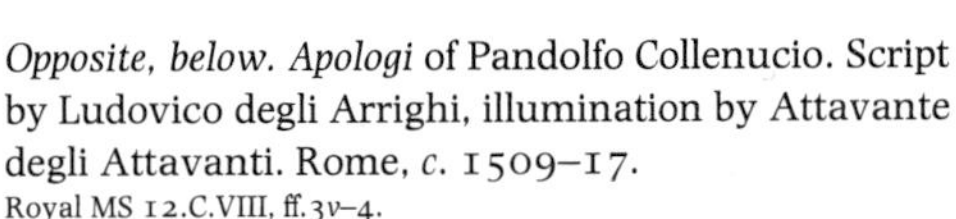

Opposite, below. Apologi of Pandolfo Collenucio. Script by Ludovico degli Arrighi, illumination by Attavante degli Attavanti. Rome, *c.* 1509–17.
Royal MS 12.C.VIII, ff.3*v*–4.

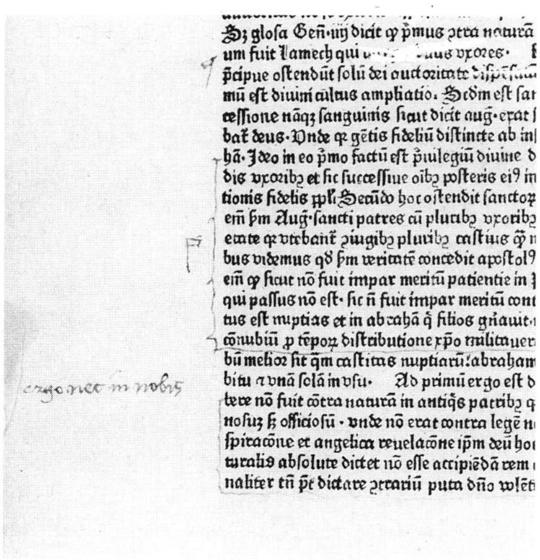

Augustinus de Ancona, *Summa de potestate ecclesiastica*, 1475. Henry VIII's copy, with his marginal annotation 'ergo nec in nobis' ('so not in our case').
IB 3131, T.10v.

book, the tract against Luther, *Assertio Septem Sacramentorum* (1521), of which the Old Royal Library copy is now in the Archbishop of Canterbury's Library at Lambeth. Many books with his signature, printed and manuscript, still survive, including the celebrated copy of Augustinus de Ancona *Summa de potestate ecclesiastica* (1475), where the author's text 'It must be said that to have several wives was not against nature among the ancients' bears Henry's note: 'So not in our case'. Other and more poignant witnesses of the King's concern are the copies, which still preserve their original bindings, of Bishop Edward Fox's *De vera differentia regiae potestatis* (1534), with the royal arms and the initials of Henry and Katherine of Aragon, and the Bible in French, printed at Antwerp in 1534, with the initials of Henry and Anne Boleyn and the inscription: 'La loye a este donne par Moyse. La grace et la verite est faicte par Iesu Christ'.

Monasteries were not the only enforced contributors to the Royal Library. Several books came from Cardinal Wolsey's library: the *Concilia generalia* (1524) bears his painted arms and Sylvester Darius's *Repetitio* of the Digest of Justinian bears a presentation inscription to Wolsey from the author. Lemaire's *Illustrations de Gaule* (1513) passed from Archdeacon William Warham to Anne's father, Sir Thomas Boleyn, and thence to the King, while Sir Thomas Elyot's *Dictionary* (1538), dedicated to the King, contains a letter from the author presenting this copy to Thomas Cromwell. A Themistius (1534) and Filelfo's *Orationes* (before 1498) belonged to James Malett, Canon of Windsor, executed for speaking against the suppression of the monasteries. A more peaceful royal association is recalled by the Princess Elizabeth's autograph translation of the Latin prayers composed by her stepmother Katherine Parr, in an embroidered binding, and presented to her father as a new year's gift on 30 December 1545.

The well-attested learning of Edward VI is preserved not only in manuscripts (*see* below, p. 46), but in the printed books that he used. There is his unique copy, on vellum and illuminated, of the Greek grammar of Daniel Talley or Tavalegus *Progymnasmata Graecae grammatices* (1547), which was presented to the prince and bears his signature. This is the only known copy, as is that of Pierre du Ploiche's *Treatise in English and French right necessary for al young children* (1551). Peter Martyr Vermigli's forbidding Oxford lecture *De sacramento eucharistiae* (1549) was annotated by the King, then still only 12 years old.

The reign of Edward VI saw a regrettable purge of 'superstitiouse bookes', which must have cost the library some fine liturgical books, and a new librarian, Bartholomew Traheron, of 'advanced protestant opinions'. He resigned on the accession of Mary, to be succeeded by John Clyffe, one of the Clerks of the Signet, who held the post until 1589. Little is known about him or about the library itself in his time – his post was evidently considered one for a court officer rather than, as in France, an eminent scholar.

It was, however, in 1553 that 'Queen Mary's Psalter', once and perhaps still in the possession of the Earl of Rutland, was sequestrated as it was on the point of being exported from the country by a customs officer, Baldwin Smith, and so came to the Royal Library. Queen Mary herself clearly used her books, as the well-worn bindings of the devotional books that belonged to her – such as *Le livre . . . des sept paroles* (1545) and N. van Ess, *Margarita evangelica* (1545) – reveal. A. a Castro, *De iusta haereticorum punitione* (1547) seems likely to have been intended for use, not ostentation, since it was apparently presented to her by Philip II's confessor, while her wedding to Philip is celebrated, with the addition of a set of autographed Greek verses, in Adrianus Junius's *Philippeis: sive in nuptias Philippi et Mariae carmen* (1554).

Queen Elizabeth, like her father, was no mean scholar, as her early gift to him attests, and the Demosthenes in Italian (1553) may have been a present from her tutor, Roger Ascham, whose signature it bears. Laurence Humphrey, President of Magdalen College, Oxford, gave her his *Optimates, sive de*

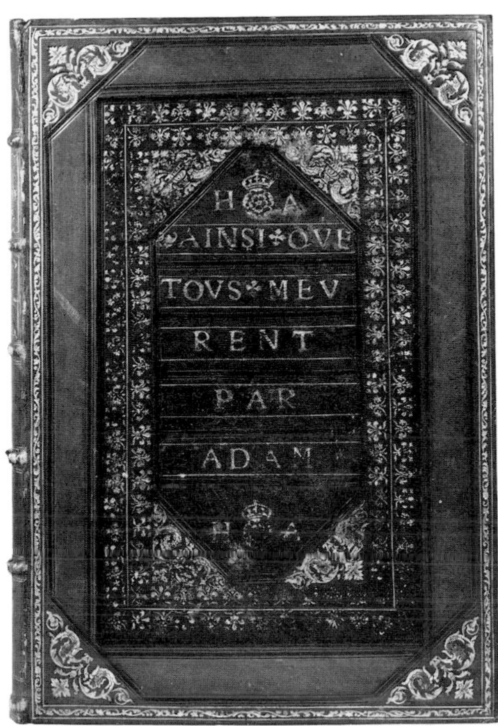

The initials of Henry VIII and Anne Boleyn, on the upper cover of a French Bible printed in Antwerp in 1534.
C. 18.c.9.

nobilitate (1560) and his edition of St Cyril on Isaiah (1563). Another early acquisition was the sole surviving copy of the 1568 edition (the first since 1510) of Sir John Mandeville's *Travels*.

The only relic giving an idea of the state of the Library as a whole in Elizabeth I's time is a sketch of a catalogue made in 1581 by Sir Thomas Knyvett, gentleman of the Privy Chamber, who later helped to protect the library from the ever-hopeful Sir Thomas Bodley. But other more powerful minds were at work on the same lines as Leland. Chief among these was Archbishop Matthew Parker (1504–75), whose collection passed to Corpus Christi College, Cambridge; and William Cecil, Lord Burghley (1521–98), some of whose books and papers still remain at Hatfield, while others were later dispersed by sale in 1687. From these, two remarkable treasures have since reached the Library, a collection of incunabular editions of the great travellers, Marco Polo (printed by Gerard Leeu at Gouda, *c.*1483–84) and the *Itineraria* of Mandeville and Johannes de Hese (printed by Cornelis de Zierikzee at Cologne), which bears a note of sums received by the Lord Treasurer on 25 October 1583 in Lord Burghley's own hand, and a copy of the official list of the Spanish Armada, captured from a Spanish boat in 1588 and annotated by Burghley.

By now, then, the shattered fragments of pre-Reformation society began to come together again, and the documentary relics of the past began to have a new significance and even importance. The change is aptly described by C.E. Wright:

> Men begin to be not only aware of the need to preserve but become very soon even intensely interested in bringing together again the material that had been scattered, and not by any means for sentimental reasons. The lead was taken by those in authority, who now realised the great importance of much of this material for the purpose of propaganda for the government's policy in church and state alike. Parker early discerned the purposes to which the writings of Aelfric and the early church historians could be put for the more secure establishing of the Ecclesia Anglicana over which he had been appointed by Elizabeth to rule, and Cecil was equally anxious to secure historical material which should feed the rising tide of nationalism and supply the groundwork of the closely reasoned state papers which were expedient to strengthen Elizabeth's position against hostile controversialists here and abroad. Both men used the opportunities which their office gave them to further the discovery and acquisition of the scattered manuscripts.

Parker's scheme, which received the support of the Privy Council in 1568, involved 'the conservation of such ancient recordes and monumentes . . . which heretofore were preserved . . . in divers Abbeyes, to be as treasure houses', but were 'nowe come to the possession of sundry private persons', by his own 'special care and oversyght'. On receipt of 'his letters or any of his learned deputies . . . requesting to have syght of any such auncient recordes', owners were required that they would 'gently impart the same: Not meaning hereby in thuse of such bookes for a tyme, to withdrawe them from your ryght and interest unto them, but after a tyme of perusyng of the same, upon promise or bonde, to make restitution of them agayne safely into your handes to be safely kept hereafter'.

Parker's aim seems to have been to build up a central registry: the means he suggested curiously anticipate the work of today's Historical Manuscripts Commission and the export licensing procedure. As such, it was a failure: Parker's real triumph lies in the manuscripts he preserved, the foundation of the Anglo-Saxon studies that have engaged antiquaries from his own day to ours, and in the stimulus given to others to follow his lead. Among these were John, Lord Lumley, who had received, by gift and inheritance, the collection of his father-in-law, Henry Fitzalan, Earl of Arundel, including most of Archbishop Cranmer's Library; Lord William Howard of Naworth; Sir Robert Cotton and Sir Thomas Bodley; John Dee, the astrologer, whose copy of Gesner's *Bibliotheca* (1545), the first organised bibliography, is in the Library;

Liber Edwardi Regis huius nominis sexti

PERMISSVM EST Ioanni Loeo ex Priuilegio Cæſariæ Maieſtatis Dauidi Tauelegi Græca Progymnaſ. ſuo prælo committere, atque vbilibet diſtrahere, vt plenius patet in monumentis ab eadem Cæſa. Maie. eidem conceſſis. Cauetur inſuper iiſdem monumentis, ne quis alius illa Progymnaſmata intra quinquennium conetur excudere, ſub pœna confiſcationis omniũ librorum, & Caroleorum florenorum quinque et viginti. Datum Bruxellæ, Anno Domini M. D. XLVI. Die XIII. Nouembris. Subſignauit Boldewijnus.

Viſus & admiſſus eſt hic libellus per P. Curtium Plebanum Theologum Louanienſem. XII. Noue. Anno quo ſupra.

Principis Eduardi ſunt hæc inſignia ſexti,
Cuius honos nomenq; precor perſiſtat in æuũ.

Κύριε σῶσον τὸν Ἐδουάρδον ἕκτον πρωτόγονον τοῦ βασιλέως.

A ij.

Daniel Talley, *Progymnasmata Graecae Grammatices*, 1547. Edward VI's copy, with his signature at top left.
C.28.a.14. Aiv–Aii.

Henry Savile of Banke; Laurence Nowell, from whom the famous manuscript of *Beowulf* passed to Cotton; Sir Simonds D'Ewes; and many others whose names will recur in the following pages.

The most immediate of these is John, Lord Lumley (1534–1609). Henry, Earl of Arundel (1511–80), whose daughter, Jane, Lumley married, had been Henry VIII's Lord Chamberlain, and led the rebellion that put Mary on the throne. He was rewarded with the Lord High Stewardship and the library of Thomas Cranmer, confiscated on Mary's accession in 1553. Arundel already had a respectable library, and believed in educating his children, who, like Lady Jane Grey and Queen Elizabeth, had a reputation for learning. Between 1556 and 1557, Arundel's wife, stepson and other daughter died, and John and Jane Lumley came from Durham (Lumley's home) to Nonesuch, the palace whose building Arundel had undertaken to complete. The library then became a shared one, the more so in 1559 when Arundel brought Humphrey Lloyd from Oxford to be his household physician and librarian. Some 70 surviving books bear Lloyd's name. All three men were members of the Elizabethan Society of Antiquaries.

Arundel was a likely suitor for the Queen's hand, but his Catholicism told against him, and he was perhaps lucky to die in his bed in 1580. Jane had died in 1577, and her husband, though he married again, was childless. Between 1590 and 1592, he made over Nonesuch, and apparently its contents with it, to the Queen, although he continued to live there and treat the library as his own. In 1596 he had it catalogued by Anthony Alcock, whose beautiful italic hand survives in the copy that he made between 1609 and Lumley's death (now Trinity College, Cambridge, MS.O.4.38). In between, Lumley gave away a number of duplicates to Cambridge University Library and the Bodleian, and to others, but when he died over 3000 works remained, to pass into the Royal collection; of these some 1500 have survived successive dispersals, 1350 in the British Library today, and 150 elsewhere.

Among this residue are many of the Library's most prized possessions. Chief among these is what remains of Cranmer's working library, in which Fisher against Luther and Erasmus on the Psalms were bound up with Greek Fathers, Basil and the two Gregories, of Nyssa and Nazianzus, and in which the controversialists of free will, Erasmus and Cochlaeus, face each other between the same covers. Here too are his great folios of the Latin Fathers, Ambrose and Augustine, and the work of influential contemporaries such as Jacques Lefèvre d'Etaples, or earlier writers of special interest such as Nicolas of Cusa. Many of these bear marginal notes in Cranmer's familiar secretary hand. Cranmer too had his share of monastic spoils, for example the early 12th-century copy of the Gospels in Anglo-Saxon from Christ Church, Canterbury, and the Augustine from Bath Priory.

Other manuscripts from the same source include the 9th-century Gospels from St Augustine's, Canterbury, the early 11th-century Life of St Swithin from Winchester and the 13th-century Bible in seven volumes from the London Blackfriars. Lumley also had part of Roger of Hoveden's chronicle, annotated by the author, the late 14th-century Lay Folk's Mass Book and Chaucer's *Canterbury Tales*. The printed books show the wide range of his intellectual interests. The vast majority are in Latin, Greek (which Jane could read better than her husband) or Hebrew. Only 7 per cent are in English, although these include some printed by Caxton, the 1481 Cicero and the 1489 Christine de Pisan, *The book of fayttes of armes*. Besides theology, which included the two great polyglot bibles (in which the texts in different languages are set out in parallel columns), the Complutensian and Plantin's, there is a more than respectable collection of the classics, including Apuleius *De aureo asino* (1510) which earlier belonged to the erratic schoolmaster–dramatist Nicholas Udall. Works of history are especially numerous, the 600 items ranging from manuscript chronicles, and Froissart in English and French, to the latest accounts of the voyages overseas, Damianus Goes on the Portuguese in India, the Jesuit Mission Relations, and the accounts of the New World by Peter Martyr and Simon Grynaeus. French and Italian literature are well represented, from Maffeo Vegio to Nostradamus. The scientific books are also remarkable, including not only medieval texts, but the up-to-date editions of Ptolemy, long runs of Apianus and Regiomontanus, and the 1566 Copernicus *De revolutionibus orbium coelestium*. Finally, there is an outstanding collection of music, including part books of Josquin Desprez, Arcadelt, Orlandus de Lassus, Ciprianus de Rore, and Palestrina, as well as Byrd and Tallis; there is also manuscript music by Lord Arundel's own musician (*see* below, p. 178).

By 1609, the Royal Library had taken a turn for the better. James I was a considerable patron of learning, as well as an author himself, and through his wife had connections with the cultivated court of Denmark. He knew and corresponded with the learned men of his time. His eldest son Prince Henry shared his tastes. It may be that Lumley gave his library to the Prince; certainly it was the Prince who took charge of it and ordered the second catalogue. The collection was pruned, losing most of its books on law and medicine in the process, the library at St James's Palace was enlarged to accommodate the residue, and many books were rebound, with the royal arms and the Prince's badges prominently displayed. Although entirely original in design, these bindings, together with those added by Prince Henry himself, with their bold (not to say garish) display of gold and silver, have a

A binding for Henry Prince of Wales (died 1612). C.74.e.3.

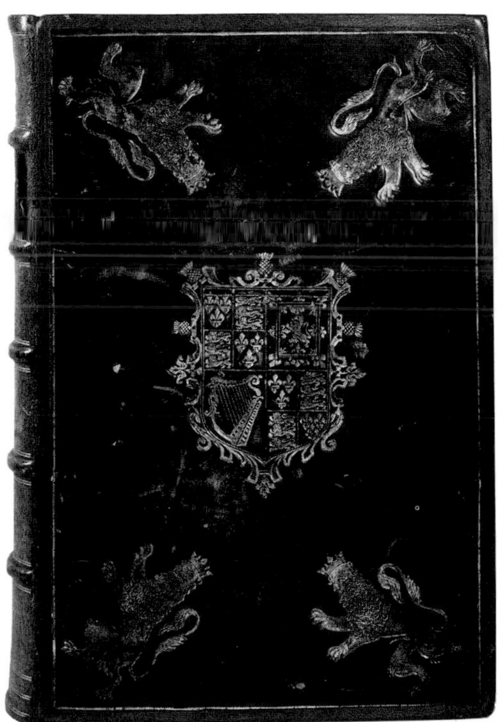

the oath of Allegiance. 3

ſitting downe againe of the Parliament, were there Lawes made, ſetting downe ſome ſuch orders as was thought fit for preuenting the like miſchiefe in time to come. Amongſt which, a forme of Oath was framed to be taken by all his Maieſties Subiects, whereby they ſhould make cleare profeſion of their Reſolution, faithfully to perſiſt in his Maieſties obedience, according to their naturall Allegiance; To the end that hereby his Maieſtie might make a ſeparation, not onely betweene all his good Subiects in generall, and vnfaithfull Traitors, that intended to withdraw themſelues from his Maieſties Obedience; But ſpecially to make a ſeparation betweene ſo many of his Maieſties Subiects, who although they were otherwiſe Popiſhly affected, yet retained in their hearts the print of their naturall duetie to their Soueraigne; and thoſe who being caried away with the like Fanaticall zeale that the Powder Traitors were, could not conteine themſelues within the bounds of their naturall Allegiance, but thought diuerſitie of Religion a ſafe pretext for all kinde of Treaſons, and re-

A 2 bellions

Triplici nodo, triplex cuneus; or, an apologie for the oath of allegiance, 1607. King James I's copy, marked up by him in preparation for a second edition.
C.45.d.23, pp.2–3.

North European look, as opposed to the Franco-Italian style of earlier English bindings.

One especial treasure that James must have brought with him from Edinburgh in 1603 is a copy of *La seconde sepmaine* (1591) of Guillaume Saluste du Bartas, whose *Divine Weeks and Works* were to be immensely popular in England. Du Bartas knew James, and in the appendix to this work had printed his translation of the King's Latin poem on the battle of Lepanto. The copy now in the Old Royal Library, however, was given to James not by Du Bartas but by James Melville (1556–1614), that intransigently presbyterian minister whose learning and charm attracted James, while his principles led to occasional and in the end irredeemable exile. *La seconde sepmaine* has Melville's signature and the date '1593' on the title page, and a leaf of verses in Melville's hand, addressed:

To the Kings Ma[ies]tie prince of
our Poets a Dixaine.

Gentle inoyne, pireless in poesie,
whome flowing fonteanes followes at the feit;
Tak mater heir, maist magnific and hie
Siemlie besetting all thy muses sweit;

Lerned, renombet, faconde royall sprite,
Birnist w[i]t[h] beauties of poetic glore;
Imploy thy penne, (I ken nane uther meit
To matche grait Bartas), as thow has done before.

So sall thy praises quhilk his harpe resounds
Transcend the skyes, throughout all Britan bounds.

This gift dates from the brief period when king and minister were closest, but the book survived its donor's disgrace soon after, and came down through James, along with the copy of Henry the Minstrel's *Actis and deidis of Schir William Wallace* (1570), the earliest copy to survive complete. Other learned men addressed their works to the King, the Czech Fradelius his *Prosphonesis* (1616), and Jean de Schelandre *La Stuartide* (1611), his hymn to James's family, with additions in his own hand.

James I, like any other author, enjoyed the opportunity of improving his work. When a second edition of his *Triplici nodo, triplex cuneus: or, an apologie for the oath of allegiance* (1607) was required, he carefully marked up his copy of the first edition for the occasion. James's other preoccupations are revealed in his copy of John Cowell's *The interpreter or booke containing the signification of words* (1607), suppressed and ordered to be burnt on 26 March 1610 on account of its absolutist interpretation of words like 'Prerogative' and 'Subsidy' (the lexicographer does not always conform to Johnson's famous definition 'a harmless drudge'), and the unique *Declaration du ... roy Jacques I pour le droit des rois* (1615).

A more congenial occasion is celebrated in Erhardus Cellius, *Eques auratus Anglo-Wirtembergicus* (1605), when James made Frederick, Duke of Wurttemberg, a Knight of the Garter; the royal copy was annotated by Sir William Dethick, Garter King of Arms at the time, and later used by Elias Ashmole, historian of the order. Other royal festivities were hymned by writers; John Forbes, the exiled minister in Holland, printed his *Genethliaca* for the wedding of Frederick V, the Elector Palatine, and James's daughter Elizabeth, the 'Winter Queen', of which no other copy survives; various writers injudiciously and prematurely praised the 'Spanish match', while Walter Quin celebrated Charles's eventual marriage to Henrietta Maria in four languages; the copy of his *Gratulatio* (1625) is, again, a unique survival.

The poet Joshua Sylvester, like Melville, admired Du Bartas, whom he translated and sent to Prince Charles, with rather less inspired verses, in 1605. Sylvester too led the chorus of lamentation at the premature death of Prince Henry in 1612 with his *Lachrymae lachrymarum*, its black pages with

A. Tuccaro, *Trois dialogues de l'exercise de sauter et voltiger en l'air*. Paris, 1599. Prince Henry's copy.
C.77.b.16, pp.137v–138.

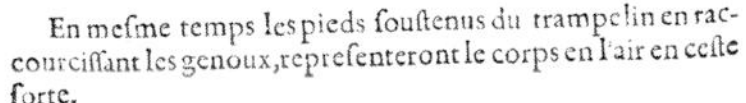
En mesme temps les pieds soustenus du trampelin en racourcissant les genoux, representeront le corps en l'air en ceste sorte.

white lettering a masterpiece of wood-engraving. Prince Henry was indeed a remarkable young man: his energy, his learning and interest in the arts, combined with an equal passion for the martial arts, riding and gymnastics, and above all his striking appearance, deeply impressed his contemporaries. Henry's copy of A. Tuccaro *Trois dialogues de l'exercise de sauter et voltiger en l'air* (Paris, 1599) shows his interest in gymnastics. James's old friend Sir William Hart addressed a poem to him in his *Ecloga* (1605), and the originality of Henry's mind can be seen in his marginalia in the works of the quietist Arias Montanus, *Humanae salvationis monumenta* (1571) and in the extraordinary compilation of J.G. Herwart van Hohenburg *Tabulae arithmeticae* (1610), whose 999 pages make it the first computer in book form.

But perhaps the collection of tracts by Henrik Rantzau is the most significant witness of the major influence on Henry's mind and character. Rantzau (1526–98), son of the heroic general, the architect of Danish independence, was a provincial governor and diplomat. He went to Scotland as early as 1560, and was closely involved in the negotiations for James I's marriage. The great house that he built was in the Renaissance classical style, with marble imported from Italy. He was a pioneering industrialist, building mills for paper and other purposes. He gathered round him learned men and writers, including Tycho Brahe, collected a library of 6300 books, including medieval manuscripts and incunables, and wrote a large number of books himself on medicine, astronomy and astrology, on history and military affairs, and poetry. His *Genealogia Ranzoviana* (1585) in the collection bears Prince Henry's signature. This paragon of the intellectual and active life must have been the hero of Henry's youth, and no doubt stimulated the great addition that Henry made to the Library.

Genealogia Ranzoviana. 1585. With Prince Henry's ownership signature.
606.c.31.

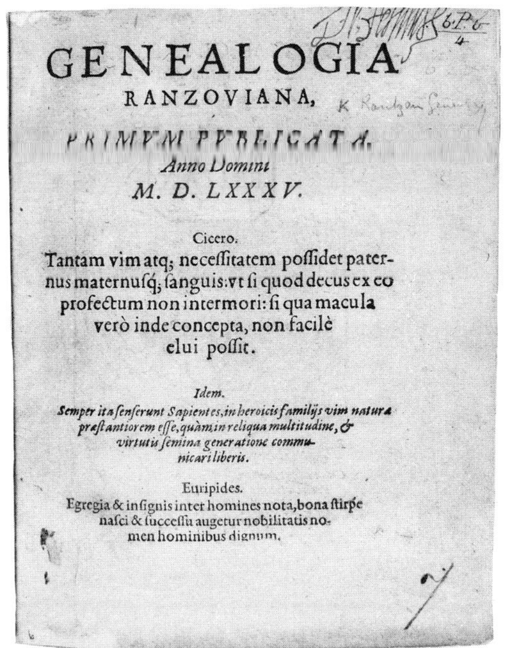
GENEALOGIA
RANZOVIANA,
PRIMVM PVBLICATA.
Anno Domini
M. D. LXXXV.

Cicero.
Tantam vim atq; necessitatem possidet paternus maternusq; sanguis: vt si quod decus ex eo profectum non intermori: si qua macula verò inde concepta, non facilè elui possit.

Idem.
Semper ita senserunt Sapientes, in heroicis familijs vim naturæ præstantiorem esse, quàm in reliqua multitudine, & virtutis semina generatione communicari liberis.

Euripides.
Egregia & insignis inter homines nota, bona stirpe nasci & successu augetur nobilitatis nomen hominibus dignum.

Henry's brother Charles was to be the greatest patron of the arts among British monarchs, despite his ill-starred reign; he was also, if to a lesser degree, a patron of letters and a buyer of books. Like his father and brother, his patronage was sought: Thomas Seget dedicated a pamphlet to James in 1622, and sent the then Prince of Wales a special copy, once again the only copy known. Charles also bought fine illustrated books, such as the *Speculum Romanae magnificentiae*, evidence of his architectural tastes. This taste was shared by Sir Henry Wotton (1568–1639), ambassador at Venice, the poet

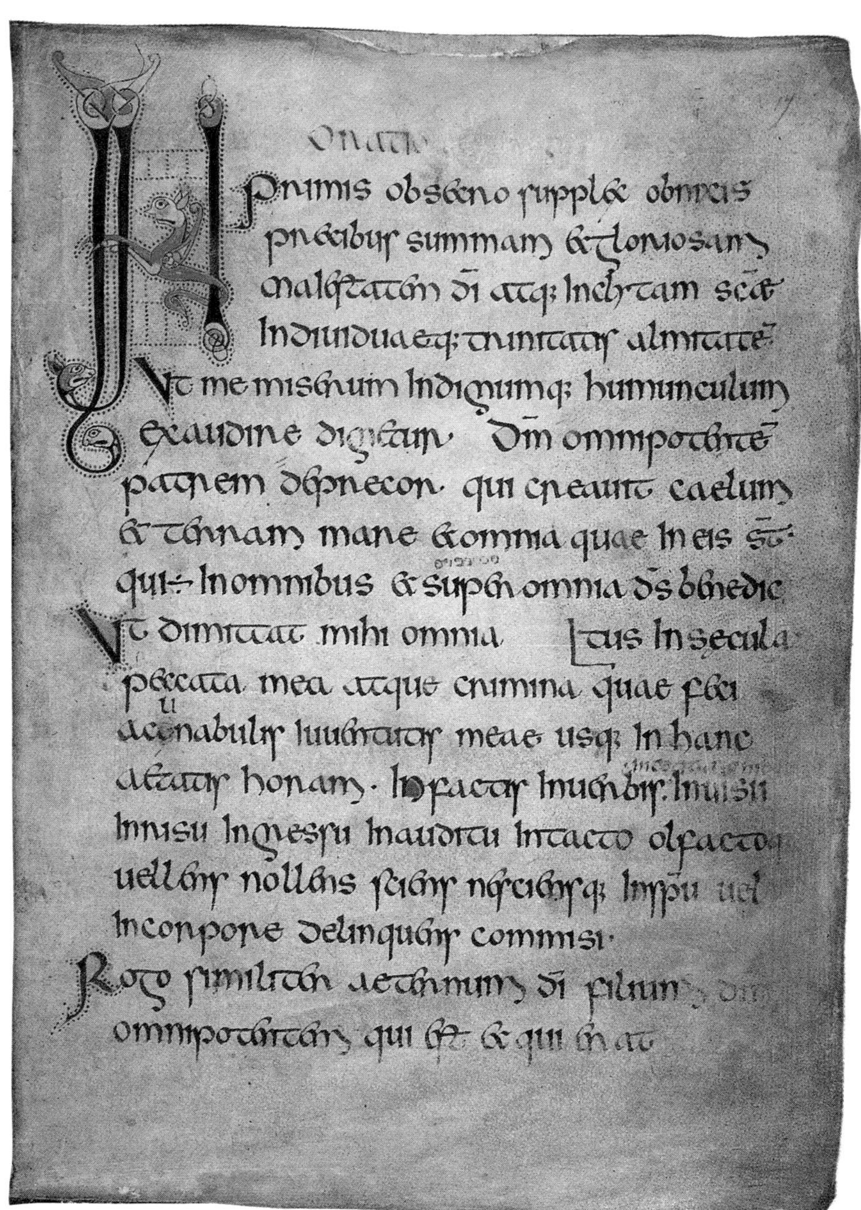

A page from an 8th/9th century prayer book from Worcester.
Royal MS 2.A.XX, f.17.

Opposite. The Codex Alexandrinus. Bible in Greek. 5th century.
Royal MS 1.D.VIII, f.41v.

who wrote 'You meaner Beauties of the Night' to the Queen of Bohemia and, on Charles's birth, 'You that on Stars do look'; he later dedicated his *Elements of Architecture* (1624) to Charles.

The Royal Librarian, who now had charge not only of the Royal Library, but also of all that Prince Henry had added to it, and the subsequent accretions, was a man fit for the task. Patrick Young, the son of James's librarian in Edinburgh, was the first scholar to be appointed to the office. With the King's encouragement he had visited Paris and met Isaac Casaubon, who later came to England (some of his books thus entered the Royal Library); he also knew Peiresc and the brothers Dupuy, and Dutch scholars, such as Daniel and Nicolas Heinsius, Gronovius and Claude de Saumaise. By these and others his reputation was spread all over Europe. In 1628 his scholarship was put to a new and exciting test with the arrival, after three years of negotiation, of the 5th-century Greek Bible presented to Charles I as a gesture of *rapprochement* between the Greek Orthodox and Anglican churches by Cyril Lucar, Patriarch of Alexandria, and hence known as the Codex Alexandrinus. Work on it, which began in 1633 with Young's edition of the Epistles of Clement (one of the Library's copies bears Young's own manuscript reconstruction of the imperfect end of the text), eventually bore fruit in the 'London

ΗΝΟΙΓΕΝΗΜΙΝΤΑΣΓΡΑΦΑΣ·
ΚΑΙΑΝΑΣΤΑΝΤΕΣΑΥΤΗΤΗΩΡΑ
ΥΠΕΣΤΡΕΨΑΝΕΙΣΙΛΗΜ ΚΑΙΕΥ
ΡΟΝΣΥΝΗΘΡΟΙΣΜΕΝΟΥΣΤΟΥΣ
ΕΝΔΕΚΑ ΚΑΙΤΟΥΣΣΥΝΑΥΤΟΙΣ
ΛΕΓΟΝΤΑΣΟΤΙΗΓΕΡΘΗΟΚΣΟ̅
ΤΩΣ ΚΑΙΩΦΘΗΣΙΜΩΝΙ ΚΑΙ
ΑΥΤΟΙΕΞΗΓΟΥΝΤΟΤΑΕΝΤΗΟΔΩ
ΚΑΙΩΣΕΓΝΩΣΘΗΑΥΤΟΙΣΕΝ
ΤΗΚΛΑΣΕΙΤΟΥΑΡΤΟΥ
ΤΜ Ι 7 ΤΑΥΤΑΔΕΑΥΤΩΝΛΑΛΟΥΝΤΩΝ
ΑΥΤΟΣΟΙΣΕΣΤΗΕΜΜΕΣΩΑΥ
ΤΩΝ ΚΑΙΛΕΓΕΙΑΥΤΟΙΣΕΙΡΗΝΗ
ΥΜΙΝ ΠΤΟΗΘΕΝΤΕΣΔΕΚΑΙ
ΕΜΦΟΒΟΙΓΕΝΟΜΕΝΟΙΕΔΟ
ΚΟΥΝΠΝΑΘΕΩΡΕΙΝ ΚΑΙΕΙΠΕ
ΑΥΤΟΙΣ ΤΙ ΤΕΤΑΡΑΓΜΕΝΟΙΕ
ΣΤΑΙ ΚΑΙΔΙΑΤΙΔΙΑΛΟΓΙΣΜΟΙ
ΑΝΑΒΑΙΝΟΥΣΙΝΕΝΤΑΙΣΚΑΡ
ΔΙΑΙΣΥΜΩΝ ΕΙΔΕΤΕΤΑΣΧΕΙ
ΡΑΣΜΟΥΚΑΙΤΟΥΣΠΟΔΑΣΜΟΥ
ΟΤΙΑΥΤΟΣΕΓΩΕΙΜΙ ΨΗΛΑΦΗ
ΣΑΤΕΜΕΚΑΙΙΔΕΤΕΟΤΙΠΝΑ
ΣΑΡΚΑΚΑΙΟΣΤΕΑΟΥΚΕΧΕΙ
ΚΑΘΩΣΕΜΕΘΕΩΡΕΙΤΕΕΧΟΝΤΑ
ΚΑΙΤΟΥΤΟΕΙΠΩΝΕΠΕΔΕΙΞΕ
ΑΥΤΟΙΣΤΑΣΧΕΙΡΑΣΚΑΙΤΟΥΣ
ΠΟΔΑΣ ΕΤΙΔΕΑΠΙΣΤΟΥ
ΤΜΑ Α 7 ΤΩΝΑΥΤΩΝΚΑΙΘΑΥΜΑΖΟΝΤΩ
ΑΠΟΤΗΣΧΑΡΑΣΕΙΠΕΝΑΥΤΟΙΣ
ΕΧΕΤΕΤΙΒΡΩΣΙΜΟΝΕΝΘΑΔΕ
ΟΙΔΕΕΠΕΔΩΚΑΝΑΥΤΩΙΧΘΥΟΣ
ΟΠΤΟΥΜΕΡΟΣΚΑΙΛΑΒΩΝ
ΕΝΩΠΙΟΝΠΑΝΤΩΝΕΦΑΓΕ
ΤΜΒ Ι 7 ΕΙΠΕΝΔΕΑΥΤΟΙΣΟΥΤΟΙΟΙΛΟΓΟΙ
ΜΟΥΟΥΣΕΛΑΛΗΣΑΠΡΟΣΥΜΑΣ
ΕΤΙΩΝΣΥΝΥΜΙΝ ΟΤΙΔΕΙ
ΠΛΗΡΩΘΗΝΑΙΠΑΝΤΑΤΑΓΕ
ΓΡΑΜΜΕΝΑΕΝΤΩΝΟΜΩ
ΜΩΣΕΩΣ ΚΑΙΠΡΟΦΗΤΑΙΣ
ΚΑΙΨΑΛΜΟΙΣΠΕΡΙΕΜΟΥ·
ΤΟΤΕΔΙΗΝΟΙΞΕΝΑΥΤΩΝΤΟ
ΝΟΥΝΤΟΥΣΥΝΙΕΝΑΙΤΑΣΓΡΑ
ΦΑΣ ΚΑΙΕΙΠΕΝΑΥΤΟΙΣΟΤΙ
ΟΥΤΩΣΓΕΓΡΑΠΤΑΙΚΑΙΟΥ
ΤΩΣΕΔΕΙΠΑΘΕΙΝΤΟΝΧΝ
ΚΑΙΑΝΑΣΤΗΝΑΙΕΚΝΕΚΡΩ
ΤΗΤΡΙΤΗΗΜΕΡΑ ΚΑΙΚΗΡΥ
ΧΘΗΝΑΙΕΠΙΤΩΟΝΟΜΑΤΙΑΥ
ΤΟΥΜΕΤΑΝΟΙΑΝΚΑΙΑΦΕ
ΣΙΝΑΜΑΡΤΙΩΝΕΙΣΠΑΝΤΑ

ΤΑΕΘΝΗ ΑΡΞΑΜΕΝΟΝΑΠΟ
ΙΛΗΜ ΥΜΕΙΣΔΕΕΣΤΑΙΜΑΡΤΥ
ΡΕΣΤΟΥΤΩΝ ΚΑΙΙΔΟΥΕΓΩ
ΑΠΟΣΤΕΛΛΩΤΗΝΕΠΑΓΓΕΛΙΑ̅
ΤΟΥΠΡΣΜΟΥΕΦΥΜΑΣ ΥΜΕΙΣ
ΔΕΚΑΘΙΣΑΤΕΕΝΤΗΠΟΛΕΙ
ΕΩΣΟΥΕΝΔΥΣΗΣΘΕΔΥΝΑ
ΜΙΝΕΞΥΨΟΥΣ ΕΞΗΓΑΓΕΝΔΕ
ΑΥΤΟΥΣΕΞΩΕΩΣΕΙΣΒΗΘΑΝΙΑ
ΚΑΙΕΠΑΡΑΣΤΑΣΧΕΙΡΑΣΑΥΤΟΥ
ΕΥΛΟΓΗΣΕΝΑΥΤΟΥΣ
ΚΑΙΕΓΕΝΕΤΟΕΝΤΩΕΥΛΟΓΕΙ
ΑΥΤΟΝΑΥΤΟΥΣ ΔΙΕΣΤΗΑΠΑΥ
ΤΩΝ ΚΑΙΑΝΕΦΕΡΕΤΟΕΙΣΤΟΝ
ΟΥΝΟΝ ΚΑΙΑΥΤΟΙΠΡΟΣΚΥΝΗ
ΣΑΝΤΕΣΑΥΤΟΝΥΠΕΣΤΡΕΨΑ
ΕΙΣΙΛΗΜΜΕΤΑΧΑΡΑΣΜΕΓΑΛΗΣ
ΚΑΙΗΣΑΝΔΙΑΠΑΝΤΟΣΕΝΤ[illegible]
ΤΕΣΚΑΙΕΥΛΟΓΟΥΝΤΕΣΤΟΝ
ΘΝ ΑΜΗΝ·

ΕΥΑΓΓΕΛΙΟΝ ΚΑΤΑ ΛΟΥΚΑΝ

A binding with all-over 'fanfare' design by Samuel Mearne, on *Holy Bible*, Cambridge 1659.
c.108.tt.6.

Polyglot', published in 1657, in which a dedication to Charles II was quickly substituted for the original one to Oliver Cromwell. But long before this Young had preoccupations other than Greek texts. The Library survived unscathed until the King's execution. Then Parliament intervened: there was a momentary threat of dispersal, as with the King's other goods; the Dutch ambassador was given some duplicates, and, more sadly, one of the greatest medieval manuscripts, the Psalter of Queen Ingeburg, was carried off to France and is now at Chantilly. Wiser counsels then prevailed, probably through the influence of the scholar and jurist John Selden. Young was allowed to retire (taking the Codex Alexandrinus with him, not to be recovered till 1664), and his place was taken by John Durie, an expatriate Scot and author of *The reformed library keeper* (1650). Durie maintained his task with some difficulty but reasonable efficiency until the Restoration, when he in turn gave place to another Scot, Thomas Ross, poetaster and tutor to Charles II's illegitimate son by Lucy Walters, the hapless Duke of Monmouth.

The Restoration proved one for the Royal Library too. Ross bought for it the library of John Morris, a wealthy amateur scholar and friend of the famous Dutch scholar, Johannes de Laet; Morris's 1500 or more volumes added some notable books to the collection. Among these were several that had belonged to Ben Jonson, including one given him by Donne's friend Rowland Woodward, a set of French tracts collected by Robert Beale, clerk of the council in Elizabeth I's reign and a copy of Milton's *Defensio pro populo Anglicano* (1651) given him by the author. Morris, a trimmer by nature, also had a copy of Maimonides that belonged to Milton's adversary, Claude de Saumaise, who had it from the great scholar Joseph Justus Scaliger. One of his more unexpected acquisitions, bought perhaps as a means of improving his German, was Hermann Bote's famous *Tyll Eulenspiegel*, printed at Strasbourg in 1515, and until recently thought to be the first edition.

Many of Morris's more important books were bound in the new French style of bright red turkey leather with a one-line rectangular panel on the covers and the royal cipher between palm-leaves at the angles. These bindings were supplied by Samuel Mearne, the Royal bookbinder, whose account was often in arrear, so much so that Evelyn wrote in 1689 to Pepys that those 'which still are lying in mercenary hands for want of two or three hundred pounds to pay for their binding; many of which being of the oriental tongues, will soone else find Jewes and chapmen that will purchase and transport them, from whence we shall never retreive them againe'. This must refer to the notable collection of Hebrew books, which may have been given to Charles II before the Restoration by Dutch Jews as an inducement to toleration. Evelyn's prophecy was only partly right: the Jew and chapman by whom they were eventually bought restored them to the Library in 1759.

Ross had abandoned the librarian's office to deputies in 1665, and he was finally succeeded in 1677 by one of them, Henry Thynne. In 1678 the last great manuscript addition to the Library was made with the purchase of over 300 books belonging to the antiquary, John Theyer (1597–1673). This contained more books of monastic provenance, mainly West Country, notably from Worcester (whence came a fine 8th/9th-century prayer book), but also from St Augustine's Canterbury, Westminster, and the North. In 1680 Evelyn visited the library at Whitehall which he says contained about 1000 volumes. One of these, judging by his description, was Queen Mary's Psalter: if so, it must have escaped the two fires, the later and worse in 1698, that destroyed the Palace. The library at St James's was more fortunate, and almost all of the books listed in Bernard's *Catalogi manuscriptorum Angliae* in 1697 exist today.

After the Revolution in 1688, Thynne may have been glad to make over the librarianship to Henri Justel, a distinguished French protestant, who had come to England before the Revocation of the Edict of Nantes, bringing some fine books. After his death in 1693, the greatest man ever to be Royal Librarian, Richard Bentley, obtained the reversion of the post and held it in conjunction with his Mastership of Trinity College, Cambridge, nominally until 1725 (when he resigned it to his son Richard, then only 16) but effectively till his death in 1742. His long tenure was marked not by acquisitions, but by ceaseless battles to obtain better accommodation for the Royal Library at St James's and later, after Sir Robert Cotton's descendants made over his collection to the nation, for both libraries. The Cottonian Library was then in Sir Robert's house, abutting the Houses of Parliament. The Cotton family settled the Library in trust in 1700, but there was prolonged negotiation about the sale of the house, on whose structure Sir Christopher Wren reported unfavourably. No doubt Bentley was trying to assert control, but it was not until 1715 that he officially became keeper of the Cottonian Library. Shortly after this he acquired a deputy, David Casley, whose merits were praised by Speaker Onslow to the Commons Committee debating Sloane's bequest (*see* above, p. 18).

The accommodation problem went from bad to worse, while the Commissioners of Works procrastinated 'because the House of Commons had lately debated the building of a new library' – no new phenomenon. In 1722, the Board of Works took a seven-year lease of Essex House in the Strand, only to abandon it for Lord Ashburnham's house in Little Dean's Yard, Westminster, partly because it was cheaper and partly because it was 'much more safe from fire'.

At two o'clock in the morning of Saturday, 23 October 1731, fire broke out in the chimney of a store below the libraries in Ashburnham House. It caught the woodwork of the room above and, although the damage to the Royal Library was slight, nearly a quarter of the Cottonian Library was destroyed or damaged. Dr Bentley, sallying out in nightgown and wig, rescued the Codex Alexandrinus; Casley assisted in the work of salvage. The books were mostly thrown out of the window, and thence removed by degrees to the unoccupied new dormitory of Westminster School and, when it was occupied, to the old dormitory then vacated.

There the books of both collections remained, ignominiously accumulating dust, while the Commons and the Commissioners of Works continued to defer decision about their future home. The younger Richard Bentley resigned his office in 1745 to Claudius Amyand, son of the King's surgeon. Casley continued to act as custodian of the sleeping library. As long ago as 1707, when the second Act of Parliament relating to Cotton House was in debate, Sir Hans Sloane had written to his friend Dr Arthur Charlett, Master of University College, Oxford:

> Here are great designs on foot for uniting the Queen's Library, the Cotton, and the Royal Society's together. How soon they may be put in practice time must discover.

Now, 50 years later, through his generosity (and unprompted by the worst bibliothecal disaster in the country's history) his wish came true.

A griffin and elephant, in a Latin bestiary. English, early 13th century.
Harley MS 4571, ff.7v–8.

3 The Cottonian and Harleian Libraries

Est animal quod dicitur elephans in quo non est con
cupiscentia coitus. Elephantē greci amagnitudine
corporis uocatum putant. quod formā montis pferat. Grece
enim mons elephio dicit̄. Apud indos autē a uoce barro uo
cant. Vnde [illegible] eius barritꝰ et dentes ebur. Rostru
autē pmuscida dicit̄ qm̄ illo pabula ori admouet &
est angui similis. uallo munitur eburneo. Nullum
hic est elaphantus

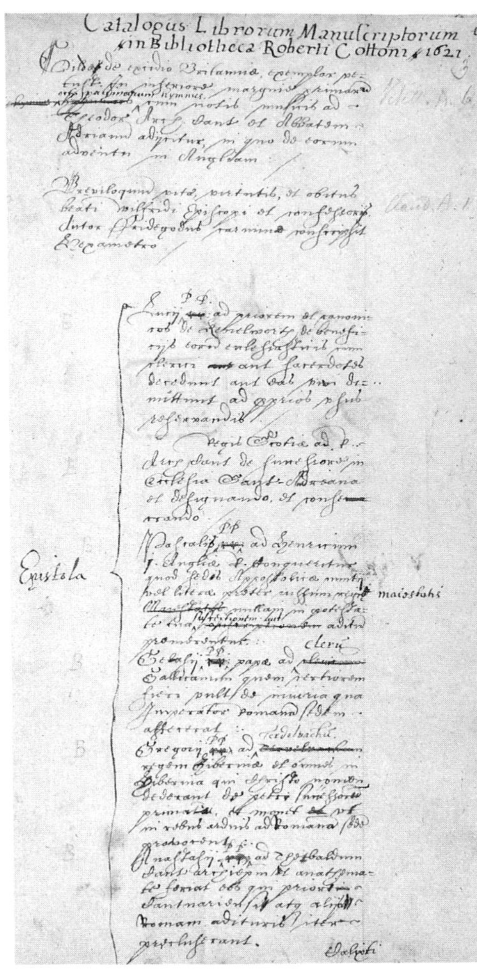
Catalogus Librorum Manuscriptorum in Bibliotheca Roberti Cottoni 1621.

Opening page of the catalogue of manuscripts in Cotton's library, 1621.
Harley MS 6018, f.3.

Portrait of Sir Robert Cotton, 1629.
Reproduced by permission of the Trustees of the British Museum.

On 13 February 1601 the Elizabethan Society of Antiquaries was due to meet but did not 'by reson of the trobles stirred by the erle of Essex'. Why should a group of scholarly men discussing antiquities find it prudent not to meet on this occasion? They were for the most part country gentlemen, keepers of records, and (in particular) heralds, as innocent a group as might be imagined. But five days earlier, as the Earl of Essex rode up Ludgate Hill, he was followed by a herald proclaiming him traitor, 'the dread word that broke the courage of many of his supporters'. Heralds and antiquaries were not impotent bystanders in the bustle of Elizabethan England. Their interest in the continuity of past and present, the links that bound generation to generation, was not, as we would say, 'academic'. These links were proofs of title, to land, power or (even) the crown. If we have reason to be glad that the College of Arms pursued its business of preserving the past, by visitations, recording documents and noting monuments, through the tumults in English society from the Wars of the Roses to the Protestant succession, we must remember that it was not an altruistic concern for posterity but a lively interest in the present that impelled them to do so.

None knew this better than Sir Robert Cotton, 'Robert Cotton Bruceus' as he habitually signed himself after 1603, emphasising his famous Scotch forebears in the reign of a Stuart king. His latest biographer points out the power that his historic collections gave him: they established the *precedents* that all parties, in government or business, needed to support their case. Thus Cotton's patron, Henry Howard, Earl of Northampton, wrote to him about debasing coin, 'though I have in my own experience observed many weighty reasones in the pointe yet I valewe muche the strength that experience of former times addes to speculation'.

'The experience of former times' lay at the root of the foundation of the Elizabethan Society of Antiquaries in 1586, under the aegis of William Camden (1551–1623), the most distinguished historian and herald of his time. Earlier he had been second master of Westminster School when Cotton was a boy there, and together in 1599 they made a journey to the North of England in search of antiquities. It also underlay Cotton's final decision to base the library, till then divided between his Huntingdonshire home and London, in new quarters between the House of Lords and the House of Commons. Between these two events Cotton grew from youth to age. The early and enthusiastic antiquary became the trusted adviser of the Earl of Northampton, the Lord Privy Seal, and later of Thomas Howard, Earl of Arundel, for whom Cotton investigated the prerogatives of the office of Constable, not for antiquarian reasons, but as the basis of his struggle with the Duke of Buckingham. The loss of that battle – not through any weakness in his precedents – proved fatal for Cotton.

But Cotton was no relentless player in the Court of Jacobean power politics. It is impossible to mistake the genuine love of antiquity for its own sake that informs his correspondence and is evident in his collection. The legend that John Dee buried the manuscripts of his work, 'and Sir Robert Cotton bought the field to digge after it', may be apocryphal, but it reveals a passion for preservation, rather than power. This is, perhaps, best shown in the petition, drawn up and signed by Cotton with two older friends and fellow-antiquaries, John Dodderidge (later Sir John; 1555–1628) and James Ley (later 1st Earl of Marlborough; 1552–1629), possibly in 1602. It deserves setting out in full, partly as the best expression of Cotton's motives in forming his collection, and partly because it is the first fully articulated scheme for a British national library. It is headed (clearly after the document itself was written) 'A proiect touching a petition to be exhibited vnto her maiesty for the erecting of her library and an Academy'.

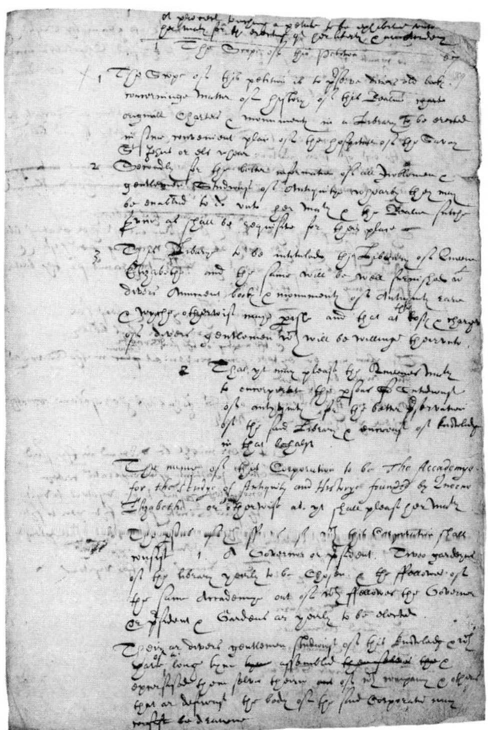

Cotton, Dodderidge and Ley's Petition.
Cotton MS Faustina E.V. f.89.

1. *The Scope of this Peticion.*

1. The scope of this peticion is to preserve divers old bookes concerninge mater of history of this Realme originall Charters & monuments into a Library to be erected in some convenient place of the hospitall of the Savoy St Johns or els whear.

2. Secondly for the better information of all Noblemen and gentlemen Studious of Antiquitye whereby they may be enabled to do vnto her Maiesty & the Realme sutche service as shall be requisite for their place.

3. This Lib[r]arye to be intituled the library of Queen Elizabethe. and the same will be well furnished with divers Auncient bookes & monumentes of Antiquity rare & wyche otherwise maye perishe and that at the costes & charges of divers gentlement which will be willinge theirvnto.

2[*sic*]. That yt may please the Queenes Maiesty to encorporate the persons studious of antiquity for the better preservation of the said Library & encrease of knowledge in that behalfe.

The name of this Corporation be *The Accademye for the studye of Antiquity and Historye founded by Queene Elizabeth.* or otherwise as yt shall please her Maiesty.

The persons & officers of which this Corporation shall consist; A Governor or President. Twoo gardeyns of the library yearly to be elected.

Their ar divers gentlemen studious of this Knowledge & which have of a long tyme aseemblid & exercised themselves theirin out of which company & others that ar desirous the body of the said Corporation may be drawne.

That yt would please the Queenes Maiesty to graunt the Custody & to comitt the care of that Library to the said Corporation according to sutche ordynaunces & Statutes as yt shall please the Queenes Maiestye to establishe.

That none shall be admitted into this Corporation or Socyety except he take the othe of the Supremacy & to preserve the said library to the best of their endeavour

That is may please her Maiesty to bestowe out of her gratious library sutche & so many of her bookes concernying history & Antiquity as yt shall please her highnes to graunt for the better furnishing of this library.

The place wher yt may please her Maiesty to appoynt for this library & the meeting of the said Society.

The place may be eyther some convenient Room in the Savoy which may well be spared, or ells in the late dissolved Monastery of St Johns of Jerusalem or otherwher whear yt shall please her Maiesty.

That their might be ordeyned in the said Letters pattentes of incorporation certeyn honorables persons to be visitors to visit the said Society from fyve yeir to fyve yeir or as often as it shall please her Maiesty to appoynt.

The names of the visitors

The Archebishopp of Canterbury being of the pryvy Covnsell, The Lord Keeper of the Great Seale, The Lord Treasurer, The Lord Admyrall, The Lord Chambrleyn, The pryncipple Secretary, The Lord Chief Justice of Englande. [This fair copied at Titu B.V. + 210.] Reasons to move the furdrance of this Corporation.

First their ar divers & sundry monuments worthe observation whearof the oryginall is extant in the hands of som privat gentleman & allso divers others excellent monumentes whearof their is no record now extant which by theise meanes shall have publick & salfe custody for vse when occasion shall serve.

The care which her Maiesties progenitors have had for the preservation of sutch ancient monuments.

Kynge Edward the first caused & comitted dyvers copyes of the Recordes and monumentes concerninge the Realm of Scottland vnto divers Abbeyes for the better preservation theirof which for the most part ar now perished or rare to be had & which provision by the dissolution of all Monasteryes is determyned.

The same King caused the libraryes of all monasteryes & other places of the Realm to be serched for the furder & manifest declaration of his titell as cheef Lord of Scottland & the record theirof now extant dothe alleidge divers Legers bookes of Abbeyes for confirmation theirof, the lik was doon in the tym of King Henry the eight.

Also when the popes auctority was abolyshed out of England by Kyng Henry the eight their was speciall care had of the searche of Antient bookes & Antiquityes for manifestation vnto the world of these vsurpations of the pope.

Also their ar divers treatises published by auctoryte for the satisfaction of the world in divers matters publicke which after they are by publik auctoryty prynted & dispersed they do after som tym become very rare for yat their is no publick preservation of historye & Antiquity of which the vniversityes being [illegible] tak little care or regard

In foreyn Covntryes whear most civility & learning is their is great regard had of the cherishing & encrease of this kinde of lerning: by publicke lectures appoynted for that purpose & their ar erected publick libraryes & accademyes in Germany Italy & ffrance to that end. Lastly this kynde of exercise shall enable divers gentleman to serve her Maiesty as agents in foreyne . . .

To this corporation may be added the Study of forreyn modern Tongues of the nations our neighbors Countryes & regard of their historyes & state whereby this Realm in a short tyme may be furnished with sundry gentlemen enabled to do her Maiesty & the realme service as agentes or otherwise to be Imployed.

Mr Cotton Mr Dodorig Mr James Lee

Nothing came of this proposal. Perhaps it was never submitted. It is possible to guess why, for the Society of Antiquaries itself came to an end shortly afterwards, for reasons recorded later by Sir Henry Spelman: 'we had notice that his majesty took a little mislike of our society; not being inform'd that we had resolv'd to decline all matters of state'. If they had declined, the option not to do so clearly existed and constituted a threat, in James I's view. Cotton's library and its formation were his response, at once daring and diplomatic, to the rejection of the 'project'.

Cotton's name is remembered today as the owner of the Cotton Genesis, a set of illustrations of the first book of the Bible dating from the 5th to the 6th century, once among the greatest of the very few surviving examples of classical book-painting, now reduced to a few sad charred fragments by the 1731 fire. The book had reached Cotton from Sir John Fortescue to whom it had been given by Queen Elizabeth. She had it from her father Henry VIII, to whom it had been presented by two Greek bishops, for the same ecumenical reasons as prompted the gift of the Codex Alexandrinus a century later. We also owe to Cotton another manuscript, of even greater importance to this country, Cotton MS. Nero D. iv, better known as the Lindisfarne Gospels, which he got from his friend Robert Bowyer, Clerk of the House of Commons. He also had the 8th-century Anglo-Saxon Psalter, once at St Augustine's, Canterbury, which he believed to be one of the manuscripts sent to St Augustine by Pope Gregory I; the Coronation Gospels, the Aethelstan Psalter, the Anglo-Saxon Pentateuch, King Alfred's translation of Orosius's *Historia Universalis*, five of the seven surviving manuscripts of the Anglo-Saxon Chronicle and the collection that contains the remarkably detailed Anglo-Saxon 'World Map' of *c*1000. Other major Anglo-Saxon sources include a collection of laws made for Archbishop Wulfstan of York, and the Durham *Liber vitae*, in use from the 9th to the 16th century. He had two of the oldest manuscripts of Bede's *Historia ecclesiastica*, both 8th/9th-century, a fine Old English Herbal, Aelfric's Homilies, and the most important of all Anglo-Saxon literary manuscripts, the unique text of *Beowulf*.

Amongst later chronicles and literature, his collection was scarcely less rich. There were, first and foremost, two of the four surviving original texts of the Magna Carta. He had examples of many of the major chronicles, including a 12th-century manuscript of Nennius, Knighton's chronicle, the 12th-century Simeon of Durham, and Thomas of Elmham's biography of Henry V. There were, as well, many monastic cartularies (Cotton too benefited from the dissolution of the religious houses), and the lives of the Welsh Saints, with the Welsh legal code of Hywel Dda. The Middle English texts included several of the *Ancrene Riwle*, Layamon's *Brut*, the Coventry Mystery Plays, and, as important for Middle English as *Beowulf* for Old English, the unique manuscript of *Pearl* and *Sir Gawain and the Green Knight*.

The Lindisfarne Gospels (detail), *c*.698. [*See* also p.8]
Cotton MS Nero D.IV. f.2*v*.

Among illuminated manuscripts and documents, beside the Lindisfarne Gospels and Aethelstan's books, he had the foundation charter of New Minster in 966, and the Prayer Book of Aelfwine and the copy of Prudentius's *Psychomachia*, both masterpieces of Anglo-Saxon drawing. Among later manuscripts were the Psalter of Henry of Blois, Bishop of Winchester, pictures of the Kings of England, *c*.1300, the French King Charles V's Coronation Book, the illuminated Admiralty Ordinances of 1413, Henry VI's Psalter, and, one of the great masterpieces of late medieval drawing, the 'Beauchamp Pageants', a series of pictures illustrating the life and achievements of Richard Beauchamp, Earl of Warwick (1388–1439), made *c*.1484–90, possibly for his daughter Anne, widow of the 'Kingmaker'.

Besides all these treasures of medieval art, history and literature, the Library was especially rich in original documents of the history of Cotton's own time, including 43 volumes for the reigns of Henry VIII and Elizabeth relating to domestic matters and negotiations with France, many of the latter annotated by Lord Burghley, and 50 more relating to other overseas affairs. He has

Top. The Vespasian Psalter. Anglo-Saxon, 8th century. The interlinear translation added in the 9th century is the earliest known copy of the Psalms in English.
Cotton MS Vespasian A.I, ff.30*v*–31.

Above. Fragment from the Cotton Genesis. Second half of the 5th century.
Cotton MS Otho B.VI. Frag.4*v*.

Right. Miniature of St John the Evangelist. From the Coronation Gospels. Carolingian, early 9th century.
Cotton MS Tiberius A.II, f.164*v*.

Page from the Anglo-Saxon Chronicle, recounting Aethelred and Alfred's defeat of the Danes in 871. 11th century.
Cotton MS Tiberius B.IV, f.33.

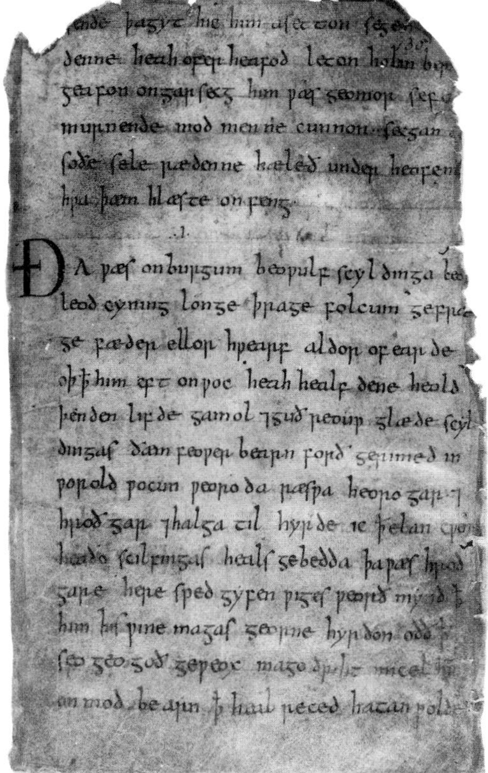

Beowulf, epic poem in Anglo-Saxon, *c.*1000.
Cotton MS Vitelius A.XV, f.133.

been blamed, in his own time and since, for appropriating material that belonged to official repositories. He was certainly unscrupulous; but he had learned to put little trust in official keepers of records and, besides, as we have seen, he saw a higher purpose for his own collection which others, notably James I, endorsed. Without him, the unique series of early royal documents, letters of Thomas More, Anne Boleyn and others to Henry VIII, Edward VI's diary, Charles V's letter to Queen Mary announcing his abdication, the documents of the end of Mary Queen of Scots and Sir Walter Ralegh's journal might have ceased to exist.

Nor were Cotton's interests restricted to Britain. He had the 8th-century St Jerome, written in France soon after 743, manuscripts from Switzerland, Holland and Italy, and a Russian Chronicle. He even possessed, most unusual at this time, some oriental material: Archbishop James Ussher gave Cotton his 'ancient copy of the Samaritan Pentateuch' in 1628; there was even a Chinese manuscript in the library. His interest in geography accounts for the manuscript of John de Castro's account of Portuguese voyages to India written in 1542, which may have belonged to Ralegh. He had friends abroad, too – Janus Gruter, Nicolas Fabri de Peiresc, to whom he sent the 15th-century manuscript of French laws, the historian Jacques Auguste De Thou, the Dutch scholar Johannes de Laet and others.

Cotton was a man of many friends: his collection was used, and borrowed from, extensively. He lent books to Ralegh, writing his *Historie of the World* in the Tower, and to Bacon for his *Henry VII*; Ben Jonson borrowed Aelfric's Homilies. He welcomed their company, and they sent him contributions for his library. This explains the wealth of letters and papers relating to antiquities, the presence too of important heraldic documents, the Camden Roll of *c.*1280 and the Caerlaverock Poem of 1300. It is pleasant for us, as it was for his contemporaries, to imagine him entertaining friends in the library room, among the presses, each one capped with the bust of a Roman emperor or empress, who gave their names to the shelves beneath, containing the all but 1000 manuscripts. Printed books (few of which now remain) presumably filled the space between. If we could leave him there, all would be well. But disaster befell him.

On 2 February 1626, his coronation day, Charles I went by river from Whitehall Palace to Westminster. Sir Robert Cotton stood waiting at the river steps of his garden, 'readie . . . to receave him with a booke of Athelstone's, being the fouer Evangelists in Lattine . . . upon which for diuers hundred yeares together, the Kings of England had solemnlie taken their coronation oath'. But – the words are those of Cotton's younger friend and rival collector, Sir Simonds D'Ewes – 'the royall barge bawked those steps soe fitlie accommodated' (a carpet had been laid) and landed at the much less convenient Parliament stairs. It was a calculated snub. Cotton was too active a parliamentarian, too close to Arundel, for the rising star, the Duke of Buckingham, and this was the result.

Worse was to follow. In 1629 he was confined, on the dubious charge of providing the copy for a seditious pamphlet ('I told you it was a MS therefore Sir Robert Cotton must have his share', the informer said with understandable if dubious logic), and his beloved library was sealed off and denied to him. His petition for its return was still unanswered when he died, it was said of grief, on 6 May 1631. The library remained closed. During the Civil War, the learned antiquaries, John Selden (who kept the key to it) and Sir William Dugdale, frequented the library and sorted and bound papers. It was returned to the family in 1650, moved to the country and brought back to London at the Restoration. No longer dangerous, it had now become an embarrassment (though small accessions were made). In 1700 Cotton's grandson established the trust that made the library over to the nation, with what result we have seen.

An original text of King John's Magna Carta, 1215.
Cotton MS Augustus II.106.

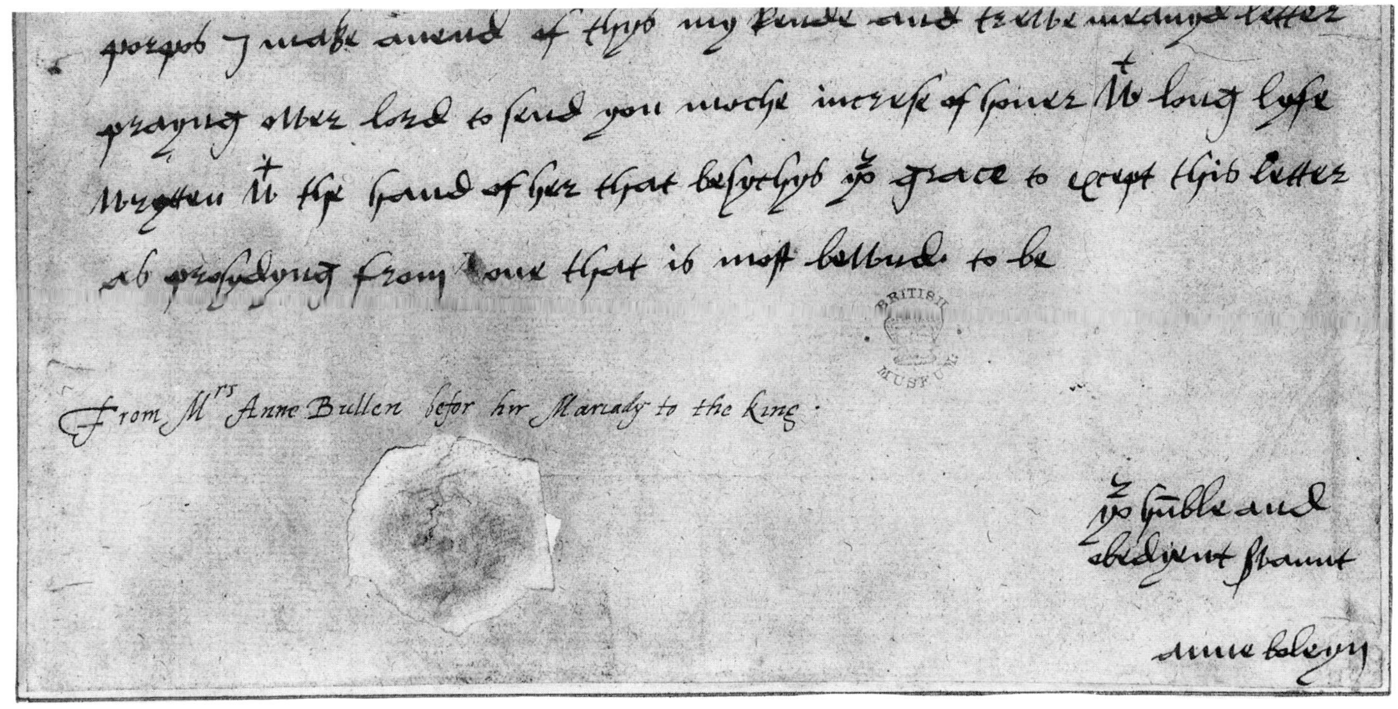

wherof I make auend of thys my rude and trwbe wrytyng letter
praying oure lord to send you moche incresse of honor with long lyfe
wrytten with the hand of her that besychys your grace to acsept this letter
as prosydyng from one that is most bounde to be

From Mrs Anne Bullen befor hir Mariady to the king

your humble and obedient servant

anne boleyn

Letter from Anne Boleyn to Cardinal Wolsey, thanking him for promoting her marriage with Henry VIII, *c.*1528 (Detail.)
Cotton MS Vespasian F.XIII, f.141.

The Tree of Jesse. From the Psalter of Henry of Blois. English, mid-12th century.
Cotton MS Nero C.IV, f.9.

A sea battle. From the 'Beauchamp Pageants', *c.*1484–90.
Cotton MS Julius. E.IV, art.6, f.18*v*.

Only a century separates the formation of the Cottonian Library from the era of Robert and Edward Harley, 1st and 2nd Earls of Oxford, who collected the far vaster group of books and manuscripts that made up the Harleian Library, whose manuscripts are now in the British Library. The elder Harley (1661–1724), Queen Anne's minister, began to collect books when he succeeded to the family estates in 1700, and did so vigorously until 1711 when he became Lord Treasurer (Prime Minister, in effect). At that point his son Edward (1689–1741), just down from Oxford, began to share in the task. In 1714 two momentous events took place: on 16 July Robert Harley was sent to the Tower, and on 31 August Edward married the heiress of the Duke of Newcastle, Henrietta Cavendish Holles. Robert was now unable to do more than help, and Edward became the main force, collecting an ever increasing mass of material until his death.

This unusual partnership was completed by a most unusual man, Humfrey Wanley (1672–1726). Wanley was the greatest palaeographer of his time. As a draper's apprentice in Coventry he spent all his spare time copying old documents and learning Anglo-Saxon. The Bishop of Lichfield sent him to Oxford, where he lived with Arthur Charlett, Master of University College; Charlett recommended him to George Hickes, the leader of the Non-jurors and the great expert on the languages of Northern Europe, and he in turn to Robert Harley, writing in 1701 that Wanley had 'the best skill in ancient hands and MSS of any man not only of this, but, I believe, of any former age, and I wish for the sake of the public, that he might meet with the same encouragement here, that he would have met in France, Holland, or Sweden, had he been born in any of those countries'.

Hickes's wish was to be fulfilled, if not in the way he expected. Wanley never published the great work he might have: instead, the 'encouragement', in the shape of confidence, friendship and almost unlimited money, made him the most powerful librarian, in point of acquisition, in Europe. In return, Wanley gave father and son the most devoted service, seeking, examining and reporting on books and documents, driving the best bargain he could with their owners, supervising access to them (he was a formidable Cerberus), studying them and supervising their binding and, on occasion, transport. Of all this he kept a diary, in his own neat and beautiful hand (as apt to copy old hands with skill and understanding), which was admirably edited by the late C.E. Wright.

Wanley's diary, like his letters, is one of the most fascinating, as well as important, documents in the history of books. We can admire the Cottonian Library, and piece together a little of its history from its present contents, but the details of its accumulation, the reason why this or that particular item came to be acquired, are as lost to us as they would have been in the Middle Ages. Through Wanley's diary, through his eyes and with the benefit of his forceful and original character, we see the Harleian Library grow. We understand why this or that book was bought and come to know the participants in the progress. The poet Pope, for example, was a friend of Edward Harley (as was Swift) and on 3 July 1723 we read in Wanley's Diary: 'My Lord sent-in a Persian MS. given by Mr Pope being a Theological Treatise written by Father San-Hieronymo Shad a Jesuit Missionary at Lahor & dedicated to Gjanghir the Great Mogol, A.D. 1609'. The manuscript, carefully docketed by Wanley, is still in the collection.

The diary is full of such instances. Here is Wanley making short work of John Warburton (1682–1759), the Lancashire antiquary, who has asked a price 'much too horribly exorbitant to be complied with' for some manuscripts.

6 July 1720: I had a Letter from Mr Warburton, pretending that a Person of Honor desire's to buy his MSS, and that he had rather Sell them to my Lord, &c. Upon Deliberation hereupon, and taking this Motion of His Person of Honor to be a mere Sham; and his Resolution to part with his Roman Altars, to be at Ten

The Harleian Golden Gospels. Carolingian, *c.*800.
Harley MS 2788, ff.108v–109.

times their Value, if he can get it; besides finding him to be extremely greedy, fickle & apt to go from his Word: I thought it would be for the best not to be too forward in Sending him any Answer, but to lett him Send or Come again to me.

7 July 1720: Mr Warburton found me out there [at the Genoa-Armes] & besought me to resume his affair, which he would again putt into my Hands; and take what I would allow: but earnestly beg'd of me to get him more Money of my Lord, than what I before brought him. I look'd Cool, made no promise, but that I would write to my Lord.

13 July 1720: Mr Warburton came to me at the Genoa-Armes, and then took me to another Tavern, & kept me up all the Night, thinking to Muddle me & so to gain upon me in Selling his MSS. &c. But the Contrary happened, & he induced to Agree to accept the Sum he offered at the first, without the Advancement of a single Farthing: and he promised to bring them to me, on the Fourteenth, by Six a Clock.

14 July 1720: Mr Warburton wrote to me that he was so disorder'd by OUR late Frolic (which, by the way, was all his Own) that he could not bring the Things til the Fifteenth by Six a Clock.

In one case, we can trace, through Wanley, the whole process of acquisition of one of the most famous of Harleian manuscripts, the Golden Gospels, one of the great Carolingian 'Codices aurei' written in letters of gold throughout and bought at the Hague, at the sale of Jean Jacques Charron, Marquis de Menars, in 1720 for 1100 Dutch Guilders. The story begins on 11 April 1720:

I agreed with Mr Vaillant [the bookseller] . . . and directed him to send into Holland for a Specimen of the Character of the Latin Gospels written all with Golden Letters, which will be sold next June in the Auction of Menars's Books.

14 May 1720: Yesterday Mr Vaillant brought me a Specimen of the Character of that Latin MS of the Gospels, which is to be sold at the approaching Auction of Menars's Books at the Hague. These Characters are all Uncials, gilded over with Gold, and appear to be formed in a very elegant Manner . . . In my Opinion, this most antient & valuable Book should be purchased at any rate.

17 May 1720: My Lord seeing a Specimen of the Character of the Latin MS of the

Gospels said to be all over written with Letters of Gold, gave Order for its being bought at Menars's approaching Auction, at the Hague, & sent over hither as soon as may be. The Commission to be given to Mr Vaillant.

4 June 1720: I wrote to Mr Vaillant to know the Price of the Golden Manuscript, & to desire it may come to my Lord as soon as possible: & I had an Answer from him to Satisfaction.

5 June 1720: Mr Vaillant sent my Lord a Letter informing him that the Antient MS of the Latin Gospels all written with Capital Letters of Gold, is actually bought in Holland for his Lordship.

6 June 1720: Mr Vaillant waited on my Lord, to apprise him of the short Time within which the Codex Aureus may be expected: and my Lord then paid him the price of it.

21 June 1720: I went to Mr Warburton & took a List of his MSS. which I sent by the Post to my Lord: together with the acceptable News that the Ship which bring's the Codex Aureus, is arrived on the Coast of England.

27 June 1720: This day the CODEX AUREUS LATINUS was cleared out of the Kings Warehouse, and delivered into my Custody.

28 June 1720: This day, by my Lords Order I drew up a short account of the said CODEX AUREUS, and sent it, by the Post, to his Lordship at Welbeck.

29 June 1720: This day, I brought the CODEX AUREUS with me, & placed it in the Library.

20 August 1720: Mr Vaillant was sent by my Lord to see how the CODEX AUREUS itself agree's with the Specimen taken from it in Holland before it was bought. And upon Sight, he own'd that it was injudiciously done.

10–11 May 1721: My Lord having condescended to lend Dr Bentley the CODEX AUREUS & the Gospels, & that other antient Exemplar . . . I carried the two MSS . . . to Dr Bentley & took his Note for them: and then went in the Cotton-Library to use some old MSS. there.

28 May 1721: Dr Bentley sent the two MSS. Books of the gospels which he Borrowed, & I returned his Note. Dr Bentley came himself, & tarried long, looking into many MSS.

27 June 1721: Dr Bentley came to thank my Lord for his Favor in lending him the CODEX AUREUS . . . Mr Elliot began to work about the CODEX AUREUS, in Order to the New Binding of it, the Cover it had in the Second Binding of it perhaps about 90 years ago, being worn out, and the whole sewing gone to decay.

13 July 1721: Mr Elliot having clothed the CODEX AUREUS in My Lords Marocco-Leather, took the same from hence this day, in Order to work upon it with his Best Tools; which he say's he can do with much more Conveniency at his house than here. This is particularly noted here, . . . in Case any ill Accident should happen.

But there was no 'ill Accident'. Elliot, the better of the two binders who 'clothed' Harleian books in the skins that were bought in bulk through Gibraltar from Wanley's stepson-in-law John Beaver, returned the book safely. It remains in the red leather binding with elaborate tooled gilt border that made 'Harleian style' a favourite term of commendation in the trade, as prized and jealously guarded now as it was by Harley and Wanley.

The whole episode (loan to Dr Bentley apart) has a surprisingly modern flavour. Wanley's evaluation makes it clear that he (and no doubt 'my Lord') saw the book not just as a text but still more as an object of antiquity and beauty: the buying of it at an auction abroad, the 'Specimen of the Character' demanded as we would photographs, the alarms of freight and customs – all this is familiar to the library or museum today. In this sense the Harleian was the first modern library. At the same time other material came, of a sort and by means with which Sir Robert Cotton would have been quite familiar. So, in the history of libraries, the Harleian stands like the statue of Janus, facing both ways: the actual transition from the old to the new is recorded in Wanley's diary.

Thus, at the beginning of Wanley's connection, he was made responsible for the purchase, in 1706, of the collection of Sir Simonds d'Ewes, a collection

Opposite, top. Robert Harley, 1st Earl of Oxford. *Centre.* Edward Harley, 2nd Earl of Oxford. *Bottom.* Humfrey Wanley.
All reproduced by permission of the Trustees of the British Museum.

The 'swan' constellation, from a copy of the *Phaenomena* of Aratus. Carolingian, 9th century.
Harley MS 647. f.5v.

made in emulation of Cotton's. Like him, D'Ewes tried to put his historic collections and knowledge to the parliamentary cause, with indifferent success; his own parliamentary journals remain an invaluable historic source for the period. Like Cotton, he had notable books from English monasteries: the beautiful Anglo-Saxon copy of the Utrecht Psalter came from Canterbury, the 9th-century copy of Cicero's *Aratea* came from St Augustine's, Canterbury, as did two collections of astronomical tracts which D'Ewes got with many other manuscripts from the estate of John Dee; he also had the great illuminated Bible from Christ Church, Canterbury, the Epistles of Alcuin from York, 9th-century and almost contemporary with the author, the copy of William of Ockham from the foundation gift to Oxford University of Humphrey, Duke of Gloucester, the Latin Chronicle of Robert of Amesbury and Robert of Gloucester's metrical English Chronicle.

Among the other large collections acquired in the heyday of Robert Harley were those of Edward Stillingfleet, Bishop of London, which included the unique manuscript of the famous domestic chronicle of Jocelyn of Brakelond, monk of Bury St Edmunds, and the book from Reading Abbey which contains the music and words of 'Sumer is icumen in'; a mass of heraldic material (a life-long interest of both father and son), including the collections of four generations of the heralds at Chester, all called Randle Holme; and the papers, including those of John Foxe the martyrologist and John Strype the historian. Besides these, Robert Harley amplified Cotton's collection of monastic cartularies, and added the indentures for masses to be said in Henry VII's Chapel

'Sumer is icumen in.' The earliest-known example of English polyphony. 13th century.
Harley MS 978, f.11v.

ut confiteantur nomini
sco tuo. & gloriemur in
laude tua ;
Benedictus dns ds isrl a se
culo & usq: in seculu. &
dicat omnis populus fiat
fiat ;

CPSALMUS ALLELUIA ·CVI·

CONFITEMINI
dno quo bonus qm
in seculum misericordia
eius ;
Dicant nunc qui redempti
sunt a dno. quos redemit
de manu inimici. de regi
onibus congregauit eos ;
A solis ortu & occasu. ab aqui
lone & mari. errauerunt
in solitudine in siccitate
uiam ciuitati habitati
onis non inuenerunt ;
E surientes & sitientes. ani
ma eorum in ipsis defecit ;
E t clamauerunt ad dnm
cum tribularentur. & de
necessitatibus eorum libe
rauit eos ;
E t eduxit eos in uiam rec
tam. ut irent in ciuita
tem habitationis ;
C onfiteantur dno miseri
cordiae eius. & mirabilia
eius filiis hominum ;
Q uia satiauit animam in
anem. & animá esurien
tem satiauit bonis ;
S edentes in tenebris & in
umbra mortis. & uincu
lis ligatos in mendicitate
& ferro ;
Q uia exacerbauerunt elo
quium dni. & consilium
altissimi irritauerunt ;
E [illegible]

Psalm 106, from the Anglo-Saxon copy of the Utrecht Psalter. Early 11th century.
Harley MS 603, f.54*v*.

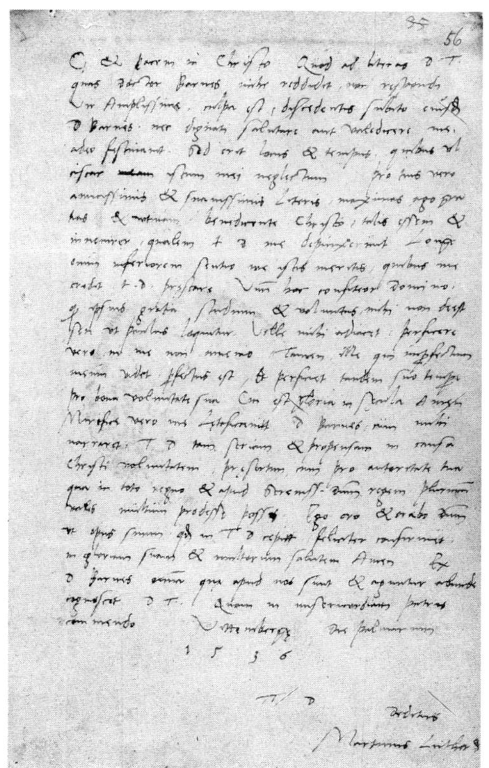

Letter from Martin Luther to Thomas Cromwell, 1536.
Harley MS 6989, f.56.

This small Manual of Prayers is believed to have been used by Lady Jane Grey on the scaffold, 12 February 1554. The notes at the foot of the page are in her hand, and addressed to her father, the Duke of Suffolk.
Harley MS 2342, ff.78v–79.

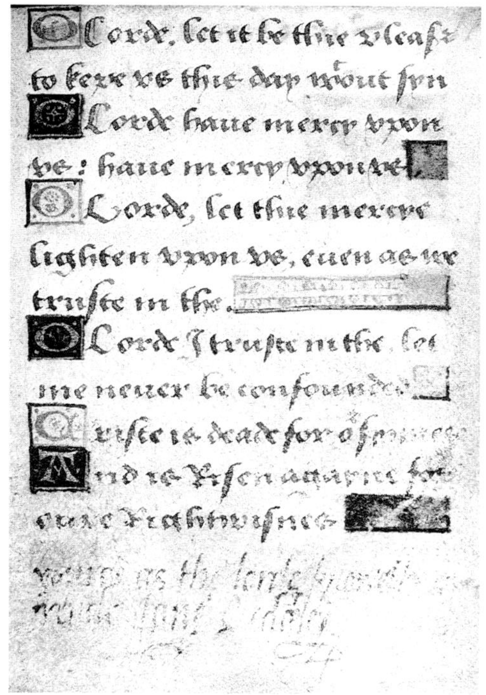

at Westminster, and Sir Edward Coke's own copy of 'Coke upon Littleton', the classic legal text. His own state papers provide a massive wealth of documentation on the political history of his time. All this set the standard for what was to follow.

With the fall of Robert Harley, Wanley's diary ceases for four years, just as he was about to visit Wimpole Hall, the house that had recently come to Edward Harley with his marriage to Henrietta Cavendish Holles and was to be his main home. The library remained in London: until January 1715 it was at York Buildings off the Strand; it was then moved to Bath Court near St James's, where it remained until 1717, when Edward Harley transferred it to the house in Dover Street which then became his London home. From 1715 Wanley and his wife lived with the library. Edward Harley was a hospitable and generous friend and patron to them, and to many others – Pope and Swift, who described his life as 'spent on study, in domestic entertainment, in conversation with men of wit, virtue and learning, and in encouraging their studies', antiquaries and scholars, William Stukeley, Richard Bentley, other collectors, Richard Mead and Hans Sloane, the poet Matthew Prior, the architect James Gibbs, who did work at Wimpole and Dover Street and designed the monument in Westminster to 'O Rare Ben Jonson' for Harley, Sir James Thornhill, and the engraver George Vertue whose industrious life owed everything to Harley – all these were welcome at Wimpole and Dover Street.

In this society Wanley moved at ease: among those with books to sell, whether owners or booksellers, he was dominant; the respect his learning and energy exacted was always turned to 'my Lord's' advantage. Nathaniel Noel, the principal bookseller he employed, was energetic, ambitious, half admired, half distrusted; relentlessly he mined the market, in Europe as well as England, in person or through his mercurial European runner, George Suttie, who found the books from Cardinal Nicolas of Cusa's library and those at Agen used by Scaliger. Wanley's policy was always to purchase privately, at first direct, later through a bookseller, or to pre-empt books to be sold at auction. If unsuccessful in the latter case, he made a hard opponent. Only the Earl of Sunderland proved difficult to beat: when he died, Wanley wrote 'I believe by Reason of his Decease, some benefit may accrue to this Library... so that, in probability, this Commodity [books] may fall in the Market; and any Gentlemen be permitted to buy an uncommon old Book for less than forty or fifty Pounds'. Sir Hans Sloane, by contrast, was commended for standing aside 'out of Respect to my Lord', so that he could buy a fine 10th-century Greek Gospels. He had his failures: the St Chad Gospels at Lichfield eluded him, and the Duke of Devonshire would not relinquish the Benedictional of St Aethelwold, which only came to the Library in 1957. But, by and large, he did not miss an opportunity. In this, as much else, Wanley was the prototype of the modern librarian.

Already in 1715 the manuscripts in the Harleian Library numbered 3000, as well as 13,000 charters and 1000 rolls, with 'numerous' printed books (grown by 1717 to 12,000): at the time of Edward Harley's death it contained 7618 manuscripts, 50,000 printed books, 350,000 pamphlets and 41,000 prints. This constitutes, quality and quantity added together, the greatest library ever made in this country; that part of it now in the British Library contains many of its greatest treasures. The letters of distinguished men – Ralegh's captivating letter to the Earl of Leicester, Luther to Thomas Cromwell, Melanchthon to Henry VIII – fill many volumes. The large collections acquired *en bloc* are full of famous books: Archdeacon Robert Burscough's, for example, contained the 11th-century 'Leofric Collectar' from Exeter, the early text of Chaucer's *Troilus and Criseyde* and the prayer book that Lady Jane Grey used in the Tower. Other royal books include the Psalter of Philippa of Hainault, Edward III's Queen, the Romance of Tristan that belonged to Richard III and the beautiful copy of Lydgate's Lives of St Edmund and St Fremund made for Henry VI.

Cicero, *De Oratore*, in the hand of Lupus of Ferrières. 9th century.
Harley MS 2736, f.40v.

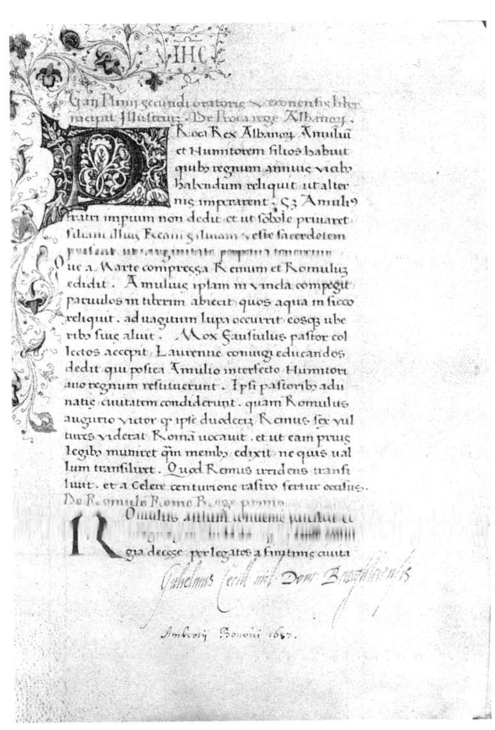

Manuscript copy of Pliny, in the hand of Thomas Candour. 15th century.
Harley MS 2471, f.1.

Among the famous English manuscripts are the 8th/9th-century collection of devotional texts once belonging to Nunnaminster (Winchester) that came to Harley from Wanley's despised boon companion Warburton. The great 10th-century Psalter from Ramsey Abbey is there; the 12th-century William of Malmesbury *De gestis pontificum* from Byland Abbey in Yorkshire was rescued by Wanley *e manibus indoctorum* – 'from unlearned hands' – in 1716. There are two of the most picturesque of 13th-century English bestiaries, and the fine illuminated Psalter made about 1220, which contains earlier miniatures, among them a picture of the murder of Thomas Becket; the unique 'King Horn' manuscript of Middle English Verse, bought with the collection of the antiquary Robert Batteley in 1723, and an important text of Thomas Walsingham's *Chronicon Anglie*, once in Archbishop Parker's collection; the imposing manuscript of Lydgate's 'Life of the Virgin' of the great John de Vere, 13th Earl of Oxford of the first creation (1443–1513), bought at the auction of Harley's competitor Thomas Rawlinson (1681–1725), and the Gospel Lectionary made for John, 5th Lord Lovel to give to Salisbury Cathedral *c.*1400, with pictures (including one of himself) by John Siferwas. Among literary texts there are the copy of the *Canterbury Tales* given to Harley by the great non-juring Bishop Francis Atterbury, Hoccleve's *De regimine principum* with its contemporary portrait of Chaucer, and Lydgate's *The Fall of Princes*, which belonged to Humphrey, Duke of Gloucester.

The Harley collection was especially rich in manuscripts of the classics, and notably in Greek manuscripts. Many of the latter came from Dr John Covell (1638–1722), Master of Christ's College, Cambridge, who as Chaplain to the Levant Company had travelled extensively in the East. Among these were the Acts–Apocalypse written in 1087, bought by Covell in Constantinople in 1677 and Euthymius Zygabenus on the Psalms, written in 1281. William Sherard the botanist Consul at Smyrna, who corresponded with Sloane, was another supplier. The earliest Greek manuscript came with the most notable of Nathaniel Noel's continental acquisitions through Suttie, the books given by Cardinal Nicolas of Cusa to the Hospital of St Nicholas at Trier. This was the Pseudo-Cyril Greek–Latin glossary written in France or Italy in the 7th century; from the same source came the manuscript of Theodore of Mopsuestia written at the abbey of Corbie in the elegant minuscule used there. The Gospels from Eller, nearby on the Moselle, were also acquired through Noel, as was the text of Cicero *De Oratore* written by Lupus of Ferrières, the scholarly 9th-century abbot. An equally important document of the transmission of the classics is the text of Lucian written for the great scholar Arethas in 914, which came via the antiquary John Bridges.

One of Noel's rivals, James Gibson, 'Scots gent buyer of books' in Wanley's words, supplied the fascinating trilingual Psalter (Greek, Latin and Arabic) written probably in Sicily before 1153 and also the 12th-century decorated text of the Sermons of St Ambrose and others written in Italy in the early 12th century. This kind of book served as the model for the script of the books written during the 'humanistic' revival of interest in the classics in the 14th and 15th century; among many notable books of this type, the most interesting is perhaps the copy of Livy annotated and partially written by Petrarch, which later passed to Lorenzo Valla; others include the Ovid owned by Coluccio Salutati and Niccolò Niccoli, the text written by Pier Candido Decembrio for Humphrey, Duke of Gloucester, the first English patron of humanism, and the Pliny written by Thomas Candour, one of the earliest English humanist scribes, probably for Thomas Winterborne, Dean of St Paul's (died 1478), and afterwards acquired by Robert Sherborne, Archdeacon of St David's, given by him to William Warham, Archbishop of Canterbury, and later in the libraries of William Cecil, Lord Burghley, and Ambrose Bonwicke.

Another of Gibson's discoveries was the manuscript of Ptolemy's *Harmonics* written in 1499. It belonged to Francesco Gaforio and Wanley consented to take it from him 'provided that he throws in the MS' with a 'little parcel' of 15

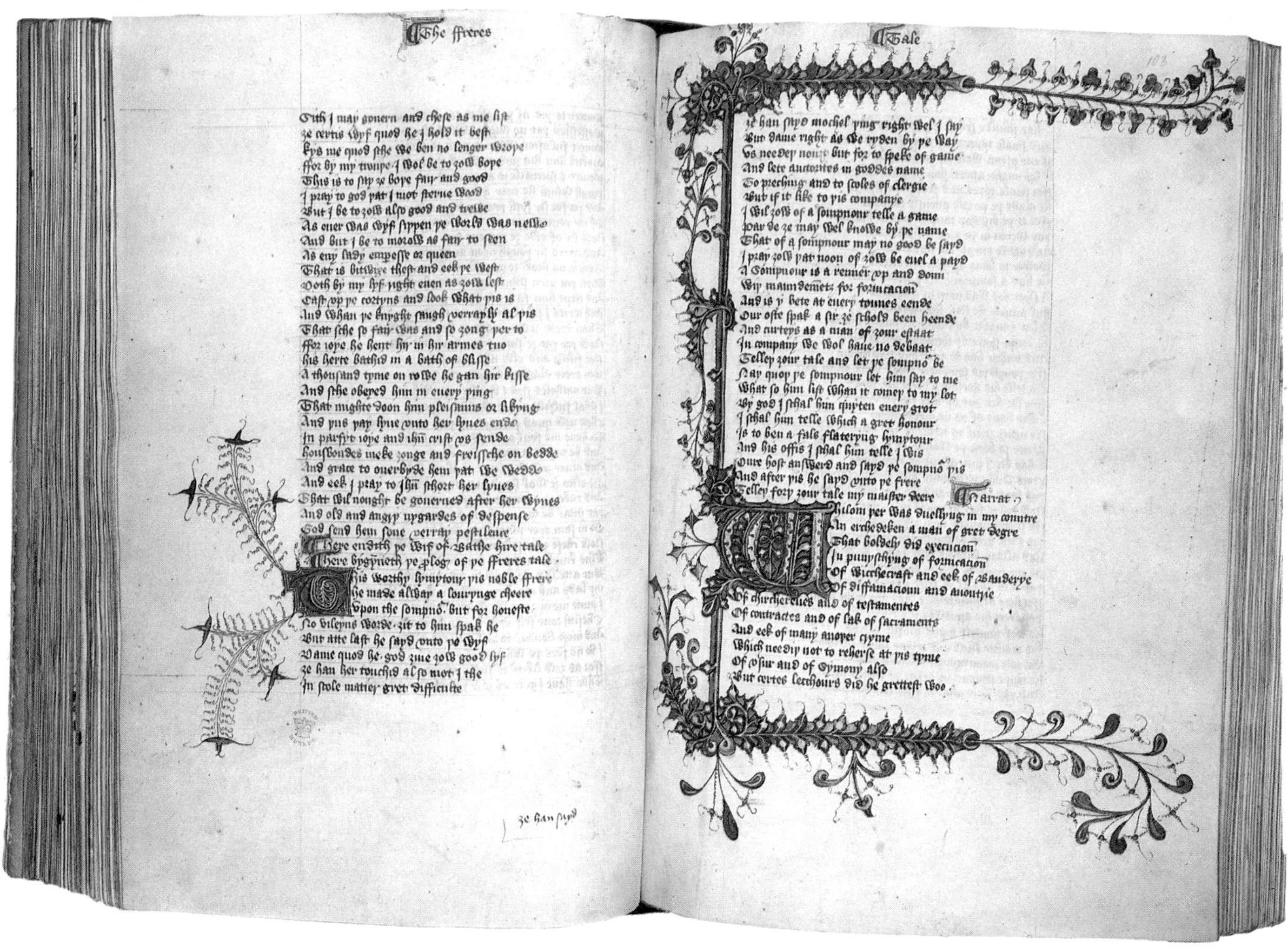

Geoffrey Chaucer, 'The Friar's tale', in a manuscript of *The Canterbury Tales*, *c.*1410.
Harley MS 7334, ff.102v–103.

other humanistic manuscripts. Among Greek books of the same period is the collection of Aristotelian texts written for Cardinal Bessarion. The beautiful italic script popularised by the humanists reached its apogee in the 16th century in the hands of Ludovico degli Arrighi and Francesco Monterchi, both represented in the Harleian collection.

One of the more provoking episodes in the Library's history was the acquisition in 1712 from the renegade Jesuit Jean Aymon (1661–1734) of manuscripts, some of which proved to have been stolen from the Bibliothèque Royale in Paris in 1707. Of these the most important, the 5th-century Codex Claromontanus, was returned by Harley in 1729. Part of another manuscript acquired from Aymon was exchanged in 1881 for 242 volumes of French State Papers transcribed for Colbert from the Loménie de Brienne Collection. Among Aymon's books that stayed in the collection were the Gospels written in Italy in the 6th century from Cardinal Mazarin's collection, the 12th-century Armagh Gospels and the illuminated Genealogies of the French Kings made for Louis XIII by Angoulême Herald. Another spectacular, if also dubious, acquisition was a Carolingian Gospels in golden letters, still at Ste Geneviève in Paris as late as 1684 but acquired in shady circumstances by James Woodman the bookseller, from whom it was bought by Wanley in 1725.

If some of the grandest French manuscripts came from dubious sources, Giovanni Giacomo Zamboni (died 1753), the London Resident for the Landgrave of Hesse-Darmstadt, was by contrast a decorous supplier, through whom came the books of the great classical scholar J.G. Graevius, among

Opposite. Portrait of Geoffrey Chaucer in Thomas Hoccleve's *De regimine principum*. Early 15th century.
Harley MS 4866, f.88.

How he þi seruaunt was mayden marie
And lat his loue floure and fructifie

Al þogh his lyfe be queynt þe resemblaunce
Of him haþ in me so fressh lyflynesse
Þat to putte othir men in remembraunce
Of his persone I haue heere his lyknesse
Do make to þis ende in soþfastnesse
Þat þei þat haue of him lest þought & mynde
By þis peynture may ageyn him fynde

The ymages þat in þe chirche been
Maken folk þenke on god & on his seyntes
Whan þe ymages þei beholden & seen
Were oft vnsyte of hem causith restreyntes
Of þoughtes gode whan a þing depeynt is
Or entailed if men take of it heede
Thoght of þe lyknesse it wil in hym brede

Yit some holden opynyon and sey
Þat none ymages schuld I maked be
Þei erren foule & goon out of þe wey
Of trouth haue þei scant sensibilitee
Passe ouer now þat blessid trinitee
Vpon my maistres soule mercy haue
For him lady eke þi mercy I craue

More othir þing wolde I fayne speke & touche
Heere in þis booke but schuch is my dulnesse
For þat al voyde and empty is my pouche
Þat al my lust is queynt with heuynesse
And heuy spirit commaundeth stilnesse

Marcantonio Flaminio, *Paraphrasi sopra li psalmi*, written by Francesco da Monterchi, 1541–60.
Harley MS 3541, ff.38*v*–39.

them the oldest surviving manuscript of Vitruvius, from St Pantaleon, Cologne, and a 10th-century Carolingian Horace, as well as important later documents, such as Van Dyck's correspondence with Junius. Important German acquisitions were the great Bible from St Maria, Worms, and the Apuleius Barbarus herbal, both 12th century. Other distinguished continental acquisitions were the 12th-century Psalter from La Charité, the Missal and Bible Chronicle of that greatest of French patrons, Jean, Duc de Berry, and the exquisite French commentary on Caesar written for François I in 1519 and brought to England by Henri Justel; the *Roman de la Rose* made for Engelbert of Nassau, the Medici copy of Petrarch's *Trionfi*, the very fine 14th-century Breviary from Val-Duchesse, near Brussels, and the great Livy illuminated for Alfonso V of Aragon and I of Naples.

Heraldry was a primary interest of both Harleys, father and son: 'I shall be glad to make the collection of Heraldic MSS as complete as possible', Edward Harley told Wanley. Manuscripts by or from the collections of most of the early heralds were acquired, including one of the arms of Knights of the Garter given by Sir William Dethick to Queen Elizabeth as a New Year's Gift in 1588, and the mass of important medieval heraldic drawing known as Sir Thomas Holme's Book. There are many collections of antiquaries' manuscripts, among them those of John Stowe, the Elizabethan chronicler of London, and Sir Robert Cotton's catalogue of his collection. Exceptional among the thousands of rolls, and most famous of all, is the Guthlac Roll, a 13th-century depiction of the life of St Guthlac in 18 tinted outline drawings, which was exhibited to the Society of Antiquaries at their meeting on 23 January 1708 at the Young Divell Tavern in Fleet Street by Peter Le Neve, and subsequently acquired by Wanley.

Two famous manuscripts are associated with the name of Thomas More. Harley MS 1860 is the autograph translation of Eusebius by More's granddaughter, Mary Basset, given by her to Queen Mary I. Finally, there is the celebrated manuscript of 'The Play of Sir Thomas More', one section of which may possibly be in Shakespeare's hand and which may have come to the Library through John Murray of Sacombe, the friend of Edward Harley and George Vertue.

Murray was a great collector of Caxtons and other early printed books, and these too engaged the attention of Edward Harley and his librarian. Wanley's interest in the history of printing was early stimulated by his acquaintance,

Opposite, above. Portrait of François I, in *Les Commentaires da la Guerre Gallique*, 1519.
Harley MS 6205, f.3*r*.

Opposite, below. William Shakespeare. Assumed autograph contribution to *The Play of Sir Thomas More*, *c.*1593–1601.
Harley MS 7368, f.9.

St Guthlac taking leave of his fellow warriors. From the Guthlac Roll. English, 13th century.
Harley Roll Y6.

F M

Le treſcreſtian Roy
Francoys
Demande a Cæſar
EN quantez parties eſt diui
ſee toute la gaule qui vous
a aultreffoiz tant donne de peine
Cæſar dictez le moy ie vous prie

I C

Cæſar reſpond
ROy liberal & pacificque vray
heritier de ma gloire et fortu

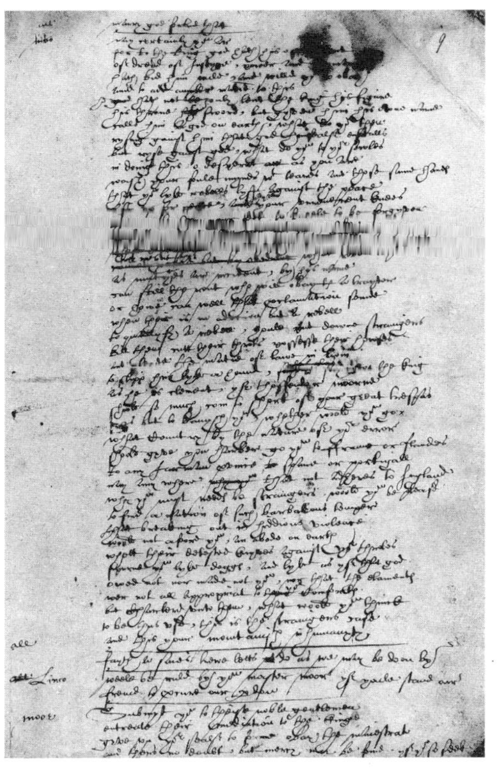

going back to 1695, with the shoe-maker and antiquary, John Bagford, who was associated with Wanley in the revival of the Society of Antiquaries in 1707, and whose collection was acquired by Harley after Bagford's death in 1716. Chiefly famous now for the broadsides known as the 'Bagford Ballads', it contains a mass of printed fragments, still not fully explored, among them a leaf of the first printed Bible, printed at Mainz *c.*1455 with 42 lines to the page, with contemporary English illumination, one of the earliest evidences of the importation of printed books into England. (Illustrated overleaf.)

The dispersal of the Harleys' main library of printed books was one of the great national tragedies of the 18th century: what was lost to Britain, in part at least, is now to be found among the treasures of the Göttingen University and Copenhagen Royal Libraries. But some at least of its contents have come later to the British Library. Among the Caxtons, of which Harley counted 42, *The Game and Play of Chess* printed by Caxton at Bruges in 1474 is now in the Library, and the first book printed at Oxford, Rufinus on the Creed (1478) is still in its original Harleian binding. One that escaped was the only perfect copy of the *Morte d'Arthur* (1485) now in the Pierpont Morgan Library, but the Harley copy, printed on vellum, of Aeneas Sylvius Piccolomini *De duobus amantibus* in a French translation (Paris, Vérard, *c.*1493) returned. Needless to say, the great collectors of later times, James West, Earl Spencer, Count McCarthy Reagh, Sir Mark Masterman Sykes and Thomas Grenville acquired many Harley books; Grenville acquired the *Catholicon* on vellum and the 1470 Rome Cicero *Ad Atticum*, and from West came the vellum copy of Bernard Breydenbach's account of his pilgrimage to Jerusalem, *Peregrinatio in terram sanctam* (Mainz, Erhard Reuwich, 1486).

All this is a fraction of what might have made the Library of the British Museum at its foundation incomparably greater than it was. But Edward Harley was too generous, too careless – Swift wrote of his 'indolence, good nature and lack of worldly wisdom'. In 1740, he was obliged to sell Wimpole, and the library there was brought up to London and set out in the new mansion that Harley had just built to house it, in twelve rooms and two galleries, in the Marylebone Road, the manuscripts remaining at Dover Street. Harley had intended to establish it as 'a public Library hereafter in or near London', but on 16 June 1741 he died. Although the sale of Wimpole had paid off a debt of £100,000, vast liabilities remained; the pictures, prints and drawings, Greek and Roman antiquities and coins and medals were sold by auction, while the printed books were sold *en bloc* to the bookseller Thomas Osborne in 1742 for £13,000 – less, it was said, than they cost to bind. Osborne commissioned the bibliographer William Oldys to prepare a catalogue of them, which was published between 1743 and 1745, and in 1742 issued 'Proposals' for the catalogue to which Samuel Johnson contributed 'An Account of the Harleian Library'. Oldys also compiled the selection from the vast collection of tracts that appeared in eight volumes between 1744 and 1746 under the title of *The Harleian Miscellany*.

As early as 1743, the non-juring historian Thomas Carte, pointing out that 'There is not a great City in Europe so ill provided with Public Libraries as London', urged that the Harleian manuscripts at least should be purchased for £20,000 and preserved for public use, but nothing came of this until Sloane's bequest and Speaker Onslow's determination revived the proposal. On 3 April 1753, as the Commons' Committee debated Sloane's bequest, Harley's sole daughter and heir, Margaret, Duchess of Portland, wrote about the manuscripts to Onslow: 'As I know it was my father's and is my mother's intention that they should be kept together, I will not bargain with the Publick'; with the further condition that 'this great valuable Collection shall be kept together in the proper repository, as an addition to the Cotton Library, and be called by the name of Harleian Collection of Manuscripts', she offered it to the nation for £10,000. The immediate result of this was described in the first chapter. Generations since have been grateful for her generosity.

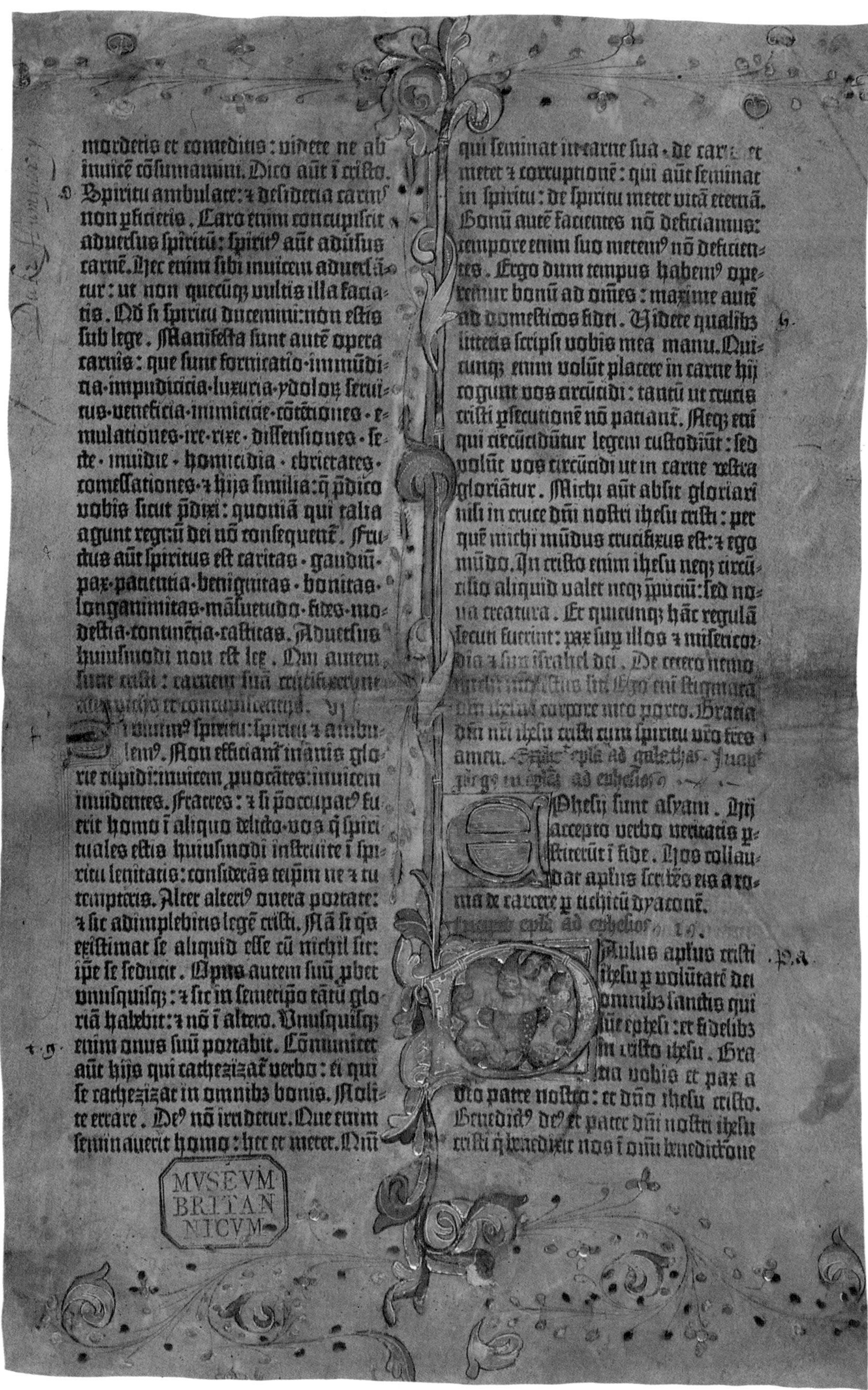

A leaf of the first printed bible (the '42-line Bible') printed at Mainz *c.*1455, with contemporary English illumination.
IC 56a.

4

Montagu House and the early years of the National Library

Montagu House, from the north, *c.*1800
BM Prints and Drawings XXVIII, no.75. Reproduced by permission of the Trustees of the British Museum.

MONTAGU HOUSE WAS set back from Great Russell Street, but parallel to it. It was 216 feet long and 57 feet high, and was joined to the wall that separated it from the street by lower wings that now served as residences for the staff. In the middle of the street wall was a gatehouse with tall gates surmounted by an octagonal tower topped with a cupola (all that survived of Robert Hooke's original building). Behind the house an elegant garden (which the Trustees were at pains to improve) stretched to a low garden wall, beyond which was still open country. To the west, a grove of limes screened the line of Gower Street (Bedford Square was not yet built); there were more trees to the east, and beyond Southampton Row.

The principal interest of the new Trustees was to put this house in order. Besides the repair to the fabric and décor already noted, presses and shelving for the books were required: 4600 feet for Sloane's books and manuscripts, 1700 feet for the Harleian, 384 feet for the Cottonian and 576 feet for Major Edwards's libraries. The division of the Museum into three sections, each with an Under-Librarian in charge, originally determined by the contents of the foundation collections, was formalised in 1758: Maty took charge of the Department of Printed Books, Morton of the Department of Manuscripts and James Empson, for long Keeper of Sloane's collections at Chelsea, of the 'Department of Natural and Artificial Curiosities'. These were the arrangements that confronted the first visitors when the Museum opened in January 1759.

For the most part they came, as now, to walk round and see what was on display. From the Entrance Hall, they went up the grand staircase, admiring the painted walls and ceiling, to the head of the stairs where the bust of Sir Hans Sloane stood. Then came the main Saloon, looking out to the north, where the cases of 'Curiosities' were displayed: there the visitor waited until one of the Officers was free to conduct him through the other rooms on the first floor: first those containing the Royal and Cottonian libraries, then the Harleian in three rooms, containing the biblical manuscripts and medals, the other manuscripts and charters, and finally the Sloane medals and manuscripts. The next two rooms, divided by the vestibule, contained the antiquities and natural history collections, whence a secondary staircase led down to the ground floor where a series of rooms, all facing north, contained the great mass of printed books from the Royal Library and Sloane's collection. Turning at the east end, the path led through the Trustees' room, and those containing Major Edwards's books and the residue of the Royal Library, back to the Hall.

Conducting visitors, at most 60 a day, was considered an exhausting task by the Officers. The Trustees' Standing Committee required them to spend four of the six hours the Museum was open thus, and 'the two vacant hours (if not thought too great a burden on the officers) might very usefully be employed by them in better ranging the several Collections . . ., and preparing catalogues for publication, which last the Committee think so necessary a work that till it is performed the several collections can be but imperfectly useful to the Public'. The Officers, however, would have preferred a day off to do this, due to 'the impossibility of applying the two spare hours in any serious study, on account of the fatigue of the other four hours' attendance'. Some concessions were made by the Trustees, but the uneasy relations between them and the staff continued.

One of the most difficult was the first Keeper of the Reading Room, Peter Templeman. The Reading Room itself was a narrow, dark room in the south-west angle of the building in the basement, ill lit by two windows. On one occasion Templeman, always concerned about his health, had left his post for the garden to get a breath of fresh air, only to be confronted by one of the Trustees who ordered him to 'Go back, Sir!' He might be forgiven, perhaps, since at the start there were not many readers. On the first day there were eight: two of them were protégés of the historian Philip Yorke, later 2nd Earl of Hardwicke (who took the chair at the meeting of the Commons Committee on 6 April 1753 that determined the acceptance of Sloane's bequest); three were divines, including Robert Lowth, later Bishop of London and Samuel Chandler, the non-conformist scholar; Samuel Musgrave, physician and classical scholar, was another, with James Stuart, antiquary, painter and architect, about to publish *The Antiquities of Athens* (1762), while the last had special 'permission to send for Books containing specimens of Cinnamon and Cassia'.

These varied interests well represent the use made of the library in these early days. Templeman soon left and was succeeded as Keeper by Richard Penneck, who held the post till 1803 and became quite a figure in the learned world. He knew Samuel Johnson, who visited the Reading Room on 8 May 1760; other early readers were William Blackstone, the author of *Commentaries on the Laws of England*; Lord Monboddo, the Scottish law-lord who speculated on the descent of man from the orang-outan; Edmund Burke, the politician, who had just started the *Annual Register*; John Wilkes, publisher of the *North Briton* and editor of Catullus and Theophrastus; Francis Hargrave, the legal historian whose library later provided the foundation of the Museum's collections on law; and Francis Douce, later Keeper of Manuscripts, who bequeathed his own collection, the first to be formed with a connoisseur's eye for medieval manuscripts, to the Bodleian Library.

Others who came were Johnson's friend, Topham Beauclerk, who lived in Great Russell Street near the Museum and, according to Horace Walpole, 'built a library which reaches halfway to Highgate – Everybody goes to see it. It has put the Museum's nose quite out of joint'. His 30,000 books, rich in plays and English literature generally, were dispersed in 1781, and some came to the Museum. Thomas Tyrwhitt, the classical scholar, editor of Chaucer, and exposer of Thomas Chatterton (who forged the medieval English poems of 'Thomas Rowley'), was another reader and later benefactor, who bequeathed his collection of classical texts, 900 volumes in all, many annotated by himself and other classical scholars. And there was another reader who came from not far away, Thomas Gray, the poet and friend of Horace Walpole, who had just moved to Southampton Row, a stone's throw from the rectory of St George's, Queen Square, whose Incumbent, William Stukeley, the antiquary who first associated Stonehenge with the Druids, was also a regular reader. On 8 August 1759, Gray wrote to his friend James Brown:

> Come and see me in my peaceful new settlement, from whence I have the command of Highgate, Hampstead, Bedford-Gardens & the Musaeum. This last (as you will imagine) is my favourite Domain, where I often pass four hours in the day in the stillness & solitude of the reading room, wch is uninterrupted by any thing but Dr Stukeley the Antiquary, who comes there to talk nonsense, & Coffee-house news; the rest of the Learned are (I suppose) in the country, at least none of them come there except two Prussians & a man who writes for Ld. Royston. When I call it peaceful, you are to understand it only of us Visiters, for the Society itself, Trustees & all, are up in arms, like the Fellows of a College, the keepers have broke off all intercourse with one another, & only lower a silent defiance as they pass by.

No doubt Gray exaggerates, but there was ill-feeling between the Keepers and between them and the staff, and the root cause of it was a chronic shortage of funds. The income from the residue of the lottery funds, the reversion of Major Edwards's bequest, and other windfalls, was grossly inadequate. In 1762 the Trustees asked Parliament for help, but despite the advocacy of Wilkes and Burke, it was never enough. Wages and the maintenance of the building accounted for all or more of the money at the Trustees' disposal; up to 1769 only £69 all told was spent on the acquisition of books. In that year the first of a series of sales of 'duplicates' took place which (as noted earlier) sadly

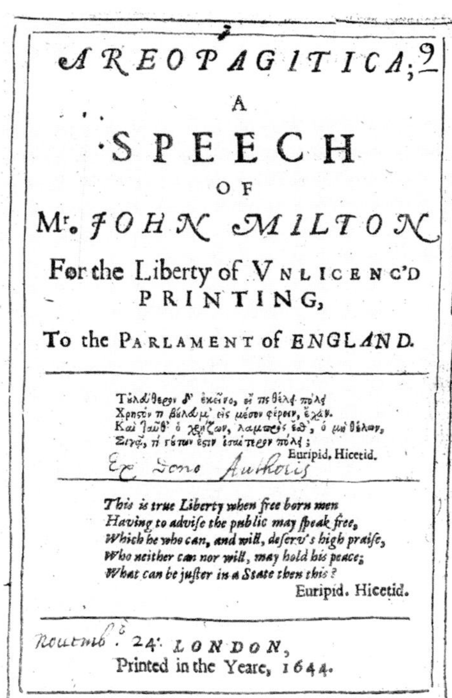
AREOPAGITICA;

A

SPEECH

OF

Mr. JOHN MILTON

For the Liberty of VNLICENC'D PRINTING,

To the PARLAMENT of ENGLAND.

Τοὐλεύθερον δ' ἐκεῖνο, εἴ τις θέλει πόλει
Χρηστόν τι βούλευμ' εἰς μέσον φέρειν, ἔχων.
Καὶ ταῦθ' ὁ χρῄζων, λαμπρὸς ἔσθ', ὁ μὴ θέλων,
Σιγᾷ, τί τούτων ἔστιν ἰσαίτερον πόλει;

Euripid. Hicetid.

Ex Dono Authoris

This is true Liberty when free born men
Having to advise the public may speak free,
Which he who can, and will, deserv's high praise,
Who neither can nor will, may hold his peace;
What can be juster in a State then this?

Euripid. Hicetid.

Novemb. 24. LONDON,
Printed in the Yeare, 1644.

Milton, *Areopagitica*. Thomason's copy, inscribed 'ex dono authoris'.
C.55.c.22(9).

depleted the historic collections without making any sizeable acquisition of new books possible; it was many years before any English books at all were purchased.

Even catalogues, vital to the Library's use, were a problem. The *Catalogue of the Harleian Manuscripts*, already all but finished (largely by Wanley) when the collection was acquired, was finished by Morton and published in 1759, but, as Gray wrote to Mason in 1759, 'I find that they printed one thousand copies of the Harleian Catalogue, and have sold four score; that they have £900 a year income and spend £1300 and that they are building apartments for the under Keepers, so I expect in winter to see the collection advertised, and all the books and crocodiles will soon be put up to auction'.

If Gray's worst predictions were not fulfilled, there remained a sad gap in the catalogues. In 1777 Thomas Astle, a Trustee and authority on the history of writing, produced a cursory catalogue of the Cottonian manuscripts, published not by the Trustees but by a bookseller, Samuel Hooper. Five years later another sympathiser outside the Museum, Samuel Ayscough, dealt with the Sloane and other manuscripts added up to 1782 in similar style. The one part of the collections which did receive a new catalogue, printed for the Trustees, was the printed books. The *Librorum impressorum qui in Museo Britannico adservantur catalogus*, a handsome piece of printing, worthy of its subject, and spacious enough to be used (as it was) for manuscript additions, appeared in 1787. It was due to Samuel Harper, who had succeeded Maty as Keeper of Printed Books, and P.H. Maty, his son, but the main work of compilation and arrangement fell on the indefatigable Samuel Ayscough, who finally joined the staff as Assistant Keeper in the year that the catalogue appeared.

Despite the lack of adequate catalogues, the number of readers grew. In 1774, Penneck's complaints proving more effective than Templeman's, the old Reading Room was abandoned for two larger, lighter and drier rooms at the north-west corner of the building, equipped with book-cases and portraits. Despite the absence of funds for acquisition, some notable accessions came, by gift or bequest, the Trustees proving energetic and generous in this respect. With the Royal Library, too, had come the presumed right to 'copyright deposit', the requirement under the 1709 Copyright Act that a copy of every work registered at Stationers' Hall should be deposited in the Royal Library, and in eight other libraries. Although the right had hardly been enforced by successive Royal Librarians, it still existed and was to have a major influence on the British Museum Library's development in the next century. It was, however, a negligible resource now.

The first major accession after the Museum opened came in 1759, from Solomon da Costa, a Dutch Jew from Amsterdam who had settled in England early in the 18th century and then came into possession of the collection of important Hebrew books acquired by Charles II but left with Samuel Mearne, the bill for binding them unpaid. Now Da Costa wrote offering them to the Trustees 'as a small token of my esteem, love, reverence, and gratitude to this most magnanimous nation; and as a thanksgiving offering, in part, for the generous protection and numberless blessings which I have enjoyed under it'. So, exactly a century after the event, the intention of the first donors was fulfilled. Among these books were the foundation of the Library's unparalleled collection of early Hebrew printing, including eight books from the first Hebrew Press at Rome (*c.*1469–72), Maimonides's *Mishneh Torah* (Rome, *c.*1480) and the Soncino Bible (1488).

Three years later came another benefaction of a very different kind, but with an oddly similar history. From 3 November 1640, George Thomason (*ante* 1602–1666), bookseller at the Rose and Crown in St Paul's Churchyard, began to collect all the pamphlets and fugitive pieces about current events that began to pour from the press following the relaxation of the Star Chamber Court regulations. It was an act of extraordinary prescience: by the time he ceased on the day of Charles II's coronation, 23 April 1661, he had

A news pamphlet in the Thomason collection, giving details of an incident during the siege of Colchester by a parliamentary army in 1648.
E.456(11).

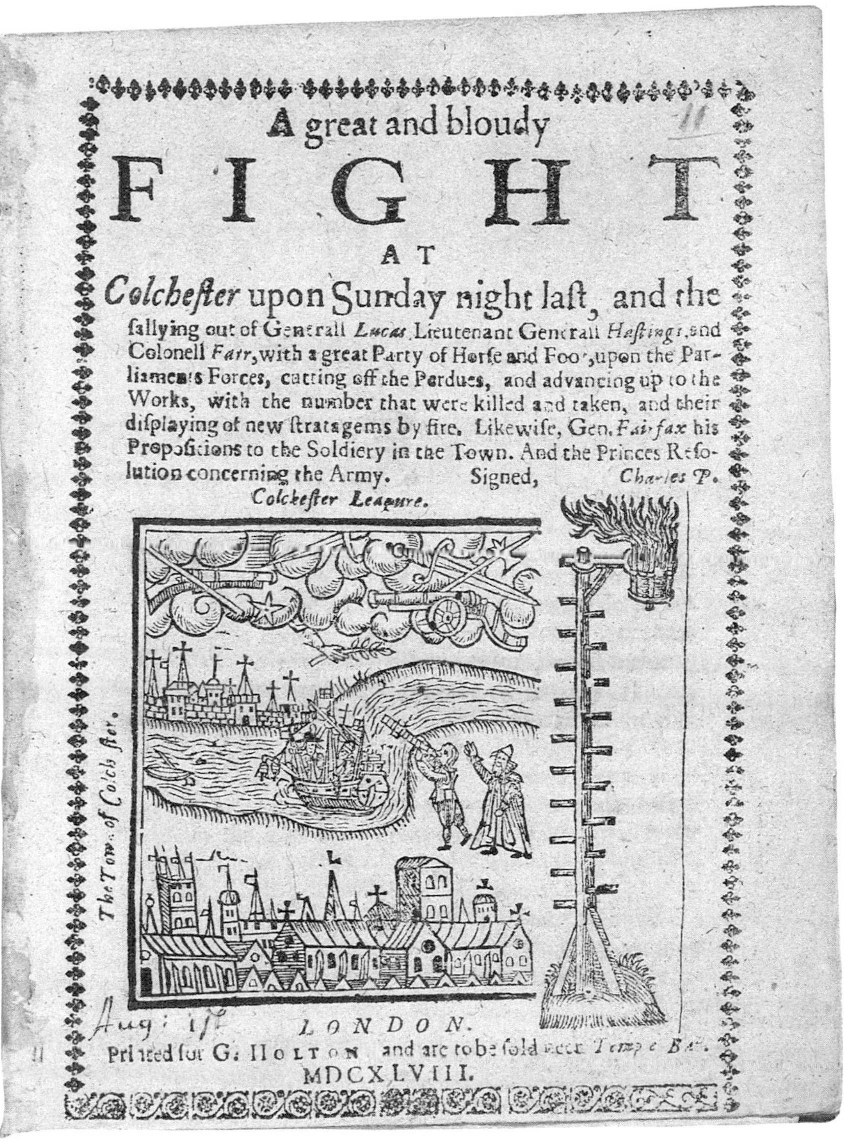
A great and bloudy
FIGHT
AT
Colchester upon Sunday night last, and the sallying out of Generall *Lucas*, Lieutenant Generall *Hastings*, and Colonell *Farr*, with a great Party of Horse and Foot, upon the Parliaments Forces, catting off the Perdues, and advancing up to the Works, with the number that were killed and taken, and their displaying of new stratagems by fire. Likewise, Gen. *Fairfax* his Propositions to the Soldiery in the Town. And the Princes Resolution concerning the Army. Signed, *Charles P.*

Colchester Leaguer.

Aug: 15

LONDON.
Printed for G. Horton and are to be sold neer *Temple Bar.*
MDCXLVIII.

Inscription by Thomason in a volume of Tracts.
E.936(8).

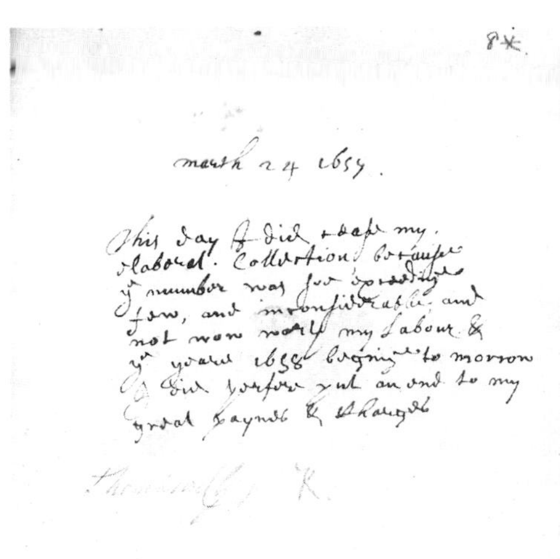
march 24 1657.

This day I did take my laboured Collection because the number was so exceeding few, and inconsiderable and not worth my labour & the yeare 1658 beginning to morrow I did therefore put an end to my great paynes & charges

accumulated 22,255 pieces bound in 2008 volumes. Thomas Carlyle, a stern critic of the British Museum, giving evidence to a Royal Commission in 1847–49, called them 'the most valuable set of documents connected with English history; greatly preferable to all the sheepskins in the Tower and other places, for informing the English what the English were in former times' – an exaggeration pardonable to the biographer of Oliver Cromwell.

This collection Thomason preserved with great care in his lifetime; providentially, he had sent it to Oxford in the care of the sympathetic Thomas Barlow (1607–91), professor of divinity and later Bishop of Lincoln, so that it escaped the Fire of London. Some time after 1676 it passed to Samuel Mearne and remained with his descendants until 1761 when Thomas Hollis (1720–74), the republican bibliophile and benefactor of Harvard University and other libraries, got to hear of it. He persuaded Lord Bute, George III's confidant, just made Secretary of State, to purchase the Thomason Tracts for £300. The king is said to have refunded Bute, who presented the collections to the Trustees in the king's name in 1762.

The chief value of the collection is its mass, as Carlyle saw, fortified by Thomason's invaluable habit of marking the exact date of acquisition on each piece. Most of the books he bought, but a few were given to him, notably Milton's *Areopagitica* (1644), inscribed 'ex dono authoris'. Here also are the prime documents of the Civil War, *The reasons of the Lords and Commons why*

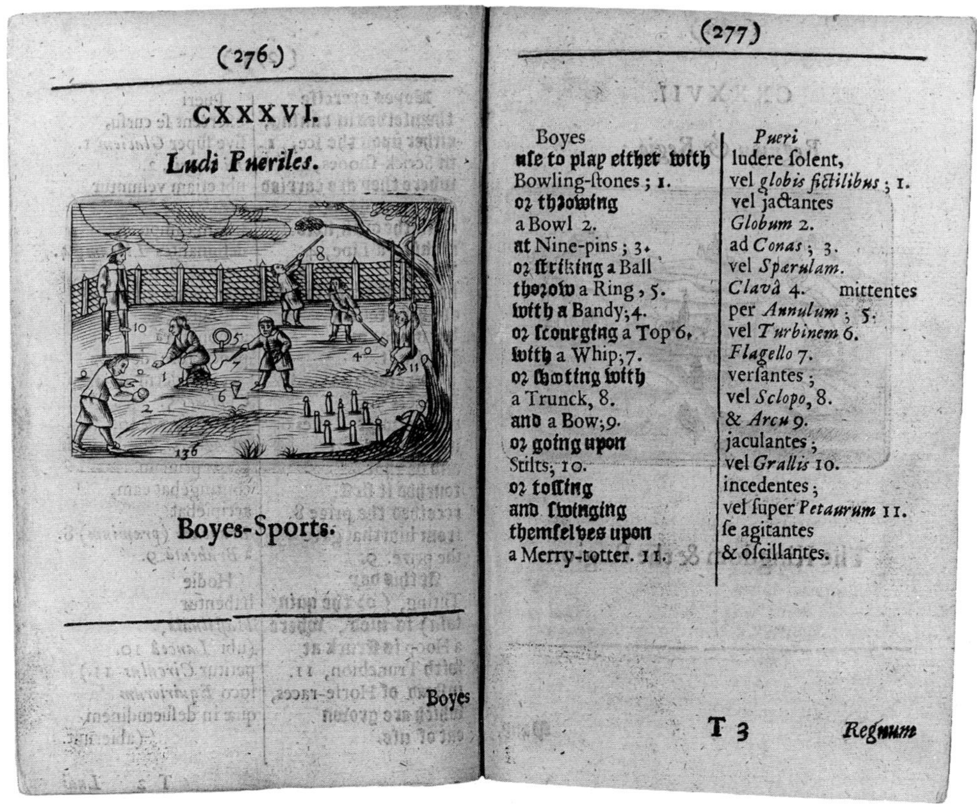

(276)

CXXXVI.

Ludi Pueriles.

Boyes-Sports.

Boyes

(277)

Boyes	*Pueri*
use to play either with	ludere solent,
Bowling-stones; 1.	vel *globis fictilibus*; 1.
or throwing	vel jactantes
a Bowl 2.	*Globum* 2.
at Nine-pins; 3.	ad *Conas*; 3.
or striking a Ball	vel *Sperulam*.
throw a Ring, 5.	*Clavâ* 4. mittentes
with a Bandy; 4.	per *Annulum*; 5.
or scourging a Top 6.	vel *Turbinem* 6.
with a Whip; 7.	*Flagello* 7.
or shooting with	versantes;
a Trunck, 8.	vel *Sclopo*, 8.
and a Bow; 9.	& *Arcu* 9.
or going upon	jaculantes;
Stilts; 10.	vel *Grallis* 10.
or tossing	incedentes;
and swinging	vel super *Petaurum* 11.
themselves upon	se agitantes
a Merry-totter. 11.	& oscillantes.

T 3 Regnum

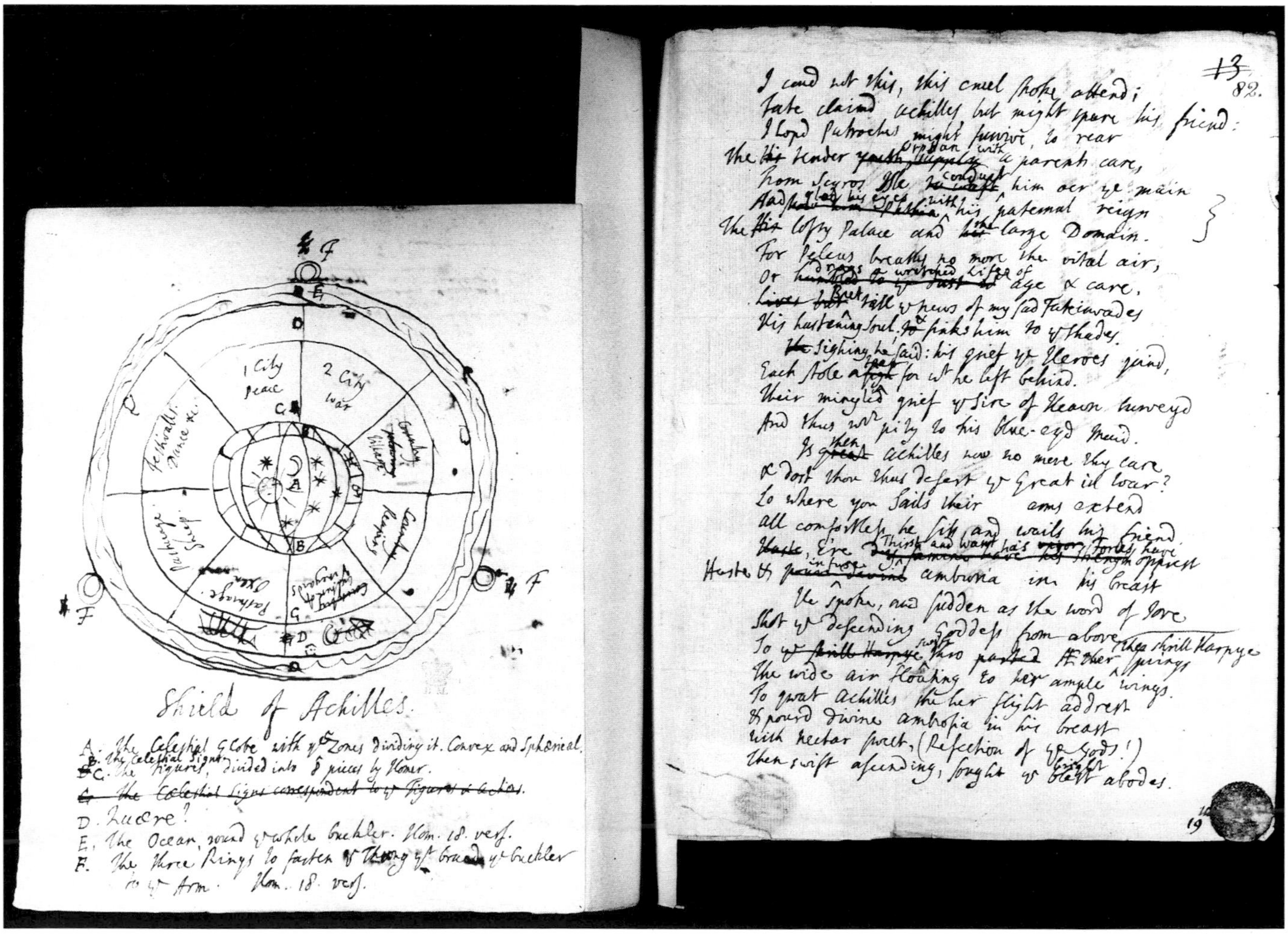

Shield of Achilles.

A. The Celestial Globe with ye Zones dividing it. Convex and Sphærical.
B. the Celestial Signs.
C. The Figures, divided into 8 pieces by Homer.
~~C. the Celestial Signs correspondent to ye Figures & actions.~~
D. Lucre?
E. The Ocean, round ye whole buckler. Hom. 18. vers.
F. The three Rings to fasten ye Thong yt braced ye buckler to ye Arm. Hom. 18. vers.

82.

I cared not this, this cruel stroke attend;
Fate claim'd Achilles but might spare his friend:
I hop'd Patroclus might survive, to rear
The tender orphan with a parent's care,
From Scyros Isle conduct him o'er ye main
And glad his eyes with his paternal reign
The lofty Palace and the large Domain.
For Peleus breaths no more the vital air,
Or drags a wretched life of age & care,
But till ye news of my sad Fate invades
His hastening Soul & sinks him to ye shades.
Sighing he said: his grief ye Heroes joind,
Each stole a tear for wt he left behind.
Their mingled grief ye Sire of Heav'n survey'd
And thus wth pity to his blue-ey'd Maid.
Is then Achilles now no more thy care
& dost thou thus desert ye Great in war?
Lo where yon Sails their arms extend
All comfortless he sits and wails his friend
Ere Thirst and Want his Forces have opprest
Haste & infuse ambrosia in his breast
He spoke, and sudden as the word of Jove
Shot ye descending Goddess from above
So swift thro Æther the shrill Harpye springs
The wide air floating to her ample wings.
To great Achilles she her flight addrest
& pour'd divine ambrosia in his breast
With nectar sweet, (Refection of ye Gods!)
Then swift ascending, sought ye bright abodes.

19

Opposite, above. Page opening from Comenius, *Orbis Sensualium Pictus*, 1659.
E.2116(1), pp.276–277.

Opposite, below. Autograph draft by Alexander Pope of his translation of Homer's *Iliad*, with his drawing of the 'Shield of Achilles'.
Add. MS 4808, ff.81v–82.

Portrait of Thomas Birch.
Reproduced by permission of the Trustees of the British Museum.

they cannot agree, 4 April 1643 and the *Declaration*, 7 April, bound together in a volume seen by the King himself, and the *Charge against Charles I* and *Proclamation for the tryall* (1649). But here too is the copy of Izaak Walton's *The compleat angler*, bought new in 1653, and the earliest English children's picture-book, Comenius's *Orbis sensualium pictus* 1659. The marks of Thomason's care and affection for his collection are clearly visible, for example in his punctual record of the circumstances in which Charles I borrowed a book and dropped it in the dirt, and of the day, 24 March 1659, when he decided to bring the collection to an end. Its subsequent history is recorded in the manuscript catalogue, made perhaps after Thomason's death and in the advertisement of the collection for sale (1685?).

Among the other early acquisitions were the transcripts of public documents made by successive Historiographers Royal, Thomas Rymer (1641–1713) and Thomas Madox (1666–1727), with those of the Rolls of Parliament and the House of Lords Journals. Besides these came the manuscripts of Dr Thomas Birch, bequeathed with some useful printed books in 1766. Birch had been 'as brisk as a bee' in all matters relating to the Museum; he is now best remembered for the £500 he left for the improvement of the librarians' salaries, but his transcripts had their importance, and some of the original documents he preserved, notably those relating to the Royal Society, of which he was Secretary, and the British Museum, are still valued today. He had important letters of Newton and Locke, the correspondence of Pierre Bayle the historian and Sir Thomas Roe, ambassador to Persia and India. Other important letters, such as Oliver Cromwell's reporting his victory at Naseby to the Speaker of the House of Commons, arrived singly, in this case 'the gift of Mr Wright' in 1750.

Arthur Onslow crowned his benefactions to the Museum with the gift of his collection of Bibles in 1768; Mrs Lucy Mallett presented the autograph draft of Pope's Homer in 1766; the original letters of Swift's *Journal to Stella* came in the same year, following Hawkesworth's first edition of the text; and in 1769 Earl Stanhope presented the Articles of the Barons, the basis of Magna Carta and the document actually sealed at Runnymede. In 1767, Joseph Banks, who had been admitted to the Reading Room at the age of 21 in August

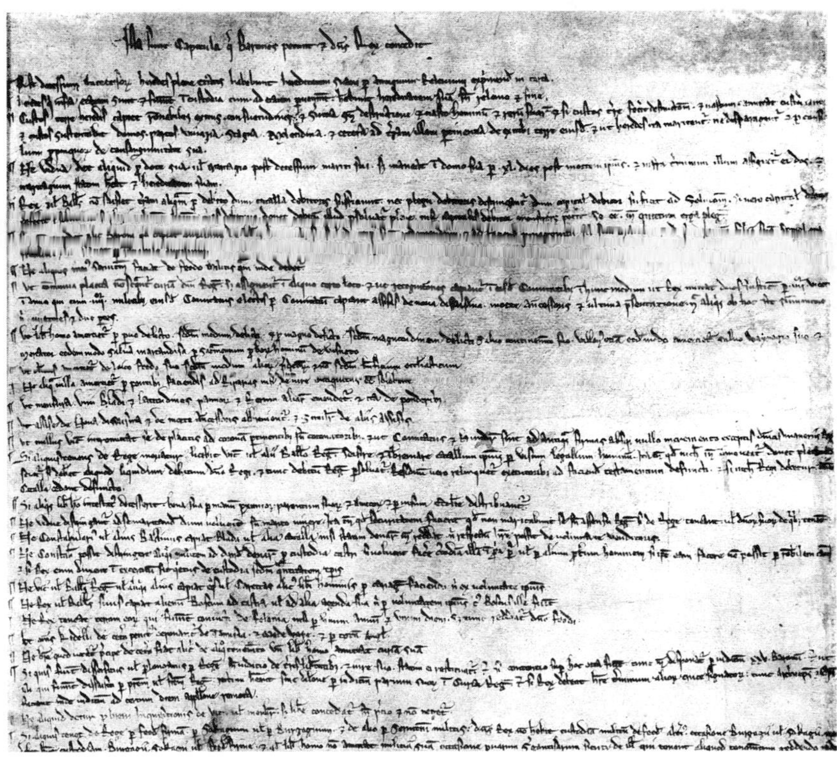

The Articles of the Barons, 1215. The document sealed by King John at Runnymede (detail, right, with Seal, above).
Add. MS 4838.

Portrait of David Garrick.
National Portrait Gallery London.

The earliest play in the Garrick Collection, *Hyckescorner*, printed by Wynkyn de Worde, ?1515. From the Astle gift volume.
C.21.c.4.

Opposite. Roubiliac's statue of Shakespeare, commissioned by Garrick for the Temple of Shakespeare at his home, Hampton House, 1758, and left by him to the British Museum.

1765, began a long career of benevolence to the Museum with the gift of Icelandic manuscripts, adding printed books in 1773. These included the first complete Bible in Icelandic, *Biblia, þad er, Øll Heilög Ritning* (Hólar, 1584), the *Landnámábok* (Skalhollt, 1688), an account of the first settlers in Iceland, and Snorri Sturluson's *Heimskringla* (Copenhagen, 1633), the first complete printing in Danish of the great chronicle of the Norse Kings.

Six years after the Banks donation came a bequest which was to have a deep and persistent influence on the future of the Library and the use of its contents. On 20 January 1779 David Garrick died, leaving to the British Museum his famous collection of early English plays, some 1300 in all, bound in 242 volumes. It was, and has remained, the largest single collection of its kind ever made. The nucleus, perhaps as much as half of the collection, had been successively accumulated by Humfrey Dyson, wax-chandler, notary and antiquary (died 1632), Richard Smith the book-collector (1590–1675; sale, 1682) and in the Harleian Library, whence it was acquired by Robert Dodsley, poet, publisher and playwright, who used it as the basis of *A select collection of old plays*, which he published in 1745–46. At some point after that, Dodsley passed it on to Garrick, who added to it substantially, notably from the collections of Lewis Theobald, the Shakespeare scholar, Narcissus Luttrell, Dulwich College and Richard Warner. An unknown benefactor gave him his copy, albeit imperfect, of Shakespeare's *Henry the Fourth, Part I* (1598). In 1763 Thomas Astle, later a Trustee of the British Museum, gave him the remarkable volume, then bound in vellum, containing six pamphlets, all unique, of early plays, dialogues and poems, *Cocke Lorelles bote*, (?1510), *A dialogue betwene the comen secretary and jalawyse* (?1560), *Everyman* (?1526–28), *Hyckescorner* (?1515), *The parliament of byrdes* (*c.*1520), and *Robert the devyll* (?1517). All these were catalogued and arranged for binding by Edward Capell, the penetrating if wayward Shakespearian scholar; others, Bishop Percy, Thomas Warton, Sir John Hawkins, George Steevens, Edmund Malone, borrowed books freely.

Since its receipt, the collection has found thousands of readers, notably Charles Lamb, who spent many happy hours with it, and in more recent time the great bibliographer, Sir Walter Greg. In 1841, Panizzi decreed that Capell's arrangement should be broken up and each volume (even Astle's) bound separately in the interests of convenience and security, which caused some controversy, then and since, although greater damage was done by the sale of duplicates in 1788. The integrity of the collection has been lost by 'perfecting', adding or subtracting leaves to make up Garrick or other copies. The situation was further confused by the transfer of similar material from other parts of the collection, notably the two volumes of Ben Jonson's *Masques* (1608–9) presented by the author to Queen Anne of Denmark from the Old Royal Library. Only one volume now survives in its original Garrick binding.

When, in April 1780, two Trustees of the British Museum went to Garrick's house to view the bequest, one of them was Joseph Banks, a Trustee *ex officio* as President of the Royal Society since 1778. It was only 15 years since he had first entered the Reading Room. Then, in 1765, Banks's voyage with Captain Cook in the *Endeavour*, his friendship with Linnaeus's pupil Daniel Solander, later Under-Librarian at the Museum and an outstanding influence on its natural history collections, and his own first expedition to Iceland when he climbed Mount Hecla, all lay in the future. From now on his long career was to continue in the public eye: his presidency of the Royal Society gave him an undisputed dominance of the scientific world in his time, and his bequest to the Library in 1820 has earned him its gratitude ever since. In 1783 and 1784, four men became Trustees, all four collectors, who were essentially private people who rarely stirred abroad. Two of them are famous: Henry Cavendish the scientist, whose notable library is now part of the great collection at Chatsworth, and Thomas Tyrwhitt the classical scholar, mentioned earlier. The other two, Sir William Musgrave and Clayton Mordaunt

Musgrave's collection stamp.

Cracherode's ownership mark

Cracherode, are hardly known, apart from the collections that they left to the Museum, both in 1799.

Sir William Musgrave's manuscripts and books, part donated in 1790, but mainly bequeathed after his death, were the basis of the biographical collections of the Library. Musgrave began collecting at a time when biography was not yet an established literary genre, although he lived to see Robertson's *Life of Charles V* and Roscoe's *Lorenzo de Medici*. Most of the books were rare and hard to come by. His collection's special value lay in its completeness. Delimiting the subject matter of the rest of the Library, as Musgrave had done, now became a matter of increasing interest and preoccupation to the Trustees and staff. The catalogue of printed books was now published, and Ayscough began the first systematic reshelving of the printed books in subject order, to which new accessions were added. The result of this was the fragmentation of the original collections, beneficial at the time but unfortunate for the historian. There was, however, clearly a feeling for the integrity of the collections of which the Library was made up. Musgrave's books were stamped with a facsimile of his signature, and the two other major collections that followed had the initials of the collector incorporated in the Museum stamp.

Of these, the most influential, then and since, was that of Clayton Mordaunt Cracherode. 'Mr C was, perhaps, the most amiable man that ever went from Westminster to Christ Church', wrote the obituarist in the *Gentleman's Magazine* in April 1799; he might have added that it was the longest journey of Cracherode's life. Born in 1730, the son of a notable soldier who commanded the marines on Anson's voyage round the world, Cracherode was educated at Westminster School and Christ Church, Oxford, of which be became a Student (fellow), and took orders in 1753. In 1762 he became perpetual curate of Binsey, but resided most of the time in London at his house in Queen's Square (Queen Anne's Gate), summering at his country house in Clapham. In 1773 Cracherode's father died and he inherited more wealth and the manor of Great Wymondley, held in Grand Serjeantry of the Crown which obliged the holder to act as Hereditary Cupbearer at the Coronation: Cracherode used nervously to enquire after George III's health from his doctor Sir George Baker, who was also his own. In London he rarely strayed further than 'Honest Tom Payne's at Mews Gate', the famous bookseller on the other side of St James's Park, or Peter Elmsley's, except when he met his friend and fellow collector George Steevens at Mudge and Dutton in the Strand, where they went to have their watches regulated.

His learning earned him the respect and friendship of scholars like Tyrwhitt. His gentleness and good manners endeared him to booksellers and his fellow-collectors, Thomas Crofts, Denis Daly, Henry Quin, Sir Joseph Banks, Sir John Thorold, and, closest of all, George, 2nd Earl Spencer. Lord Spencer (1758–1834), his friend and neighbour at Spencer House, St James's, was younger than Cracherode, who, however, instantly recognised his quality, and, as Lord Spencer placed his first order at Peter Elmsley's shop, said (according to Spencer's panegyrist, the Rev. T.F. Dibdin): 'I'll almost venture a wager of my Tyndale on vellum against any book in the Royal Collection, that this same young nobleman becomes in due time a first rate collector'. When Cracherode died, Lord and Lady Spencer, with his other friend, Shute Barrington, Bishop of Durham, received mourning rings by his will and attended the private funeral in Westminster Abbey with his sister Anne, the sole heir to an estate still substantial after almost 50 years of collecting books, coins and medals and shells.

All this, including Anne Boleyn's copy of the Tyndale New Testament, printed on vellum in Antwerp in 1534, with the royal arms painted on the title page and ANNA REGINA ANGLIAE painted in red on the gilt edges, came to the British Museum. It was the first collection thus acquired of books that had been consciously sought and treated as treasures. Despite

A binding by Roger Payne on Aldus's first printed book, Lascaris, *Erotemata*, 1494–5.
IA 24382.

the wealth of earlier accessions, all, however old or beautiful, had been acquired as useful, if only as evidence of the past. Cracherode's collection treated books, as it did coins and medals or the exquisite shells (for which he paid as much as coins, with intent to found, as he did, the Museum's systematic collection), as objects of aesthetic importance as well as for use. He was fortunate in his time, since books of this sort were available as they had not been before: he was even more fortunate in the combination of learning, taste and a good eye that led him to profit so well from the opportunities that came his way.

He was, for example, the first English collector to collect books bound for Jean Grolier, the most enterprising and persistent patron of the great 16th-century bookbinders. Cracherode had 20, of which perhaps the Jenson Pliny, 1476, is outstanding. Two at least came from the collection made later by the President Jacques-Auguste de Thou, finally sold in 1784 after the death of the Prince de Soubise. Cracherode had over 100 books from his sale, including the presentation copy of Scaliger's Manilius (1599) bound in the special Turkish-patterned morocco used for the most distinctive De Thou bindings. Nor were these accidental purchases, the random result of buying books from the sales of French connoisseurs: Cracherode also sought out the rarer bindings of Grolier's contemporary Thomas Mahieu, of which he had five, notably

7
5
6
8
9
10
3
4
1
2
15
16
11
12
21
22
13
14
19
17
18
20

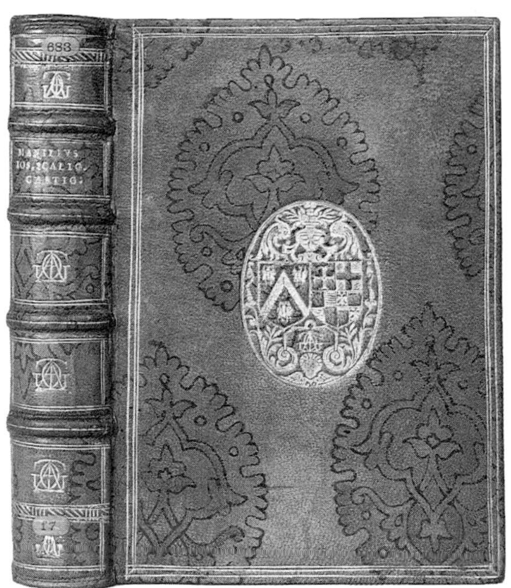

A gold-tooled and stencilled binding for Jacques Auguste de Thou, with his arms impaling those of his second wife, Gasparde de la Chastre.
683.f.7.

the Sweynheym and Pannartz *Caesar* (1469) bound in brown morocco, and the Aldine *Hypnerotomachia Poliphili* (1499), the most famous of 15th-century Italian illustrated books; his acquisition of the Florentine *Anthologia Graeca* printed on vellum (1494) in a contemporary (and probably local) binding shows a taste far in advance of his time.

Not that he despised the work of contemporary binders. He was an early patron of the German binders who came to London, such as Hering and Walther, but his favourite was Roger Payne, who bound his copies of the first book printed by the great Venetian printer, Aldus, Lascaris *Erotemata* (1494–95), in olive green morocco and Cicero, *De Oratore* (Rome, Ulrich Han, 1468) in red, both with his elegant coat of arms. The first of these came, with the first book printed at Venice, Cicero, *Ad familiares* (1469), from the sale of Denis Daly, the Irish politician, in 1792. One of the most enterprising acts of connoisseurship can be seen in Cracherode's copy, printed on vellum, of Lambin's Lucretius (1563), one volume still in its original blue morocco binding, the other rebound in careful facsimile. His early printed books included the Mainz Cicero (*De officiis*) and the Lamoignon copy of the 1462 Bible printed on vellum. He had four Caxtons including *The myrrour of the world* (*c.*1480) and the *The boke of Eneydos* (1490), the first Virgil printed in English. He had a notable collection of bibles and prayer books, ranging from the Complutensian Polyglot in a magnificent De Thou binding (which he left to his friend Barrington, after whose death it passed to the Museum in 1828) and Thomas Cranmer's Catechism (1548) to Baskerville's Prayer Book, bound by Payne, and the facsimile of the Codex Alexandrinus (again on vellum), edited in 1786 by C.G. Woide, one of the most learned of the under-librarians and notable as the first of many such facsimiles to issue from the Library. Two other notable association copies were the presentation copy of the *Gospels*, printed in 1571 at Archbishop Parker's behest, this copy bound by the émigré French binder Jean de Planche for presentation to Queen Elizabeth by John Foxe, and the similar binding on Parker's own *Flores Historiarum*. It was Cracherode also who bought the unique illuminated copy on vellum of the first English edition of Lily's Grammar (1542); this was translated by the same Daniel Talley, whose Greek grammar, similarly adorned, belonged to Edward VI.

The list of *editiones principes*, editions of the classics, the great English theologians (Cracherode's Jeremy Taylors were famous), of books from famous collections and in notable bindings, association copies such as Mme de Pompadour's first edition of *Il Cortegiano*, is endless. But Cracherode did not just collect old books: he had the great Ibarra *Don Quixote* (1780) in a fine binding, and among his last acquisitions were George Vancouver's *A Voyage of discovery to the north Pacific Ocean* (1798), the great folio Edward Young *Night Thoughts*, illustrated by William Blake, and his friend Sir Uvedale Price's *Essay on the Picturesque*, both also printed in 1798. His interest in shells is testified by some exquisite colour plate books, such as Born's *Testacea musei Caesarei Vindebonensis* (1780). He had the first editions of Plato and Palladio, Hakluyt and Captain Cook, of *Paradise Lost* and *The Shepheard's Calendar*.

It was, in short, a collection as important as it was beautiful. From the first, the Museum treated it as something special and select. It was accorded, and has retained ever since, a special room to itself; unlike the previous collections acquired, it was not divided up by subject and dispersed into the general library collection. The quality of Cracherode's books, and the sense of connoisseurship, applied as much to binding and condition as to text, and paying particular attention to the interest of books in association with famous former owners, was something new to the Museum. It made it a force to be reckoned with in the era of great connoisseurs who dominated the first half of the 19th century, the era of the Roxburghe sale in 1812 (a 'cometary year' to Dibdin). A new energy and authority began to make itself felt in the collection of the major monuments of the national literary heritage and of the world at large.

Coloured plate in Born's *Testacea musei Caesarei Vindebonensis*, 1780.
678.k.14, T.13.

Tho Stringers Journall Continued A° 1718.

5

The East India Company, its Records and Library

IN JANUARY 1799, not long before Cracherode's death and the bequest that had such a signal influence on the British Museum, Charles Wilkins, then 50 and already well-known as an orientalist, addressed a letter to the Court of Directors of the East India Company:

> GENTLEMEN,
>
> Having heard that your Honorable Court has lately passed the very laudable resolution appropriating a portion of the new buildings at the India House to the purpose of an Oriental Museum, I humbly presume upon the little knowledge and experience I acquired in those matters which seem the natural objects of your design, during a residence of nearly sixteen years in the Company's employ in Bengal, to make you a tender of my advice and assistance; not only in digesting such a plan as shall render the institution a public benefit, but in classing and arranging such books and productions of Nature and Art, as are, or may be collected, and, finally, (if such an employ should be found necessary) to take charge of the Museum, and give up my whole attention towards rendering it a Monument of the Taste, as well as of the Munificence of its Founders.
>
> I have already committed to paper a sketch of my ideas of what the Museum, to be useful, as well as ornamental, should principally consist; but as it might be deemed officious in me to communicate it unasked, and when, perhaps, it has been anticipated by one more perfect, that, with any other services in my power, is reserved for your commands.
>
> I have the honor to subscribe myself,
>
> Gentlemen,
>
> Your most obedient
>
> Humble Servant,
>
> CHAS WILKINS.
>
> Fitzroy Square,
> No. 33,
> January 1799.

The 'sketch of a plan for an Oriental Museum' that he subsequently forwarded recalls the structure and content of the original British Museum. He envisaged, first, 'A Library, to consist of Manuscripts and Printed Books'; 'A Cabinet of Natural Productions . . . Animal, Vegetable and Mineral'; 'Artificial Productions', the raw material of silk and cotton and every stage of their manufacture, sugar, salt-petre, borax machines and tools used in the manufactures of Asia; and 'Miscellaneous Articles', 'curiosities, chiefly presents . . . as cannot conveniently be classed under any of the former heads'. Wilkins needed the firm support of Warren Hastings before he was eventually able, in 1801, to secure the Court's agreement to the scheme and his own appointment as 'Librarian to the Oriental Repository' with the proviso 'that Mr Bruce the Company's historiographer be always permitted to have free Access to the Books and papers contained there in'. The original impetus of which Wilkins wrote came in a 'Public Letter' from the Court to its servants in India of 25 May 1798 which announced 'our disposition for the encouragement of Indian literature'; adding 'that the Institution of a public Repository in this Country for Oriental Writings would be useful, and that a thing professedly of this kind is still a bibliothecal desideratum here'.

Although Wilkins did not take up office until 1801, and it was not until 1817 that he added the Register of Indian Records to his charge, it was thus in the last but one year of the 18th century that the need to preserve the records and documents of India, the largest and most influential of England's colonial ventures, was publicly acknowledged, and the foundation laid of what is now the India Office Library and Records.

In fact, the need (like that which brought about the British Museum) had a long, complex history. Robert Orme (1728–1801), who had returned to England in 1760 after a career in the East India Company's service, published

Title page from the journal, dated 1712–13, of Isaac Pyke, Captain of the *Stringer*.
IOLR MSS Eur.D.5.

in 1763 the first volume of his *Military transactions of the British nation in Indostan*: his continuing research was officially supported by the Directors in 1769 and they awarded him an annuity in 1772. His bust by Nollekens, made in 1774, is in the Library. When pressed by Henry Dundas to appoint a Historiographer in 1793, the Directors pointed out that Orme already occupied this post, but Dundas's nominee John Bruce was promised the reversion to which he succeeded in 1801 on Orme's death. The office of 'Register and Keeper of the Indian Books, Records, Accounts, and other Papers deposited in the room usually called the Book Office' had been created at the recommendation of the Company's Committee of Correspondence on 26 March 1771. This, in turn, arose from the creation of the post of 'Examiner of the Indian Correspondence and Records' in 1769, a function thus detached from that of the Company's Secretary and in 1776 made independent of that office. The subordinate offices of Register and Keeper of Records, now combined, now detached, were variously involved in the custody of documents, either historic (defined in 1787 as pre-1765) or contemporary.

Warren Hastings, by Thomas Banks, 1790
IOLR F.659.

There are two strands at work here, the commercial and political, and the literary and scholarly; both were, in different degrees, historic in approach. The year 1765 was a critical one for the East India Company. It was the year of Clive's return to India, of the final defeat of the combine of Mir Kasim, erstwhile Nawab of Bengal, Shah Alam the Mughal Emperor, and the Nawab of Oudh, and of the Company's assumption of *diwani*, the right to collect the imperial revenue in Bengal; in short, 1765 saw the Company change from a commercial to a political force, a change confirmed in 1772, when Warren Hastings 'stood forth as Dewan', taking over the responsibility for the actual collection of revenue and the administration of justice. Hastings's success in tempering the confusing and confused objectives of commerce and politics laid the foundation of British rule in India, but the complication of the Company's relations with the Government in the period between the Regulating Act of 1773 and Pitt's India Act of 1784 led to his impeachment, although he was finally acquitted in 1795. His bust, by Thomas Banks, carved in 1790 during the ordeal of his seven-year trial, was given to the Library in 1949.

Simultaneously, but independently, there had grown up a new interest in the culture and languages of the sub-continent. The old interest in oriental languages depended, if in various ways, on the need both to study the holy writ of Judaism and Christianity, and to promote it. By the second half of the 18th century, several generations of servants of the East India Company had moved from mere acquaintance with Persian, 'the official court-language of the Mogul Empire, and the *lingua franca* of India as a whole', to an appreciation of the literature and art of the Mughal empire and its Persian predecessors. Increasing involvement in the religious and legal complexities of India had also brought them into contact with Hindu culture and thus with Sanskrit. This was a new discovery, all the more exciting since the documents recorded in it and its own linguistic roots were of great antiquity, so much so as to throw new light on the antecedents of the languages of Western Asia and Europe.

This discovery was almost wholly due to Sir William Jones (1746–94), acknowledged in his lifetime and ever since as the founder of western Sanskrit studies, and in his proposition of the theory of Indo-European languages the founder of modern linguistics. He began his life as tutor to Cracherode's young friend John, son of the first Earl Spencer, the future book-collector. This relationship was mutually beneficial: Jones was able to learn Arabic and Persian well enough to translate a life of Nadir Shah brought to England in 1768 by Christian VII of Denmark. In 1771 he published his *Grammar of the Persian language*, which Samuel Johnson sent to Warren Hastings in Calcutta, and in 1774 the *Poeseos Asiaticae commentariorum* which finally established his reputation. In the interval he had become an equally successful jurist. He wanted to become a judge in the new Supreme Court in Calcutta, but, due to

Fort William, Calcutta, by George Lambert and Samuel Scott, *c.*1731.
IOLR F.45.

his open opposition to the war against the American colonies, did not succeed until 1783.

The same war, and apprehension of French designs on India, had vastly extended English contacts with and experience of the sub-continent. Jones found a new interest in the Indian past, as much due to the need to understand the local legal codes as to antiquarianism. He flung himself into the task. With Hastings he founded the Asiatic Society of Bengal. Every aspect of Indian life, from its languages to natural history, engaged his passionate attention. He translated the *Hitopade Sā* and *Sākuntalā* and in 1794 published the *Institutes of Hindu law*. His early death was mourned by the pandits who admired his legal capacity, as well as the English in India and the scholarly world of Europe. He had opened a window on a whole new world of culture: its impact (curiously anticipated in William Collins's *Persian eclogues*) can be seen in Beckford's *Vathek*, Goethe's *West-œstliche Divan* and Coleridge's *Kubla Khan*.

The treasures that are now in the India Office Library and Records reflect this complex and diverse heritage. The East India Company, granted its first charter in 1600 (only surviving in one abstract and in later copies), sent out its voyage on 13 February 1601; it headed for the East Indies and the spice trade, and it was not until 1608 that the first servants of the Company landed at Surat and went to the Mughal emperor's court. They were not the first; the Portuguese under Vasco da Gama had arrived in 1498 and over the next two decades D'Albuquerque, the architect of Portuguese empire, had established a series of posts which effectively controlled maritime trade across the Indian Ocean, the Persian Gulf and from the East Indies. Energy and superior military force maintained this dominance throughout the 16th century, but

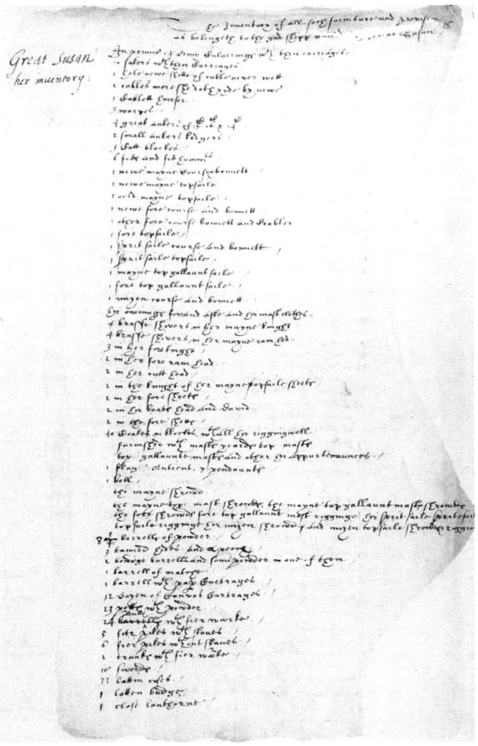

Inventory of the ship the *Great Susan*, 26 September 1600, from the first minute book of the East India Company.
IOLR B/1, f.15.

Portugal itself was overstrained and after its absorption by Spain in 1580, its influence waned. The Dutch who followed were more interested in the more profitable East Indies from which they effectually excluded the English. The East India Company was thus forced from the outset to study Indian trade and customs to steal a march on its predecessors. This interest was reciprocated; as soon as Jahangir recognised the English naval superiority over the unpopular Portuguese, he was willing to grant trading facilities. Surat was the English headquarters from 1613 to 1687; other factories were established on the Coromandel Coast at Masulipatam in 1611 and in 1640 at Madras. Bombay came to the English Crown in 1661, was occupied in 1665, and leased to the Company in 1668. Calcutta was founded in 1690. The latter, which became the centre of British influence, is depicted as it was *c.*1731 in one of the paintings commissioned from George Lambert and Samuel Scott of the British settlements in India.

The real wealth of the collections lies in the voluminous records maintained by the Company, 'the best historical materials in the world', wrote James Grant Duff in his *History of the Mahrattas* (1826), and calculated by Sir William Foster as amounting to 48,000 volumes. To this the papers of the official government agencies, the Board of Control (1784–1858) and India Office (1858–1947) and other related bodies, have added substantially, so that the collections are now estimated at over 250,000 volumes, files and boxes, with 40,000 maps, 70,000 official publications and 14,000 volumes and boxes of private papers. The reasons for this abundance are described by Foster:

> The distance separating the Company from its servants in the East, and the jealous care with which it supervised their actions, necessitated full explanations by correspondence: while the system of administration in the Company's settlements and territories, which from the first took the form of a Council, also favoured a full disclosure of the motives underlying every decision of importance. In its final development, proposals were largely made in written minutes, which often, in controverted questions, provoked equally argumentative minutes of dissent; and these were entered at full length upon the records of the Council meetings (termed 'Consultations' or 'Proceedings'), transcripts of which were regularly sent home... In early days these were accompanied by separate volumes containing copies of all letters received or sent; in later times such correspondence was either entered on the Consultations, or, in cases of special importance, transmitted as enclosures to dispatches. Since equally careful, though more concise, records were kept at home of the proceedings of the Court of Directors and of the various Committees into which it divided itself, it is obvious that, had the archives of the East India House survived in their entirety, we should now be in possession of full information regarding the transactions both at home and abroad.

That they do not is due to the nature of the Company. Its growth was largely unplanned, or at least undetermined by considerations other than the commercial needs of the moment. Despite the caution that dictated the elaborate system of documentation, once the need was passed the documents tended to be neglected.

In 1682, the Court Minutes refer uncomfortably to the 'old books and papers which are in a confused manner layd in the upper garret of the [East India] House'. In 1720 the Secretary was directed to sort the documents and put them in a proper repository, probably the origin of the 'Book Office' mentioned above. When Pitt's India Act created the Board of Control in 1784, yet further duplication occurred, since all correspondence had to be officially approved, while the exigencies of the moment demanded that the Board should receive unofficial warning, in the form of 'Previous Communications', as well as official notice in the form of 'Drafts', of the Despatches which the Directors planned to send to India. Between 1858, when the Crown took over the government of India from the Company, and 1860 over 300 tons of papers judged obsolete and mostly duplicate were sent for waste.

Three East Indiamen, drawn by Captain William Wilson in the log book of the *Suffolk*, December 1756.
IOLR L/MAR/B/397D, f.89.

What survives, however, confirms Grant Duff's verdict, the more so since it also includes the documents of the Company's other overseas interests, its long and profitable connection with China, its posts that stretched from Borneo to St Helena, the logs and ledgers of the voyages of the 'East Indiamen', the vessels freighted by the Company, the registers of baptisms, deaths and marriages in India and other personalia, and the wonderful collection of maps already mentioned.

Among the many historic documents preserved in this great archive is the first of the unbroken series of Court Minute Books, 198 volumes in all from 1599 to 1858. On the first page of the first volume the names of the subscribers to the first voyage (with the sums they invested) are listed, and subsequent pages record the fitting out of the first small fleet of five ships to sail to India. These first voyages were as much explorations as trading ventures, and before long reached Japan, where the Company's factory was established at Hirado, near Nagasaki. One of the most notable exploratory voyages was Weddell's to the North Pacific in 1637, recorded in a volume of the Company's 'Consultations' and correspondence relating to China and Japan. War was always a threat, whether in Europe or the East, and the success of the Commonwealth Navy against the Dutch brought problems which the Company referred to Cromwell for help. Peace under Charles II brought the royal grant of Bombay (part of Catherine of Braganza's dowry) in 1668 for which the company paid an annual rent of £10. The Tally Stick for the first payment, made on 27 March 1669, still survives.

Up to 1657, the capital for each voyage (the 'Stock') was raised and accounted for separately and finally distributed, but in that year the 'New General Stock', a permanent capital, increased but never distributed, began, and with it the Company became a permanent and unitary force. It was perhaps resentment of its monopoly that led to the creation of a rival 'English Company Trading to the East Indies' which received its royal charter in 1698. Competition benefited neither Company, however, and in 1702 they began to cooperate under a joint Court of Managers, finally amalgamating in 1709; the arms granted to the 'New Company' became those of the 'United East India Company', which documents and the flags on ships and factories made familiar throughout the East.

The Company's obsession with documentation extended to the logs of the ships that they freighted, many of which provided a pictorial as well as documentary record of the Company's maritime activities. Captain Francis Stanes

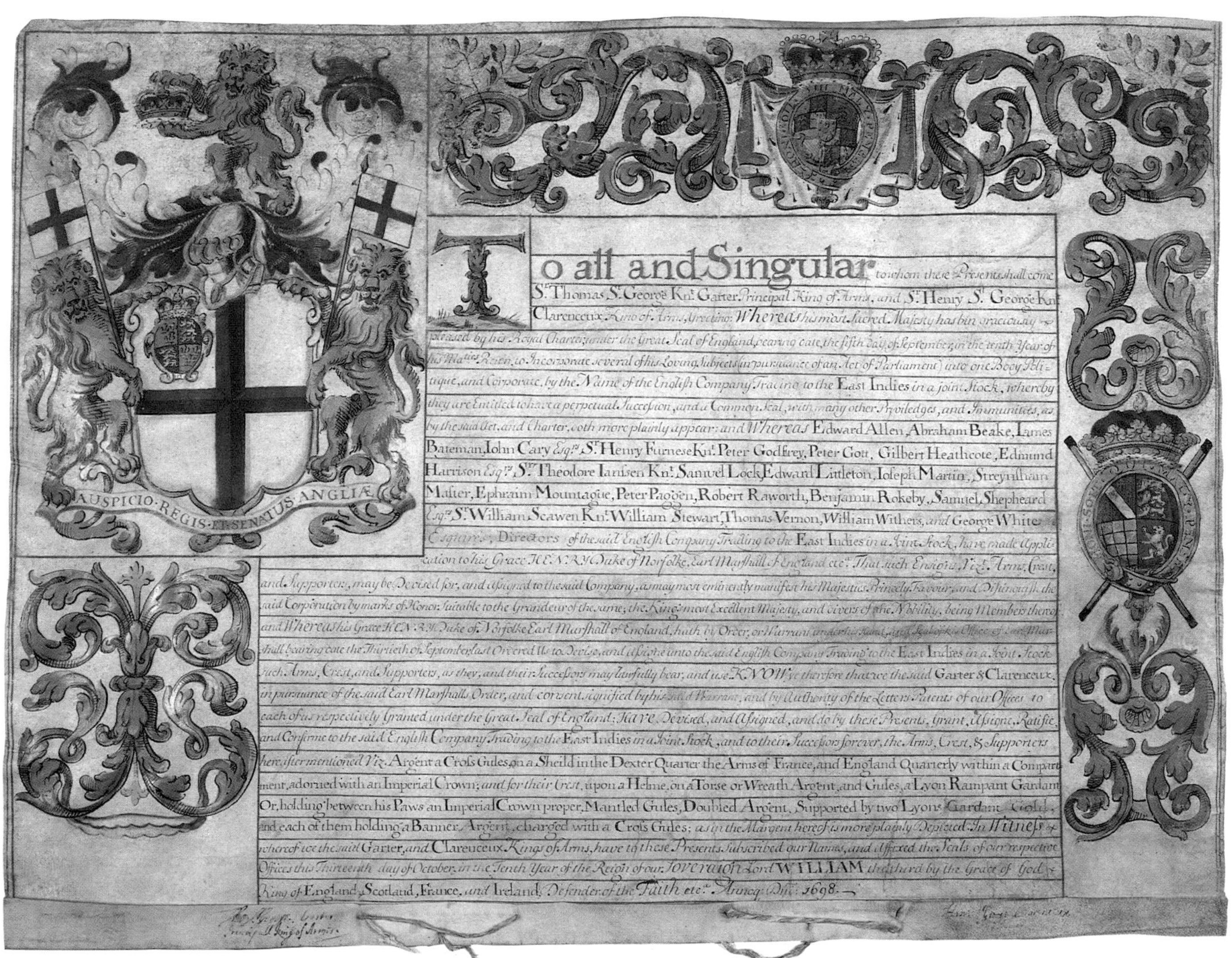

AUSPICIO REGIS ET SENATUS ANGLIÆ

To all and Singular to whom these Presents shall come S^r. Thomas S^t. George Kn^t. Garter, Principal King of Arms, and S^r. Henry S^t. George Kn^t. Clarenceux King of Arms, Greeting: Whereas his most Sacred Majesty has bin graciously pleased by his Royal Charter, under the Great Seal of England, bearing date the fifth day of September, in the tenth Year of his Maties Reign, to Incorporate several of his Loving Subjects (in pursuance of an Act of Parliament) into one Body Politique, and Corporate, by the Name of the English Company Trading to the East Indies in a joint Stock, whereby they are Entitled to have a perpetual Succession, and a Common Seal, with many other Priviledges, and Immunities, as by the said Act, and Charter, doth more plainly appear: and Whereas Edward Allen, Abraham Beake, James Bateman, John Cary Esq^rs. S^r. Henry Furnese Kn^t. Peter Godfrey, Peter Gott, Gilbert Heathcote, Edmund Harrison Esq^rs. S^r. Theodore Jansen Kn^t. Samuel Lock, Edward Littleton, Joseph Martin, Streynsham Master, Ephraim Mountague, Peter Paggen, Robert Raworth, Benjamin Rokeby, Samuel Shepheard Esq^rs. S^r. William Scawen Kn^t. William Stewart, Thomas Vernon, William Withers, and George White Esquires, Directors of the said English Company Trading to the East Indies in a Joint Stock, have made Application to his Grace HENRY Duke of Norfolke, Earl Marshall of England etc^a. That such Ensigns, Viz^t. Arms, Crest, and Supporters, may be Devised for, and Assigned to the said Company, as may most eminently manifest his Majesties Princely Favour, and Distinguish the said Corporation by marks of Honor suitable to the Grandeur of the same; the King's most Excellent Majesty, and divers of the Nobility, being Members thereof: and Whereas his Grace HENRY Duke of Norfolke Earl Marshall of England, hath by Order, or Warrant [illegible] Marshall bearing date the Thirtieth of September last Ordered Us to Devise, and Assigne unto the said English Company Trading to the East Indies in a Joint Stock such Arms, Crest, and Supporters, as they, and their Successors may lawfully bear, and use. KNOW ye therefore that we the said Garter & Clarenceux, in pursuance of the said Earl Marshalls Order, and consent signified by his said Warrant, and by Authority of the Letters Patents of our Offices to each of us respectively Granted under the Great Seal of England; HAVE Devised, and Assigned, and do by these Presents, Grant, Assigne, Ratifie, and Confirme to the said English Company Trading to the East Indies in a Joint Stock, and to their Successors forever, the Arms, Crest, & Supporters hereafter mentioned Viz. Argent a Cross Gules, on a Sheild in the Dexter Quarter the Arms of France, and England Quarterly within a Compartment, adorned with an Imperial Crown; and for their Crest, upon a Helme, on a Torse or Wreath Argent, and Gules, a Lyon Rampant Gardant Or, holding between his Paws an Imperial Crown proper, Mantled Gules, Doubled Argent, Supported by two Lyons Gardant Gold, and each of them holding a Banner Argent, charged with a Cross Gules; as in the Margent hereof is more plainly Depicted. In Witness whereof we the said Garter, and Clarenceux Kings of Arms, have to these Presents subscribed our Names, and affixed the Seals of our respective Offices this Thirteenth day of October, in the Tenth Year of the Reign of our Soveraign Lord WILLIAM the third by the Grace of God King of England, Scotland, France, and Ireland, Defender of the Faith etc^a. Annoq: Dni: 1698.

[illegible] Garter Principal King of Arms

[illegible] Clarenceux

Grant of Arms to the New East India Company, 13 October 1698.
IOLR A/1/58.

Messages from Warren Hastings, 7–14 September 1781, smuggled out of the fort of Chunar in quills. IOLR MSS Eur.B.253.

drew his ship, the *Rochester*, in the harbour at Chusan, and the flying fish he landed, with equal enthusiasm and accuracy. Isaac Pyke, commander of the *Stringer* in 1712, clearly thought it politic to record the reverence with which his cargo was unloaded in Bombay, while the more conventional log of the *Suffolk*, under Captain William Wilson, records the coastal topography of his voyage to Madras and China in 1755–57, and includes a splendid sketch showing the *Suffolk* and her sister ships the *Houghton* and *Godolphin* with whom she formed a convoy for the homeward voyage. The care and accuracy with which these logs were kept was vital to navigation in unsurveyed waters, but Wilson's elegant calligraphy shows the pride he took in his work (which also involved a successful fight with French men-of-war off the Cape of Good Hope).

The wonderful documentary wealth of the Company's archives provides many examples of the report of major historic events by the principal participants, such as Clive's letter of 8 September 1765 announcing to a friend the acquisition of the *diwani* of Bengal, Bihar and Orissa. The career of Warren Hastings, who laid the foundations of British rule in India and gave it its special mixture of principle and common sense, sympathy and detachment, is fully recorded in the Company's official archives. His private papers are to be found in the British Library's Department of Manuscripts. The letters that he wrote while besieged in Chunar Fort in September 1781 after the revolt of Raja Chait Singh at Benares, on slips of paper so small that they could be rolled up and put in quills to be smuggled through the lines, are vivid testi-

Chinese junks in the harbour of Chusan, drawn by Captain Francis Stanes in the log book of the *Rochester*, December 1711.
IOLR L/MAR/B/137B, ff.150–51.

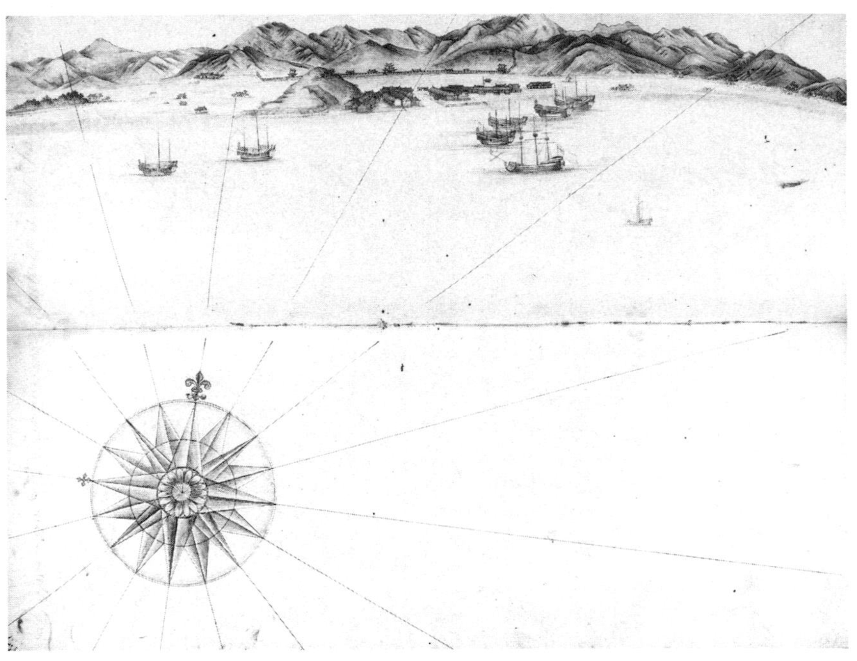

mony of his turbulent period of office, which led ultimately to his impeachment.

Mapping the territories with which it traded and which it later controlled was always an important part of the Company's activities, out of which grew the Survey of India, one of the major monuments of the British Empire. James Rennell's *Bengal Atlas* of 1780 and 1781 was the progenitor of this. Its large scale and unprecedented accuracy and variety of detail reflect the Company's need for precise knowledge of the land which it had conquered – the same need that had called forth the 'Domesday Book' in England seven centuries earlier. The engraved plates of many of the maps used for the first and subsequent editions of the *Atlas* are still preserved.

If Rennell's work was the forerunner of the Survey of India, its continuation depended in turn on a steady succession of new surveys of unmapped areas. The long overland march from Bengal to Surat undertaken by Colonel Goddard, sent with reinforcements to the Bombay Presidency during the Maratha war in 1778–79, provided an opportunity, seized by two engineer officers, for surveying the route. William Knox's brief 'Residency' at Nepal (1803–5) provided a similar opportunity. Other maps were acquired by the Company's servants; Orme had his own collection, including maps of Clive's campaign in 1757.

Still further back is the work of earlier Portuguese surveyors such as that preserved by Sir Hans Sloane (see above, p. 17). Between 1779 and 1790 Alexander Dalrymple (Hydrographer to the East India Company, 1779–1810) compiled an important series of sea charts based on his official examination of the ship's logs in East India House. His successor as Hydrographer was another noted geographer James Horsburgh. He held the post from 1810 until his death in 1836, and compiled from manuscript maps the great *Atlas of India* (1827 onwards), on the quarter-inch scale, continuing James Rennell's pioneering work of the 18th century.

Opposite, above. 'The Delta of the Ganges with the Adjacent Countries', a plate from *A Bengal Atlas*, by James Rennell, London 1780.
IOLR X/998/1.
Opposite, below. The Mughal Emperor Shah Alam II conveying the grant of the Diwani of Bengal, Bihar and Orissa to Lord Clive, August 1765. By Benjamin West, early 19th century.
IOLR F.29.

The Company also commissioned or accepted works of art to mark its history and purposes, or to honour its greatest servants: for example the vast canvas by Benjamin West, depicting Shah Alam granting the *diwani* of Bengal to Clive; the fine portrait of the Marquis Cornwallis, Governor General 1786–93, by A.W. Devis in 1792; the most unusual picture of the Persian Ambassador, Nakd Ali Beg, painted in 1626 by Richard Greenbury – the

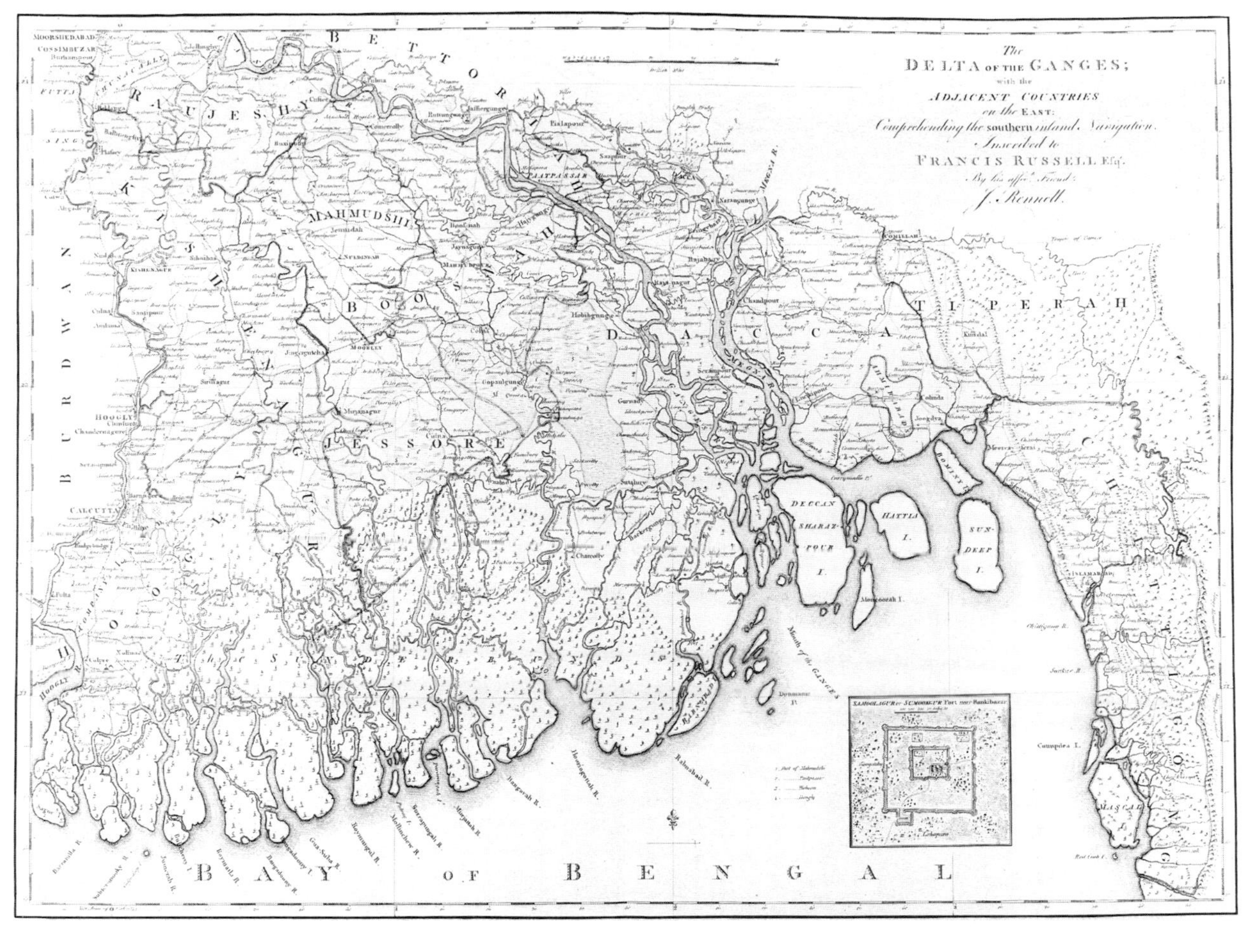
The DELTA of the GANGES; with the ADJACENT COUNTRIES on the East: Comprehending the southern inland Navigation. Inscribed to FRANCIS RUSSELL Esq. By his affec. Friend: J. Rennell.
BETTORIA
RAUJESHY
MAHMUDSHY
BOOSNAH
DACCA
TIPERAH
JESSORE
BURDWAN
HOOGLY
CALCUTTA
DECCAN SHABAZPOUR I.
HATTIA I.
SUNDEEP I.
BAY OF BENGAL

Above. Warren Hastings's copy of Amir Khusraw's poem *Laylá va Majnūn*, copied 1506.
IOLR Ethé 1204, ff.1–2.

Left. A poet presenting his poem to two patrons, a persian *diwan* from the Johnson Collection, *c*.1314.
IOLR Ethé 913, f.16.

earliest painting in the collection; or the beautiful overmantle sculpture executed in 1728 by Michael Rysbrack for East India House, illustrating the commercial wealth of India.

The main wealth of the literary and artistic collections of earlier Indian culture entered the collection in the 19th century, but three in particular were formed in the 18th century and may be associated with the foundation of the Library, presaged in 1798. Richard Johnson served the Company from 1770 to 1790, spending the years 1783 to 1787 as Resident at Hyderabad. Returned to England, he sold to the Company his collection of over 1000 oriental manuscripts and another 1000 Indian miniatures in 1807, which included the remarkable collection of Persian *diwans*, notably that of the year 1315/714, with its Persian verse texts, and the oldest surviving manuscripts of Amir Khusraw. Warren Hastings's collection, which came in 1809, was also distinguished by its Persian manuscripts, such as the copy of *Laylá va Majnūn*, written by the famous scribe Sultan Ali Mashhadi for the Sultan of Herat in 1506, later in the libraries of Shah Jahan and Alamgir, and finally acquired by Hastings.

In 1806, the Library received from the Marquis Wellesley, Governor General from 1798 to 1805, 197 volumes from the library of Tipu Sultan, taken at the capture of Seringapatam in 1799. These included Tipu's extraordinary autograph diary of his dreams and his collection of Qur'ans, one possibly as early as the 14th century.

Finally, the Europeans made their own distinctive contribution to the many different methods by which texts were transmitted, through the printing press and movable type technology. Introduced to serve the designs of European missionaries and administrators, ironically the press later played an enormously important role in the Indian cultural and religious renaissance and ultimately in the dissemination of nationalist ideas and aspirations. During the later 18th century, publishing was concentrated in the three British settlements of Madras, Bombay and Calcutta. The Library possesses, for instance, the earliest known example of printing at Bombay, a handbill of 1772 advertising a panacea quaintly named '*Diogo's drops*', once in the collection of the bibliomane Sir Thomas Phillipps. Calcutta became the main centre of publishing, and there Sir William Jones, with his fellow scholar Nathaniel Brassey Halhed, produced the first volume of the transactions of the newly formed Asiatic Society of Bengal, *Asiatick researches* in 1788. Other examples of European literary activity in Calcutta are the *Oriental magazine* and the *Asiatick miscellany* which both appeared in 1785. The patronage of the East India Company was a great stimulus to the study of Indian languages and in particular to the development of founts of type in original Indian scripts. Perhaps the most evocative evidence for this are the punches of the types, engraved by English punch-cutters following models supplied from the East, for the Devanagari, Bengali, Modi and Gujarati scripts, preserved in a wooden box belonging to Charles Wilkins. Some he brought back to England on his return in 1786, others he had engraved later; and the Bengali at least were certainly used for printing Indian texts in England before his death in 1836. The adaptation of Indian scripts to typographic form was not the least of his achievements.

The appointment of Wilkins marks, then, a turning point not only in his career but in the East India Company's history, as it changed its purely commercial, detached and on the whole ephemeral view of its present purpose and future to one of long-term and political involvement. Wilkins's career spanned this change, and to some extent typifies it. Born in 1749 in Somerset, he went out to Bengal in 1770 and, having learned Bengali and Persian, embarked on Sanskrit in about 1778. He soon made sufficient progress to translate the *Bhagavadgītā*, encouraged by Warren Hastings, who arranged for it to be printed at the Company's expense in 1785.

Wilkins's maternal uncle was the famous engraver Robert Bateman Wray, and this connection may explain his interest in the task of converting oriental script to type. The first product of it was his friend Nathaniel Halhed's *Grammar of the Bengal language* (1778) printed in Bengali characters. In 1786 Wilkins was obliged, for reasons of health, to return home to Bath. Thirteen years later, and now living in London, he wrote the letter that spurred the Company to implement its decision of 1798, and, in 1801, the Library came officially into existence. His career, thereafter, is part of the history of the East India Company and its Library and Records. Part of the latter fell to his charge in 1817. The collections and the staff engaged to deploy them grew. Wilkins was made an honorary Doctor of Civil Law by Oxford University, and the Royal Society of Literature awarded him its medal as the Prince of Sanskrit Literature. He was largely responsible, with Henry Colebrooke, for the foundation of the Royal Asiatic Society in 1823. His publications continued, among them the *Grammar of the Sanskrita language* (1808), which became the official textbook of the Company's College at Haileybury. In 1836 he died, old and honoured all over the world; his family gave his own oriental manuscript collection to the Library.

The Library that he had done so much to establish continued to grow and expand; and so did the Records, both of the Company and the Board of Control. Their later history is the subject of Chapter 11.

Opposite, above. Tray of metal matrices for casting movable type to print Oriental scripts, prepared in England to patterns supplied by Sir Charles Wilkins, *c.*1800. The matrices are still in the original wrappers labelled by Wilkins; also illustrated are some of Wilkins's pattern cards.
IOLR.

Opposite, below right. Title page of *A Grammar of the Bengal Language*, by Nathaniel Brassy Halhed, Hoogly 1778.
IOLR T 6863.

Opposite, below left. Diogo's Drops, a handbill printed at Bombay 1772.
IOLR V 23500.

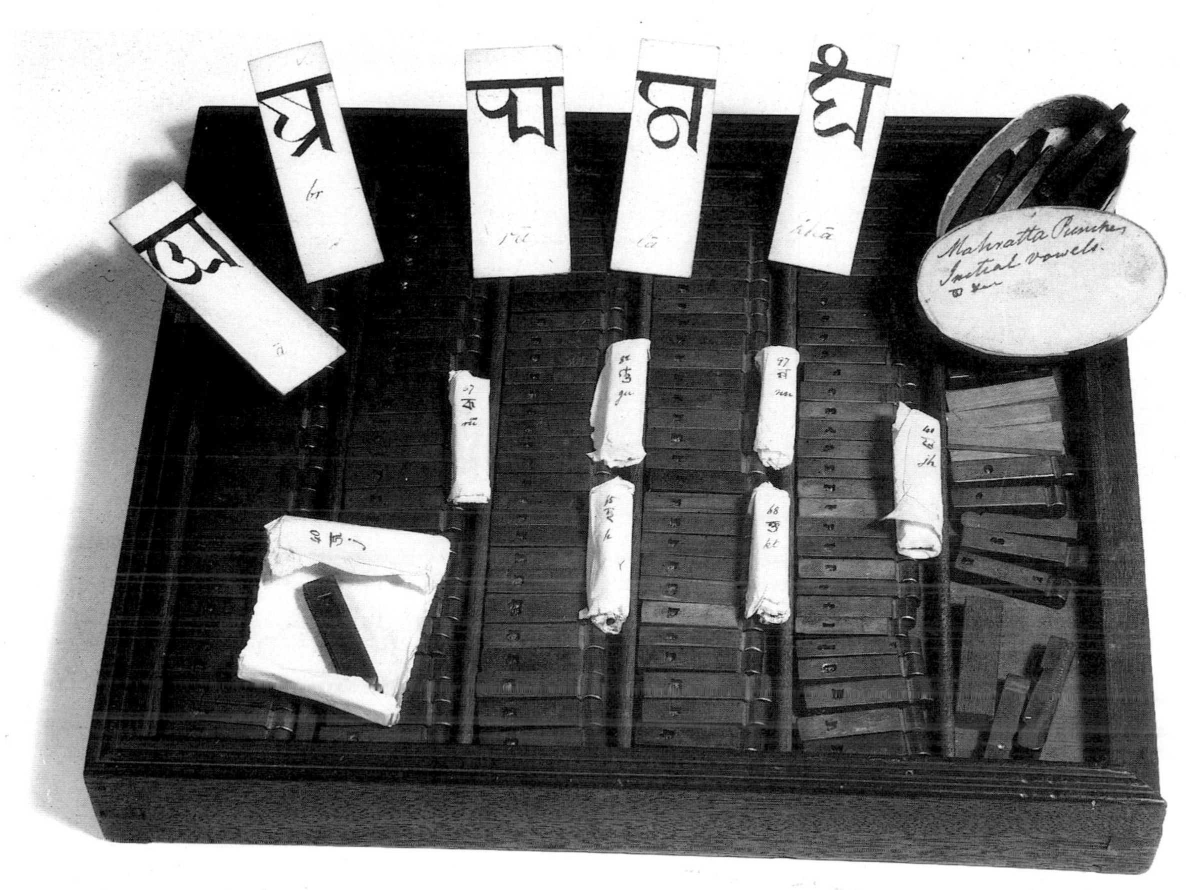

বোধপ্রকাশং শব্দশাস্ত্রং
ফিরিঙ্গিনামুপকারার্থং
ক্রিয়তে হালেদঙ্গ্রেজী

A
GRAMMAR
OF THE
BENGAL LANGUAGE

BY
NATHANIEL BRASSEY HALHED.

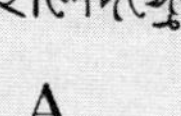

ইন্দ্রাদয়োপি যস্যান্তং নযযুঃ শব্দবারিধেঃ।
প্রক্রিয়ান্তস্য কৃৎস্নস্য ক্ষমোবক্তুং নরঃ কথং॥

PRINTED
AT
HOOGLY IN BENGAL

M DCC LXXVIII.

DIOGO'S DROPS.

FROM many Years experience found far to excel any of the kind ever yet offered, the intrinsick value and good effect of which has been, and is, daily experienced by many distinguished families in these parts and many others; it has cured above three hundred persons of divers complaints, without the least return or symptom of their disorder, the truth of which he can bring many instances exhibited here, and only begs a fair trial, being truly confident, his composition having such ingredients therein, that its excellent qualities will admit of no comparison, and must infallibly gain the true approbation, and undoubtedly will excite the admiration of the curious.

The Use and Method of taking DIOGO'S DROPS.

They are an immediate remedy for the Cholera Morbus, in these parts stiled the Mort de Chien, generally attended with fatal consequences: To be taken in a tea [illegible] [illegible] it away, if not then, repeat the same agreeable to the age of the patient, and it will have its true effect.

Also very good for the head ach, violent coughs, diseases in the stomach, for worms, violent gripings, vomitings, purgings, fluxes, all kind of fevers, for the Uterine or Fits of the Mother, and convulsions in these complaints: To be taken in tea, congee, gruel, &c. or any warm liquid that will cause perspiration: Likewise very good for a depraved appetite and indigestion; to be taken in a little brandy or any spirituous liquor: And in fractures, compound fractures, green wounds, &c. these drops to be applied to the parts affected, with the lint dipt in this liquid, or the bandages wet with the same. From twenty years to eighty, about thirty drops, being equal to a tea spoon full; from eight years to twenty, half the above quantity; for infants, from four to eight drops.

N. B. To prevent counterfeits, the true Original Drops are sealed with the maker's Cypher.——Price of the bottle twenty rupees, with directions for using.

Diogo de Miguel [illegible]

BOMBAY: Printed at the house of Mr. James Tod, where all manner of printing work is carefully and expeditiously executed. 1772.

6

The New Century: The King's Library

THE TURN OF the 18th century marked an era in the fortunes of the British Museum and its Library in several ways. The Cracherode and Musgrave bequests had strengthened the collection of printed books immeasurably; the vast and heterogeneous wealth of Sloane's collection and the Old Royal Library had been given a new direction, both in terms of modern books and the monuments of early and later printing. In 1796 the Earl of Hardwicke, the last survivor of the original Trustees, died. In 1799 Charles Morton, the Principal Librarian and last of the first three Under-Librarians, also died, to be succeeded by Joseph Planta.

Planta had succeeded his father, Andrew Planta, the first Assistant Keeper of Natural History in 1758 who had transferred to printed books in 1765, on his death in 1773. He was to serve the Museum and Library for no less than 54 years, and the mark that he set upon it in that long period was greater than any save that of Antonio Panizzi, whose better-publicised achievements have tended to diminish those of his predecessors.

The Planta family were Swiss protestants who settled in London in 1752, Andrew becoming pastor of the German Lutheran church and Reader to Queen Charlotte. Court and Museum connections may have given Joseph Planta a good start, but his own abilities must have been manifest in 1776 when he not only succeeded Morton as Under-Librarian and Keeper of Manuscripts, but also Matthew Maty (who had succeeded Gowin Knight as Principal Librarian in 1772) as Secretary of the Royal Society.

The men who served under Planta were also more distinguished than their predecessors. Robert Nares, Keeper of Manuscripts from 1799 to 1807, was an eminent philologist. Francis Douce, who succeeded him in 1807, formed the most remarkable collection of illuminated manuscripts of his time, anticipating those of later generations, which was lost to the Museum Library when he resigned in 1812. Henry Ellis, who joined the Museum Library in 1800, succeeded Ayscough as Assistant Keeper of Printed Books in 1805, became Keeper in 1806 and followed Douce as Keeper of Manuscripts in 1812. He was one of the editors of the *editio maxima* of Dugdale's *Monasticon* and his original *Letters illustrative of English history* drew on the Library's manuscript resources; his work on the 'Domesday Book' is the source of modern study since. He succeeded Planta as Principal Librarian in 1827. Thomas Maurice, Assistant Keeper of Manuscripts from 1799 to 1824, was the author of *Indian Antiquities* and a Sanskrit specialist. Henry Baber, editor of the Old Testament portion of the Codex Alexandrinus facsimile (begun by Woide), was Keeper of Printed Books from 1812 to 1837, and distinguished not least for the respect in which he was held by such diverse figures as Planta, Ellis and Panizzi.

Planta himself found time for scholarship, including two substantial works on the history of his native Switzerland. But his principal contribution lay in the reorganisation that he initiated through Committees of the Trustees in 1805 and 1806. This laid down clearer definitions and responsibilities for the administration of the Museum; for the first time the Departments of Antiquities, Coins and Medals, and Prints and Drawings were given independent status, and the need for scholarship in foreign languages in filling vacancies was made obligatory. The structure of the British Museum that lasted until 1973 was laid down in the first decade of the 19th century.

Another innovation came in the publication of catalogues, of the Cottonian manuscripts (1802), the revision of the Harleian catalogue (1808–12), the Hargrave (1818) and Lansdowne (1819) manuscripts, and most important, the new catalogue of printed books in seven octavo volumes (1813–19), undertaken by Baber and Ellis and their assistants in record time.

It was also in Planta's reign that the right to the deposit of all books 'entered at Stationers' Hall' under the 1709 Copyright Act, assumed to have been transferred with the Old Royal Library, was established in the Museum's

Previous page. View of the King's Library. Roubiliac's statue of Shakespeare can be seen at right.

Portrait of Joseph Planta.

William Petty, 1st Marquess of Lansdowne.
National Portrait Gallery London.

favour. A series of legal decisions in the last quarter of the 18th century had maintained the rights of the copyright libraries not only to books 'entered' but also to unregistered books. Spurred on by Edward Christian, the University of Cambridge prosecuted a bookseller for failing to deliver a book and won its case. The Trustees of the British Museum took counsel's opinion on the transfer of the Old Royal Library's right, which was given in their favour. In 1812–14, despite a petition from the booksellers to Parliament, further pressure resulted in the passing of the Copyright Act (1814), in which the Museum's right to deposit copies was definitively established.

This came at an opportune time. The Museum's parliamentary grant of a biennial £3000 had remained unaltered from 1774–75 till 1800. Thereafter the grant had been made annual, and increased steadily from 1805 to 1815, rising to over £10,000 in 1816, the year that the Elgin Marbles were received. But most of this increase had been accounted for by the need for buildings to house the growing collections, among which books were less conspicuous now than antiquities, such as the notable bequest of the Towneley Marbles in 1805. In 1812, the Trustees, petitioning parliament, had emphasised the weakness of the Library as 'very defective . . . in that part of the collection which respects the British Islands and the several possessions of the British Empire', and had been rewarded with an annual grant (which, however, only lasted till 1815) of £1000 to make good the deficiency through acquisitions.

But apart from this grant, and the grants made for special acquisitions, the funds available for adding to the Library were very small. The operation of the Copyright Act in the Museum's favour was vital to its growth. Old habits died hard, however: although there was a brisk increase in deposits – the annual figure leapt from 50 to 500 – this was a drop in the ocean of what the Museum was entitled to receive. Like the other libraries, it was obliged to employ a collector to go to Stationers' Hall, and not until another Copyright Act in 1842 laid the obligation on publishers for books 'to be delivered for the use of the British Museum' was it able to assert its right effectively.

Despite all this, the years following the Cracherode and Musgrave bequests were in no way barren. In 1805 the great collection of William Petty, Earl of Shelburne and 1st Marquess of Lansdowne (1737–1805), was put up for sale. In an age of party politics, his independence of mind made him almost universally unpopular. His ability as a negotiator (to him was due the credit for the peace that ended the American War of Independence) and as an orator was only matched by his inability to conceal his own belief in his superiority. He began his political life by supporting Lord Bute; he ended it by supporting Warren Hastings. No man in his time knew more or reflected more deeply on the roots of political action in his own or other times.

His house in Berkeley Square had been open to writers and artists as well as politicians, and he collected there a splendid library of printed books and manuscripts, maps, prints and drawings, as well as a notable gallery of pictures and ancient statuary, the last acquired through Gavin Hamilton. He began to collect historic documents seriously after his first retirement from public life. His great opportunity came four years after his second retirement in 1769, frustrated by lack of support for conciliation of the American colonists. In 1773, at the sale of James West, Deputy Treasurer of the Inner Temple and President of the Royal Society (1704–73), the greatest of all the book-collectors who profited by the dispersal of the Harleian printed books, Shelburne bought 122 manuscript volumes, all but one the private papers of William Cecil, Lord Burghley. These had been retained after Burghley's death by his secretary, Sir Michael Hickes, and had passed from Hickes's great-grandson to the distinguished bookseller, Richard Chiswell. He sold them to the historian John Strype (1643–1737), whose work was based on the enormous collection of original documents put together during a long life, at the end of which they were bought by West. This collection, joining the already rich resources of the Cottonian and Harleian historic documents, has made the Library a prime resource for students of Elizabethan history all over the world.

Besides this, Shelburne acquired two other historical *fonds* of substantial size. Fifty volumes of the papers of the Jacobean statesman Sir Julius Caesar (1558–1636), out of a total of 187 that had been sold off between 1744 and 1757, were patiently reassembled by the antiquary Philip Carteret Webb (1700–70) and bought on his death by Shelburne; the Library has continued to acquire further volumes whenever they have become available. The third large collection was the 107 volumes of materials on English church history of Bishop White Kennet (1660–1728), whose collections on the spread of Christianity in America passed to the Society for the Propagation of the Gospel.

But Shelburne's interest ranged far wider than the documents of English history. His interest in genealogy and heraldry led him to acquire important material in this field, which again fitted well with the Cottonian and Harleian collections, including, for example, the Yorkshire collection of Wanley's old antagonist John Warburton. In the Lansdowne manuscripts, there was also some important medieval heraldic and tournament material, such as that included in Sir John Paston's 'Great Book', and some notable medieval books, such as the 12th-century Psalter of Henry the Lion, the beautiful English psalter, also 12th-century, from Shaftesbury, the very fine Bible in French, perhaps the presentation copy from the translator Raoul de Presles to Charles V, which later belonged to the Duc de Berry, and a fine illuminated copy of the *Canterbury Tales*, probably from the North of England. A 15th-century Italian copy of Columella, *De re rustica* was bought by Lord Shelburne for its practical use rather than for the elegance of its script and decoration. Finally, among the manuscripts of more recent date is one of special interest to the Library, as well as all scholars of English bibliophily, namely the diary of Humfrey Wanley (*see* p. 48).

The Lansdowne manuscripts were destined to be auctioned with all Shelburne's other collections, which were sold off in 1806. The Trustees of the British Museum, however, petitioned Parliament to prevent the dispersal of the manuscripts, and in 1807 a parliamentary grant of £4925 enabled them to acquire the collection. The Trustees' own resources, still slender, were used for the purchase of the Combe collection of bibles in 1804, and for the great classical scholar Richard Bentley's collection of classical texts, many of them annotated by him, bought from his grandson Richard Cumberland in 1807 for £1000. The same sum sufficed for the modern European literary texts, 4300 in number, bought in 1813 from Pierre Louis Ginguené, author of *Histoire littéraire d'Italie* (1811–19). The foundation of another collection, a treasure built up over many years, came in 1817 when a mass of 'tracts', pamphlets, broadsides and periodicals printed during the French Revolution and put together by Colin, Marat's publisher, was bought on the recommendation of John Wilson Croker. The period of the Revolution and the Napoleonic wars was as productive of printed matter as the English Civil War, and Croker became its Thomason; the collection of this material became his life-work, and was bought from him in two parts, in 1831 and 1856. Altogether, there are 48,579 pieces in the three series, one of the richest documentary resources for the period in the world.

All these acquisitions cost relatively small sums, compared with the £4578 paid by the Museum for the library of 20,000 books, the herbarium and mineral collection of Baron von Moll in 1815–16. Two other important acquisitions were made, like the Lansdowne manuscripts, through parliamentary grants. In both cases, however, it was the owners, not the Trustees, who petitioned Parliament. In 1813, the widow of France Hargrave, a distinguished parliamentary lawyer, obtained a grant of £8000 for his substantial library of legal manuscripts and printed books, which laid the basis of the

Opposite. Page from the Psalter of Henry the Lion, 12th century.
Landsdowne MS 381(pt.1), f.8.

MOYSES
MALACHIAS

Bust of Charles Burney by Joseph Nollekens.
Reproduced by permission of the Trustees of the British Museum.

Above. Joseph Banks.
Reproduced by permissioin of the Trustees of the British Museum.

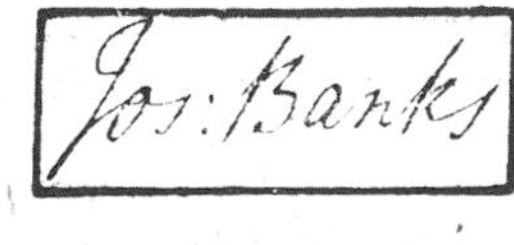

Above. Library stamp of Joseph Banks.

Library's important legal collections. A similar procedure was followed by the family of the Rev. Charles Burney (1757–1817), son of Dr Charles Burney, the author of the *General History of Music*, and brother of Fanny Burney. The younger Burney, a successful schoolmaster in later life, atoned for a misdeed in his youth (like another great collector, James Orchard Halliwell, he stole some books from Trinity College, Cambridge), by putting together three collections, each one of which has proved to have far greater importance than was realised at the time. The sum asked for was £14,000: Parliament reduced this to £13,500, and took £3–4000 off the Museum's general annual grant as well as withdrawing the annual Special Book Fund of £1000.

Harsh though these conditions were, the Burney collection has justified its acquisition many times over. The main part consisted of 525 manuscripts and about 13,000 printed texts of the Greek and Latin classics, ranging in date from the late 7th-century Origen in Latin from Corbie and the 11th-century Towneley Homer, to the correspondence of the great scholar Isaac Casaubon and Burney's own notes for his work on Greek metre. There were also important texts of the Greek orators and illuminated manuscripts, among them the fine Byzantine Gospel-books and the 13th-century Bible of Robert de Bello and a collection of the works of the Greek orators and the Codex Crippsianus from Mount Athos, the earliest manuscript of speeches of the minor Attic orators. Besides these were many annotated and interleaved texts, used by later scholars, whose full riches remain to be exploited. They include books used by Henri Estienne and Richard Bentley, the latter joining the books bought from Richard Cumberland in 1807.

The importance of the Burney classical collections was appreciated at the time. But his other two collections, of newspapers and playbills, were lightly regarded in 1817. Burney began collecting newspapers in his youth, buying the issues for each day or week and binding them up in a single chronological sequence. Later, perhaps because he bought complete runs of back issues, he arranged them conventionally (as we would think), binding each title separately. He also added retrospectively, beginning with the first proper 'coranto', *News from Holland* (1619), as well as some earlier 'news' pamphlets. The result, some 1800 volumes, London papers from their inception, the English provincial press from 1712, Scottish from 1708, Irish from 1691, as well as important runs of American papers, notably the *New England Courant*, on which Benjamin Franklin worked, has become one of the main staples of the historian of the English world in the 17th and 18th centuries. The 349 volumes of playbills, cuttings and portraits, equally neatly organised, laid the foundation for the study of the English theatre in the 18th century. To it too, later acquisitions have been added to form the best collection of English playbills in the world.

A smaller but not less influential bequest was the collection of over 2000 works on Italian history, genealogy and topography given by the distinguished antiquary Sir Richard Colt Hoare of Stourhead (1758–1838), much used by Italian historians both before and after the unification of the nation. The collection has been kept together, and the donor's own catalogue of it, with his presentation inscription, is also preserved.

The last two great acquisitions made during Planta's librarianship both came by gift or bequest. Sir Joseph Banks, as President of the Royal Society, had been an official Trustee of the British Museum since 1778 and a benefactor as early as 1765. Ever since his expedition to Iceland in 1772, with Daniel Solander, then Assistant Librarian in the Natural History Department, his own collections on botany, zoology and the sciences in general, and on travel and discovery, had been formed in conjunction with the Museum's collection (*see* p. 68). Latterly, when Jonas Dryander, another Swede, succeeded Solander and drew up a catalogue of Banks's library, it was with the intention that his should join the Museum's books.

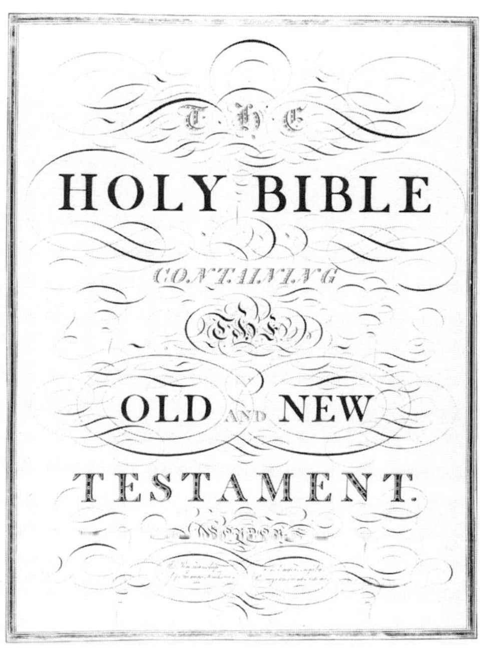

Engraved title-page from calligraphy by T. Tomkins in Macklin's Bible, 1800.
681.K.1–7.

CORANTE, OR, NEVVES FROM
Italy, Germanie, Hungarie, Poland, Bohemia and France. 1621.

News pamphlet of 1621 in the Burney Collection.
C.55.1.2.

It is hard to do justice to the wealth of the Banks collection, except by saying that for a generation or more it was the scientific section of the Museum Library. Banks's contemporaries sent him their books, such as Lavoisier, who gave his *Traité élémentaire de chimie* (1789), and Buffon, whose great *Histoire naturelle* (1749–1807) he possessed complete. He had a special wealth of Scandinavian books, those of his admired Carl Linnaeus, *Flora Suecica* (1745), travel books, such as Pehr Kalm *En resa til Norra America* (1753–61) and atlases such as Pontoppidan *Den Danske atlas* (1763–81). His many colour-plate scientific books, for example the *Flora Danica*, edited by Von Oeder, published in Copenhagen from 1761 and Andrews, *Roses* (1805–28), were, like Sloane's, specially coloured for him. He had a beautiful copy of the great monument of English botanical illustration, Robert Thornton's *Temple of Flora*; the magnificent title page was the work of Thomas Tomkins, the great calligrapher, who also presented to the Library his *magnum opus*, a copy of Macklin's Bible (1800), with his own calligraphic titles, and a bust of himself by Sir Francis Chantrey. The Banks bequest, which came through his last assistant Robert Brown, who remained to supervise the collections, was a treasure so immediately useful, and so much used, that both the individual quality of the books and the overall value of the collection as evidence of the extent of Banks's influence at a seminal time in the history of European science came to be overlooked. It is only recently that it has been possible to give the Banksian library the individual treatment it deserves, and thus to enable the study of the advance in scientific history that it represents.

Banks's library might have enjoyed a better fate if it had not been put so soon to such extensive use. If, like the Cracherode collection, Banks's had been kept separate from the general library, it would have been better, both for study of the collection as such and for the books themselves. From the Trustees' point of view, however, the library was of secondary importance to Banks's herbarium, which, joined with those of Sloane and Moll, made the Museum in this respect second only to the Jardin des Plantes in Paris; the matter was further complicated by the fact that the entire collection was left to Brown for his lifetime with reversion to the Museum. Any prospect of preserving the collection as a unit, however, was lost almost immediately by the accession of an even greater collection, the library of George III by the gift of his son, George IV, announced to the Prime Minister, Lord Liverpool, in a letter of 15 January 1823.

When, in 1751, the future George III succeeded his father as Prince of Wales, he inherited a not inconsiderable library, for Prince Frederick (as we have seen) was a person of some cultivation and taste. George himself, however, was something more: 'the most judicious of collectors', in the words of the antiquary Thomas Amyot (1775–1850), who had good opportunity to judge. He was, perhaps, first and foremost, a collector of prints and drawings, and his first librarian, Richard Dalton, was an artist. But when he came to the throne, three years after his grandfather had given the Old Royal Library (whose loss he can hardly have felt personally) to the Museum, he began to set about building a major library. In 1763 he bought for £10,000 the second and best of the three great collections of books made by Joseph Smith (1682–1770), for years British Consul in Venice. Smith's first collection of manuscripts had been bought by Lord Sunderland as long before as 1720, and since then he had been able to use his mercantile and diplomatic connections to assist the many Englishmen who came to Venice to buy anything from ancient statuary to contemporary pictures, as well as to form his own collection. In 1755 Smith printed a catalogue of his library, a copy of which formed the basis of the present transaction and bears Richard Dalton's note 'Received', dated at Venice, 28 January 1763. What George III bought, then, was the cream of almost half a century of collecting, not only the books but the drawings which remain the wealth of the Royal Collection at Windsor, notably those by Canaletto, whose patron Smith was for many years. The

Reinagle pinx^t. Earlom sculp^t.

Tulips

London Published May 1 1798, by D^r. Thornton

Plate from Hevelius, *Selenographia*, 1647.
48.f.5, Fig.R.

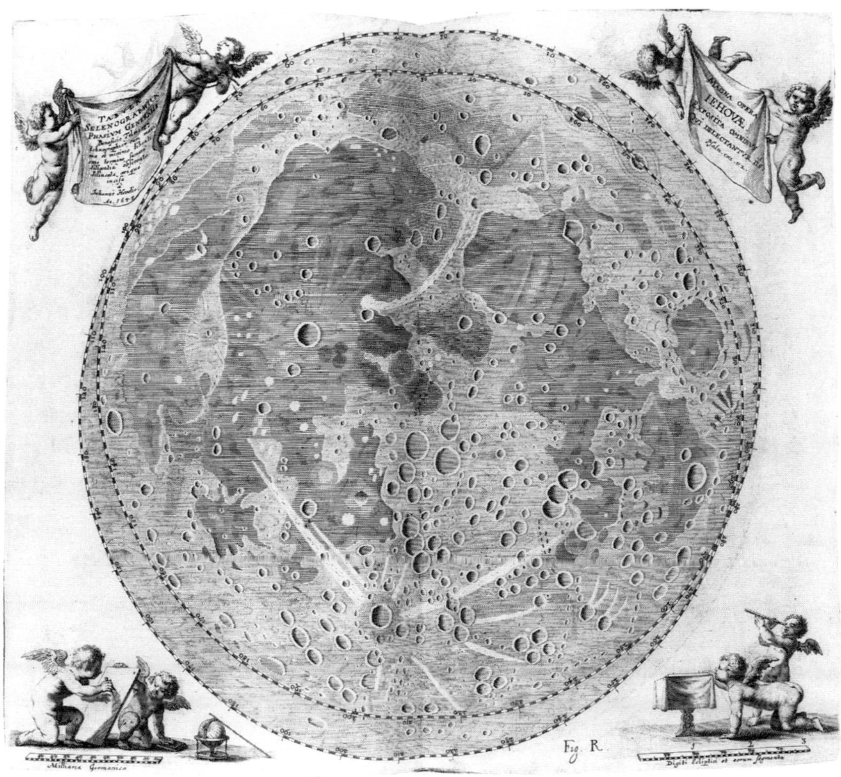

library was rich in early printed books and history and literature of Europe, but especially that of Italy. No single Italian library, even now, can boast equal wealth.

In all this, George III took close and personal attention: it was very much his own collection. In 1774, he appointed a full-time librarian, Frederick Augusta Barnard, allowing Dalton to concentrate on the collection, as rapidly growing, of art and antiquities. Barnard was not a scholar but the son of a royal servant (and godson of the King's sister, not, as once suggested, the King's natural half-brother) and became Page of the Back Stairs in 1761; he remained in charge of the royal library until his death in 1830 at the age of 87. He conducted the day-to-day business of the library, but George III kept in close touch with his main agent, George Nicol, the royal bookseller. The library was open to scholars, even those, like Joseph Priestley, of whom the King disapproved: a more welcome reader was Samuel Johnson, who had his famous meeting with George III in his library in February 1767. Johnson remained a valued friend and adviser, writing to Barnard, recommending to him the policy that 'a royal library should have the most curious edition, generally the first, the most splendid, and the most useful, generally one of the latest', of any book of which more than one edition existed, and emphasising the need for books on law, 'a regal study', the literature of every country, and a comprehensive collection of maps.

So it was that George III acquired the cream of the collections of Anthony Askew, James West and John Ratcliffe (sold in 1772, 1773 and 1776). Askew's books included a remarkable sequence of early editions of the classics and Italian literature, and West's early English literature, notably plays, and the Mainz *Catholicon*; from West and Ratcliffe came no less than 43 English incunables, and the further gift by Jacob Bryant in 1782 made the royal collection uniquely rich in the work of the first English printer. Through Nicol, books were bought at the Paris auctions: one such was a presentation copy of Hevelius's *Selenographia* (1647) to Louis XIV's minister, Jean-Baptiste Colbert, and bound by him in red morocco with his arms. Other books came from James Edwards, Nicol's neighbour in Pall Mall, and both bought from Alexander Horn of Ratisbon, the first bookseller to specialise in early German

Opposite. 'Tulips'. From Thornton's *Temple of Flora*, 1798.
10.TAB.40 (pt.3).

To the Reader.

This *Figure*, that thou here ſeeſt put,
It was for gentle *Shakeſpeare* cut;
Wherein the *Graver* had a ſtrife
With *Nature*, to out-doe the *Life*:
O, could he but have drawn his *Wit*
As well in *Braſſe*, as he has hit
His *Face*; the *Print* would then ſurpaſſe
All, that was ever writ in *Braſſe*.
But ſince he cannot, *Reader*, look
Not on his *Picture*, but his *Book*.

B. J.

M^R. WILLIAM
SHAKESPEAR'S
Comedies, Hiſtories, and Tragedies.
Publiſhed according to the true Original Copies.
The third Impreſſion.
And unto this Impreſſion is added ſeven Playes, never before Printed in Folio.
viz.

Pericles Prince of *Tyre*.
The *London Prodigall*.
The Hiſtory of *Thomas* L^d. *Cromwell*.
Sir *John Oldcaſtle* Lord *Cobham*.
The *Puritan Widow*.
A *York-ſhire* Tragedy.
The Tragedy of *Locrine*.

LONDON, Printed for *P. C.* 1664.

Title opening of the 1664 Third Folio of Shakespeare's plays. Charles II's copy. 80.1.13.

books and to distinguish them by their types. Contemporary books came from every country in Europe. The library also contained over 400 manuscripts, including a few of medieval date.

George III spent some £2000 a year on his library, a level of expenditure maintained by his trustees during the Regency, and continued after his death by George IV. At this point, the library consisted of 65,259 volumes and 868 boxes of pamphlets, later bound up in 19,000 volumes. A printed catalogue (the cost of which George IV also paid) was prepared by Barnard and issued in five volumes between 1820 and 1829.

The wealth that thus came to the British Museum can only be suggested. Although some of the greatest treasures were retained in the royal collection as heirlooms, no reservation was put on Charles II's copy of the Third Folio (1664) of Shakespeare, two magnificent royal bindings by Samuel Mearne, the copy of Hogarth's *Analysis of Beauty* (1753) presented by the author to George III as Prince of Wales, or Johnson's *Dictionary* (1755). Among the early English books were Caxton's first edition of Chaucer's *Canterbury Tales* (1476) and the only known copy of Robert Green's *Pandosto* (1588). Early Italian books included the first edition of Castiglione, *Il cortegiano* (1528) and a 'Canevari' binding. Among the bibles were the Plantin Polyglot (1564) printed on vellum for the Duke of Alva and the English Polyglot (1657), whose acquisition particularly pleased Johnson. There is also the unique 1535 Rabelais *Pantagruel*. Early science is represented by Tycho Brahe's *Epistolae astronomicae* (1596), Napier's primary tract on logarithms, *Mirifici logarithmorum canonis descriptio* (1614), Galileo's *Dialogo* (1632) and Copernicus *De revolutionibus orbium caelestium* (1543).

Modern science was not forgotten: Volta's *Lettere* (1777) are there, and the reprehensible Dr Priestley's *Observations on different kinds of air* (1774–77). Herbals include Fuchs, *De historia stirpium* (1542) and – a late purchase – Redouté, *Les roses* (1817–24). Other contemporary works added to the library were Adam Smith's *The Wealth of nations* (1776), Chateaubriand's *Génie du Christianisme* (1802) and Herder's *Ideen zur Philosophie der Geschichte der Menschheit* (1784–91).

The collection of Scandinavian books was also remarkable, including Thurah *Den Danske Vitruvius* (1746–49), with its fine architectural plates, the illustrated Danish translation of the classic *Utopia*, Holberg's *Niels Klims underjordiske Reise* (1784), and the first Finnish dictionary, Juslenius's *Suomalaisen sana-lugun coetus* (1745), as well as notable Icelandic books, among them the first secular book printed in Iceland, *Lögbok Islendinga* (1578). Even more exotic imprints were the Gospels in Tamil printed at Tranquebar in 1714 and Nathaniel Halhed's *A grammar of the Bengal language* (1778), the first book to be printed in Bengal.

George III's interest in his overseas possessions, evinced by Collins's *An account of the English Colony in New South Wales* (1798–1802), the *Plan of the association for promoting the discovery of the interior parts of Africa* (1788), and the critical document of Canadian history, the *Statement respecting the Earl of Selkirk's settlement upon the Red River* (1817), is, ironically, nowhere better displayed than in the documents of the American War of Independence. Samuel Johnson's *Taxation no tyranny* (1775) is there, but so is *A collection of state-papers relative to the first acknowledgement of the sovereignty of the United States of America* by 'An American' (1782), Benjamin Franklin's olive branch. A memento of more peaceful times, Harvard University's congratulatory verses on the King's accession in 1760, *Pietas et gratulatio Collegii Cantabrigiensis apud Novanglos* (1761) is still in the collection.

All this is a mere sketch of the scope of a collection which gave the library of the British Museum its present character as a repository of printed books, both ancient and modern, second to none in the English-speaking world. It had been by no means certain that the library would come to the Museum. It was rumoured that George IV had intended to sell the collection to the Czar, or that the House of Commons, a Committee of which was deliberating on the King's letter, would recommend some other destination. The Trustees, who with commendable promptitude had in 1823 commissioned from Robert Smirke a design for the new building that would clearly be needed, held their breath. But on 23 April 1827 the Committee issued its verdict, that 'the Public will derive the greatest benefit from placing this noble donation under the care of the Trustees of the Museum', on condition that it be 'kept distinct and entire' and 'a separate room should be appropriated for its reception'. Parliament had already anticipated this decision in one sense by voting the necessary funds for the new building, erected between 1823 and 1827 and latterly fitted for the accommodation of the King's Library, which finally arrived in August 1828.

Joseph Planta, who had served the Museum for 54 years, and had lived to see the happy outcome of Parliament's deliberation and the completion of the King's Library gallery, just missed the final fruition, for he died on 3 December 1827, aged 84. He had been Principal Librarian for 28 years, and he was succeeded by the Keeper of Manuscripts, Henry Ellis, who was to serve the Museum for even longer than his predecessor. It was, however, to be a very different place in the second quarter of the 19th century.

Geoffrey Chaucer, *The Canterbury Tales*. The copy of Caxton's first edition (the first book printed in English), 1476, bound for George III.
167.c.26.

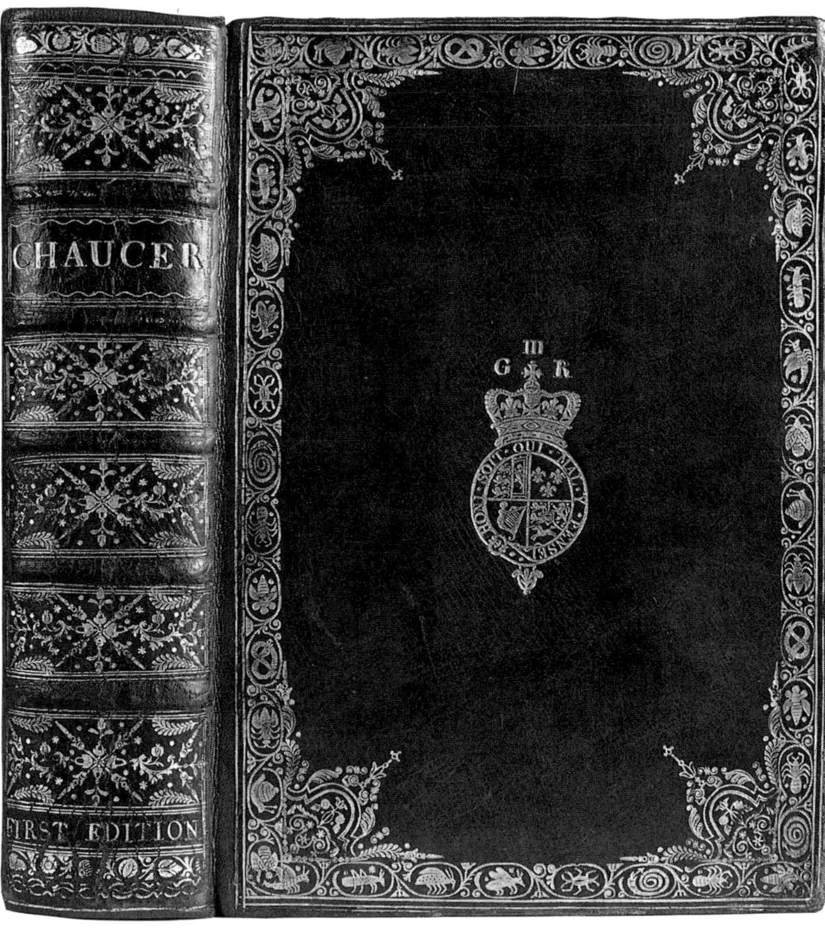

Below. Polyglot bible printed by Plantin on vellum, 1564.
6.h.4.

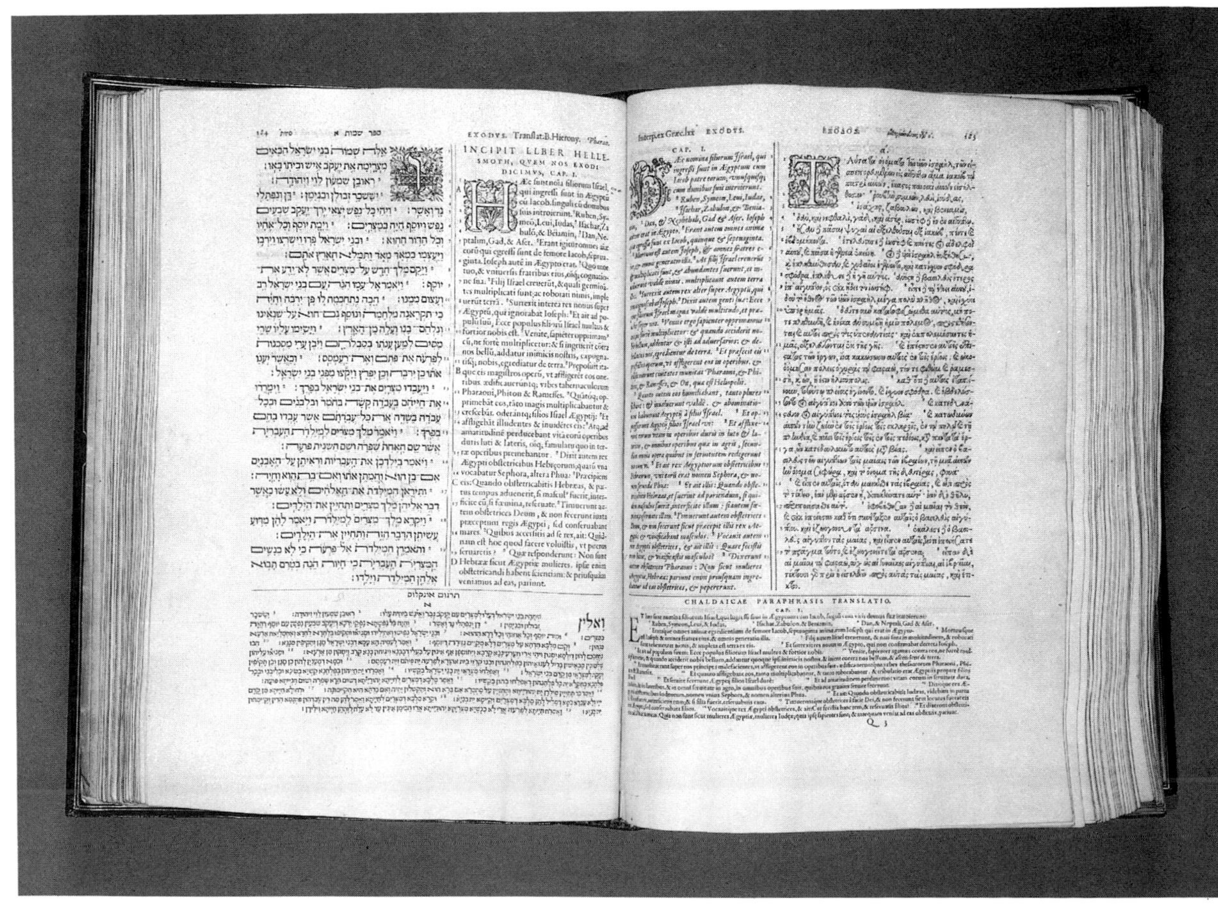

7

Antonio Panizzi and the Department of Printed Books in the 19th Century

T.H. Shepherd, 'The New Reading Room', *c.*1838.
BM Prints and Drawings 1938–11–12–1. Reproduced by permission of the Trustees of the British Museum.

Opposite. The Arch Room, 1841.
Maps C.26.f.7.

In 1803, the year that Richard Penneck died after 43 years in charge of the Reading Room, the increasing number of readers meant that more space was required, and a larger room next to the old one was fitted up for the purpose. But the pressure steadily increased. By 1810, 2000 readers a year were recorded, by 1825 22,800, and in 1835, 100,000 came: it was not only the accession of the King's Library that dictated the need for a new building. Smirke's plan had, from the outset, envisaged the extension of the Montagu House site to a complete quadrangle. The east wing, mainly accommodating the King's Library, was built first, with the eastern end of the south range, comprising three rooms destined for the Department of Manuscripts; two, however, were immediately used as Reading Rooms, accommodating 120 readers. The western wing, built to accommodate the rapidly increasing Natural History and Antiquities Departments (the latter now including the Elgin Marbles), was already under construction. At this point Parliament refused to fund further extension, and it was not until 1833 that the north wing began to be built, to be completed in 1836. The whole of the collection of printed books (except the King's Library) was now transferred to these new quarters, some 250,000 volumes in all. In 1838 the two easternmost rooms were equipped and opened as reading rooms, holding 168 readers; a contemporary view shows that this was none too large a space. Finally, the north wing was completed with an extension to the west, beyond the confines of the quadrangle, with a double gallery, the present Arch Room. Montagu House was demolished in 1845, and Smirke's whole plan, with its handsome classical façade, completed in 1852.

It is not, perhaps, surprising that this gradual and complicated progress, taking place as it did at a time of rapid growth of population and industry and of social unrest, should have generated complaint. This found public form in the Parliamentary Enquiry of 1835–36 and the Royal Commission, set up in 1847, whose report in 1850 brought public criticism to an end. The Enquiry was occasioned by a relatively trivial circumstance, the complaint of a member of staff dismissed for incompetence: it was seized as an opportunity by those who wished for more professional representation, especially of the nascent interest in the sciences, on the Museum's Board of Trustees. The results of the Enquiry were neither radical nor conclusive: but its effects on the staff and Trustees were greater.

The principal recommendations were that there should be no basic change in the composition of the Board; that there should be more and better consultation between Board and staff; that Parliament should be more generous in its grants; and that the staff should be properly paid and hold 'no other situation conferring emolument or entailing duties'. None of these worked in the manner intended. Sir Henry Ellis, conservative by nature and principle, could see nothing wrong with the status quo and had said so at the Enquiry. Although this was satisfactory neither to the critics nor the staff, it drew him closer to the Trustees (whose preference for a classified, rather than alphabetic, catalogue he shared). He had a powerful ally in Josiah Forshall, Keeper of Manuscripts and Secretary to the Board, who now gave up the former post and as Secretary was able to influence the Trustees to a very marked degree. The Keepership of Manuscripts was thus vacant, and at the same time the edict against pluralism forced Henry Baber, the Keeper of Printed Books, to retire to the country living which he also held. The two vacancies were filled by two remarkable men, Frederic Madden and Antonio Panizzi. Their energy transformed the departments over which they presided; their mutual antipathy pervaded the whole Museum so that, in the words of A.N.L. Munby, it 'resembled internally a seething cauldron on the surface of which the aged and genial Sir Henry Ellis bobbed like a bewildered cork'.

Antonio Panizzi was the victor in this feud, and in much else: to him is due the credit for making the Library the great treasure-house of books that it became in his lifetime; he gave it the character it bears today. Born near

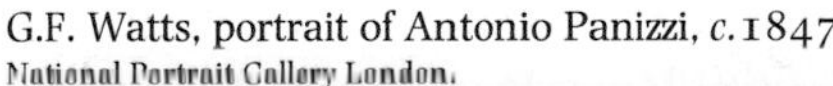

G.F. Watts, portrait of Antonio Panizzi, *c.*1847.
National Portrait Gallery London.

Modena in 1797, his life-long passion for the independence of Italy brought a promising legal career to an end in 1823, when he fled to London under sentence of death. Encouraged by William Roscoe, the great Liverpool patron of all things Italian, he taught Italian there, returning to London as Professor of Italian at the newly-founded University. In 1830 he became a reader at the British Museum and was appointed an Extra Assistant Librarian in the Department of Printed Books in 1831. As such he was subordinate to Henry Francis Cary, the translator of Dante and Assistant Keeper since 1826. But in 1837 when Baber retired, Cary was passed over on account of his age and health, and Panizzi became Keeper.

Panizzi had made his objectives very clear to the Parliamentary Enquiry. 'Public opinion is exercised only upon one of the purposes for which the British Museum was instituted: that is upon its establishment as a show place', he said. 'Unfortunately as to its most important and most noble purpose, as an establishment for the furtherance of education, for study and research, the public seem almost indifferent.' Asked if he regarded it as 'a very secondary object to keep up the Library even if it could be done, with a full supply of all the modern British and foreign works', he gave a memorable reply:

I would not say a very secondary object; but if I am to choose, I would say that it is of less importance for the library of the British Museum to have common modern books, than to have rare, ephemeral, voluminous and costly publications, which cannot be found anywhere else, by persons not having access to great private collections. I want a poor student to have the same means of indulging his learned curiosity, of following his rational pursuits, of consulting the same authorities, of fathoming the most intricate inquiry, as the richest man in the kingdom, as far as books go, and I contend that Government is bound to give him the most liberal and unlimited assistance in this respect. I want the library of the British Museum to have books of both descriptions; I want an extra grant for those rare and costly books which we have not, and which cannot be bought but upon opportunities offering themselves. Then the annual grant should be increased for modern books, that is books printed from about the beginning of last century.

Moved by a higher sense of his responsibilities than those whom he addressed, Panizzi set about his task. His energy was already attested, the speed and accuracy of his cataloguing having already engaged the surprise and admiration of the Trustees. His first task was to establish order in the Reading Room, with an established routine for the requisition and return of books. Next came the removal of the books from Montagu House to their new quarters, and with it the opportunity of reclassifying and shelf-marking the books by subject. This was achieved with the aid of Thomas Watts (1811–69), the ablest of the group of assistants that Panizzi built up, and with John Winter Jones and Richard Garnett (the elder) his most loyal supporters. Then came the clash with the Trustees over the Catalogue. They determined on a printed catalogue, however inaccurate, Panizzi holding out (with eventual success) for a single but accurate copy. After 10 years, loyally spent trying to bring about the Trustees' vacuous wishes, during which time he had to bear the blame for the errors of the volume that did appear, the Trustees gave way and asked Panizzi 'to proceed with the utmost despatch in the compilation of a full and complete catalogue in manuscript'. Another hazard was the casual enforcement by Forshall, as Secretary to the Trustees, of the much improved Copyright Act of 1842, which at last gave the Museum the right to every printed book published in the British Isles.

On the other hand, there were some solid advances, notably in acquisitions. Between 1801 and 1832 the funds available for the purchase of printed books had averaged only £600 a year, including the special grants (apart from them, the Trustees' allocation had been barely £200). From 1834–35 regular annual grants were made, and a total of £2944 was recorded in the following year. As soon as the classified reshelving was com-

Contemporary print showing the demolition of Montagu House in progress prior to the erection of Smirke's facade, 1845.
Maps c.26.f.7.

plete, Panizzi and Watts began a survey of the Library, section by section, detailing the deficiencies in each. This was presented to the Trustees together with a request for extra purchase funds of £10,000 for old books, £5000 for new books, plus a grant of £2500 for binding, over a period of 10 years. Although Panizzi did not get all he asked (£10,000 rather than £15,000), this level of funding was maintained for over 40 years. At last the Museum was able to command the resources to build the collection that Panizzi had envisaged.

It was not a moment too soon. The sale of the collection of Richard Heber (1773–1833), the greatest book collector of his time, took place between 1834 and 1837, and the Museum was able to strengthen its holdings of early English literature, even though the cream of the collection was bought by William Henry Miller, the founder of the Britwell Court library, from which, 80 years later, the Library was able to acquire some at least that it had missed. Now more substantial purchases were possible at the sales of the Duke of Sussex and Benjamin Bright (1843–45); at the latter one of its greatest treasures was acquired, the collection of some 1200 broadside ballads known from its first collector, the famous Duke of Roxburghe, as the 'Roxburghe Ballads'. Oriental printed books, as well as Hebrew, were added, the great collection of Luther tracts begun; from Lord Guildford's collection came an unrivalled series of ancient and modern Greek books. Booksellers, not only in Britain, but all over the world, sensed the new vitality. The Museum's main agents, successively Thomas Rodd, Thomas Thorpe, Thomas and William Boone, F.S. Ellis and, last and greatest, Bernard Quaritch, served its needs manfully; Adolphus Asher of Berlin combed all northern Europe; and, in 1845, at the introduction of the historian Jared Sparks, the American bookseller Henry Stevens 'drifted in', to lay the foundations of the greatest collection of American books outside the United States. Among the major acquisitions by purchase made at this time was the Richard Heber collection of catalogues of book-sales, bought from Thomas Thorpe in 1838 for 50 guineas. The existing collection, stretching back to the earliest English

C. Manzini, portrait of Thomas Grenville, 1841.
National Portrait Gallery London.

Dedication inscription by Panizzi to Grenville, in his edition of Boiardo *Sonetti e Canzone*, 1835.

DELLA PRESENTE EDIZIONE SONOSI
TIRATI SOLI CINQUANTA ESEMPLARI
DA NON ESSER POSTI IN COMMERCIO.

No. 2

All' Onorevolissimo Sig.r
Tommaso Grenville

In argomento di rispetto
e gratitudine
l'editore

20 maggio 1835

auction sale catalogues bought by Sloane in his youth, was now strengthened and brought up to-date, thus laying the foundation of the Library's present unrivalled series. Other major acquisitions included the Hebrew bible on vellum printed at Naples *c.*1492, two Caxtons, the French *Recueil des histoires de Troye*, and *The fables of Esope* (1484); the first copies of the Indulgence printed by Gutenberg *c.*1455 and of Columbus's letter to Ferdinand and Isabella announcing the discovery of America, printed at Rome in 1493, as well as copies of Shakespeare's *Lucrece* (1594), *Venus and Adonis* (1594) and *Sonnets* (1609). Perhaps most remarkable of all was a volume in the long, thin format called 'agenda', containing 64 'sotties' or farces in French, all printed between 1540 and 1550, the majority unique.

The new encouragement offered by more generous purchase funds was great, but greater still was the bequest – the last great donation received by the British Museum Library – of the library of Thomas Grenville (1755–1846). This, too, was entirely due to Panizzi. Italian literature was the bond that had drawn the old Whig politician and the emigré scholar together. It is possible that the link was first made by Ugo Foscolo, poet and patriot, who had presented his *Ultime lettere di Jacopo Ortis* (1817) to Grenville, and had befriended his young fellow exile on his first arrival. Certainly they were acquainted by 1829 when Grenville lent Panizzi the texts of Ariosto and Boiardo, editions of which Panizzi published, dedicating Boiardo's *Sonetti e canzone* (1835) to Grenville. The friendship grew; Panizzi helped Grenville with the acquisition of his library, as his notes in the books themselves testify. But Grenville's eventual decision to bequeath the books to the Museum, communicated under seal of secrecy to Panizzi, came as a deeply moving surprise. Grenville had been a Trustee of the Museum, like Cracherode, but took a low view (shared by Panizzi) of their deliberations.

The bequest, when it came, finally put the Museum in the first rank among the libraries of the world. Grenville had been collecting for over 50 years. His copy on vellum of the first (42-line) Bible had come from the great 18th-century French collector Girardot de Préfond. His range was as generous as that of the King's Library, his care to select the best copy as great as that of Cracherode; in total number his 20,240 volumes came between the two. Like Heber, he had a particular interest in early printing in all the vernacular languages of the world. His collection of the printed records of travel and discovery had no equal, before or since.

In early printing, besides the 42-line Bible, he had the 1457 Mainz Psalter and the Harleian copy of the *Catholicon*, the unique complete copy of the *editio princeps* of Ovid, printed at Bologna by Baldassare Azzoguidi in 1471, his favourite among all his books. There was a finely illuminated copy of the Jenson Pliny of 1472, and the same printer's very rare pocket *Officium Beatae Virginis Mariae* (1474). The collection was rich in European literature, including two famous chivalric romances, *Tirant lo Blanch*, printed at Valencia in 1490 and the *Cronica del famoso cavallero Cid Ruy Diez Campeador* legend of 'the Cid', (Burgos 1512), the first editions of Louise Labé's exquisite *Oeuvres* (1556), and of Montaigne's *Essais* (1586) and *Don Quixote* (1605).

In Italian literature he had Luigi Pulci's unique *Morgante maggiore* (Florence, 1482), the 1516 first edition of Ariosto's *Orlando furioso* and that of Tasso's *Gerusalemme Liberata* (1580), as well as Tasso's *Rime* (1581) with the autograph corrections of Aldo Manuzio the younger; a fragment of wood said to be from the door of Tasso's cell at Ferrara is mounted in the case in which the book is kept.

In English literature, he ranged from the Caxton *Canterbury Tales* and Ben Jonson's copy of George Puttenham's *Arte of English poesie* (1589), from the best surviving copy of Shakespeare's *Sonnets* (1609) and John Donne's *Poems* (1633) in a binding with Charles I's arms, to a very scarce edition of Defoe's *Robinson Crusoe* (1719–20) in serial form and the large-paper copy of Warburton's edition of Pope (1751) that had belonged to John Wilkes, bibliophile

The Cooper of Norfolke:

OR,

A pretty Iest of a Brewer and the Coopers Wife: And how the Cooper served the Brewer in his kind. To the tune of, The Wiving Age.

Attend my Masters, and listen well
Unto this my Ditty, which briefly doth tell
Of a fine merry Iest which in Norfolke befell:
A brave lusty Cooper in that Countie did dwell,
And there he cry'd Worke for a Cooper,
Maids ha'ye any worke for a Cooper?

This Cooper he had a faire creature to's wife, (life,
Which a Brewer i'th Towne lov'd as deare as his
And she had a tricke, which in some wives is rife:
She still kept a sheath for another mans knife,
And often cornuted the Cooper,
While he cry'd, More worke for a Cooper.

It hapned one morning the Cooper out went,
To worke for his living, it was his intent:
He trusted his house to his wives government,
And left her in bed to her owne hearts content,
While he cry'd, What worke for a Cooper,
Maids ha'ye any worke for a Cooper?

And as the Cooper was passing along,
Still crying and calling his old wonted song,
The Brewer, his rivall, both lustie and yong,
Did thinke now or never to doe him some wrong,
And lie with the wife of the Cooper,
Who better lov'd him than the Cooper.

So calling the Cooper, he to him did say,
Goe home to my house, and make no delay,
I have so much worke as thou canst doe to day:
What ever thou earnest, Ile bountifully pay.
These tidings well pleased the Cooper,
Oh, this was brave newes for the Cooper.

Away went the Cooper to th'house of the Brewer,
Who seeing him safe at his worke to indure:
Thought he, now for this day the Cooper is sure,
Ile goe to his wife, her green-sicknesse to cure:
Take heed of your forehead, good Cooper,
For now I must worke for the Cooper.

So straight waies he went to the Coopers dwelling,
The goodwife to give entertainment was willing,
The Brewer & she like two pigeons were billing:
And what they did else they have bound mee from
He pleased the wife of the Cooper, (telling:
Who better lov'd him than the Cooper.

But marke how it happened now at the last,
The sun-shine of pleasure was soone over-past;
The Cooper did lacke one of's Tooles, and in haste
He came home to fetch it, and found the doore fast:
Wife, open the doore, quoth the Cooper,
And let in thy husband the Cooper.

Now when the goodwife and the Brewer did heare
The Cooper at doore, affrighted they were:
The Brewer was in such a bodily feare,
That for to hide himselfe he knew not where,
To shun the fierce rage of the Cooper,
He thought he should die by the Cooper.

The good wife perceiving his wofull estate,
She having a subtill and politicke pate,
She suddenly whelm'd downe a great brewing Fat,
And closely she cover'd the Brewer with that:
Then after shee let in the Cooper,
What's under this Tub? quoth the Cooper.

HANC TVA PENELOPE
lento tibi mittit ulixes.
Nil mihi reſcribas:
attamen ipſe ueni.
Troya iacet certe danais inuiſa puellis.
Vix priamus tanti: tota q; troya fuit.
O utinam tunc cum lacedemona claſſe petebat
Obrutus inſanis eſſet adulter aquis.
Non ego deſerto iacuiſſem frigida lecto:
Nec quererer tardos ire relicta dies.
Nec mihi quaerenti ſpatioſam fallere noctem
Laſſaret uiduas pendula tela manus.
Quando ego non timui grauiora pericula ueris!
Res eſt ſoliciti plena timoris amor.
Inte fingebam uiolentos troas ituros.
Nomine in hectoreo pallida ſemper eram.
Siue quis anthilocum narrabat ab hectore uictum
Anthilocus noſtri cauſa timoris erat.
Siue meneciadem falſis cecidiſſe ſub armis:
Flebam ſucceſſu poſſe carere dolos.
Sanguine tlepolemus lyciam tepefecerat haſtam.
Tlepolemi laeto cura nouata mea eſt.
Deniq; quiſquis erat caſtris iugulatus achiuis:
Frigidius glacie pectus amantis erat.
Sed bene conſuluit caſto deus ęquus amori.
Verſa eſt in cineres ſoſpite troia uiro.
Argolici rediere duces. altaria fumant.
Ponitur ad patrios barbara pręda deos.
Grata ferunt nymphę pro ſaluis dona maritis.
Illi uicta ſuis troica facta canunt.
Mirantur iuſtiq; ſenes: trepidę q; puellę.
Narrantis coniux pendet ab ore uiri.
Iamq; aliquis poſita monſtrat fera pręlia menſa.
Pingit & exiguo pergama tota mero.
Hac ibat ſymois: hic ē ſigeia tellus:

Above, left. 'The Cooper of Norfolk'. A broadside ballad in the Roxburghe Ballads collection.
C.20.f.7, vol.1.

Above, right. Page from Grenville's unique complete copy of Azzoguidi's Ovid, printed at Bologna 1471, with contemporary decoration.
G.10035.

as well as radical politician, whose editions of Catullus and Theophrastus were also in Grenville's collection. Franklin's *Opuscules* (Lyons, 1795) again showed politics tempered with bibliophilic prudence.

The section on American voyages was especially rich, with an unequalled collection of 'Columbus letters' and almost all the documents of the discovery: these included the first account of Pizarro's victories, the voyages of Cartier, Vespucci, Smith's propaganda pamphlet for the new colony in Virginia and Wood's In Massachusetts. Outside the New World, he had the first edition of Marco Polo (1477), unexpectedly in German, and Richard Jobson's *The golden trade* (1623), describing the River Gambia for the first time. Among the long section of bibles and liturgical works were the Complutensian Polyglot, and the only known fragment of Tyndale's first English New Testament, printed at Cologne in 1525, as well as the 42-line Bible and the Mainz Psalter.

His illustrated books ranged from the 1481 Florence Dante with all 19 engravings, said to be after Botticelli, and the *Hypnerotomachia Poliphili* (1499) in a magnificent 16th-century binding by Claude de Picques for Thomas Mahieu, to Zacharias Heyns's *Const-thoonende juweel*, printed at Zwolle in 1607–8. Other splendid bindings include Simonetta's 'Sforziada' (Milan, 1490) bound for Ludovico Sforza, 'il Moro', Duke of Milan, the Lascaris edition of the *Anthologia Graeca* (Florence, 1494) printed on vellum in a contemporary binding, and the *Tragedie* of Lodovico Dolce (Venice, 1560) bound for the Doge Marco Foscarini.

But perhaps the most distinctive element of his collection were the books printed in exotic places or languages, for example Dinko Ranjina's *Piesni*

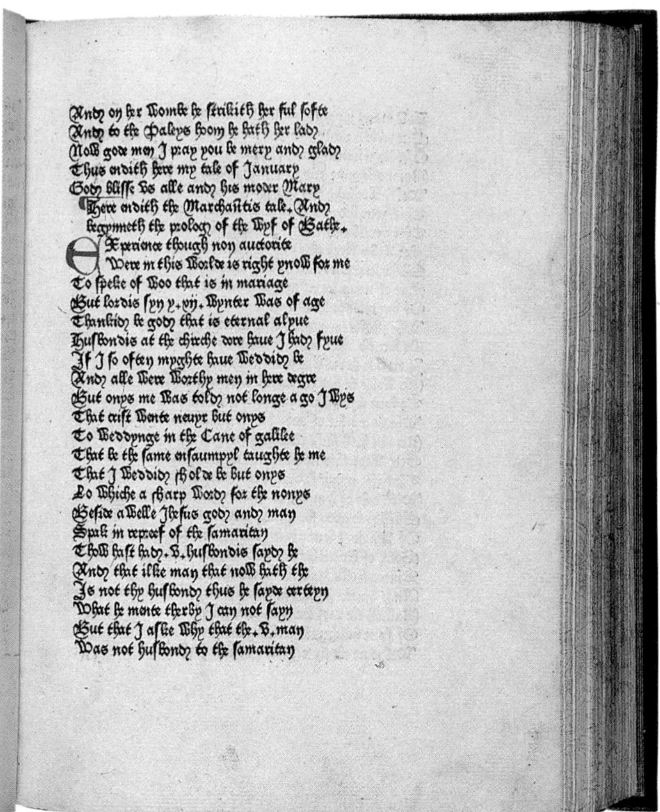

Andy on her Wombe he strikith her ful softe
Andy to the Paleys hom he hath her lady
Now gode men J pray you be mery andy glady
Thus endith here my tale of January
Gody blisse vs alle andy his moder Mary
Here endith the Marchantis tale. Andy
begynneth the prolog of the Wyf of Bathe.
Experience though non auctorite
Were in this Worlde is right ynow for me
To speke of Woo that is in mariage
But lordis syn x.vij. Wynter Was of age
Thankidy be gody that is eternal alyue
Husbondis at the chirche dore haue J hady fyue
If J so often myghte haue Weddidy be
Andy alle Were Worthy men in here degre
But onys me Was toldy not longe a go J Wys
That crist Wente neuyr but onys
To Weddynge in the Cane of galilee
That be the same ensaumpyl taughte he me
That J Weddidy sholde be but onys
Lo Whiche a sharp Wordy for the nonys
Beside a Welle Jhesus gody andy man
Spak in repreef of the samaritan
Thow hast hady .v. husbondis sayde he
Andy that ilke man that now hath the
Is not thy husbondy thus he sayde certeyn
What he mente therby J can not sayn
But that J aske Why that the .v. man
Was not husbondy to the samaritan

CAII PLYNII SECVNDI NATVRALIS HISTORIAE LIBER .I.

CAIVS PLYNIVS SECVNDVS NOVOCOMENSIS DOMITIANO SVO SALVTEM. PRAEFATIO.

IBROS NATVRALIS HISTORIAE NOuitium camœnis quiritium tuorum opus natum apud me proxima fœtura licentiore epistola narrare constitui tibi iucundissime imperator. Sit.n. hæc tui præfatio uerissima: dum maxio cõsenescit in patre. Nãq; tu solebas putare esse aliqd meas nugas: ut obiicere moliar Catullum conterraneũ meum. Agnoscis & hoc castrẽse uerbum. Ille enĩ ut scis: permutatis prioribus syllabis duriusculũ se fecit: q̃ uolebat existimari a uernaculis tuis: & famulis. Simul ut hac mea petulãtia fiat: quod

Above, left. Opening page of 'The Wife of Bath's Tale' in Caxton's 1476 edition of *The Canterbury Tales*.
G.11585, f.124.

Above, right. Opening page of Jenson's 1472 edition of Pliny, *Historia Naturum*.
G.9382, f.1.

raslike, printed in Florence in 1563 before the author's return to Dubrovnik. Further afield, he had the Library's only example of the early Portuguese press at Goa, Garcia de Orta's *Coloquios dos simples* (1563), and the *Guia do pecador*, printed at the Jesuit press at Nagasaki in 1599. Other missionary texts included the Gospels and Acts in Malay printed at the instance of Robert Boyle in 1677 and both the New Testament (1661) and Bible (1663) translated by John Eliot for the conversion of the American Indians and printed at Boston. Nearer home, he had the first Finnish grammar, Vhael *Grammatica Fennica* (1733) and Ole Worm's *Rúnir: seu Danica literatura antiquissima* (Copenhagen, 1636). Finally, there were a few important scientific books, notably Otto von Guericke's *Experimenta nova Magdeburgica de vacuo spatio* (1672).

Grenville died on 17 December 1846, and on 28 January 1847, an icy day with driving snow, the books began to arrive, to be installed (at Ellis's suggestion) in the West Room next to the Manuscript Saloon. This provoked a new and crucial explosion in the feud between Madden and Panizzi. The new room had been promised to Madden; he had already begun to install select manuscripts in it, thus relieving the other overcrowded rooms of his Department. Panizzi demanded the whole room and, ignoring Madden's suggestion that the Grenville books could be double-banked, like his manuscripts, made his point by leaving the surplus on tables or planks or even on the floor, where they were viewed with distress by Grenville's old servant, who had helped his master dust the books for many years, always using a white duster. Although asserting that the arrangement was only temporary, the Trustees ordered Madden to remove the manuscripts, nor was he more successful in claiming Grenville's manuscripts for his Department, notably the volume of 12 paintings on vellum of the Triumphs of the Emperor Charles V, then ascribed to Giulio Clovio, which were its principal treasure; they only came to the Department of Manuscripts in 1890, exchanged with the Department of Printed Books for the printed part of Bagford's collections from the Harleian Library. Panizzi had won. Grenville's printed books remain where they were put, their

Opposite. Illuminated page from the 1455 '42-Line Bible'.
C.q.d.4.

Incipit prologus sancti iheronimi
presbiteri i parabolas salomonis

Iungat epistola quos iungit sacerdo-
cium: immo carta non diuidat: quos
xpi nectit amor. Cōmētarios in osee.
amos. et zachariā malachiā. quoq;
poscitis. Scripsissē: si licuisset pre vali-
tudine. Mittitis solacia sumptuum.
notarios nr̄os et librarios sustenta-
tis: ut vobis potissimū nr̄m desudet
ingeniū. Et ecce ex latere frequēs turba
diuersa poscētiū: quasi aut equū sit me
vobis esurientibȝ aliis laborare: aut
in racione dati et accepti. cuiq; preter
vos obnoxius sim. Itaq; lōga egrota-
tione fractus. ne penitus hoc anno re-
ticerē. et apud vos mutus essem. tridui
opus nomini vr̄o consecraui. interp-
tationē videlicet triū salomonis vo-
luminū: masloth qd hebrei parabolas.
vulgata editio pūbia vocat: coeleth.
quē grece ecclesiasten. latine cōcionatorē
possumus dicere: sirasirim. qd i linguā
nr̄am vertit canticū cāticorū. Fertur et
panaretos. ihū filii sirach liber: et alius
pseudographus. qui sapientia salomonis inscribit. Quorū priorē hebra-
icum reperi. nō ecclesiasticū ut apud la-
tinos: sed parabolas pnotatū. Cui iūcti
erāt ecclesiastes. et canticū canticorū: ut
similitudinē salomonis. nō solū nu-
mero librorū: sed etiā materiarū gene-
re coequaret. Secūdus apud hebreos
nusq; est: quia et ipse stilus grecam
eloquētiā redolet: et nōnulli scriptorū
veterū hūc esse iudei filonis affirmāt.
Sicut ergo iudith et thobie et macha-
beorū libros. legit quidē eos ecclia. sed
inter canonicas scripturas nō recipit:
sic et hec duo volumina legat ad edi-
ficationē plebis: nō ad auctoritatem
ecclesiasticorū dogmatū cōfirmandam.
Si cui sane septuaginta interpretum
magis editio placet: habet eā a nobis
olim emēdatā. Neq; eni noua sic cu-
dim⁹: ut vetera destruam⁹. Et tamē cū
diligentissime legerit. sciat magis nr̄a
scripta intelligi: que nō in terciū vas
trāsfusa coacuerit: sed statim de prelo
purissime cōmēdata teste: suū saporē ser-
uauerit. Incipiunt parabole salomonis

Parabole salomonis
filii dauid regis isrl:
ad sciendā sapienti-
am et disciplinā: ad
intelligenda verba
prudentie et suscipi-
endā eruditionē doctrine: iusticiā
et iudiciū et equitatē: ut detur paruulis
astutia: et adolescenti sciencia et intel-
lectus. Audiēs sapiēs sapientior erit: et
intelligēs gubernacula possidebit. Ani-
aduertet parabolam et interpretatio-
nem: verba sapientiū et enigmata eorū.
Timor dn̄i principiū sapientie. Sapien-
tiam atq; doctrinam stulti despiciūt.
Audi fili mi disciplinā pr̄is tui et ne
dimittas legem mr̄is tue: ut addatur
gracia capiti tuo: et torques collo tuo.
Fili mi si te lactauerint peccatores: ne ac-
quiescas eis. Si dixerit veni nobiscū.
insidiemur sanguini. abscōdam⁹ tedi-
culas cōtra insontem frustra. degluti-
amus eū sicud infernus viuentē et inte-
grum. quasi descēdentē in lacū: omnē
preciosā substanciā reperiem⁹. implebim⁹
domus nr̄as spoliis. sortem mitte no-
biscum. marsupiū sit unum omniū
nr̄m: fili mi ne ambules cū eis. Pro-
hibe pedem tuū a semitis eorū. Pedes
eni illorū ad malū currūt: et festināt ut
effundant sanguinem. Frustra autem
iacit rete ante oculos pēnatorū. Ipi q̄ȝ
contra sanguinē suū insidiantur: et

TRIVMPHVS

ce ligatura alla fiſtula tubale, Gli altri dui cũ ueterrimi cornitibici concordi ciaſcuno & cum gli inſtrumenti delle Equitante nymphe.

Sotto lequale triũphale ſeiughe era laxide nel meditullo, Nelq̃le gli rotali radii erano infixi, deliniamento Baluſtico, gracilifcenti ſepoſa negli mucronati labii cum uno pomulo alla circunferentia. Elquale Polo era di finiſſimo & ponderoſo oro, repudiante el rodicabile erugine, & lo incẽdioſo Vulcano, della uirtute & pace exitiale ueneno. Summamente dagli feſtigianti celebrato, cum moderate, & repentine riuolutiõe intorno ſaltanti, cum ſolemniſſimi plauſi, cum gli habiti cincti di faſceole uolitante, Et le ſedente ſopra gli trahenti centauri. La Sancta cagione, & diuino myſterio, inuoce cõſone & carmini cancionali cum extrema exultatione amoroſamente laudauano.

**
*

PRIMVS

EL SEQVENTE triũpho nõ meno mirauiglioſo dl primo. Impo che egli hauea le q̃tro uolubile rote tutte, & gli radii, & il meditullo de fuſco achate, di cãdide uẽule uagaméte uaricato. Ne tale certam̃te geſtoe re Pyrrho cũ le noue Muſe & Apolline ĩ medio pulſãte dalla natura ĩpſſo.

Laxide & la forma del dicto q̃le el primo, ma le tabelle erão di cyaneo Saphyro orientale, atomato de ſcintillule doro, alla magica gratiſſimo, & longo acceptiſſimo a cupidine nella ſiniſtra mano.

Nella tabella dextra mirai exſcalpto una inſigne Matrõa che dui oui haueua parturito, in uno cubile regio collocata, di uno mirabile pallacio, Cum obſtetrice ſtupefacte, & multe altre matrone & aſtante Nymphe Degli quali uſciua de uno una flammula, & de laltro ouo due ſpectatiſſime ſtelle.

**
*

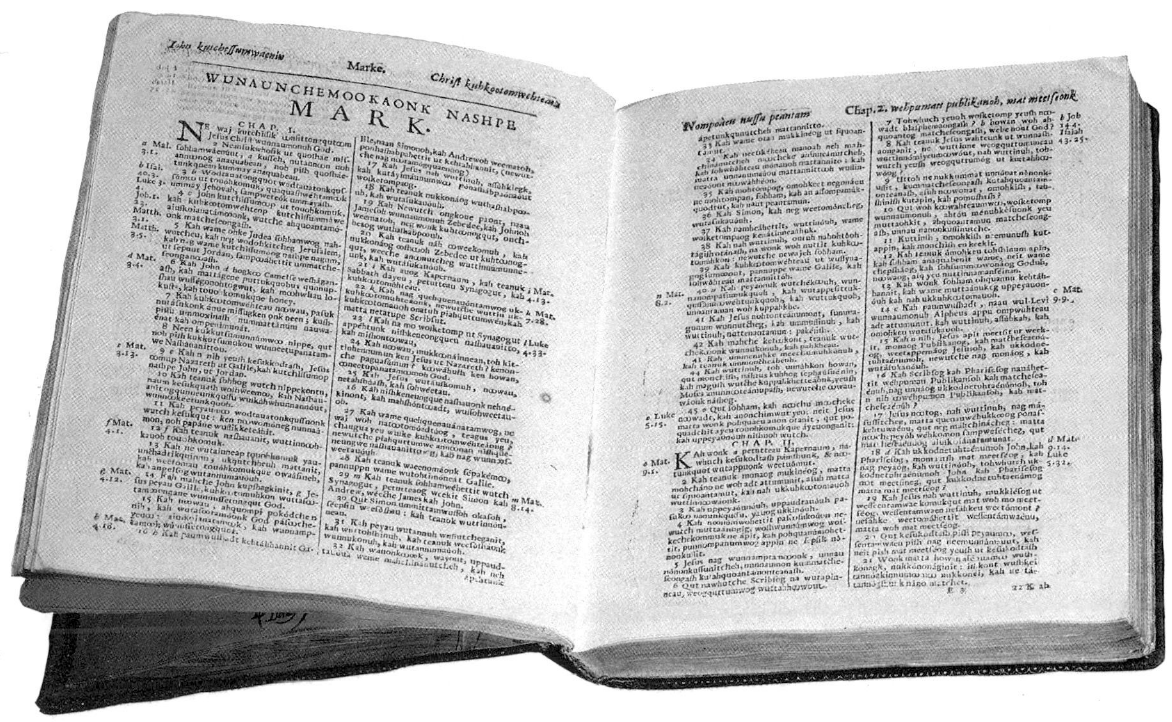

Opposite, above. Page opening from *Hypnerotomachia Poliphili*, Venice 1499.
86.K.49.

Opposite, below. John Eliot's American Indian New Testament. 1661.
G. 12160.

Right. Dante, *Inferno*. Canto XIX. Engraving after Sandro Botticelli. Florence, 1481.
G.10874.

Below. Title-page of *Guia do Pecador*, Nagasaki, 1599.
G.11929.

GVIA DO PECADOR.

御出世以来千五百九十九年

慶長四年閏三月中旬鏤梓也

IN COLLEGIO IAPONICO SOCIETATIS IESV.
Cum facultate Ordinarij, & Superiorum.
ANNO 1599.

beautiful bindings still adorning the walls that visitors to the Library's public rooms first see.

No sooner was the Grenville Library safely shelved than the Museum was faced with a new threat, the Chartist mob who, it was thought, might attack the Museum building, which was promptly fortified and defended by the staff, and with a new inquisition, this time in the form of a Royal Commission. This was formally requested by the British Association and other scientific bodies, expressing dissatisfaction with the lack of scientists among the Trustees. In fact, several Trustees elected in the previous ten years, notably Henry Hallam the historian, W.R. Hamilton, Sir John Herschel, Dean Buckland and Macaulay, were men of letters or science, and two ulterior factors lay behind the challenge thus expressed: the first was the continuing dissatisfaction with the Museum's administration, and the second was Panizzi's prolonged battle with the Royal Society over the catalogue of its library a decade earlier, which, despite his eventual success, had left him enemies there. Panizzi himself welcomed the test to which his own actions were put. The Commission vindicated his stand over the catalogue, despite the fact that its own secretary, John Payne Collier (soon to be confronted with the evidence of his forging of literary evidence), published an attack on it.

Furthermore, despite the neglect of the Natural History Department, the Commissioners concentrated their criticism on the administration, and in particular the irresponsible and casual action of the Secretary, Forshall. They recommended that the post of Secretary should be abolished, and Forshall resigned. Finally, Panizzi persuaded the Trustees to give him authority to enforce the provisions for deposit in the 1842 Copyright Act; although this made him new enemies in the book trade, he was soon able to enforce the delivery of books to the Museum, and the number of items deposited almost trebled within the decade.

The treasures that have poured in through the operation of the Copyright Act are too many to number. Every major work of literature, every new novel, all the articles in scientific periodicals that have charted the great innovations and inventions in Britain over the last century or more, now rest on the Library's shelves. Two examples must suffice. There is the first published edition of *Alice in Wonderland*, printed by Richard Clay for Macmillan & Co. after Lewis Carroll had rejected the first printing by the Oxford University Press because Tenniel's famous illustrations were badly printed. The first published edition was received under the Copyright Act and stamped in November 1865. It was first shelved under 'fiction' and only later removed to one of the select cases; it was nearly a century before it was followed by the 'pre-first' Oxford edition. Secondly, there is Captain F. Rivière's *Manual for the practice of company drill* (1862), a small pamphlet of no great length, but accompanied, on deposit, by a rosewood box which opens to reveal 'military

Circle of Giulio Clovio. 'The Battle of Mühlberg 1547', in *The Triumphs of Charles V*.
Add. MS 33733, f.15.

figures on a mechanical base', an enchanting set of neatly painted wooden figures who march and turn as you move the levers of the 'mechanical base'. It is quite as ingenious as any of the White Knight's inventions: surely nothing in *Alice* is quite so improbable as the deposit of such an object among the books at the Copyright Receipt Office.

Finally, Panizzi was able to turn his attention to the last and most vexatious cause of criticism, the Reading Room. The centre of Smirke's quadrangle, a desert described by Thomas Grenville, with some irony, as 'the finest mason's yard in Europe', had long been seen as a possible site, and the idea of a circular reading room had actually been proposed. But the exact dimensions, the cast-iron structure, and the decision to equip the 'quadrants', the interstices between the circular reading room and the inner sides of the quadrangle, for book storage, again using modern cast-iron construction, which provided more light and (it was then thought) a better guarantee against fire – all this was due to Panizzi. The scheme was put to the Trustees on 5 May 1852: just under five years later, on 2 May 1857, it was formally opened to almost universal applause. Even Thomas Carlyle, a sturdy critic of the Museum, was moved to praise. It was a double triumph for Panizzi; the year before he had succeeded Sir Henry Ellis, who retired at the age of 78, as Principal Librarian. From now until his own retirement in 1866, he was in unquestioned command, with generous space for readers and books at his disposal.

When Panizzi retired, the British Museum could look back on 30 years of incessant activity and change, sometimes violent change. Panizzi had been a great and strong leader, liked and admired by those he trusted, but always formidable: those who opposed him, the incompetent, or those he simply disliked were brushed ruthlessly aside. But his last decade was one of relative

Opposite. Giovan Pietro Birago, frontispiece to Giovanni Simonetta's *Sforziada*, Milan 1490.
G.7251.

LIBRO PRIMO DELLA HISTORIA DELLE COSE FACTE DALLO INVICTISSIMO DVCA FRANCESCO SFORZA SCRIPTA IN LATINO DA GIOVANNI SIMONETTA ET TRADOCTA IN LINGVA FIORENTINA DA CHRISTOPHORO LANDINO FIORENTINO.

NE TEMPI CHE LA REGINA GIOVANNA SEconda figliuola di Carlo Re regnaua: perche era succeduta nel regno Neapolitano a Latislao Re suo fratello: elquale partì di uita sanza figliuoli: Alphonso Re daragona con grande armata mouendo di Catalogna uenne in Sicilia: Isola di suo Imperio. La cui uenuta excitò gli huomini del Neapolitano regno a uarii fauori: & a diuersi consigli: & non con piccoli mouimenti di quel regno: Impero che Giouāna Regina per molti & uarii suoi impudichi amori era caduta in sōma infamia. Et desperandosi che lei femina potessi adempiere lofficio del Re: & administrare tanto regno: fece a se marito Iacopo di Nerbona Conte di Marcia: elquale per nobilita di sangue: & belleza di corpo: ne meno per uirtu era tra Principi di Francia excellente. Ma accorgendosi in breue che quello desideraua piu essere Re: che marito: & quella non molto stimaua: mosso da feminile leuità lo rifiutò: & priuò dogni administratiōe. Questo fu cagione chel suo regno: elquale per sua natura è prono alle dissensioni & discordie: arrogendouisi e nō honesti costumi della Regina: ritornò nelle antiche factioni & partialita: & cominciò ogni giorno piu a fluctuare & uacillare. Erano alcuni a quali nō dispiaceua la signoria della dōna: perche benche il nome fussi in lei: loro nientedimeno comādauono. Altri desiderauano: che Lodouico tertio Duca dangiò: figliuolo di Lodouico elquale era nomato Re di Puglia: & di uiolante: nata della Reale stirpe daragonia: fussi adoptato dalla Regina. Costui poco auāti pe conforti di Martinò tertio sōmo Pontefice: & di Sforza Attendolo excellentissimo Duca in militare disciplina: & padre di Francesco Sforza de cui egregii facti habbiamo a scriuere era uenuto a liti di Campagna: Et cōgiuntosi Sforza: hauea mosso guerra alla Regina. Ma quegli che repugnauano a Lodouicho: metteuano ogni industria: che Alphonso fussi adoptato in figliuolo della Reina: acciò che in Napoli fussi tal Re: che con le sue forze & di mare & di terra potessi resistere alla possa de Franciosi. Adunque in cosi uehemēte contentione de baroni: & piu huomini del regno: Alphonso chiamato dalla Reina in herede & compagno del regno: diuēne nō solo illustre: ma anchora horribile: Et el nome Catelano elquale insino a quegli tempi nō era molto noto & celebre se non a popoli maritimi: ma inuiso & odioso: cominciò a crescere . & farsi chiaro . [illegible] Lodouico & da Sforza [illegible] ogni giorno piu erono oppressi: el Re & la Regina: che diffidādosi nelle proprie forze: conduxono Braccio Perugino: el quale era el secondo Capitano di militia in Italia in quegli tēpi cō molte honoreuoli cōditioni: & maxime

Military figures, with their box, which accompanied F. Rivière's *Manual for the practice of company drill*, 1862, when deposited at the Copyright Receipt Office.
Cup.900.tt.35.

peace. John Winter Jones, his faithful adjutant, succeeded him as Keeper of Printed Books, and again as Principal Librarian when he retired, and continued Panizzi's work. In particular, the purchase grants, which Panizzi had earlier been forced to have reduced, for want of shelf-space, were restored, and the net of acquisition was spread ever wider and more vigorously.

The hero of this campaign, still too little celebrated, was Thomas Watts (1811–69). He was a self-taught scholar, with a natural gift for languages: according to legend, he picked them up while working as an attendant at a bathing pool, the Peerless Pool, City Road, which his family owned. The Parliamentary Enquiry drew him to the Museum in 1836: he wrote an article about it, which anticipated the idea of the round Reading Room, and also recommended the acquisition of some Russian books, then hardly represented in the collection. Panizzi was impressed, and recruited him to the staff. He had the same appetite for work. Besides acquisitions in every language, he was responsible for the complete reshelving of the Library, and devised the 'elastic system' of press-markings which enabled new acquisitions to be added within an ever-expanding subject classification. In addition, he became Superintendent of the Reading Room and succeeded Winter Jones as Keeper in 1866. His short reign was, characteristically, distinguished by the acquisition of the Siebold Japanese collection and two collections of Mexican books. Watts once wrote without exaggeration, 'In Russian, Polish, Hungarian, Danish and Swedish [and he could have added others], with the exception of

Photograph of the Round Reading Room under construction.
Maps C.26.f.7.

The Reading Room, shortly after its opening.
From *The Illustrated London News*, 9 May 1857.

Opposite, above left. The *True Encounter*, the first illustrated English news pamphlet, containing a contemporary account of the battle of Flodden, 1513.
C.123.d.33.

Opposite, above right. Sheets of Edward Raban's Hornbook, Aberdeen *c.*1636.
C.38.d.2(68).

Opposite, below. Tourneur, *The transformed metamorphosis*, 1600.
C.40.b.56.

perhaps fifty volumes, every book that has been purchased by the Museum within the last three-and-twenty years has been purchased at my suggestion. Every future student of these literatures will find riches where I found poverty'. Like Panizzi himself, Watts set and achieved the goal of making the Museum the 'second-best library in the world' – second, that is, only to the combined national libraries of each country.

A glance at the records of acquisitions shows how successfully Panizzi's ideal of acquiring not only common, but 'rare, ephemeral, voluminous and costly publications', and Watts's extension of the Museum's coverage into every language, were achieved. In 1847, for example, the year in which the accession of the Grenville collection was gratefully recorded, the Museum, which already possessed two copies of the first edition of Dante, printed at Foligno in 1472, and had just acquired the edition printed in the same year at Mantua with the Grenville collection, was able to buy the *third* (and rarest) edition printed in 1472, that of Venice.

From Libri's sale came the first book printed in France, the *Epistolae* of Gasparino Barzizza, printed at the Sorbonne press in 1470 and the Museum's unique copy of the Italian verse translation of the Columbus letter by Giuliano Dati. In the same year came the first great accession of Chinese books, the collection of John Robert Morison the younger, 476 works in 11,509 volumes. Next year, it was the turn of Hebrew, with the acquisition of the 4420 volumes of the H.J. Michael collections, with (for good measure) six of the seven editions of the Cranmer Great Bible, all printed between 1539 and 1541, 130 Irish proclamations of 1685–91, and Ramusio, *Primo Volume*, 1550, in one of Thomas Mahieu's elegant bindings. Finally, in 1849, at the Stowe (Duke of Buckingham) sale, the collection of 600 ballads and broadsides made by the great 17th-century collector Narcissus Luttrell was bought. Besides these major acquisitions were 'a complete collection of Danish Law', 'the whole of the works on Russian History and Topography', while 'None of the works of the minor German metaphysicians... are any longer deficient'.

This catalogue of achievements was continued. As the century wore on, the collection of incunables, already great, became unapproachably the best. Eleven specimens of 15th-century block books and broadsides, the texts printed not from type but from woodcut blocks, came in 1872 from the Weigel collection; and in 1895 great excitement was caused by the acquisition of what was thought to be one of the original blocks for the *Speculum humanae vitae*. (It turned out, however, to be a later copy made *c.*1710 for the typographic historian John Bagford.) A vellum copy of Bonifacius *Decretales*, the first major text of canon law to be printed (Mainz, Fust and Schoeffer 1465), was acquired in 1879, while in 1882 the second edition (1477) of Boccaccio's *Ninfale* followed, with the illustrated Czech Bible of 1489 in 1888 and the beautiful illustrated Bible in the Italian translation of Niccolò de Malermi (1490) in 1897. The Epistles and Gospels printed at Utrecht in 1479 by Johan Veldener, who supplied Caxton's types, came in 1882; in 1891, the 'Valdarfer Boccaccio', the first edition of the *Decameron*, printed at Venice in 1471, which caused a sensation when a copy of it sold for £2260 at the Roxburghe sale in 1812, and the *Octoechos*, the Orthodox liturgy printed at Cetinje in Montenegro in 1494; in 1892 the beautiful book of hours printed by Matthias Moravus at Naples in 1486, and the *Bible historiée*, the first book printed in France with illustrations (Lyon, 1477) in a contemporary binding. In 1898, the long-lost collection of Maurice Johnson (founder of one of the oldest provincial antiquarian societies, the Spalding Gentlemen's Society), rich in 15th-century English books, provided two Caxtons and no less than 10 pieces printed by Wynkyn de Worde not in the Museum's collection.

Among other English books, the cream of the Shakespearian scholar James Halliwell's play quartos, including his *Hamlet* (1603), was purchased from him in November 1858 for £1000. The 'Dyson Pageants', the collection of Lord Mayor's pageants and poems by Anthony Munday, Thomas Dekker,

A 'Luttrell Ballad'.
C.20.f.5.(119).

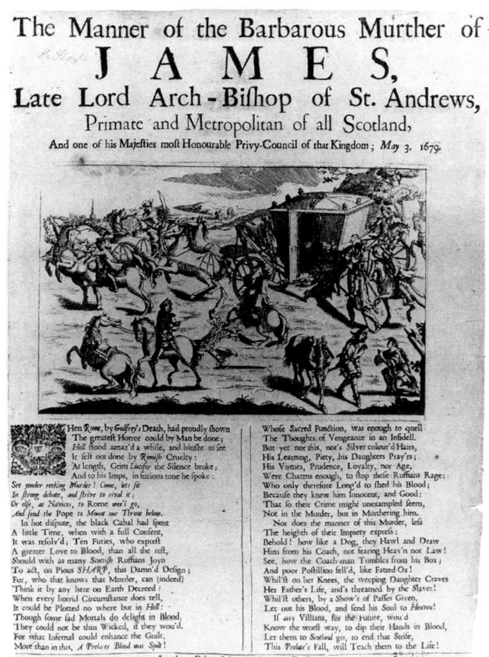

The Manner of the Barbarous Murther of
JAMES,
Late Lord Arch-Bishop of St. Andrews,
Primate and Metropolitan of all Scotland,
And one of his Majesties most Honourable Privy-Council of that Kingdom; *May* 3. 1679.

WHen *Rome*, by *Godfrey's* Death, had proudly shown
The greatest Horror could by Man be done;
Hell stood amaz'd a while, and blusht to see
It self out done by *Romish* Cruelty:
At length, Grim *Lucifer* the Silence broke;
And to his Imps, in furious tone he spoke:
See yonder reeking Murder! Come, lets sit
In strong debate, and strive to rival it;
Or else, as Novices, to Rome *wee'l go,*
And send the Pope *to Mount our Throne below.*
In hot dispute, the black Cabal had spent
A little Time, when with a full Consent,
It was resolv'd; Ten Furies, who exprest
A greater Love to Blood, than all the rest,
Should with as many *Scottish* Ruffians Joyn
To act, on Pious *SHARP*, this Damn'd Design;
For, who that knows that Murder, can (indeed)
Think it by any here on Earth Decreed?
When every horrid Circumstance does tell,
It could be Plotted no where but in *Hell*:
Though some sad Mortals do delight in Blood,
They could not be thus Wicked, if they wou'd.
For what Infernal could enhance the Guilt,
More than in this, *A Prelates Blood was Spilt!*

Whose *Sacred* Function, was enough to quell
The Thoughts of Vengeance in an Infidell.
But yet nor this, nor's Silver colour'd Hairs,
His Learning, Piety, his Daughters Pray'rs;
His Virtues, Prudence, Loyalty, nor Age,
Were Charms enough, to stop these Ruffians Rage:
Who only therefore Long'd to shed his Blood;
Because they knew him Innocent, and Good:
That so their Crime might unexampled seem,
Not in the Murder, but in Murthering him.
Nor does the manner of this Murder, less
The heighth of their Impiety express:
Behold! how like a Dog, they Hawl and Draw
Him from his Coach, not fearing Heav'n nor Law!
See, how the Coach-man Tumbles from his Box;
And poor Postillion fell'd, like Fatted Ox!
Whil'st on her Knees, the weeping Daughter Craves
Her Father's Life, and's threatned by the Slaves!
Whil'st others, by a Show'r of Passes Given,
Let out his Blood, and send his Soul to *Heaven*!
If any Villians, for the Future, wou'd
Know the worst way, to dip their Hands in Blood,
Let them to *Scotland* go, to end that Strife,
This *Prelate's* Fall, will Teach them to the Life!

London, Printed for *J. S.* and *B. H.* 1679.

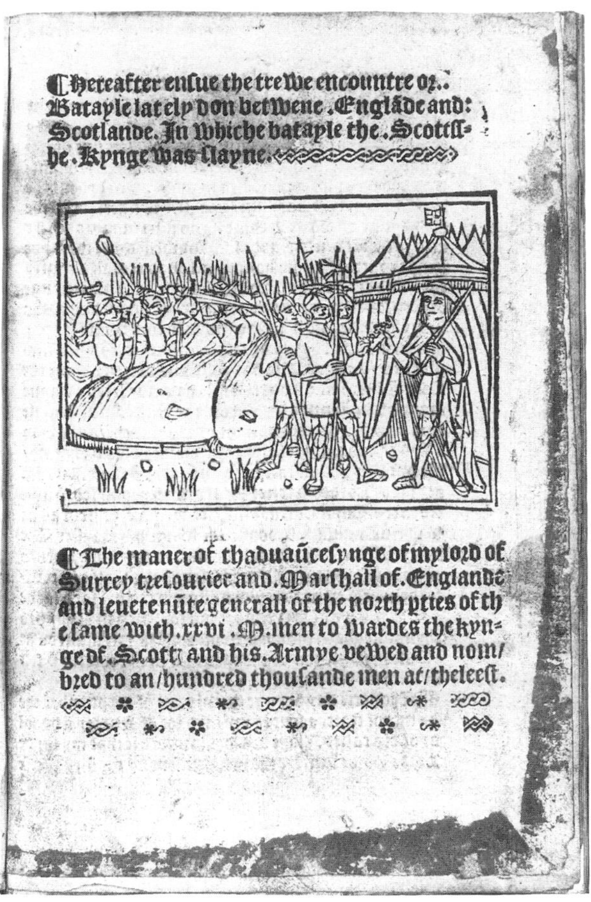

¶ Hereafter ensue the trewe encountre or. Batayle lately don betwene. Englãde and. Scotlande. In whiche batayle the. Scottsshe. Kynge was slayne.

¶ The maner of thaduauncesynge of my lord of Surrey tresourier and. Marshall of. Englande and leuetenũte generall of the north ptes of the same with. xxvi. M. men to wardes the kynge of. Scott; and his. Armye vewed and nombred to an hundred thousande men at the leest.

Aabcdefghiklmnop qrstuvwxyz,:.

In the Name of GOD the Father, the Sonne, and of the holy Ghost, Amen.

Our Father, which art in Heaven, Halowed be thy Name: Thy kingdome come: Thy Will be done on Earth, as it is in Heaven: Give vs this day our dayly Bread: And forgive vs our trespasses, as wee forgive them that trespasse against vs: And leade vs not into temptation, But deliver vs from Evill: For thine is the kingdome, the Power, and the Glorie, for ever, and ever, Amen.

Aabcdefghiklmnop qrstuvwxyz,:.

In the Name of GOD the Father, the Sonne, and of the holie Ghost, So be it.

Our Father, which art in Heaven, halowed be thy Name: Thy kingdome come: Thy will be done on Earth, as it is in Heaven: Give vs this day our dayly Bread: And forgive vs our Trespasses, as wee forgive them that trespasse against vs: And leade vs not into temptation, but deliver vs from Evill: For Thine is the kingdome, power, and glorie, for ever, Amen.

The Author to his Booke.

O were thy margents, cliffes of itching lust;
Or quotes to chalke out men the way to sinne;
Then were there hope, that multitudes wold thrust
To buy thee: but sith that thou dost begin
To pull the curtaines backe, that closde vice in,
Expect but flowts: for t'is the haire of crime,
To shunne the breath that doth discloude it sinne.
What? (will he say) a recluse from the time?
Nor canst thou hope that thy weake ioynted rime
Shall please the more, because it shrowdes it selfe
Vnder his shade, whose mighty armes do clime,
Eu'n to the highest heau'n; disdaining pelfe;
For heau'nly mindes, the brightlier they do shine:
The more the world doth seeke to worke their tine:
This onely be thy hope; to please the best:
And to be safe from malice of the rest.

To the Reader.

IT may be (Reader) I may gall those men, (touch;
Whose golden thoughts think no man dare them
It may be (too) my fearelesse ayre-plume-pen,
May rouse that sluggish watch, whose tongues are
[illegible]
Yet were *Apelles* heere, he could not paint
Forth perfectly the worlds deformities;
For as the troubled mind, whose sad complaint
Still tumbles forth, halfe breathed accenties,
Th'*Idea* doth confuse and chaoize:
So will the *Chaos* of vp-heaped sinne
Confound his braine, that takes in hand to lay
A platforme plainly forth, of all (that in
This *Pluto*-visag'd-world) hell doth bewray,
When death or hell, doth worke it liues decay:
So perfect is our imperfectionesse,
For imperfection is sinnes perfectnesse.

A 3

Les Louanges de Bacchus.
ousiours vn puissant Dieu dompte l'humaine audace,
advint que Bacchus voulant passer en Naxe.
Et que les Mariniers qui le prindrent au port,
Au lieu de le passer Iusques a l'aultre bord,
ntreprindrent felons (a leur honte & Ruyne)
'enlever fierement sa personne Divine.
Afin d'en abuser mais la Divinité,
Ne voulant endurer telle meschanceté.
it tout soudainement que leurs puissantes Rames,
evindrent grands serpans ayans & corps & ames.
Et que leur grand Batteau en vigne fust changé,
Chargeé d'vn doux fruict prest a estre mangé.
Quoy estant faict soudain la Mariniere bande,
F 4 Se

Page opening from Meynier, *Naissance et triomphes esmerveillables du dieu Bacchus*, Paris ?1610.
C.30.a.26.Sig.F4.

Thomas Middleton, Thomas Churchyard and others, put together by the Elizabethan notary Humfrey Dyson was bought in 1868. In 1871, the Museum acquired the 72 leaves representing 13 works printed by Caxton, three unknown hitherto, retrieved from the fragments of the binding of a Caxton Boethius at St Albans School by William Blades, while in 1874 Lydgate's *Fall of Princes*, printed by Richard Pynson in 1494, 'was rescued from a tobacconist's shop at Lamberhurst; portions of it had been cut out to wrap up tobacco and snuff'. From the Laing sale came complete sheets of four different editions of the Horn Book, or children's reader, printed by the first printer at Aberdeen, Edward Raban, *c.*1636, and in 1878 the still unique copy of the first English newsletter announcing the Battle of Flodden in 1513.

The collection of rare 16th and 17th-century pamphlets, often then thought to be unique (although other copies have since appeared, many at the Britwell Court sales), was an object of continuing energy. They included such oddities as *Maroccus exstaticus* (1595), the account of Banks's wonderful horse, and John Witherings's *Orders lawes and ancient customs of Swanns* (1632). Perhaps the most memorable acquisition was that of 26 such pamphlets, from a cache found in 1867 in a cupboard at Lamport Hall in Northamptonshire, where they had probably rested since they were new. Among them was the unique copy of Cyril Tourneur's *The transformed metamorphosis* (1600), and of the rest, which included the first edition of Marlowe's *Hero and Leander* (1598), only one or two other copies are known.

The first edition of Bunyan's *The Pilgrim's Progress* (1678) was bought in 1884, and other works by him added, notably the rare *Book for Boys and Girls* (1686), the foundation of a collection of Bunyan now unsurpassed. The earliest known London Directory (1677) was acquired in 1871, and in 1892 Dryden's *Rival Ladies* (1664) and Farquhar's *The stage coach* (1705), both then thought to be unique. Among later works, the author's own annotated copy of Smollett's *Travels* (1766), and Byron's *Poems on various occasions* (1807) were acquired; the rare works of Shelley were persistently sought and found, and very rare modern books, such as George Darley's *Nepenthe* (1835) and Tennyson's *Enid and Nimuë* (1857) were also added.

Among continental books, the beautiful illustrated Josephus (Lyon, 1566) was bought in 1879. The Hamilton Palace sale in 1881–82 produced wonderful books from William Beckford's collection, notably Aretino's *Opera nova*, the first French translation of *The Pilgrim's Progress* (1685), Le Roy *La vertu enseigńee par les oiseaux* (Liege, 1653) and Meynier *Naissance et triomphes esmerveillables du dieu Bacchus* (Paris, ?1610), the last two among the rarest of illustrated books. Marvellous Spanish books came from the Seillère and Hérédia sales, including the romance *Caballero platir* (1533), Ovid's

Title-page of the first edition of Bunyan's *The Pilgrim's Progress*, 1678.
C.37.d.61.

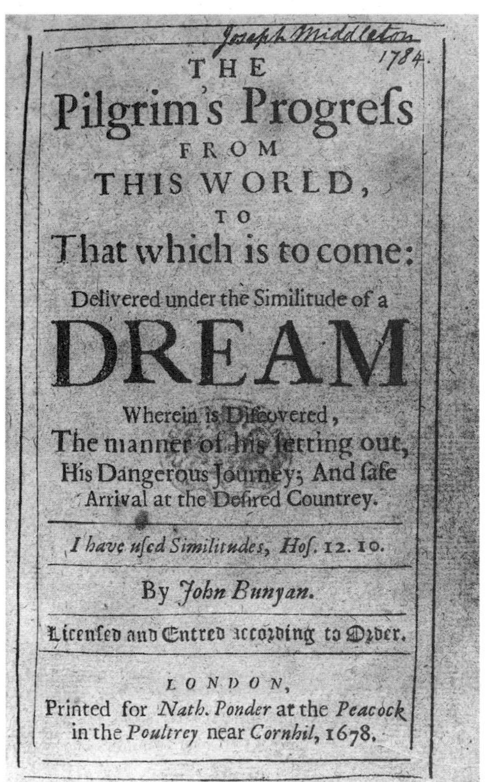

Joseph Middleton 1784.

THE
Pilgrim's Progress
FROM
THIS WORLD,
TO
That which is to come:
Delivered under the Similitude of a
DREAM
Wherein is Discovered,
The manner of his setting out,
His Dangerous Journey; And safe
Arrival at the Desired Countrey.

I have used Similitudes, Hos. 12. 10.

By *John Bunyan.*

Licensed and Entred according to Order.

LONDON,
Printed for *Nath. Ponder* at the *Peacock*
in the *Poultrey* near *Cornhil*, 1678.

Qu. If all the Art I have, or power can do it,
He shall be found, and such a way of justice
Inflicted on him: A Lady wrong'd in my Court,
And this way rob'd, and ruin'd?
The. Be contented Madam,
If he be above ground I will have him
Ag. Fair virtuous Maid, take comfort yet and flouriſh,
In my love flouriſh: the ſtain was forc'd upon ye
None of your wills, nor yours; riſe, and riſe mine ſtill,
And riſe the ſame white, ſweet, fair ſoul, I lov'd ye,
Take me the ſame.
Mer. I kneel and thank ye, Sir,
And I muſt ſay ye are truly honourable:
And dare confeſs my Will, yet ſtill a Virgin;
But ſo unfit and weak a Cabinet
To keep your love and virtue in am I now,
That have been forc'd and broken, loſt my luſtre,
I mean this body, ſo corrupt a Volume
For you to ſtudy goodneſs in, and honor,
I ſhall intreat your Grace, confer that happineſs
Upon a beauty ſorrow never ſaw yet:
And when this grief ſhall kill me, as it muſt do,
Only remember yet ye had ſuch a Miſtriſs;
And if ye then dare ſhed a tear, yet honour me:
Good Gentlemen, expreſs your pities to me,
In ſeeking out this villany; and my laſt ſuit
Is to your Grace, that I may have your favour
To live a poor recluſe Nun with this Lady,
From Court and company, till Heaven ſhall hear me,
And ſend me comfort, or death end my miſery.
Qu. Take your own Will, my very heart bleeds for thee.
Ag. Farwell *Merione*, ſince I have not thee.
I'll wed thy goodneſs, and thy memory.
Leo. And I her fair revenge.
The. Away: let's follow it,
For he is ſo rank i' th' wind we cannot miſs him. *Exeunt.*

Scæna Quarta.

Enter Crates *and* Conon.

Cra. *Conon*, you are welcome home, ye are wondrous (welcome,
Is this your firſt arrival?
Co. Sir, but now
I reacht the Town.
Cra. Y'are once more welcome then.
Co. I thank ye, noble Sir,

Marginal annotations by S.T. Coleridge in his copy of Beaumont and Fletcher's play *The Queen of Corinth*.
C.45.i.7, p.A4*v*.

Metamorphoses in Catalan (1494), and the only known copy of the first edition of the romance *Amadís de Gaula* (1508), found in Ferrara in 1872.

It was a wonderful period for acquiring the early romances of chivalry, and the R.S. Turner sale and the two sales from the Bibliotheca Lindesiana in 1887 and 1889 proved especially productive. From the latter came *Baudouin de Flandres* (Lyons, 1478), the French illustrated *Guy of Warwick* (1525), and also such *exotica* as the first Armenian Psalter (1565) and Bible (1666) and the Bible in Georgian (1743), as well as Paprocki *Ogrod Krolewski* (Prague, 1599), the *rara avis* of Polish historiography. Other out-of-the-way imprints included the Bible in Malagasy, printed at Antananarivo in 1830–35, very rare since most copies were destroyed during the Christian persecution. A run of the *Hobart Town gazette* from 1846 was bought in 1873, and in 1897 a copy of *Michael Howe, the last and worst of the bushrangers* (1818), the first book printed in Tasmania.

Books annotated by their authors or other distinguished hands were a notable feature of the collection. Athenaeus (1556) annotated by Tasso was acquired in 1875, and Porson's copy of the same text in 1892; another example of his beautiful hand is in Prosper Marchand's *Cymbalum mundi* (1753), bought from the Mitford Sale in 1873. Coleridge's copy of Cary's Dante, acquired in 1877, was the foundation of the now large collection of books annotated by the poet and philosopher. Erasmus's copy of Herodotus (1502), the Elzevir family bible, bound by the great Dutch binder Magnus, the Prussian General Von Bulow's critique of the campaign of 1800, annotated by Napoleon, Charles Lamb's copy of the 1679 Beaumont and Fletcher, Leigh Hunt's own *Imagination and Fancy*, the copy of Southey's *History of Brazil* given by him to Coleridge, and Baron's *Illustrations of the enquiry respecting tuberculous diseases*, copiously annotated by Edward Jenner – all have provided important and unique evidence of their owners. The foundation of scholarly investigation of the history of bookbinding was laid with the acquisition of Felix Slade's collection in 1869.

Altogether, the catholicity and range of what was acquired can only evoke our wonder, a century later. Old and rare books are, perhaps, more easily appreciated, but imagine the versatility that brought in Gutierrez *Dialectica resolutio*, printed at Mexico in 1584, with a title page border from the first English *Book of Common Prayer* (1549); the second and third volumes of Monstrelet's *Chronicques* printed on vellum in Paris *c.*1498, replacing those missing in Henry VII's copy; 'J.V.W.', *Zilveren Echt-zang aan den Heere J.G.F. Myners en de weledele Vrouwe Elisabeth Hamilton* (1771), printed on satin and bound in silk embroidered with silver; or a copy of the Sternhold and Hopkins Psalter (1633) in a contemporary needlework binding in an embroidered bag, with 'a pair of richly worked kid gloves'; not to mention Eadweard Muybridge's *Animal Locomotion* (1887), that monument of early motion photography.

This, then, gives some idea of the contribution of Panizzi and his successors in the acquisition of printed books. One of Panizzi's achievements had been to recover the selection of staff from the hands of the Civil Service, and the steady improvement in the quality of the staff, and their aptitude for the great task, was more and more marked. Among the best known of these was Richard Garnett, the legendary superintendent of the Reading Room whose memory, which seemed to embrace not only every book in the Museum but its precise place on the shelf, was the wonder of all the many readers, of whom first 300, and then, as more accommodation was made, as many as 450, filled the seats there. Where earlier in the century, Porson, collating classical manuscripts, Scott, at work on *The Minstrelsy of the Scottish Border*, Southey, translating Spanish romances, or Lamb, reading the Elizabethan dramatists, had once put up with cramped conditions for the sake of the treasures that surrounded them, a new generation came to enjoy vastly increased resources in much greater comfort. Swinburne and Sir Henry Newbolt came, Sir Leslie Stephen

The Whole Booke of Psalmes, London 1633. Embroidered binding and bag.

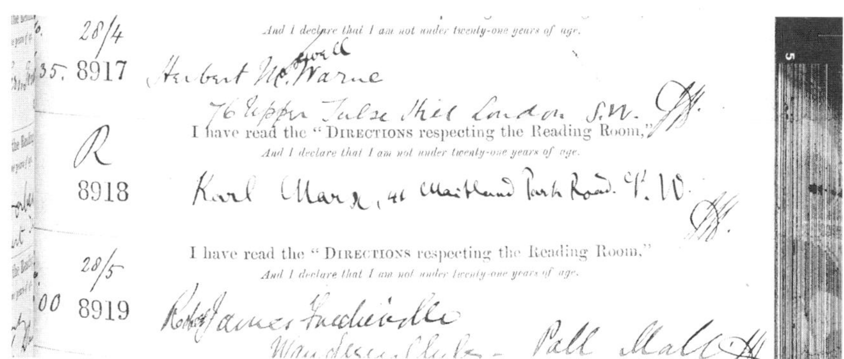

And I declare that I am not under twenty-one years of age.

8917 Herbert McWarne

76 Upper Tulse Hill London S.W.

I have read the "DIRECTIONS respecting the Reading Room."

And I declare that I am not under twenty-one years of age.

8918 Karl Marx, 41 Maitland Park Road. N.W.

I have read the "DIRECTIONS respecting the Reading Room."

And I declare that I am not under twenty-one years of age.

8919

Pall Mall

Karl Marx's signature in the Reading Room admissions register, 28 November 1877.

wrote his history of 18th-century thought, Thomas Hardy pursued architectural research. Scientists, at peace with the Museum now, used its new resources, and revolutionaries, from Panizzi's Italian friends the Rossettis to the anarchist Kropotkin (who loyally presented his own works to the Library), came to work and plan a new world. Most famous of all was Karl Marx, a great bibliophile and a regular reader from 1850. He too became a donor, and, amongst all the treasures acquired in the 19th century, not least is the copy that he gave of *Das Kapital*, 'Zweite verbesserte Auflage', Hamburg, 1872.

8

The Department of Manuscripts in the 19th Century

'The legend of the Fleurs-de-Lys'.
The Bedford Hours. Paris, *c.*1423.
Add. MS 18850, f.288*v*.

Portrait of Sir Frederic Madden.

As Panizzi was to the Department of Printed Books and the Library as a whole, so was Sir Frederic Madden (1801–73) to the Department of Manuscripts. Madden has, on the whole, had a bad press. While his scholarly attainments are undeniable (and attested by his publications), his reputation has suffered from his legendary feud with Panizzi and – wonderful source though it is – his diary. It takes two to make a feud, and, unfortunately for Madden, Panizzi won: those who have justly praised Panizzi have felt obliged to denigrate his enemy. The diary, too, into which Madden poured his innermost thoughts for 54 years (1818–72) is too good a source, its words too lively and well chosen, for the historian to resist, even when he knows that the words, and sometimes the facts recorded, are *ben trovato*. The diary was the safety-valve to Madden's tumultuous thought and suppressed vigour: it is dangerous to judge the power of the engine by the outrush of steam.

Madden's reputation as a palaeographer was made while he was in his twenties. He had collated the manuscripts of Cædmon while at Oxford and worked on the catalogue of Lord Leicester's manuscripts at Holkham. In 1826 he joined the British Museum, first working in the Department of Printed Books on the abortive class catalogue, but from 1828 to 1866 he was in effective charge of the Department of Manuscripts, first as Assistant to Forshall, who was increasingly taken up with his duties as Secretary, and from 1837 as Keeper. The structure of the Department and the continuous tradition of scholarship in it are due to his energy, scholarly care and devotion.

At first all went well. Madden's edition of *Havelok the Dane* (1828) established him as a medievalist. He became a Fellow of the Society of Antiquaries at once, of the Royal Society and a founder member of the Athenaeum Club in 1830, a Knight of the Guelphic order (KH) in 1832 and a full Knight Bachelor in 1833. *Havelok* was followed by *William and the werewolf* (1832), the *Gesta Romanorum* (1838) and *Syr Gawayne* (1839). He was an excellent departmental head, conscientious and industrious; his eye for the hands of past ages and his ability to read and date them were as marked as Wanley's. He was in the forefront of the critical study of manuscripts, notably in the early use of photography.

All seemed set for a brilliant career. That Madden did not achieve it, or what he considered his due in his lifetime, was the result of a number of factors: a prickly personality, a capacity for taking offence and retaining it, a dangerous facility with sharp words (was it wise to write, even to Sir Thomas Phillipps, on the brink of succeeding as Keeper, that if he did not he would resign and 'however low a state I sink to, I should thank God for having saved me from the infamy of being Archbishop of Canterbury', who as senior Trustee was to sign his certificate of appointment two weeks later, if (irritatingly) two days after he had done the same for Panizzi?) – all these had some bearing on it. But bad luck counted for much: his long and loyal association with Forshall, with whom he edited the text of the Wycliffe Bible, published in 1850 and still of value, compromised him with Forshall's administrative errors, while Panizzi's own combative nature equalled his own. Finally, there was simply the trend of the times: printed books, neglected hitherto, became, with the Industrial Revolution, the main object of a new interest, the spread of learning (hitherto considered to be adequately preserved in manuscript), to a new and growing population. It was Panizzi's fortune, and Madden's bad luck, to coincide with this new trend.

Within his department, there was plenty to engage Madden's attention. The Claudius Rich collection of manuscripts and coins from the Near East had been acquired in 1825, followed by the Halhed collection in 1830. In 1826, Adam Wolley's remarkable topographical and genealogical collection on Derbyshire had come to join Cole's on Cambridgeshire and Burrell's Sussex material (1796). Topography was further strengthened by the bequests of drawings and other material by the Very Rev. Sir Richard Kaye, Bt, Dean of Lincoln (1809) and Thomas Kerrich (1828). Lord Frederick Campbell, Lord Clerk Register of Scotland from 1768, bequeathed a remarkable collection of medieval charters in 1816. Finally, the King's Manuscripts (that is, the manuscript part of George III's library) had come, bringing with it some important historical papers, for example, the autograph of Samuel Johnson's tragedy *Irene*, some fine 15th-century manuscripts of Italian provenance from Consul Smith, an *Iliad* and a Virgil and a 15th-century Dutch *Biblia Pauperum*. Much of this still awaited cataloguing; and when Madden succeeded as Keeper, older skeletons in other cupboards were found – the charred remains of Cottonian manuscripts and the 'refuse' of the Harley collection.

Madden was, however, fortunate in his assistants: William Cureton who resigned in 1849 to become a Canon of Westminster and eventually Royal Trustee of the British Museum, John Holmes who catalogued the maps but was distrusted by Madden, and Edward Bond, who eventually succeeded him. He was fortunate, too, in the availability of material for sale: the dissolution of religious houses, the French Revolution and the Napoleonic wars had dislodged more old books, manuscript and printed, than the market could absorb. One of Madden's main achievements, despite lack of funds and unsympathetic Trustees, was to make his department a nationally respected institution for the acquisition of manuscripts as well as the first authority on them. This is all the more remarkable since, after his early years in the department, there were no major gifts or special accessions of the sort that had given the Library its early fame as a repository primarily of manuscripts.

Daniel Mytens, portrait of Thomas Howard, 2nd Earl of Arundel, in his sculpture gallery.
National Portrait Gallery London.

The two major accessions, the Bridgewater bequest and the Arundel manuscripts, that came to the Department of Manuscripts in 1829 and 1831 were, however, of major importance, the one prospective, the other retrospective. In 1666, John Evelyn persuaded the grandson (later 6th Duke of Norfolk) of Thomas Howard, Lord Arundel, to present his grandfather's great collection to appropriate permanent homes: the famous Arundel marbles went to Oxford, half the manuscripts to the College of Arms and the other half and the printed books to the Royal Society. With the refoundation of the Society of Antiquaries in 1717–18, the universality of the Royal Society had diminished, and by the early 19th century, its interests now concentrated on the sciences, the Arundel manuscripts were no longer relevant to its new function. An agreement was concluded in 1831 whereby the manuscripts, minus the orientalia and a Howard chartulary which were returned to the family, were transferred to the Museum in exchange for £3559 in cash and 2072 printed books duplicated by copies received with the King's Library. This, with the final sale in the following year, was the last occasion when 'duplicate' printed books in any number were released, a practice which has done the Library more harm than good, and reputedly caused Lord Fitzwilliam to bequeath his collection to Cambridge University rather than the Museum in 1816.

Thomas Howard, 2nd Earl of Arundel (1586–1646), was the great-grandson of the Earl of Arundel whose collection passed, through Lord Lumley and Henry, Prince of Wales, to the Old Royal Library. He was a friend and contemporary of the members of the Elizabethan Society of Antiquaries; as Earl Marshal, he was Cotton's last patron and, like him, suffered from the disfavour of James I and Charles I. In the 1630s, restored to favour, he went as ambassador to Holland, Germany and Vienna, urging the restoration of the Palatinate to Charles I's nephew, the son of the Winter Queen. A loyal royalist, he escorted Henrietta Maria to the Continent in 1642 and remained in Padua until his death. His collection thus contains, like Cotton's, a number of the great monuments of medieval English literature and history, notably the autograph manuscript of the unique text of *The ayenbite of inwit* (remorse of conscience), written *c.*1340 by Michael of Northgate, monk of St

Augustine's, Canterbury, where it was preserved until the dissolution. He also had a psalter with a commentary in English by Richard Rolle of Hampole, the 14th-century poet and mystic, a book of romances, including *Guy of Warwick* and *The Seven Wise Masters*, a 13th-century collection of devotional texts with an English verse bestiary, and an early manuscript of the chronicle of Henry of Huntingdon (*c.*1080–1155).

Most notable of his early English manuscripts are two Anglo-Saxon psalters, one from Christ Church, Canterbury, *c.*1012–23, written and probably illuminated by Eadui Basan, and the other from New Minster, Winchester, *c.*1060–80, with an old English gloss and a fine crucifixion which is one of the latest Anglo-Saxon drawings. He also had the magnificent De Lisle Psalter, one of the great monuments of English 14th-century illumination, and the elaborate 15th-century missal bequeathed to the City church of St Lawrence, Old Jewry, by William Melreth, Alderman of London, in 1446. Two manuscripts belonged to Henry VII, a collection of astrological tracts, and the *Tabula Cebetis* and other pieces presented to the King by Philippus Albericus, later given by the 'Winter Queen' Elizabeth to Lord Carew.

So far, his collection parallels those of his ancestor and Sir Robert Cotton. But his travels abroad and his passionate interest in ancient and modern art brought in new and surprising treasures. His greatest coup came in 1636 when he bought at Nuremberg the residue, not acquired by the city, of the library of its famous Renaissance citizen, the humanist Wilibald Pirckheimer (1470–1530). How many of the manuscripts of obviously German origin came from this source is hard to say, but it must be a considerable number. A number were written by his father, Johann Pirckheimer, to whom still more had come from the Mainz charterhouse and Eberbach Abbey. The 8th-century patristic anthology in insular script, at Würzburg in the 13th century, the 9th-century collection of medical tracts, and a whole range of 10th- and 11th-century texts, notably a handsome Athanasius, suggest a common source.

On the other hand the 10th-century fragments of Isidore are certainly Spanish, and there are some early Italian manuscripts, notably the Sallust with an introductory epistle by Amandus, elected Bishop of Vigilia in Apulia in 1153, in Beneventan script. There is a remarkable set of letters of Italian humanists, some of which certainly came through Pirckheimer. But the very fine humanistic Columella and the Diodorus Siculus, with the epistles of Aeneas Sylvius Piccolomini and Cristoforo Buondelmonte, written for Raphael de Mercatellis, Abbot of St Bavo, Ghent, must have been acquired by Lord Arundel independently. Three separate anthologies of medieval Latin verse of the 13th and 14th centuries, one English, one German and one Italian, can only be separate acquisitions and reflect a taste rare before the 19th century. The two 16th-century collections of medical tracts in Erse and some notable Greek manuscripts – a 10th/early 11th-century Gospels, a Hesiod and Euripides of 1420, a set of 16th-century grammar texts, the notebook of the German humanist, Johannes Cuno, accumulated during his work at the Aldine Press in Venice – all reflect an equally eclectic taste. Most famous of all is the celebrated notebook of Leonardo da Vinci, the so-called 'Codex Arundel', the best evidence of the individual taste of the most remarkable connoisseur of the 17th century.

The other deeply influential accession to the department came on the death of Francis Henry Egerton, 8th Earl of Bridgewater (1756–1829). The eccentric son of the Bishop of Durham, he also took orders but spent most of the latter part of his life in Paris. He was a prince of the Holy Roman Empire before succeeding to the Bridgewater title in 1823. His small but much loved collection of manuscripts he bequeathed to the Museum, together with funds for purchasing additions to the collection, which were increased by a further bequest in 1838 from his cousin Charles Long, Lord Farnborough. The Bridgewater and Farnborough funds thus provided an independent source of

Opposite. Scenes from the life of Christ. The De Lisle Psalter. English, 14th century.
Arundel MS 83, f.124.

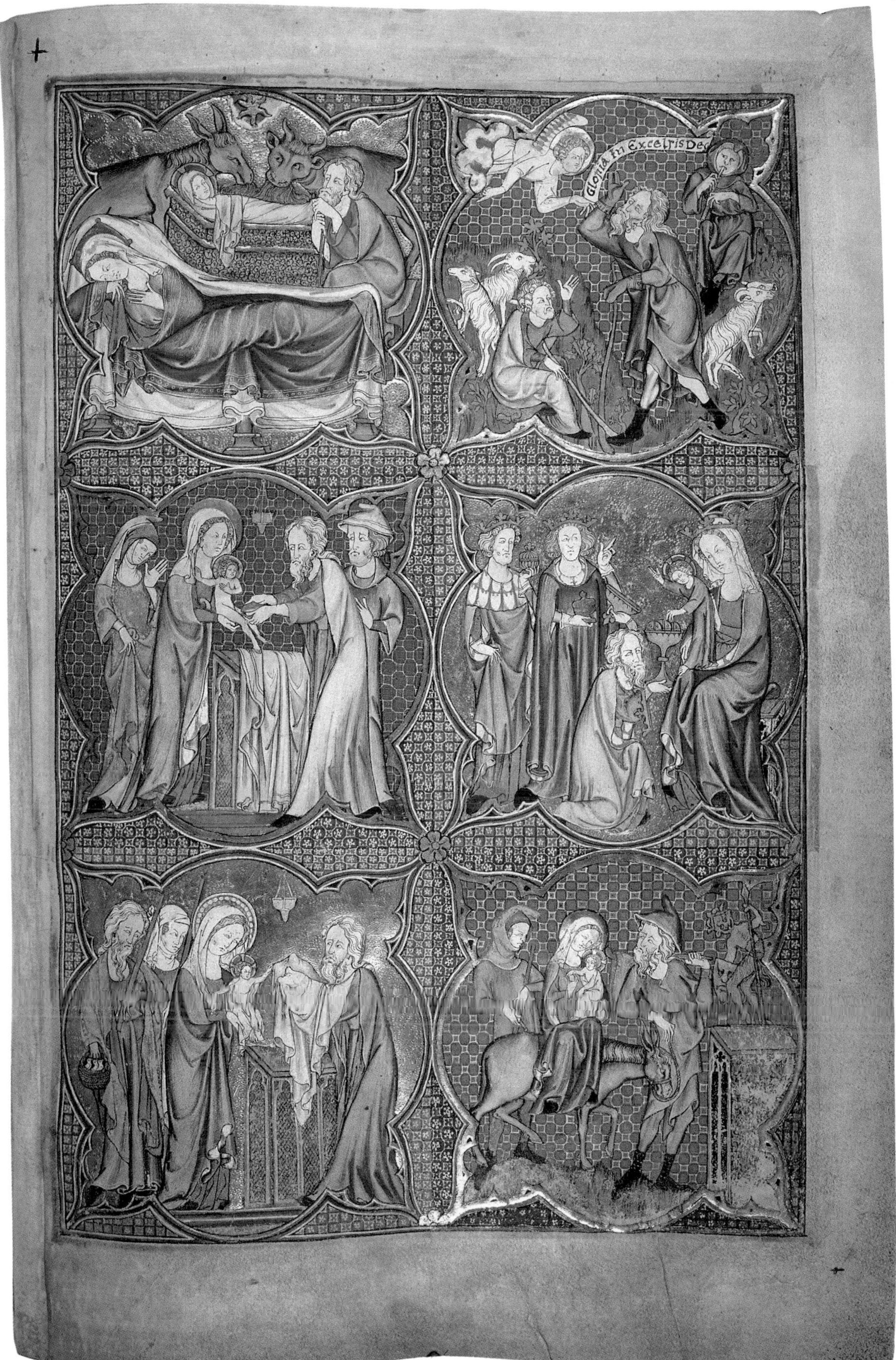
Gloria in excelsis Deo

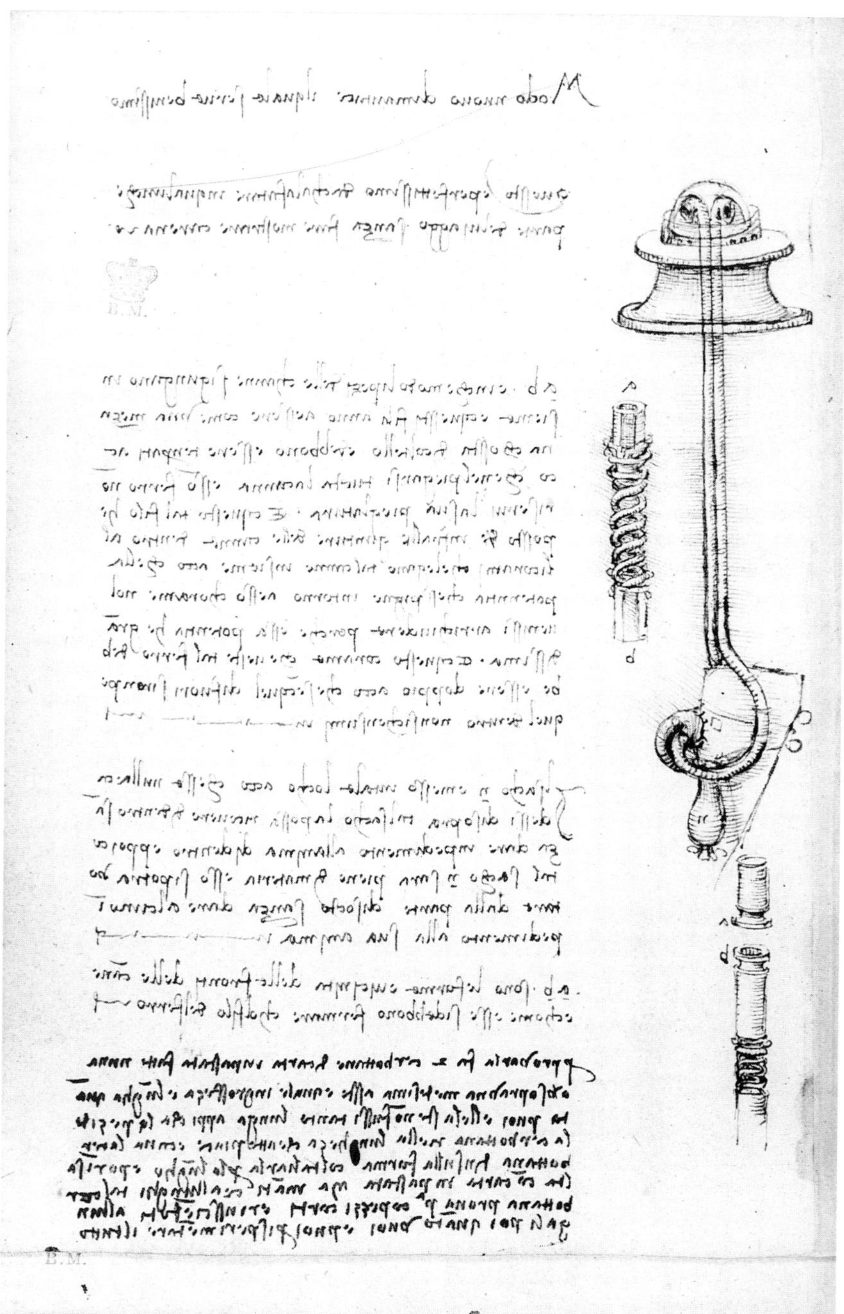

Leonardo da Vinci (died 1519). Autograph notebook known as the Codex Arundel. The notes are in Leonardo's characteristic 'mirror-writing', running from right to left.
Arundel MS 263, f.24v.

money for the purchase of manuscripts important to the collection but lying beyond the ordinary resources available. The Egerton manuscripts (so called after the founder) have thus grown from a small nucleus, consisting mainly of the correspondence of the French and Italian writers, scientists and statesmen of the 16th to 18th centuries, including letters of Montaigne and Galileo, with some charters; they form one of the main constituent collections of the department.

The variety of the acquisitions thus made is considerable. Egerton himself had one Hebrew manuscript; to this was now added a Pentateuch written in Spain or Portugal in the 14th century on 75 strips of leather. Another remarkable early acquisition was the autograph collection of plays, 1624–28, by Lope de Vega, as was the 9th-century Gospels in Caroline minuscule from Tours. Madden's own interests can be seen in the fine Bible, in John Wycliffe's English translation, made for Thomas of Woodstock, Edward III's youngest son. There followed the late 9th-century Gospels of St

Luke and St John, one of the monuments of Franco-Saxon illumination, a 14th-century copy of the *Roman de la Rose*, one of the most popular of medieval romances, the *Passion of St Margaret*, a very early illustrated manuscript of Dante's *Divina Commedia*, and the 9th-century Anglo-Saxon Bible (Sapiential Books), part minuscule, part half-uncial.

The Egerton funds made possible the acquisition of illuminated manuscripts on a scale hitherto beyond reach, a fact recorded in the name 'the Egerton Master' given to the artist of the Hours of René of Anjou. The Melissenda Psalter, one of the major examples of book-painting from the crusader kingdom, in a binding that retains its original ivory plaques, was another early Egerton manuscript. Two outstanding herbals were also acquired, one the *Tractatus de herbis* made in Apulia early in the 14th century, the other the magnificent book, with pictures by Jacopo Filippo, a masterpiece of early naturalistic plant-drawing, made for Francesco Carrara at Padua *c.*1400.

A melon plant, from the Carrara Herbal. Padua, *c.*1400.
Egerton MS 2020, f.161*v*.

Above. The Hours of René of Anjou. French, 15th century.
Egerton MS 1070, ff.29v–30.

Opposite. The Egerton Genesis. English, 14th century.
Egerton MS 1894, f.3.

Below. Signature of William Shakespeare on the 1613 Blackfriars mortgage-deed. (Enlarged.)
Egerton MS 1787.

The Egerton funds were also used for the purchase of more recent literary autograph manuscripts. Thus, the first part of Sterne's corrected draft of *A Sentimental Journey* was acquired in 1853, as was Nelson's last letter to Lady Hamilton, written on the eve of Trafalgar. Manuscript poems by Burns were joined by his autobiographical letter to Dr John Moore of 1787, while the first two cantos of *Childe Harold* and other Byron autographs became Egerton MSS 2027–30. Historic papers included some of Charles I's letters from Carisbrooke Castle and the 1613 mortgage deed (once in Garrick's collection) of a house in Blackfriars, bearing the signature of 'William Shakespeare, of Stratford upon Avon, gentleman'. Egerton MS 2015 is a collection of autograph letters including important ones by Titian and Ariosto, while Egerton MS 2380 contains notable letters by composers, Haydn among them. The manuscript of the medieval Irish *Tale of Deirdre*, written by members of the O'Mulconry (O Maoilchonaire) family, hereditary scribes of Connaught, in 1517 is Egerton MS 1782. Lastly, there are two illuminated manuscripts that must have been specially dear to Madden's heart; the little book of hours painted by 'egregius pictor Franciscus' and the still more important 'Egerton Genesis', a spectacular Bible picture-book of the early 14th century, whose provenance – was it French or English? – was to engage scholarly attention for almost a century.

All these were obtained during or just after Madden's keepership from the income of the original Bridgewater and Farnborough bequests, something under £10,000 in value. It is ample testimony to the skill, both economic and scholarly, with which the money was spent. It is, however, only a cross-section, if a particularly interesting one, of the whole range of acquisition during the 19th century. Although Madden frequently complained, sometimes with reason, of the meanness of the Treasury and the incomprehension of the Trustees, the purchase grant, fixed at £700 in 1837, was doubled in 1843, and by 1848–49 had reached £3000. True, the Treasury refused to

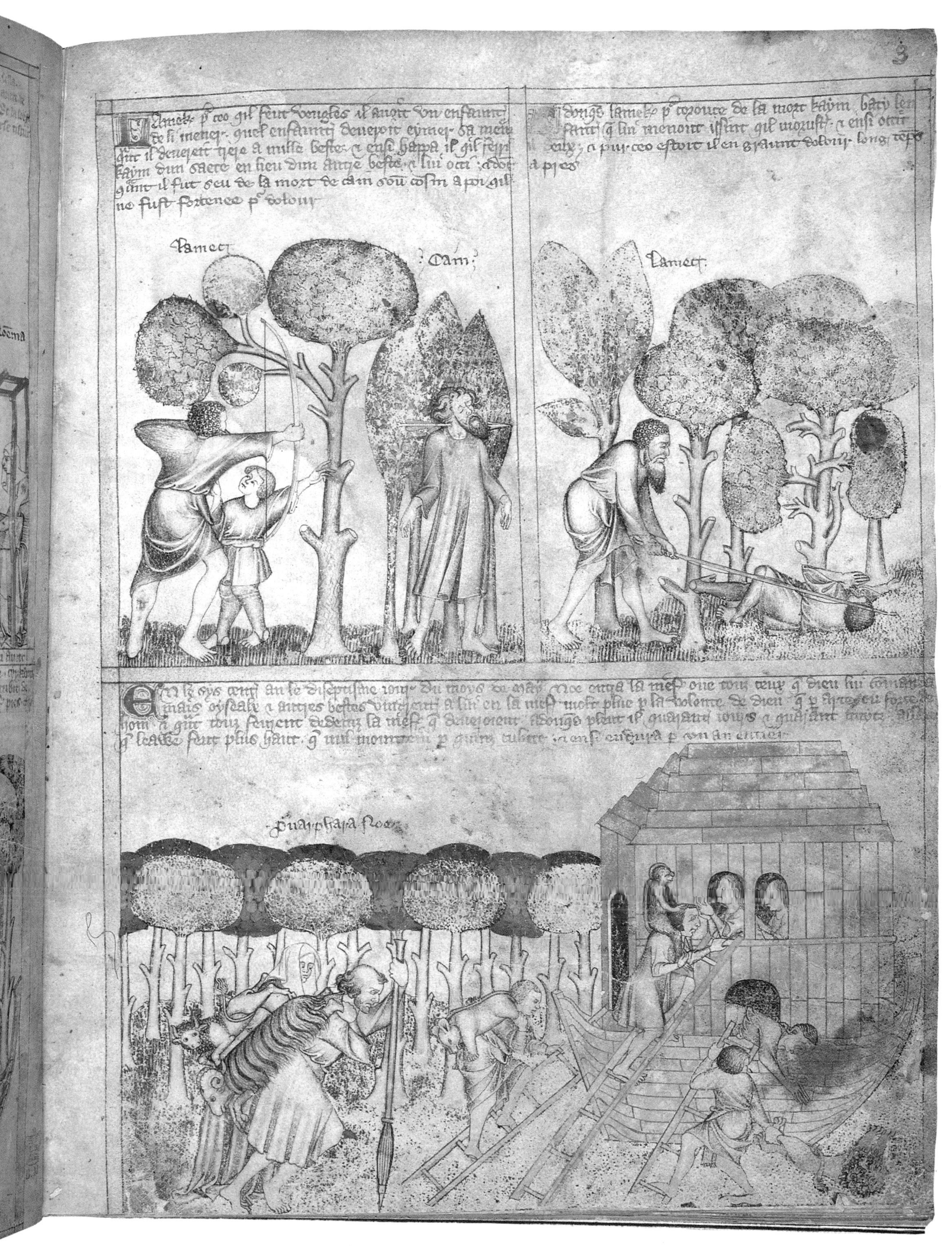
3
Lamech
Cain
Lamech

Letter from Queen Elizabeth I to the future King James I, signed 'your Loving and frendely sister Elizabeth R.' January 1603.
Add. MS 18738, f.40v.

Letter of Michelangelo, signed 'Michelangelo, sculptor'. [1512.]
Add. MS 23140, f.37.

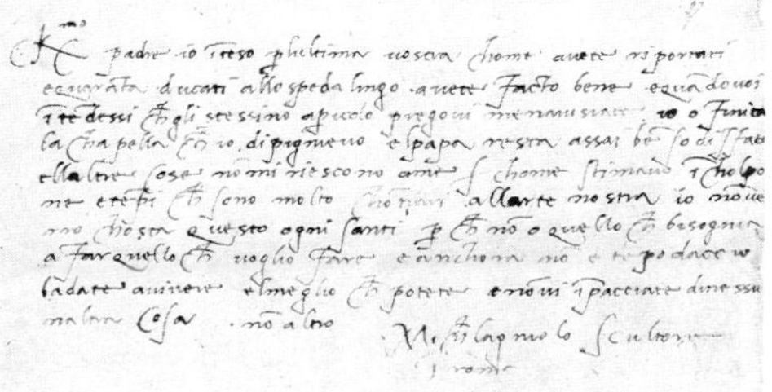

provide £1500 for special purchases at the Duke of Sussex and B.H. Bright sales, and were equally unresponsive to repeated appeals for help in 1846 to buy the first and perhaps most remarkable collection made by Guglielmo Libri, scholar and book-thief, which had passed to the Duke of Buckingham's library at Stowe. (Libri, it may be remarked, was another bone of contention between Madden and Panizzi, the former convinced that he was 'a great rogue' and as a foreigner one of 'an ungrateful humbugging set', the latter unwilling to believe ill of a fellow exile in the cause of Italian liberty.) Worst of all, when the Duke of Buckingham was obliged to sell the whole Stowe collection and the Treasury did give its consent, the Museum was forestalled by Lord Ashburnham, whose brusque *hauteur* was only equalled by his voracity as a collector.

But there were considerable victories to be set off against occasional defeat. There was, for example, the Moutier Grandval Bible, the Vulgate text revised by Alcuin of York, Abbot of Tours, between 796 and 801, and itself written and illuminated at Tours about the middle of the 9th century, which was a *cause célèbre* at the 1835–36 Enquiry, whose witnesses criticised the Trustees for not buying it for £1500; it was finally bought for £750. Bishop Samuel Butler's manuscripts, advertised for sale after his death by Christie's in 1841, were bought *en bloc* before the sale. This brought 280 manuscripts of biblical and classical texts, Greek and Latin, among them the 7th-century *Moralia* of Pope Gregory I, written in the elegant Luxeuil minuscule, the fine Acts, Epistles and Apocalypse written in Caroline minuscule at St Gall in the abbacy of Hartmut (872–83), the abbot himself having added the apocryphal epistle of St Paul to the Laodiceans, and the beautiful Greek illuminated 'Lives of the Saints' by Simeon Metaphrastes, 11th to 12th century.

Among the later manuscripts, there were the copy of Seneca written out by the early Florentine humanist, the Chancellor Coluccio Salutati, the beautiful copy of the work of the Greek astronomer, Aratus, written and perhaps illuminated by Demetrius Damilas, the first Greek typographer, and an equally beautiful Lucretius by the scribe Joannes Rainaldus Mennius.

In the 1840s also came further papers of Sir Julius Caesar from Horace Walpole's collection at Strawberry Hill, and a large increase of Elizabethan and other letters from the sale in 1846 of the autograph collector William Upcott. The Duke of Sussex and Bright sales were not neglected, in the event. Important Spanish and Portuguese manuscripts came from the collections of Lord Kingsborough and Robert Southey. Most striking of all was the acquisition of oriental Christian manuscripts from the monasteries of the Nitrian Desert in Egypt. Robert Curzon, whose collection came to the Library in 1917, made the first successful expedition to buy manuscripts there, followed by the Coptic scholar Henry Tattam. In 1842–43 Tattam was commissioned by the Museum to return: the Syriac manuscripts that he brought back were a major accession, on which William Cureton founded his career as an orientalist (*see* below, p. 146). The music manuscripts bequeathed by Domenico Dragonetti and the Arabic and Persian books given by the heirs of William Yule were other significant acquisitions. The collection made by the antiquary Bezze of *alba amicorum* of German scholars of the 16th and 17th centuries, ancestors of the modern autograph album, was an unusual and picturesque as well as novel addition to the department; they were bought in 1850. The *album* of Hieronymus Koler of Nuremberg, 1562–75, is a fine example. Madden added consistently and substantially to the Bezze *fonds*, which is now one of the finest collections of such material in the world.

In the second half of the century, the pace and scope of acquisition increased still further. Letters were bought singly – a fine one from Queen Elizabeth I to the future James I, written just before her death, for example – or in large collections. The original papers of the General Inquisition of Spain, Prince Rupert's correspondence, those of the Duke of Lauderdale, the 1st Earl Granville, and the Marquis of Pombal as ambassador in London, 1739–41 –

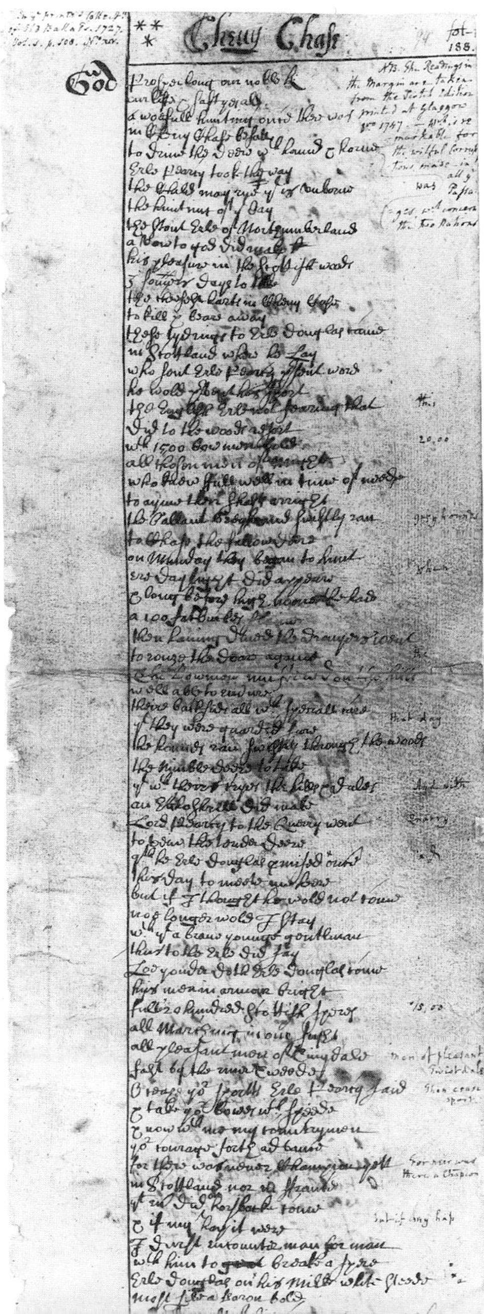

'Chevy Chase', from the anonymous mid-17th century collection of ballads known as the 'Percy Folio'. The margins are filled with annotations by Bishop Thomas Percy, who rescued the manuscript from burning.
Add.MS 27879, f.94.

all these added notably to the Museum's historic resources. The letters of Sir Frederick Haldimand are invaluable for the early history of the British in Canada; Sir Hudson Lowe's relate to Napoleon's captivity on St Helena; the correspondence of Sidney, Earl of Godolphin and Thomas Osborne, Duke of Leeds and Earl of Danby, are the inner history of the Cabal. Perhaps the most important of all were the papers of Warren Hastings, the main resource for the history of the establishment of British rule in India, with the Indian papers of Richard, Marquis Wellesley, the brother of the future Duke of Wellington: besides the documents of his administration, we find Johnson's letter to Hastings, soliciting help for Hoole, the translator.

The first instalment of the Paston Letters, the most famous collection of medieval domestic letters, came in 1868. The Davy and Dawson Turner collections further enriched the Museum's holdings of East Anglian history and topography. Here, too, are Burns's letters, given by Archibald Hastie, the original book of ballads, 17th century, from which Bishop Percy drew his *Reliques of ancient English poetry*, and Francis Place's extraordinary collections relating to the early 19th-century movement for social and political reform. Francis Bacon's notebook, and John Locke's diary for 1679; Lamb's transcripts of the Garrick plays, given by his publisher Edward Moxon in 1835, and a document signed by Spenser; Chatterton's 'Rowley' forgeries and the original 'Letters of Junius'; Wren on the monument to the Great Fire, Hogarth on his own prints, Cowper on Johnson, and Milton's agreement with his printer for 'a poem intitled *Paradise Lost*', no less important now, these were all especially valuable at a time when not many major documents of English literary history were available.

Amongst similar material from Europe, there was the 14th-century manuscript of Dante from the Milanese Archinto library, the letters of Michelangelo and an autograph sonnet; a collection of letters by painters, including Sebastiano del Piombo, Rembrandt and Poussin; Boiardo's *Canzoni* and the autograph of Tasso's *Torrismondo*.

All these might seem remarkable enough, but the mid-19th century was the golden age for the acquisition of early and medieval manuscripts. The Nitrian monastery of St Mary Deipara produced 6th-century palimpsests of the Gospels of St Luke and St John in the original Greek and Coptic. Early classical manuscripts included the 10th-century Juvenal and 11th-century Caesar. Among major illuminated manuscripts, the great Bibles from Stavelot, 1094–97, Parc, 1148, and Floreffe, mid-12th century, were all acquired now. Other later French treasures included a 13th-century psalter and a Gospel-lectionary in the same style as the Sainte-Chapelle service books; and a notable 14th-century Apocalypse. A set of striking illustrations of Sir John Mandeville's travels came from 15th-century Bohemia, and a fine *La somme le roy* from Paris.

The Flemish manuscripts run from the 12th-century missal from St Bavo, Ghent to the so-called 'Golf Book', written and illuminated probably about 1520 and attributed to the leading studio of the day, that of Simon Bening. Among Italian books, there was the 12th-century Psalter in Beneventan script, the pictures by Niccolò de Giacomo of Bologna in Simone de Cascia's *L'Ordine della vita cristiana*, two remarkable manuscripts connected with Doge Cristoforo Moro, his election covenant and Bernardo Bembo's panegyric to him, both dated 1462; and the four-volume St Augustine on the Psalms written and illuminated for Ferdinand of Aragon in 1480. The Stuart de Rothesay Hours decorated by Giulio Clovio fully justifies the artist's reputation as the last great master of book-illumination. From Spain came the 9th-century Isidore, the Lives of the Saints written in Burgos in 919, and the spectacular illustrations of the copy of Beatus on the Apocalypse made at Silos in 1109.

There were, too, a considerable number of important English manuscripts, from the 10th-century St Petroc Gospels onwards. There were the Psalters of

Nuremberg. Watercolour from an *album amicorum* of Magnus Weickmann of Hersbruck, 1746.
Egerton MS 1451, f.26*v*.

Alfonso, son of Edward I, and John Grandisson, Bishop of Exeter, given by him to Isabella, daughter of Edward III; two manuscripts of *The Prick of Conscience*, Lydgate's *Thebes*, and the vast anthology of 14th-century verse known as the Simeon Book. Ranulf Higden's *Polychronicon*, a fine copy made for Richard Beauchamp, Earl of Warwick (died 1439), was bought at the sale of Archbishop Tenison's library in 1865. The sad fragments, once in the possession of Philip Hanrott, of a magnificent missal made for the Carmelite convent in London at the beginning of the 15th century, whose reconstruction by Margaret Rickert is a landmark in the study of the subject, were acquired in 1875. There were also two royal books, Edward VI's autograph treatise on the Sacrament of the Lord's Supper, written in French in 1549, and James I's poems, some in the handwriting of Prince Charles, and with his father's corrections.

If any single episode in this catalogue of acquisitions might be seen as outstanding, the purchase of the Tobin manuscripts in 1852 must be it. Sir John Tobin, a Liverpool merchant, had a small but choice collection which he gave to his son, the Rev. John Tobin, in 1838. Sir John died in 1851 and shortly afterwards his collection was bought by the London bookseller William Boone. There were altogether seven manuscripts, all good, but three 'of the first rank'. Madden had had his eye on them since he had first seen them at Liverpool in 1835, and Boone was soon in touch with him. Madden did his best to bargain, encouraged by the Trustees, but ended up paying Boone's full price, £3000. So it came about that two of the greatest of late medieval illuminated manuscripts, the Bedford Hours, made for the wedding of John, Duke of Bedford and Anne of Burgundy in 1423, and the Hours made in Flanders for the Infanta Joanna (daughter of Ferdinand and Isabella) soon after her marriage to the Archduke Philip in 1496, (illustrated on p. 141) came to the Library, with the Hours of François de Dinteville, Bishop of Auxerre, in 1525, once in the collection of the greatest of English connoisseurs, William Beckford, and four other manuscripts, any of which would have been outstanding in other company.

All this was achieved amid the confusion and stress caused by the rapid growth of the whole Museum and the building works and moves that entailed, only partially relieved by the removal of the Natural History Department to South Kensington in 1880–83. In 1860 Madden had asked for six assistants to keep up with the work, but there was no space for them to work in. When Madden retired in 1866, he could none the less look back on almost 40 years of systematic progress, in the growth of the collections, in the standard of cataloguing, and – last but not least – in the crucial task of salvaging the charred remains of Cottonian manuscripts, damaged in 1731. Madden

Opposite. Astronomers at the top of Mount Athos. Page from The Travels of Sir John Mandeville. Bohemia, 15th century.
Add. MS 24189, f.15*r*.

was succeeded by Edward Bond, who had been Assistant Keeper since Holmes's premature death in 1854. For 12 years he had borne the brunt of ever-increasing accessions and Madden's increasing disillusionment. He got on well with Panizzi, and became the channel of communication between the department and the Principal Librarian. Now he had his chance to reform the department. Like Madden, he was fortunate in his subordinates: Edward Maunde Thompson had joined in 1861, and Edward Scott in 1863; George Warner was to follow them in 1871. With them he made up the arrears of the catalogue, postponing publication, however, until he had created the class catalogue, a subject index of the collection, all the more valuable since the catalogues of the early parts of the collection were so often defective. The invention of photography and the consequent facsimile printing processes revolutionised palaeography: a set of *Facsimiles of Ancient Charters* in the department was published in 1873–78. Another product was Bond and Thompson's decisive redating of the Utrecht Psalter to the 9th century in what was the first full-scale photographic facsimile of a medieval manuscript: together they pioneered the work of the Palaeographical Society in making facsimiles of early manuscripts available.

Finally, in 1885, some resolution of the space problem was achieved. As long ago as 1823, William White had bequeathed funds for improving the building, but subject to a life interest that only expired in 1879. In the previous year Bond succeeded Winter Jones as Principal Librarian and was able to apply the money to the extension of the department, filling the space between the Manuscript Saloon and the Keepers' Residences at the east corner of the site. The small bindery there was demolished and a larger building erected for it to the north of the Arch Room. Now at last the department had a Students' Room for the consultation of manuscripts and working rooms for staff, as well as more and better storage space for select manuscripts. It was Bond also who introduced electric lighting to the Library, as early as 1879, an important improvement in days when a fog-ridden London might cause the Museum to be closed and candles were a constant fire-risk. When Bond retired in 1888, Maunde Thompson succeeded, Scott following him as Keeper of Manuscripts, and together they saw the century out, while Warner built up the department's reputation for scholarship with a series of important publications for the Museum, the Palaeographical Society and its successor (which he founded), the New Palaeographical Society, and the Roxburghe Club. It was a strong team, and it was needed, for the last quarter of the century saw a substantial further growth in the collection of manuscripts.

Aristotle (died 322 BC). *Constitution of Athens*. *c.* AD 100. (Detail.)
Papyrus CXXXI(3).

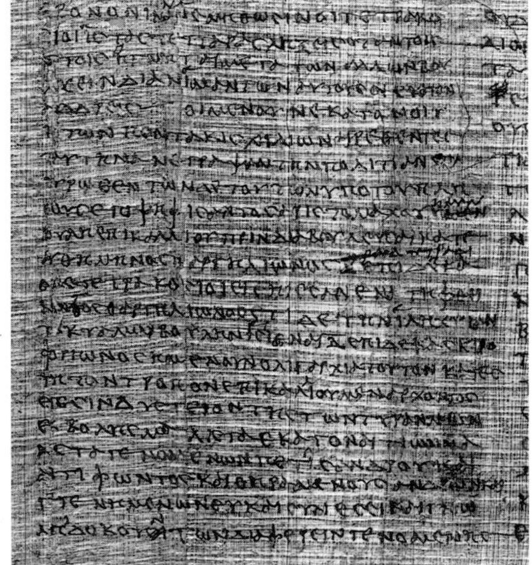

One important new class of accession to the collections was papyri. Until now, specimens of papyrus were considerable rarities: in 1865 Queen Victoria donated two of the charred rolls from Herculaneum that had been given to George IV when Prince of Wales, but significantly they were deposited in the Department of Antiquities and were not transferred to Manuscripts until 1882. Now the sands of Egypt began to reveal papyrus fragments (but well-preserved) in quantity. The Egypt Exploration Society was formed to excavate the sites scientifically, and B.P. Grenfell, A.S. Hunt and D.G. Hogarth took charge of the work, the findings being distributed to various libraries, notably the Museum. It began in 1879 with the purchase of the Orations of Hyperides, 1st century BC, and the substantial (eight feet long) section of Book 24 of the *Iliad*, 2nd century, known as the Bankes Homer. In the years that followed came the hitherto unknown texts of Aristotle on the Constitution of Athens and the Mimes of Herodas, both 1st century, fragments of Plato's *Phaedo* and Euripides's lost play *Antiope*, both of the 3rd century BC. In addition, there was a substantial part of the works of the poet Bacchylides, also hitherto unknown, of the 2nd century BC. Both the Constitution of Athens and Bacchylides were edited by F.G. Kenyon, who joined the department in 1889. Besides major literary finds, there were a whole host of other papyri,

The Bankes Homer. 2nd century AD. (Detail, much reduced.)
Papyrus CXIV(E).

official and private, as important as documents of the history of Egypt under the Ptolemies and in Roman times, as of Greek and Latin script.

Again, the historical sources in the library were enormously amplifed by the arrival of substantial archives: the papers of Charles I's Secretary of State Sir Edward Nicholas and of John Wilkes; original letters received by the Council of the North and the vast collection of Pelham and Holles papers, centred on the papers of the Duke of Newcastle, the most durable of 18th-century politicians (died 1768), given by the Earl of Chichester; papers of the Earls of Auckland (the 2nd Earl was the famous Viceroy of India) and Hardwicke; General Gordon's, including his Khartoum diary, acquired while his death was still current news; and (a major acquisition) a batch of Nelson's papers, acquired from Lord Bridport in 1895. Historic documents, smaller but equally important, were Henry VIII's ordinances for his household, the property of successive Lord Chamberlains, the Earl of Worcester and Henry, 9th Earl of Arundel, papers relating to the Armada, and a further group of the Paston Letters.

It was a particularly rich period for English literary manuscripts. The autograph manuscript of Cavendish's *Life of Wolsey*, the commonplace book of that exotic Elizabethan Gabriel Harvey, Milton's family bible and Locke's commonplace book, particularly interesting since he invented the indexed system for such works; autograph manuscripts of Sir Thomas Wyatt and George Eliot, the latter containing most of her novels, bequeathed by the author; the drafts of Coleridge's poems, some later printed in *Sibylline Leaves*; Charlotte Brontë's juvenile *The Spell*; and the journal and letters of Gilbert White of Selborne; all these are remarkable. Among important acquisitions of letters were those of his father-in-law Sir Richard Browne to John Evelyn, Jeremy Bentham's correspondence, and, particularly appealing, the original letters from Dorothy Osborne to Sir William Temple. The Gibbon centenary exhibitions led to the acquisition of the card index of his library and his letters and journals. But the most remarkable of all the literary manuscripts acquired in this period were those of Keats: the set of autograph poems including 'Isabella: or the Pot of Basil', and the long series of his letters to his sister Fanny, presented by her daughter Rosa Llanos Keats.

It is hard to set a lesser importance on a group of medieval manuscripts beginning with two major Merovingian manuscripts, the 7th-century Homilies of St Augustine in Luxeuil script and the 8th-century Laon *Moralia* of St Gregory, but in quantity if not quality the ordinary acquisitions in this field were less remarkable. True, there were a whole series of 9th-11th century Mozarabic liturgies from Silos, complementing the great Beatus on the Apocalypse, any one of which would be outstanding, and an Exultet roll, a 12th-century Easter liturgy of which few examples exist outside Italy. Among later manuscripts were the very fine illuminated Durandus *Rationale*, Italian, *c.*1400, from the Firmin Didot Sale, and the magnificent Hours of Bona Sforza, the gift of John Malcolm of Poltalloch. Another memorable gift was the

February. From the 'Golf Book'. Bruges, *c.*1520.
Add. MS 24098, f.19*v*.

manuscripts collected by the architect William Burges, among them a fine 13th-century French Bible.

One unusual acquisition linked England with one of the greatest works of European literature, the Commentary on Dante's *Divina Commedia* compiled by Giovanni Bertoldi, Bishop of Fermo, during the Council of Constance in 1416–17 for his fellow bishops, the Cardinal de Saluces, Nicholas Bubwith, Bishop of Bath and Wells, and Robert Hallam, Bishop of Salisbury. The English manuscripts themselves included two major Anglo-Saxon manuscripts, the Grimbald Gospels, written by Eadui Basan at Christ Church, Canterbury, early in the 11th century, and Aelfric's *Grammar*; the *Encomium Emmae Reginae* with a drawing of the author presenting his book to Queen Emma is of Norman origin. Later books included the 15th-century Barber Surgeons Guild Book of York, with its remarkable illustrations, a fine 13th-century illustrated Apocalypse and the York Mystery Plays. There was, too, an outstanding Irish manuscript, the life of St Bridget, Abbess of Kildare, by St Ultan, of the 9th century.

The topographical collections include the notes of many generations of antiquaries, often accompanied by drawings of surprising quality. There are two remarkable series of drawings, those of Samuel Grimm (1733–94) and Edward Blore (1787–1879), John Carter's for his *Ancient Buildings*, 1764–1817, and the extraordinary set of over 10,000 drawings by John Chessell Buckler and his father and son, John and Charles Alban Buckler. Other significant acquisitions included a notebook on seven wooden tablets

Opposite. March. Calendar miniature by Simon Bening. Bruges, *c.*1540. (Enlarged.)
Add. MS 18855, f.108.

1 Augusti 1588

C Howard George Cumberland

Fra: Drake

Hampstead Tuesday

My dear Fanny,

I have just written to Mr Abbey to ask him to let you come and see poor Tom who has lately been much worse. He is better at present—sends his Love to you and wishes much to see you. I hope he will shortly—I have not been able to come to Walthamstow on his account as well as a little Indisposition of my own.—I have asked Mr A. to write me. if he does not mention any thing of it to you, I will tell you what reasons he has though I do not think he will make any objection. Write me what you want with a Flageolet and I will get one ready for you by the time you come.

Your affectionate Brother
John—

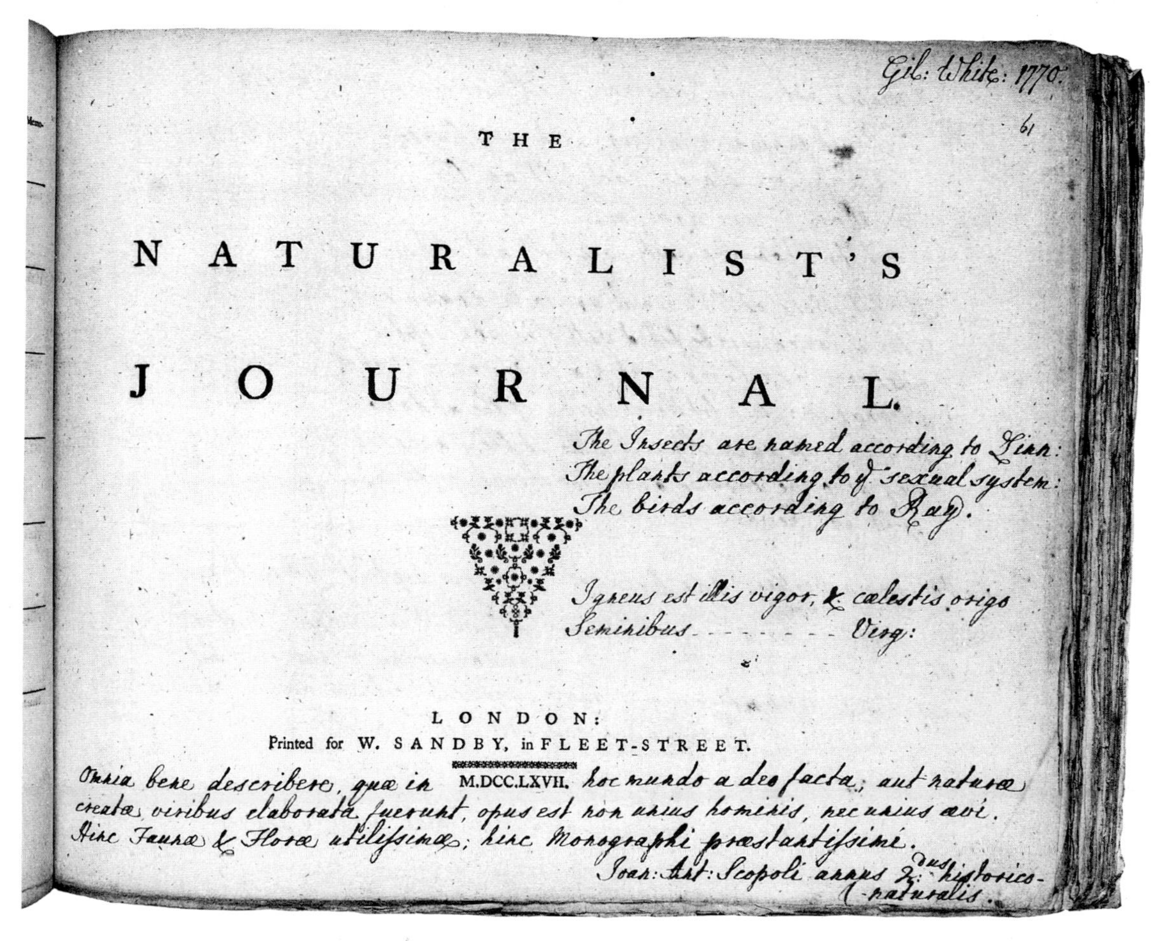

Gil: White: 1770.

THE
NATURALIST'S
JOURNAL.

The Insects are named according to Linn:
The plants according to ye sexual system:
The birds according to Ray.

Igneus est illis vigor, & cœlestis origo
Seminibus - - - - - - - Virg:

LONDON:
Printed for W. SANDBY, in FLEET-STREET.
M.DCC.LXVII.

Omnia bene describere, quæ in hoc mundo a deo facta, aut naturæ creatæ viribus elaborata fuerunt, opus est non unius hominis, nec unius ævi. Hinc Faunæ & Floræ utilissimæ; hinc Monographi præstantissimi.
Joan: Ant: Scopoli annus 2dus historico-naturalis.

Opposite, left. Signed resolution of a council of war of the commanders of the English fleet which opposed the Spanish Armada in 1588.
Add. MS 33740, f.6.

Opposite, right. Letter from John Keats to his sister Fanny, *c.*1818.
Add. MS 34019, f.5.

coated with wax, 3rd century, an extraordinary survival, a Mexican picture chronicle compiled 1576–1607 (since transferred to the Museum of Mankind) and a vast railway map of Australia, 12 feet by 9½ feet.

The period was, however, chiefly distinguished by two major acquisitions, the Stowe manuscripts and the Rothschild Gift. Lord Ashburnham, who had cut the Museum out when the Duke of Buckingham's collection was for sale in 1848, died in 1879, and his entire collection was offered to the Museum for £160,000. After protracted negotiation, the Museum was enabled to buy the 993 Stowe MSS alone for £50,000 in 1883. These included the *Liber vitae* of New Minster, written *c.*1016–20, with three fine drawings, and the Norwich Breviary, *c.*1325. Among the historical sources were the earliest text of the Chronicle of William of Newburgh, *c.*1200; Elizabethan letters, including Sir Philip Sidney's to Burghley; Robert Cecil's account of the Gunpowder Plot; the letters of the Duke and Duchess of Marlborough to the Secretary of State James Craggs; and Robert Harley's to George I. Two manuscripts preserved their original 'girdle book' bindings, with a strap and ring attachment – Pierre Sala's poems with his portrait by Jean Perréal, and the Psalms with a portrait of Henry VIII in a gold and black enamel binding, which by tradition, wrong but romantic, was said to have been given by Anne Boleyn on the scaffold to one of her maids. There was an astonishing wealth of heraldic manuscripts which had belonged to the great Garter King of Arms, John Anstis (1669–1744); they included a major masterpiece of medieval heraldry, the Garter Book of William Bruges, the Order's first King of Arms, with 26 drawings of the Founder Knights, *c.*1430. Finally, perhaps the greatest of all the Stowe treasures was the collection of 64 early charters, 42 of them Anglo-Saxon: notable among these are the Charters of Queen Aethelgyfu to Christ Church and King Aethelred II's to his bondman Aethelred. The acquisition of the Stowe manuscripts can now be seen as a landmark in the history of the Library, last of a series of collections of which Cotton's was the first and greatest.

A Roman wooden tablet coated with wax, still bearing writing. 3rd century.
Add. MS 33270.

At the time almost equal prominence was given to the bequest of Baron Ferdinand de Rothschild (1899), perhaps because its 14 manuscripts were all illuminated. The outstanding book, one that gave most delight in the Museum, was one volume of the Breviary of John the Fearless, Duke of Burgundy (died 1419) the rest of which was already in the Harleian collection. Other remarkable books included the Breviary of Daniel Birago, the Exposition of the Apostles' Creed presented by the author, Pierre de Valtan, to Charles VIII of France and a French *Decameron*, later in the possession of and bound for the Protector Somerset. The Rothschild bequest added notably to the Library's collection of pictorial 15th-century manuscripts, which, due to the high prices they had attracted throughout the century, had not come to it as freely as earlier manuscripts.

The period that stretches from Nares's Keepership to that of Scott is, all things considered, one of consistent and remarkable growth for the Department of Manuscripts, as remarkable, if on a smaller scale, as that of the Department of Printed Books. If, in terms of money for acquisitions or public notice, it played second fiddle to the larger department, its achievement is the more remarkable. The credit for this largely belongs to Madden: over nearly 30 years his energy and learning converted a valuable if heterogeneous assemblage into a truly national collection. His also is the credit for setting a high standard of cataloguing, and establishing the tradition of punctual attention to small details on which so much rests: he was by no means as bad a departmental officer as his detractors have made out. If his success was diminished by uneasy or bad relations with the Trustees, the case is probably overstated in his diary.

Opposite. Gilbert White's autograph annotations on the tite-page of his journal for 1767.
Add. MS 31846, f.61.

He would no doubt have dwelt on his failures – the Stowe collection in 1848, or the series of missed opportunities at Libri's sales – rather than the

Opposite, above. The Hours of Joanna of Castile. Bruges, 1496–1506. (Reproduced approximately same size as the original.)
Add. MS 18852, ff.14v–15.

Opposite, below left. Giovan Pietro Birago, decorated text page from the Hours of Bona Sforza. Milan, about 1490.
Add. MS 34294, f.334.

Opposite, below right. Jean Perréal. Portrait of Pierre Sala in *Emblesmes et Dévises d'Amour*. Lyons, *c.*1500.
Stowe MS 955, f.17.

great successes, like the Tobin purchase. Oddly enough, he seems (perhaps because he knew the collector too well, and had suffered so much from his opposition in the sale room) to have made little attempt to attract the greatest of all 19th-century collections, that of Sir Thomas Phillipps, to his department, whether by gift, purchase or bequest. In 1831–32 Phillipps made overtures for purchase and even drafted a will in the Museum's favour, but nothing came of it. In 1861 Panizzi tried again, after Phillipps's long negotiations with Oxford broke down, with no more success, though it brought him and Madden into cordial relations for once.

Finally, after Phillipps's death, negotiations in 1874–76 between his Trustees and the Museum, in which Bond and Lord Acton took part, again led to nothing. The dispersal of the collection, which lasted more than a century, is perhaps the greatest of all losses to the national collection.

On the other hand, the careful acquisitions of a century had added an almost equal wealth to the collection, and the consistency with which it had been developed had given it a strength beyond even the greatest adventitious acquisition. One example alone must suffice. Out of some 46 surviving Anglo-Saxon books from Winchester, 27 are now in the Department of Manuscripts: 19 of these were in the Cottonian, Harleian and Old Royal Libraries, but 7 more were acquired in the 19th century (one, and perhaps the greatest, the Benedictional of St Aethelwold, has been added since). It was no mean achievement, and it typifies the growth of the collection overall.

Catalogue of Edward Gibbon's library, written on the backs of playing-cards. Many of the books from his library still exist, dispersed among different collections.
Add. MS 34716.

SPECVLVM
CONSCIENCIE

Antate dno
canticum no
uum: laus ei
in ecclesia sanctoru.
Letetur israel in eo
qui fecit eu: 7 filie si
on exultent in rege
suo. Laudent nom
eius in choro in tim
pano: 7 psalterio psal
lant ei Quia bnpla

9

The Development of Oriental Collections

Sir Hans Sloane's catholic tastes, predictably enough, led him to acquire specimens, at least, of writing in non-European languages. On 12 February 1703, James Cunninghame, Physician to the East India Company's Factory at Chusan in China, wrote forwarding such specimens which he described thus:

> In the foresaid Box there's for yourself a Chinese Common Prayer Book, which I procured from the Bonzes at Pu-to', the Lord's Prayer Belief and 10 Commandements translated into Chinese by the Jesuites, a description of Pu-to' in Chinese, & a Draft of the River of Ning-po done by a French Father who resides there.

These can be identified as Sloane MS 4090 amongst others and in the years that followed Sloane acquired other Chinese material – three dictionaries, notes, a deed, a palm leaf and a wooden tablet, partly in Old Javanese and partly in Chinese. Besides these, he had one Syriac manuscript, four Sanskrit, several Hebrew, among them a translation of Aristotle's *Historia animalium* and other tracts, mostly on physiology, Spanish, *c.*1400, the Leipnik *Haggadah* which he may have bought new in 1740, some Armenian, Georgian and even some Japanese material.

More surprisingly, there is oriental material in both Cottonian and Harleian collections. Cotton had a Samaritan manuscript, three Anglo-Jewish charters, a collection of tales with some medical prescriptions in Chinese and a letter and account book in Japanese. The Harleian collection also contained a Syriac manuscript, from the Jesuit college at Agen, over 130 Hebrew manuscripts, including the magnificent *Mishneh Torah* written in 1471–72 by Solomon ibn Alzuk, bought in 1725 from Bernard Mould who had acquired it in Smyrna, and a bible, written in Italy *c.*1300, 34 Turkish manuscripts, including a unique 'Wonders of the World', four Armenian manuscripts and examples of Chinese and Japanese, including some contemporary Chinese tea-shop advertisements.

Richard Bentley acquired for the Old Royal Library the materials collected by Thomas Hyde (1636–1703) for his *Historia religionis veterum Persarum*, mainly Persian and Avestan MSS of Zoroastrian literature, but again including some Chinese material. Among the printed books was the *editio princeps* of the *Mishneh Torah*, printed at Rome *c.*1480; the remarkable restoration of Hebrew books by Solomon da Costa in 1759 has been noted above (p. 38). The Banks collection contained some Japanese books, and the Lansdowne manuscripts some Hebrew, as well as a set of 24 maps of the Chinese provinces and Chinese Tartary, with a plan of the imperial city of Peking. The King's Library manuscripts included a fine Hebrew bible, written at Solsona in Spain, 1384. The Egerton and Arundel collections added a few more Hebrew and Syriac manuscripts.

All these acquisitions had come casually, as appendages to collections great in other respects. Although the Museum had had one orientalist of repute on its staff since 1782 in C.G. Woide, editor of the New Testament of the Codex Alexandrinus, and another from 1799 to 1824 in Thomas Maurice, the Sanskrit scholar, no great attempt was made to improve the position. True, the manuscripts, mainly Persian and Sanskrit, of Charles Hamilton (1753–92) and Nathaniel Brassey Halhed (1751–1830) were

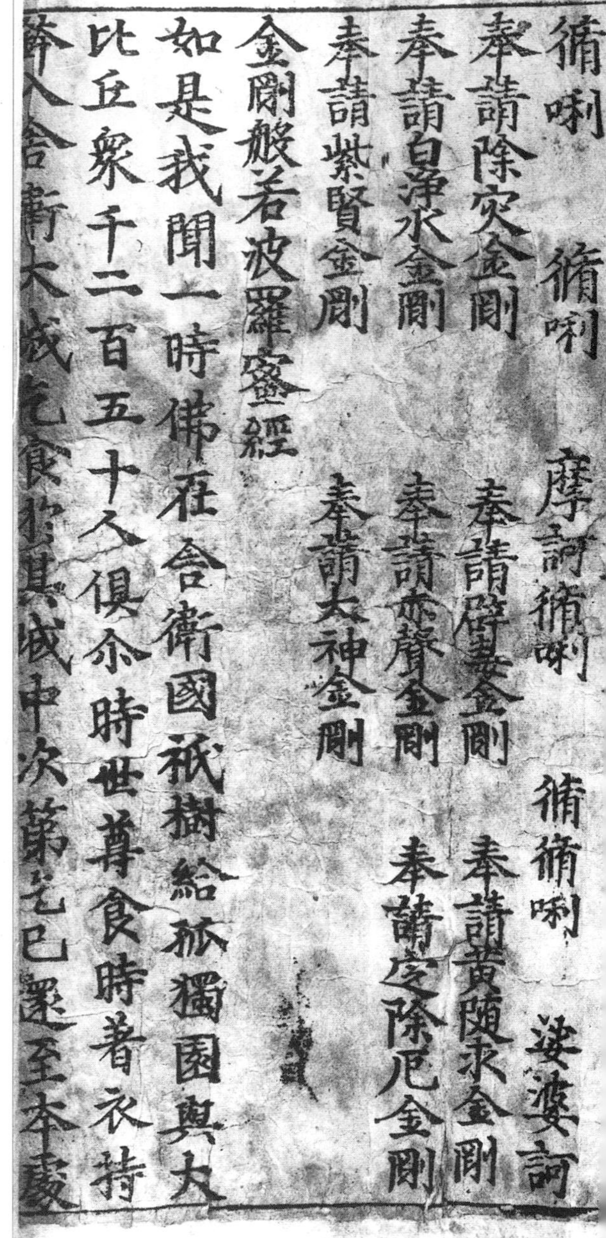

脩唎脩唎摩訶脩唎脩脩唎娑婆訶

奉請除灾金剛 奉請辟毒金剛 奉請黃隨求金剛

奉請白淨水金剛 奉請赤聲金剛 奉請定除厄金剛

奉請紫賢金剛 奉請大神金剛

金剛般若波羅蜜經

如是我聞一時佛在舍衛國祇樹給孤獨園與大

比丘衆千二百五十人俱尒時世尊食時著衣持

鉢入舍衛大城乞食於其城中次第乞已還至本處

Frontispiece to the Diamond Sutra, the world's earliest dated printed book, AD 868.
Or. 8210/P.2.

bought in 1794 and 1796, with a large set of manuscripts of the Vedas, the first to reach Europe, from Colonel Antoine Polier; while among the loot from Napoleon's army brought to London after the Battle of the Nile were a number of Arabic manuscripts, which thus escaped the more energetic French orientalists then building up the collection at what is now the Bibliothèque Nationale.

It was Josiah Forshall, not yet the discredited Secretary to the Trustees, who set on foot a more active policy. He succeeded Maurice in 1824. The following year the Museum's holdings were dramatically altered by the acquisition of the collection of Claudius Rich (1786–1821), the East India Company's Resident in Baghdad. A brilliant linguist, Rich had travelled extensively in the Near East, studying archaeological remains with a prescience that identified the site of the ancient Nineveh long before Layard and others had excavated it. His collection had been formed by rescuing from neglect what he found. As he himself wrote: 'Manuscripts are fast perishing in the East and it is almost the duty of a traveller to rescue as many as he can from destruction'. Rich's

Above. The Hebrews building cities for the Pharaohs of Egypt. From the Barcelona Haggadah. Mid-14th century.
Add. MS 14761, f.30*v*.

Opposite, top left. Noah's Ark. From the North French Miscellany. *c*.1280.
Add. MS 11639, f.523*v*.

Opposite, top right. Four Biblical scenes. From the Golden Haggadah. North Spain, *c*.1320.
Add. MS 27210, f.11*r*.

Opposite, below left. Decorated first word of the Book of Deuteronomy. From the Duke of Sussex German Pentateuch.
Add. MS 15282, f.238*r*.

Opposite, below right. The Lisbon Mishneh Torah, 1471/1472.
Harley MS 5698 (Vol.1), f.11*v*.

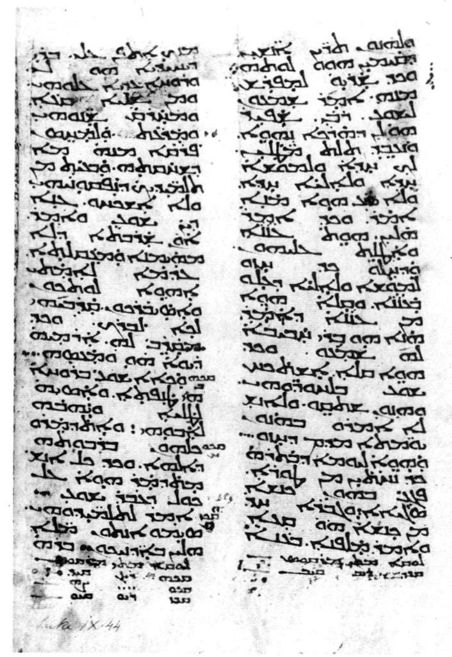

A Syriac fragment of St Luke's Gospel.
Add. MS 14451, f.49r.

coins and antiquities were the foundation of the Museum's Western Asiatic collections; the manuscripts were an even more substantial acquisition. The Trustees petitioned Parliament which sanctioned the purchase of the collection from Rich's widow for £7500. It contained over 300 each of Arabic and Persian manuscripts, 124 Turkish, 66 Syriac and Karshuni, two Armenian and one Ethiopian manuscript.

It was the Syriac manuscripts that engaged Forshall's attention, and he set to work to catalogue them with the aid, when he became Keeper in 1827, of Friedrich Rosen, Professor of Oriental Languages at University College. The catalogue was finally published in 1838, the first notice to the scholarly world of the Museum's new wealth. Among the books thus described are some of the earliest Peshitta Bible texts, and the Jacobite and Nestorian versions, including a Nestorian New Testament dated 768. Of particular interest too were the 12th-century illuminated Syriac Gospel lectionaries, of which Add. MSS 7169–70 are notable examples. In his catalogue Forshall was obliged to describe the collection as still inferior to those at Oxford, Paris, or the Vatican, but the next acquisition was to alter this.

Most of Rich's Syriac manuscripts had come from the area of Mosul. Those that Tattam brought back from St Mary Deipara at Souriani in the Nitrian Desert had originated at Edessa, near Mosul, and had migrated to Egypt in the 10th century. Tattam made his first visit to Egypt in 1834 and brought back a number of books which he sold to the Museum. His next expedition, in 1842–43, was financed by the Museum, and he was able to bring back what he supposed to be the residue, 317 volumes, although subsequently more were found and eventually recovered. They proved to be even more important than was first believed. By now William Cureton had succeeded Forshall as Assistant Keeper under Madden: originally an Arabist, he had had to learn Syriac, but did so to great effect. Although worsted in the controversy following his claim that the Nitriana copy of the Epistles of St Ignatius was the only authentic text, he correctly identified some gospel fragments as predating the Peshitta text. He published this, together with a palimpsest fragment of the *Iliad*, and the newly-discovered text of the 'Festal Epistles' of St Athanasius. Even more important were the earliest Pentateuch manuscripts, one written at Edessa, AD 411/12, the other signed by the scribe, the deacon John, at Amida in 463. The earliest dated manuscript was the Epistle of Titus, Bishop of Bostra, against the Manichaeans, 411; the latest was dated 1292.

Forshall was also responsible for beginning the serious acquisition of Hebrew manuscripts, buying 10 manuscripts at the sale of Adam Clarke, the biblical critic and author of the *Bibliographical Dictionary* in 1834. In 1839, however, several books from the Reina Library at Milan were bought, among them a fine 14th-century German bible (Prophetic Books), but also including what is still the most remarkable Hebrew book in the collection, the 'North French Miscellany', the Pentateuch with its *haftarot* and *targum*, and many other liturgical and poetical texts, including 41 full-page bible pictures of a quality comparable with the best French work of the period (*c.*1280), most of which are (unusually) circular. Another major source of acquisitions was the Duke of Sussex sale, from which came the Pentateuch, written and perhaps illuminated by the scribe Hayyim, *c.*1300, a bible made in Catalonia, *c.*1350, an Italian Pentateuch, *c.*1320, and the bible, also of Italian origin, signed and dated 1448 by the scribe Moses Akrish. Just before this sale, the Museum also acquired two notable manuscripts from the great booksellers, Payne and Foss – the decorated *Haggadah* made, probably in Barcelona, *c.*1350 and another *Haggadah*, written and illuminated *c.*1460–75 by Joel ben Simeon Feibusch, a scribe from the Rhineland who had visited Italy, the influence of whose artists can be seen in his work.

Other notable accessions followed. The Coburg Pentateuch, written and vividly illustrated by Simhah ben Samuel Halevi in 1395, the 13th–14th century Pentateuch with *haftarot* and *megillot*, with the *masorah* in picturesque micrography, and the same text, splendidly illuminated in Spain, *c.*1400; the Siddur written and illustrated at Forli, 1383 and two *Machzorim* (festival prayer books), both illuminated, one South German *c.*1320, the other Italian, *c.*1400.

In 1865, a major acquisition, both as to quantity and quality, was made through Adolphus Asher of Berlin, the Museum's energetic German bookseller. This was the manuscript collection of Joseph Almanzi, collected both by him and Hayyim Joseph David Azulai. The price was £1000, astonishingly little even for the time, especially since the collection included not only three of the books described above but also the Golden Haggadah, one of the grandest of all Hebrew manuscripts, with a set of biblical illustrations, four to a page, of very high quality, probably painted in or near Barcelona, *c.*1320.

The printed Hebraica had never been neglected. Da Costa's benefaction had awoken an interest that was maintained. Of 106 Hebrew incunables recorded in David Goldstein's *Hebrew incunables in the British Isles: a preliminary census*, only 18 are not in the British Library; most of them were acquired in the 19th century to add to the already considerable number in the foundation collections. In 1848 the number of Hebrew books was enormously increased by the accession of the H.J. Michael collection, formed in Hamburg and containing 3970 works in 4420 volumes. It included some remarkable incunables, among them Jacob ben Asher, *Orah Hayim* (1485), the first book printed in Portugal, and the Avicenna printed at Naples in 1491, the first printed book in Hebrew on medicine. There were also a large number of books, hitherto unknown, printed in Poland and Turkey in the 16th century, and books annotated by great Hebrew scholars, from Azariah de Rossi and Bezalel Ashkenazi in the 16th century to contemporary scholars such as Heidenheim, A. Eger and Michael himself. The books annotated by the great 18th-century Rabbi Jacob Emden were of especial importance. With this in hand, the Museum was fortunate in engaging in 1855, through the introduction of Adolphus Asher, the services of one of the greatest Talmudic scholars of his time, Emmanuel Deutsch, who, in his short career (he died in 1870), left a lasting mark on the work of the Museum and on Hebrew scholarship as a whole.

Of the other languages of the Christian East, Coptic was hardly represented at this point, nor was Ethiopic until the gift of 74 volumes by the Church Missionary Society in 1846 provided the basis for a first catalogue. Manuscripts in Armenian and Georgian, however, were both acquired early, and two notable additions were made in the 19th century, the 11th-century *Lives of the Saints* associated with the Georgian monastery at Jerusalem and the fine illuminated Armenian New Testament, written at Sis in 1280. In 1836, Panizzi secured a Parliamentary Grant for the purchase of all the books printed at the Mechitarist covent on the island of San Lazzaro at Venice, much visited by English travellers from Byron to the present day.

Arabic had scarcely been represented in the foundation collections, although a handsome Turkish Qur'ān, 13th–14th century, in *Naskhī* script came in 1766. It was now significantly advanced by the accession of Rich's manuscripts, which included an illuminated Qur'ān on vellum in Eastern Kufic script of the 11th or 12th century, and an unusually early example of small *Naskhī* script in another illuminated Qur'ān dated AH 427 (AD 1036); both originated in what is now Iraq, where Rich doubtless acquired them. The Reina Library, in addition to its memorable Hebrew manuscripts, was also the source of two more fine Qur'ān manuscripts, one copied in Spain in the 11th century in Andalusian *Maghribī* script and another in Eastern Kufic, with an illuminated frontispiece, probably 10th century.

All these were now catalogued by Cureton, whose first speciality was Arabic. Further gifts and purchases came from the descendants of Major William Yule, in the East India Company's service, in 1845; from the missionary Dr Sternschuss in 1851; and from Colonel Robert Taylor, Rich's

successor as Resident at Baghdad (1852). More manuscripts were added: the *Maqāmāt al-Ḥarīrī* (Assemblies of al-Ḥarīrī), an anthology of adventure stories, illustrated, from the 13th century, *al-Wāfībi-al-wafayāt*, a biographical dictionary in three volumes by Ṣalāḥ al-Dīn Khalīl ibn Aybak al-Ṣafadī, 14th–15th century, and one of the finest of all surviving *Qur'ān* manuscripts written in gold, *Thuluth* by Muḥammad ibn al-Waḥīd and illuminated by Aydughdī ibn 'Abd Allāh al-Badrī for the Mamluk Sultan Baybars II, in Egypt, AH 704 (AD 1304).

Although Arabic block printing dates back to the 10th century, movable type printing in Arabic has always been dependent on western technology and was originally used largely for books produced in the west for scholarly or evangelistic purposes. Most of them are represented in the Library's collection, from the *Horologium breve* (*Kitāb ṣalāt al-sawā'ī*) printed at Fano in 1514, the first book to contain Arabic printed from movable type; among them are the first edition of the famous *Canon medicinae* of Avicenna (Ibn Sīnā, *al-Qānūn fī al-ṭibb*), printed at the Typographia Medicea in Rome in 1593, and, in the Old Royal Library, the rare *Specimen characterum arabicorum* of the Plantin Press (1595), bound with a copy of Jacob Christmann's *Alphabetum arabicum*. The first printing in the Muslim world was in Hebrew: David and Samuel Ibn Nahmias printed the *Aba'ah Turim* of Jacob ben Asher at Constantinople in 1493. The first press in the east to use Arabic type (other than the Christian Lebanese missionary presses) was that of Ibrahim Muteferrika, a Hungarian convert to Islam, who edited and printed at Istanbul in AH 1145 (AD 1732–33) his Turkish *Cihan-nüma*, the first atlas printed in Arabic characters. Oddly enough, the credit for fully acclimatising printing in the Arab world is due to Napoleon: the French set up three presses in Egypt, and that of the orientalist J.J. Marcel continued to print his *Grammaire Arabe-Vulgaire* while under siege by the British and Turkish troops. This initiative led to the setting up of the first commercial press by the Khedive Muḥammad 'Alī at Bulaq in 1821.

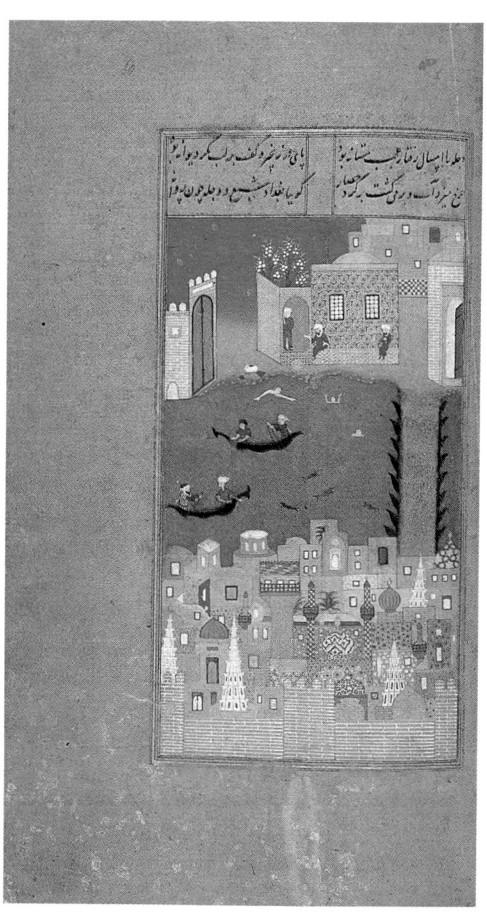

Persian had been better represented in the early collections than Arabic, and at least 150 manuscripts were in the collection before the accession of Rich's books, thanks to Hamilton, Halhed, and the bequest by John Fowler Hull of another collection made by one of the East India Company's servants, James Grant. Among Rich's manuscripts were a fine *Ẓafar-nāma*, the life of Tīmūr (Tamerlane) by Sharaf al-Dīn 'Alī Yazdī, written at Shiraz, AH 929 (AD 1423), with Safavid miniatures, in which fragments of mother-of-pearl are used as a medium, and the Ḥafiẓ written at Shiraz AH 855 (AD 1451), whose decorated pages are an early example of the 'chinoiserie' style. Other important manuscripts were added over the next 40 years, from the collections of Yule (267 manuscripts, 252 of them in Persian, mainly acquired while he was the Company's Assistant Resident in Lucknow and Delhi) and Cureton (106 Persian out of 156 manuscripts, bought in 1864). They included the anthology of poetry, completed AH 873 (AD 1468) at Shemakha in northern Azerbaijan, a rare and outstanding example of 'Turkman' illumination and book painting; the famous illustrated copy of the *Anvār-i Suhaylī* made for the Emperor Jahāngīr, AH 1016 (AD 1610–11) and three poems by Khwājū-yi Kirmānī, written by Mīr 'Alī Tabrīzī in Baghdad, AH 978 (AD 1396) for Sultan Aḥmad Jalā'ir, with paintings in the first mature Persian style by Junayd.

The *Khamsa* of Niẓāmī, copied in AH 846 (AD 1442), with 19 Timurid paintings made 50 years later at Herat, some by the most famous of all Persian painters, Bihzād, was acquired in 1864 and the Miscellany of Iskandar Sultan, an unusual illustrated Timurid work, completed AH 813–14 (AD 1410–11) in Southern Persia, came with the collection of Sir John Malcolm, the great Indian administrator and diplomat, received between 1862 and 1865. The collection of Dr Sternschuss provided the earliest then known *Shāhnāma* manuscript, 13th century, bought at Shiraz in 1848.

Opposite, above. Mesrop Xizanc'i. Portrait of Ss Peter and Paul. From an Armenian New Testament of 1218 (this illumination 1618).
Add. MS 18549, f.161*v*.

Opposite, below. Flooding in Baghdad. Poetical anthology in 'Turkman' style, completed AH 873 (AD1468) at Shemakha.
Add. MS 16561, f.60.

Right. Illuminated page from a Mamlūk Qur'ān. Egypt. AH 704 (AD1304).
Add. MS 22406, f.1v.

Sultan Mehemmed II 'Fatih'. Portrait in *Kiyafet ül-insaniye*. Ottoman Turkish, AH997 (AD1588/9).
Add. MS 7880, f.42*v*.

The Harleian collection had contained one exotic illustrated Turkish manuscript, as we have seen, and Sloane's contained another, the *Paşaname*, İbrahim Tulu'ī's verse account of the exploits of Ken'ân Paşa in Roumelia and Crimea, 1616–19, written for Sultan Murad IV, shortly after the events described and with five miniatures. With the Rich collection came *Kısas ul-enbiya*, an early 14th-century account of the lives of the prophets, a text of major philological significance, and Seyyid Lokman, *Kifayet ül-insaniye* (description of the Ottoman Sultans), dated AH 997 (AD 1588–89). Other remarkable books include the *Humayun-name*, 'Ali Çelebi's Turkish version of the *Kalīla va Dimna* fables, 16th century; *Nusretname*, Mustafa Âli's chronicle of the Ottoman conquest of Georgia in 1578, dated AH 990 (AD 1582), with miniatures in a style at once realistic and decorative; and the *Senglah*, or Turkish-Persian dictionary compiled by Muḥammad Mahdī, a secretary of Nādir Shah.

Of the languages of India, a few were represented in the early collections, and this was hardly improved (with one or two notable exceptions, such as a letter of Ḥaidar 'Alī, in Kannada, presented in 1789 and some Tamil manuscripts) in the first half of the 19th century, since the Library of the East India Company was the natural repository for the material that became available. This was particularly true of Sanskrit, although Sloane had six and Halhed added 14 more manuscripts. It was not until the 1840s that a manuscript of real quality, the illustrated *Rāmāyaṇa* made in Udaipur, for Rāṇa Jagat Siṅgh of Mewar, in 1650–53, was acquired from the Duke of Sussex's collection. The same was true for the modern Indian languages, with the romance *Pemnem* in Dakhni Urdu, made in Bijapur, 1591–1600, acquired in 1847, regarded as unquestionably the finest and most beautiful work to survive from the early Deccani period. From the collection of Horace Hayman Wilson (1786–1860), first Boden Professor of Sanskrit at Oxford and Wilkins's successor at the India Office Library, came in 1866 a notable specimen of calligraphy, the *Nasr-i Benaẓīr*, while that of another distinguished orientalist, William Erskine (1773–1852) provided the *Qiṣṣah-yi Shāh Bahrām va Bāno Ḥusn* in Gujarati characters in 1865.

Title-page of the Tamil Old Testament printed at the Danish missionary station at Tranquebar, 1777.
Or.71.d.6, p.1a.

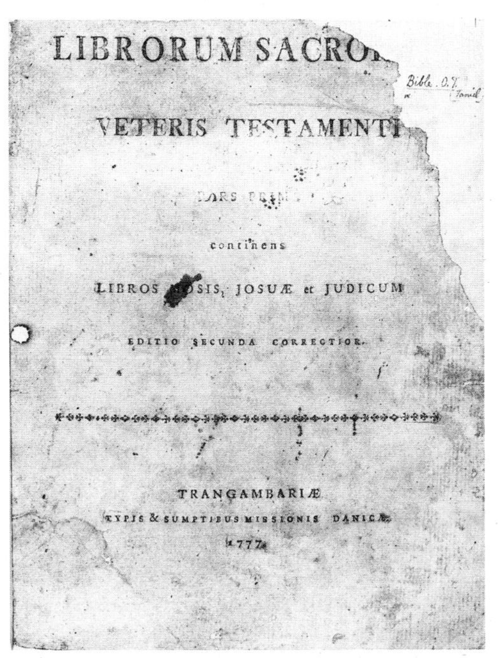
LIBRORUM SACRO
VETERIS TESTAMENTI
continens
LIBROS SIS, JOSUÆ et JUDICUM
EDITIO SECUNDA CORRECTIOR.
TRANGAMBARIÆ
TYPIS & SUMPTIBUS MISSIONIS DANICÆ
1777.

In Tamil, there is an almost complete set of the products of the press set up in 1714 at the Danish missionary station at Tranquebar by Bartholomaeus Ziegenbalg (1682–1719), whose own remarkable manuscript *Verzeichnis der Malabarischen Bücher* was bought by Sloane in 1726. Ziegenbalg was a German pietist sent out to India by King Frederick V in 1706. Through A.W. Boehm, Chaplain to Prince George of Denmark, he interested the Society for the Propagation of the Gospel in this work, for which (through the East India Company) the Society provided books, a press and types. Some of the books printed at Tranquebar were presented to Elisabeth Sophia, George I's sister, and came with the Old Royal Library, no doubt at the instance of Boehm.

It is remarkable that some of the earliest collections contained manuscripts from different parts of remote Southeast Asia, and from Sri Lanka also. Among these are the earliest dated Burmese manuscript in the British Library collections, a single palm leaf inscribed with a permit to trade granted by King Sandawizaya of Arakan in 1729, a Malay-English vocabulary dated 1731, and a Sinhalese palm-leaf manuscript with painted wood covers of *jātaka* stories. Many more manuscripts were acquired in the course of the 19th century in an increasing range of languages. From island Southeast Asia came Batak, Buginese and Javanese as well as Malay manuscripts, while from the mainland came manuscripts in Mon, Shan, Cambodian and Lao as well as in Burmese and Thai. Several fine collections formed by British scholar-administrators were also acquired. Malay manuscripts came from John Crawfurd (purchased in 1842), Burmese manuscripts from Sir Arthur Phayre (in 1886), and over 2000 Sinhalese manuscripts from Sir Hugh Neville (acquired in 1904). Few manuscripts from island Southeast Asia are illustrated but a Javanese *Pawukon* (Astrology Treatise) with delicate coloured

Siddhattha is borne away in the night by the gods. (Detail.) Ritual text from northern Thailand. Late 19th century. Wooden cover boards with lacquer and gold floral decoration.
Or. MS 14025.

figures of gods and goddesses is a notable exception. A bark divination manual with text in Mandailing-Batak and red and black diagrams is a fine example of an unusual type of manuscript still in use among the Batak soothsayers of Sumatra.

The first major document of Thai civilisation to be acquired was the album of drawings by the artist Bun Khong, *c.*1820, commissioned by James Low, an officer in the Company's service for 32 years in Malaya. These remarkable pictures illustrate the Buddhist cosmology, as well as Thai festivals and birth tales, and zodiacal pictures for divination; although designed for European use, they reflect traditional exemplars. This very full pictorial record came to the Library in 1866, after Low's death in 1852. From Vietnam, there is an important manuscript in 10 volumes of rare plays and legends written in *Nôm* script, and acquired in 1894.

Although the Chinese material remained slight, the interest in Chinese civilisation and 'chinoiserie' in the latter part of the 18th century brought in a few things – a seal, a specimen of Chinese music and a vocabulary. It was, however, one of Sloane's acquisitions, a translation of most of the New Testament, copied 'at Canton in 1737 and 1738 by order of Mr. Hodgson, junior', and subsequently given by him to Sloane that was, indirectly, the cause of the Museum's first major accession of Chinese books. It was this that provided Robert Morrison (1782–1834), the first great English sinologist, with the means of studying Chinese. The remarkable library that Morrison collected during his lifetime in China was offered for £2000 to the Museum on his death in 1834, but, having just bought the 'Alcuin Bible' for £750, it was in no position to accept, and the books went to the University of London. However, Morrison's son, John Robert Morrison (1814–43), Chinese Secretary to the Colonial Secretariat at Hong Kong, put together an equally large library, which was bought by the Foreign Office after his premature death and given to the Museum by Lord Aberdeen, then Foreign Secretary, in 1846. It largely consisted of contemporary copies of works covering a vast range of subjects: its maps and genealogical works are especially notable. This, with the Hull bequests, and 'Five cases of Chinese books brought from the seat of the late war in China as presents by Her Majesty, December 1843', remained the main resource for Far Eastern literature until the latter part of the century.

European military involvement in China in the mid-19th century led to some notable acquisitions – in particular, items looted from the Old Summer Palace (Yuan Ming Yuan, or Garden of Perfect Brightness) in 1860 by British and French troops. Sir Harry Knollys, who served under General Sir Hope Grant in 1860, and edited his memoirs which describe the arrival of the British forces at the Yuan Ming Yuan, donated leaves from a manuscript album of court costume, identical with the woodblock illustrations to the *Huang chao li qi tu shi* (*see* p. 163); and an elaborate lacquer-cased and silk-wrapped manuscript by the Qianlong Emperor himself 'On the recognition of one's faults' (*Zhi guo lun*), was apparently taken by the commander of the French troops, General Montauban, and acquired by the Library from a French dealer in 1906. Amongst other items presumed to emanate from the Old Summer Palace are a number of beautifully produced manuscript archive volumes relating to the Qing house, the *Da Qing tai zong wen huang di shi lu*, the record of the Manchu emperors dated 1638, still in its handsome original brocade binding.

When Cureton retired in 1850, his post as an orientalist remained unfilled, but Charles Rieu, who had studied under Silvestre de Sacy at Paris and joined the Museum staff as a Supernumerary Assistant in 1847, gradually took his place. In 1850, the Royal Commission recommended a separate Department of Oriental Manuscripts, which having been set up in 1867 remained until 1892, when the oriental printed books were added to its charge. In 1865 the first sinologist to join the Museum staff arrived – Robert Douglas, who succeeded Rieu in 1892. The establishment of the new Department coincided

The Holy Family, from a 10th-century Sahidic codex. Or. MS 6782, f.1v.

with the arrival of four important collections, all received in 1868.

Napier's campaign in 1867 against King Theodore of Ethiopia was an opportunity not missed by the Trustees, who sent R.R. Holmes, son of John Holmes, with the expedition. After the fall of Magdala a library of about 1000 volumes was found, of which 350 were selected by Holmes. They included a number of illuminated manuscripts, among them a hymn-book, 18th century, and a very decorative gospel-book, showing marked signs of western influence. On Archdeacon Tattam's death in 1868, the Museum purchased a number of books from his library, adding the first substantial body of Coptic books to its collection. In 1883 a further large find was made in Egypt; the bulk went to Paris, but several important manuscripts came to London. Finally, E. Wallis Budge, who joined the then Department of Egyptian and Assyrian Antiquities in 1883, brought back another cache discovered at Atripe in 1888. From these, the Library acquired the early Sahidic biblical codex on papyrus, 4th century, the small Apocalypse on vellum, 5th century and the 10th-century illuminated codex.

Colonel George William Hamilton (1867–68) had amassed a considerable quantity of Persian and Indian manuscripts after the Indian Mutiny, many from the library of the Kings of Oudh at Lucknow, of which 352 volumes were bought by the Museum. Others followed from the collections of Sir Henry Rawlinson (1877), Sir Henry Elliot (1878) and Garcin de Tassy (1878). Sidney Churchill, Persian Secretary at the British Legation at Tehran, acting as agent for the Museum, purchased 240 manuscripts between 1883 and 1895. Throughout the period, Sir Augustus Wollaston Franks (1826–97), Keeper of British and Medieval Antiquities and the most catholic collector of his time, added generously to the Sanskrit holdings.

The Department today can take pride in a collection of matchless importance in all branches of Central and South Asian literature. The oldest are the several hundred wooden tablets in Prakrit, of the 2nd to 3rd centuries, found in China with many other wooden documents, such as the letters from two Buddhist monks, but there are also the oldest surviving complete Sanskrit text, a Buddhist medical work, written on Central Asian paper in the 4th century, and the earliest paper manuscript from South Asia, the Lotus Sutra from Gilgit, 6th–7th century. Another unusual early survival is a leaf of a *pothi* manuscript of a Buddhist text in Gupta script in ink on silk, 6th century, found in a *stupa* at Bash-Koyumal in Xinjiang.

Manuscripts in Soghdian script derived from Syriac, and brought to Central Asia by Nestorian Christians, include the *Nīlakaṇṭha-dhāraṇī* in alternate lines of Soghdian and Gupta (Indian) script, *c.*650–750; another bilingual work is the block-printed *dhāraṇī* in Uyghur with Gupta glosses, *c.*1000. Many of these came from the famous expeditions made by Sir Aurel Stein to China and Central Asia.

There is also an important collection of illuminated Buddhist manuscripts from eastern India and Nepal. Among them are three early palm-leaf manuscripts from eastern India, the *Kāraṇḍavyūhasūtra*, 1100, and the two copies of *Prajñāpāramitā*, one datable *c.*1130–50, with 69 miniatures, and the other of great importance for its beauty and for its firm provenance, from the monastery of Vikramaśīla, with six miniatures. Many of the finest examples of this kind come from Nepal, among them a manuscript of two Sanskrit hymns, written in gold ink on blue paper, with six miniatures, dated 1184, the earliest known example of its type. One such *pothi* manuscript has a fine wooden cover showing the Buddha preaching to two disciples, *c.*1120. The *Pañcarakṣā* from Kathmandu, dated 1676, is a decorative example of later Nepali work. Later manuscripts from India proper include the *Sarvasiddhāntatattvacūḍāmani*, a finely illuminated treatise on the astronomical systems of India, Islam and Europe masquerading as a horoscope, by Durgāśaṅkara Pathaka, Benares, *c.*1839.

There are also examples of illuminated manuscripts in the other languages

The fabulous region of Himavant, from a Burmese Buddhist cosmology. Illustrated paper book in 59 folds. 19th century.
Or.Ms 14004, ff.34–35.

of South Asia. In Assamese, there are two texts, the *Dharmapurāṇa* and *Brahmakhaṇḍa*, written on large sheets of aloe bark and heavily illustrated, both presentation copies to kings of Assam, in 1736 and 1836 respectively; in Rajasthani, the *Hitopadeśa*, the famous collection of fables, illuminated for Jasvant Singh of Uniara, 1761; in Hindi, a *rāgamālā* set with illustrations of musical modes, *c.*1760; in Oriya, the *Rādhākṛṣṇakeli*, the tale of the love of Krishna and Radha, illustrated, on palm leaves, *c.*1630; and in Urdu, Nuṣratī's *Qaṣīda*, a panegyric addressed to 'Abd Allāh Quṭbshāh of Golconda, *c.*1650, the margins of its pages decorated with alternating floral patterns and arabesque and geometric designs in gold and colours.

Tibetan manuscripts of great textual significance include the *Arja-deva-vajra-kalisvari-nama-mantra-tantra-raja* (the *rgyud 'bum* of Vairocana), a 17th–18th-century copy of one of the first series of translations done in Tibet of the primary Buddhist texts.

A unique and very fine work is the almost complete set of the 108 volumes of the *Kanjuṛ (bKa'-'gyur)* or Buddhist Canon, written in manuscript in gold ink on black paper in the 17th century. Later calligraphy can be seen in the collected works of Five Sakyapa Lamas, an 18th- or 19th-century copy of a text produced as a gift for the Mongol Emperor, Kublai Khan (1260–94). It contains the early history and doctrine of the Sakyapa (*Sa-skya-pa*) school of Tibetan Buddhism (the third oldest sect), as set out in the works of five of its hereditary Head Lamas. A Sakyapa Head Lama submitted Tibet to Mongol suzerainty in 1244, and was appointed Regent. The calligraphy of this manuscript is especially noteworthy. It is written in three separate scripts: first in *lantsa* (decorative Sanskrit characters) in black ink, followed by a phonetic transliteration into Tibetan characters in red, and finally a translation into Tibetan in cursive script in black.

Printing from carved wooden blocks was extensively practised in Tibet: an example is the *Ma-ni- bKa'-'bum* (Hundred Thousand Precepts) produced in the 16th or 17th century.

Two unusual items are the edicts (*bKa'-shog*) written in manuscript on yellow silk and issued by the Fifth Dalai Lama and the Third Panchen Lama in the 17th and 18th centuries respectively. Both of these silk scrolls are illuminated, and written in an elegant Tibetan script: the edict of the Third Panchen Lama includes an interlinear translation in Mongolian. The edict of the Fifth Dalai Lama was issued at Lhasa in 1656, and is a proclamation reserving grazing rights within the Nag-chu-kha (Black-water) area of Central Tibet, defined in detail by reference to its boundaries, for the use of local and other nomads specifically authorised by the Tibetan Government to exercise such rights. The edict of the Third Panchen Lama was issued at Tashilhunpo in 1775. It constitutes a passport authorising safe travel within and beyond Tibet by the monk for whom it was issued, and invites donations on the occasion of a monastic degree-giving ceremony. It was issued at the behest of the Abbot of Ga-Idan monastery, whose predecessor had been a special teacher of the Seventh Dalai Lama, who had in turn taught the Third Panchen Lama.

As recently as 1984, a rare collection of 16 manuscripts relating to the indigenous Bon religion of Tibet was added to the British Library collection.

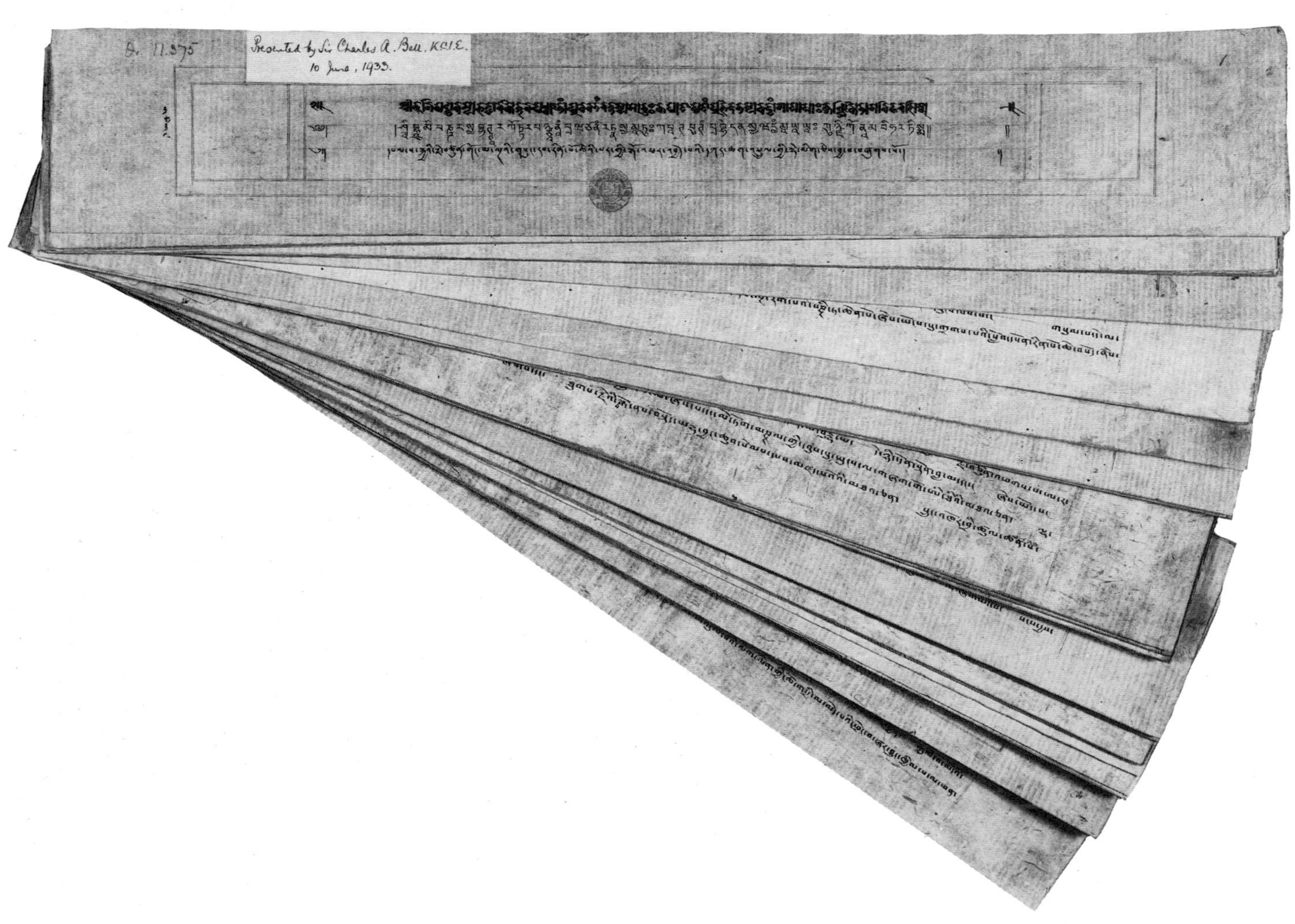

The works of the Five Sakypapa Lamas. Tibetan, 18th or 19th century.
Or. 11375.

Copper charter in Tamil and Sanskrit, recording a grant in the year AD 769/770.
Ind.Ch.4.

This acquisition consists of manuscript copies of earlier works dating from the 15th or 16th century to the present day.

The variety of media for the transmission of texts in the subcontinent is considerable, and one not so far mentioned is metal plates: the Library holds a series of 67 charters incised on copper in a variety of Indian scripts and from various parts of India, and from as far away as Java. One such is in Tamil (Vaṭṭeḻuttu) and Sanskrit (Grantha) and records a grant in the year 769/70. Or.12018 is a copper plate with an inscription in Telugu on one side and representations of the seven crafts and their assistant divinities on the other, of late medieval date. Even more distinguished are the Maunggun plates, long strips of gold, inscribed with Buddhist texts in Pali in early Pyu script (5th century), which were discovered near Prome in Burma in 1896.

Burmese manuscripts are often decorative and use various media. A fine and rare example is the Buddhist ordination text, or *Kammavācā*, with decoration and text in inlaid mother-of-pearl. There are also elaborately decorated *Kammavācā* manuscripts on ivory and on metal sheets, as well as on the more usual gilded and lacquered palm leaves. An 18th-century *Kammavācā* is particularly notable for its delicate interlinear decorations of leaves and birds.

Silvering was also used to decorate Burmese palm leaves, as in a text of the Buddha's first sermon. Unique to Burma are manuscript wrapping ribbons with dedicatory inscriptions and Pali verses woven into them by a process which is now a lost art. The illustrated folding books (*parabaik*) are vivid in colour and execution. Many illustrate scenes from the life of the Buddha or the *jātaka* stories of his previous lives. Most date from the 19th century but two finely-painted late 18th-century manuscripts of the life of the Buddha, collected originally by Henry Burney, British Resident at the Court of Ava from 1829–37, have recently been acquired. One of the finest examples of Burmese manuscript painting is the huge folding book, *Pageant of King Mindon*, dated 1867, while an illustrated copy of the *Rāmāyaṇa* (*c.*1870) is important not just for its artistic quality but as one of the few known Burmese manuscripts depicting this Indian epic.

Some of the Sinhalese palm-leaf manuscripts are illustrated, such as the *jātaka* (birth tale) of Buddha's former life as Vidhura, *c.*1830. Another interesting object from Sri Lanka is the pictorial scroll *c.*1769–1805 of the procession of Buddha's tooth, which was influenced, like Low's Thai pictures, by European style. Other Thai manuscripts include the 18th-century (as such, unusually early) *Mahābuddhaguṇa* in Pali, in folding paper form with fine illustrations, or palm-leaves such as the *Padatthayojanā* on 449 leaves with mother-of-pearl inlaid boards, *c.*1830. An example of similarly elaborate work from Laos is a *Kammavācā*, with raised gilt and inlaid cover boards.

All these manifestations of the art and literature of Buddhism in and near India are a reminder that the early Mughal rulers of India exercised an alien, though generally tolerant, hegemony. Although local languages, scripts and artistic styles had their influence, the works copied and illustrated for the Mughals were in Persian. Most of the Library's major monuments of Mughal work have been acquired since 1867. Outstanding is the great *Khamsa* of

Above. The Pageant of King Mindon. Burmese, 1867. Or. MS 12013, f.1.

Opposite. Majnūn visited in the desert by his mother and Salim. From the *Khamsa* of Niẓāmī, made for the Emperor Akbar, completed AH 1005 (AD 1595). Or. MS 12208, f.150r.

Below. Manuscript wrapping ribbon with woven verses. Upper Burma, 19th century. Or. MS 11767/ribbon

Niẓāmī, made for the Emperor Akbar and finished AH 1004 (AD 1595), with 38 miniatures and marginal decoration throughout of birds, plants and mythical beasts, bequeathed to the British Museum in 1958 by C.W. Dyson-Perrins. Other superb imperial manuscripts are the lavishly illuminated – if now incomplete – *Dārābnāma* (Exploits of Dārāb) made for Akbar *c.*1580–85, the *Bāburnāma* (Life of the Emperor Bābur), with 143 paintings, and the *Akbarnāma*, with 40 miniatures, completed *c.*1602–5, just before Akbar's death, with slightly later marginal decoration on the title-page. Two earlier manuscripts of great quality are the *Gulistān* with pictures partly Mughal and partly Bukhara work, 1567, and the *Sharafnāma*, part of the Alexander Romance of Niẓāmī, made for Nuṣrat Shah, Sultan of Bengal, at Gaur in 1531–32.

Of the Persian manuscripts which were the antecedents of the great illuminated Mughal books, many had already entered the collection before the Department of Oriental Manuscripts was formed in 1867. Since then, however, the activity of Sidney Churchill, the Museum's Tehran agent, provided more. There is a notable early text of the *Kalīla va Dimna*, the most durable of all fable collections, this copy finished at Shiraz in AH 707 (AD 1307); its miniatures, apparently unique, have great, if primitive, charm. A later Shiraz manuscript is the four narrative poems, dated AH 800 (AD 1397), with spectacular miniatures, rare examples of their style. One of the greatest of the

اندام دلش شکسته شد خورد
ز اندیشه او بدست و پا مرد
سر تا قدمش بمهر مالید
بر سر و رخ پدر بمالید
گشت پسر پر ز غبارش
گه کند ز پای خسته خارش
گه شست باب دیده رویش
گه برد بشانه کلک مویش
می برد بهر کناره دست
گاه آبله سود و که ورم بست
چون کرد ز روی مهربانی
با او ز تلطف آنچه دانی

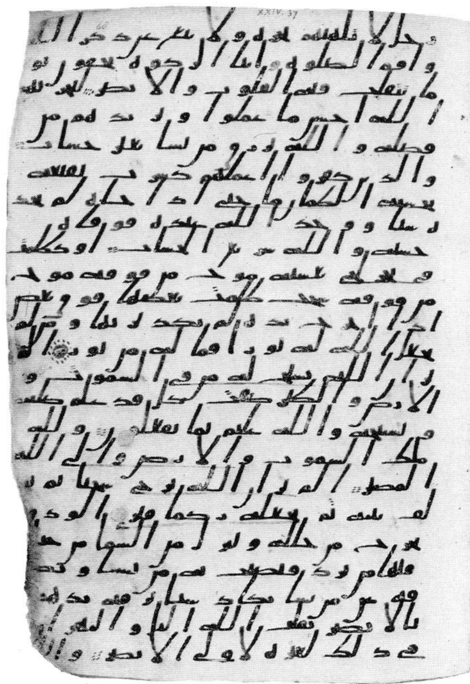

Page from a very early manuscript of the Qur'ān, written in Medina or Mecca, probably in the 8th century AD.
Or. MS 2165, f.67v.

later Herat School manuscripts is another *Khamsa* of Niẓāmī dated AH 900 (AD 1494–95), whose 21 Bihzād studio miniatures include some by the master himself. Finally there is yet another *Niẓāmī*, perhaps the most famous of all Persian manuscripts, made at Tabriz in AH 946–50 (AD 1530–43) for the Safavid Shah Ṭahmāsp; of its 17 miniatures, 14 are contemporary and of legendary quality, while the three added in AH 1086 (AD 1675) are outstanding of their kind; the binding is later still, but an admirable example of Qajar lacquer work.

The Turkish collections contain one remarkable manuscript with pictures strongly influenced by the Persian Tabriz school of illumination, the *Garayib us-sıgar*, a collection of early lyric poems by the writer, scholar and statesman 'Alī Shīr Navā'ī, finely illuminated and with six miniatures, in the Eastern Turkish literary language (Chagatay, ancestor of modern Uzbek) *c.*1520. One of over 100 manuscripts in the important E.J.W. Gibb Bequest (1901) was the *Divan* of Baki, *c.*1570, with nine paintings, several of which appear to portray the poet himself. To these may be added the very rare history of Chingiz Khan and his descendants, *Tevariḫ-i güzide* (selected chronicles), Füzuli's *Hadikat us-suada* (Lives of the Prophets and Muḥammad's family) of the 16th–17th centuries, and 'Five Poems' of Şeyḫî, late 15th century, one of the very few manuscripts from the earliest period of Ottoman painting. One later graphic monument of Turkish history is the collection of 1800 photographs in 51 albums, selected from Sultan Abdülhamid II's collection of over 30,000, depicting numerous aspects of contemporary Turkey, from the treasures of the Topkapı Palace to a group of anatomy students complete with cadaver, presented in 1893 by the Sultan, together with about 300 printed books, all in uniform polychrome bindings.

The Library's Arabic manuscripts have increased significantly in number in the last 120 years. Sir Henry Rawlinson, Alexander Jaba, Russian Consul at Erzerum, Sir Charles Murray, Consul General in Egypt from 1844, Alfred von Kremer, Dr Edward Glaser, who acquired manuscripts in Yemen, and E.W. Lane, the Arabic lexicographer, all made notable contributions. Others came from the Stowe collection, the Curzon manuscripts bequeathed by his granddaughter Baroness Zouche in 1918, and the so-called Sultan's Library from Constantinople (1920); between 1926 and 1934 R.S. Greenshields gave a number of fine illuminated manuscripts, mostly Arabic, with some Persian.

The important collection of Qur'ān manuscripts now include the very early copy in *al-Mā'il* script, probably 8th century, and written in Mecca or Medina and an early illuminated copy in Kufic made in North Africa, 9th century. Early eastern manuscripts include one in Qarmatian Kufic, 11th–12th century, several in *Maghribī* script from Morocco, AH 975 (AD 1568), and Spain, 12th century, and in the elegant *Rayḥānī* script, Egypt 14th century, and India or Afghanistan, 16th century. Among the finest in the world are two in *Muḥaqqaq* script, with particularly fine illumination, a copy of section 25 in gold *Muḥaqqaq* script, made for the Īl-Khānid Sultan Ūljāytū, Iraq, AH 710 (AD 1310), and the complete Qur'ān made in Egypt in the 14th century with more than 2000 unique ornaments; and a most splendid Qur'ān in seven volumes copied in gold *thuluth* script by Muḥammad ibn al-Waḥīd, the great court calligrapher to Sultan Baybars, which is the only complete work in his hand to have survived.

Among secular manuscripts, the Dioscorides Materia Medica (*Kitab Dioscorides fī mawādd al-'ilāj*) dated AH 735 (AD 1334), the Aristotelian *De natura animalium (Na't al-ḥayawān wa-manāfi'ihi)*, 13th century and the *Ṣuwar a-kawākib al-thābitah*, a treatise on the fixed stars, by 'Abd al-Raḥmān ibn 'Umar al-Ṣūfī, 14th century, all reflect the importance of science in the Muslim world. The *Maqāmāt al-Ḥarīrī*, or book of adventures, is represented by the second oldest copy, AH 557 (AD 1162), inscribed by the grandson of the author, Qāsim ibn 'Alī al-Ḥarīrī, and the illustrated copies of *'Ajā'ib al-*

Right. View of Istanbul. A photograph from Sultan Abdülhamid II's collection. Late 19th century.
Sultan Abdülhamid Albums, no.8.

makhlūqāt wa-gharā'ib al-mawjūdāt (Wonders of Creation) which date back to the late 12th and 16th century. History provides the chronicle of the campaigns of Muḥammad, the *Kitāb al-Maghāzī* of al-Waqidī, AH 564 (AD 1169), and *Zubdat al-Tawārīkh*, a history of the Seljuks' dynasty by Sayyid Ṣadr al-Dīn 'Alī ibn al-lmām Abū al-Fawāris Nāṣir, a unique 14th-century text. Among the important biographical collections is the unique autograph *Wafayāt al-A'yān* of Ibn Khallikān, AH 672 (AD 1273), and among dictionaries the lexicon of Ibn Duraid, in a copy partly made in the 10th century, almost during the author's lifetime.

The Hebrew collections had also grown markedly, their scope broadened by acquisitions from outside the European market, which provided most of the early treasures. In 1882, a large collection of Karaite manuscripts, originating partly at Hit near Baghdad and partly in Cairo, and biblical texts in Hebrew written in Arabic characters, were acquired in Jerusalem. The major part of the collection of Moses Gaster, born in Rumania and subsequently Chief Rabbi of the Spanish and Portuguese Synagogue in London, was acquired in 1925. The Cairo Genizah, some of which came to the British Museum, provided part of the lost Hebrew text of Ecclesiasticus, and also the autograph text in the hand of the great 12th-century scholar and canonist, Moses Maimonides.

From these and other sources have come the 10th-century Pentateuch from Iraq, and another from San'a in Yemen, dated 1469, with the 'carpet' pages characteristic of oriental manuscripts from whose ancestors derive the similar pages found in insular manuscripts like the Lindisfarne Gospels. A number of fine 14th-century manuscripts include two illuminated *Haggadot*, one from Catalonia, *c.*1360, the other probably from Barcelona, *c.*1350, and the Law Code or legal decisions of Isaiah ben Elijah of Trani in Apulia, written and illuminated in Italy and dated 1374. The great Lisbon Bible, written by Samuel Ibn Musa and completed in 1482, with its beautiful illumination and micrography, was bought from Benjamin Cohen of Bukhara. There is also an elaborate *Ketubah* or marriage contract, a masterpiece of early Italian Baroque, made at Modena in 1557. A most unusual recent acquisition, bought at the auction of the great collection of David Solomon Sassoon in 1975, is the *Fathnāma*, a poetical paraphrase in Persian (but written in Hebrew characters) of the books of Joshua, Ruth and Samuel by 'Imrānī of Shiraz, with pictures by a Persian artist, 17th century.

Below. Page from an Arabic treatise on the fixed stars, *Ṣuwar al-kawakīb al-thābitah*. 13th century AD.
Or. MS 5323. f.45*v*.

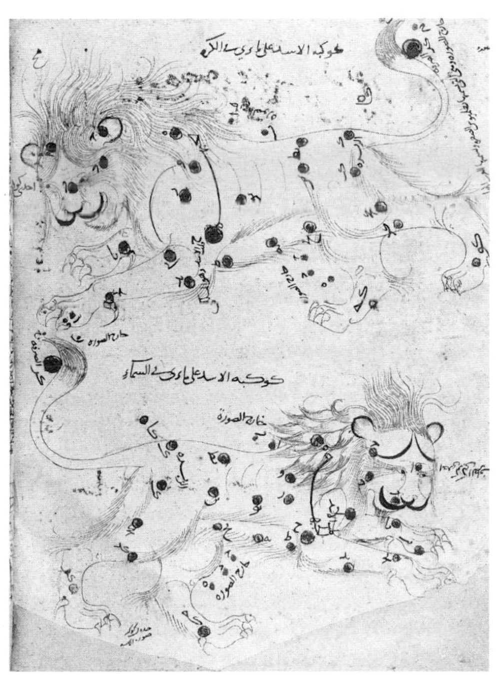

Above. Coloured woodblock print from the Ten Bamboo Studio, Nanjing, *c.*1643. [See page 164].
Or.59.a.10.

Opposite. A keepsake from the cloud gallery. Painting on paper. Chinese, 1750. [See page 164.]
Add. MS 22689.

When Sir Robert Douglas (as he became) succeeded Rieu in 1892 and the oriental printed books joined the manuscripts in the newly constituted Department of Oriental Manuscripts and Printed Books, he was well placed to take charge of the last great accretion of material, this time from the Far East. The Chinese and Japanese collections, hitherto of moderate importance, were now to become, like the others, among the greatest in the world. Douglas had already produced a catalogue of the Chinese books (then over 20,000) in 1877, and followed it in 1898 with another of Japanese books, which had grown enormously through the acquisition of the collections of Philipp Franz von Siebold (1868), Sir Ernest Satow (1884) and William Anderson (1882–1900). The Stein collection (*see* below) then transformed the Chinese collections and engaged first Douglas and then Lionel Giles (Keeper, 1929–40). Lionel Barnett, Keeper 1908–29, maintained the tradition of scholarship in the Semitic and Indian languages, and in more recent time Kenneth Gardner (Keeper 1957–70) has achieved the same position in Japanese.

The preeminence of British holdings of masterpieces in all the book arts of South Asia, and those of the British Library in particular, is due to one fact: the almost two centuries of British rule in India. The simple need for information about an unfamiliar country grew to embrace a sympathetic interest in every aspect of the civilisation of the subcontinent, which spread to its cultures, the Muslim culture of the Near and Middle East, and the Buddhist culture of Central Asia. The British Library is now the major beneficiary of this interest. Similarly, its preeminence among the world's repositories of the oldest recorded documents of Central Asia and the Far East is due to one fact: the extraordinary collection of material brought back from Central Asia by Sir Marc Aurel Stein in three successive expeditions, 1900–1, 1906–8 and 1913–16. Stein's journeys are recorded in his own great volumes, and the story of the archaeological exploration of the area between Kashgar and Dunhuang between 1890 and 1930 is told in Peter Hopkirk's *Foreign devils on the silk road*. Suffice it to say here that what was found transformed not only the department's collections of early Asian material, but the whole history of the documents of human civilisation.

Some of the most remarkable discoveries were, as we have seen, documents in scripts and languages other than Chinese, and the oldest of these (2nd–3rd century), from Niya, are in Prakrit written in *kharoshthi* script on wooden boards (paper, perfected in China by AD 105, had yet to acquire currency in Turkestan). The oldest Chinese documents, however, are not from the Stein collection, but the Couling-Chalfant collection of oracle bones, probably originating from sites of the Shang capital at Anyang, and dating from *c.*1000 BC. But the main wealth of the Stein collection is the astonishing mass of documents from the 'Caves of a Thousand Buddhas' at Dunhuang, consisting of some 7000 relatively complete scrolls and as many fragments. It is hard, even now, fully to comprehend the magnitude and antiquity of this cache: every scrap of paper predates the earliest paper document in the west, some by seven centuries. The vast majority of these are manuscript, but among them are 20 printed documents, of which one, the world-famous 'Diamond Sutra' of AD 868, is the earliest complete and dated printed 'book' in the world. It cannot, in fact, be by any means the earliest such document ever made: it is 16 feet long, with an elaborate frontispiece and a sophisticated text layout, and the colophon, which dates it precisely (11 May 868) also records that it was printed for free, and therefore presumably wide, distribution; none of this suggests a process then primitive. There are other early examples of printing in the department, notably the *Lei feng ta* scroll of 975, found walled up in the Lei feng pagoda in Hangzhou, or the sheet of multiple stamped images of Buddha (whose multiplication was itself an act of piety) from Dunhuang, perhaps 8th century; but none are as important as the Diamond Sutra.

The manuscripts from Dunhuang consist mainly of Buddhist devotional works, although the secular texts, primarily administrative documents, provide a valuable historical record of the area in the 6th to 10th centuries. The documents on paper go back to the early 5th century or earlier; the *Prātimokṣasūtra* ('rules for monks') is the earliest to bear a date – 406. One particularly interesting survival is the *Ratnakūṭaparipṛcchasūtra* ('Gem-heap Sutra'), 8th century, still attached to its original wooden roller and with its blue silk tie, a tribute to the preservative qualities of the dry cold of the dark cave in which it was kept for so long. The *Vajracchedikā Prajñāpārimitāsūtra* (Diamond-cutter perfection of wisdom) of the 10th century contains four pages of powerful drawings, and the *Saddharmapuṇḍarīkasūtra*, 9th–10th century, contains drawings in ink tinted with colours. The *Fo shuo shi wang jing* (Sutra of the 10 kings) has some splendidly vigorous drawings in the same style. All this can give only the merest suggestion of the wealth of material, which will continue to engage scholarly attention for years to come.

Besides the Stein collection, the department also holds some 600 other

Woodblock illustration from the 1728 imperial encyclopaedia, *Gu jin tu shu ji cheng*. 125023.b.1.

manuscripts and 200 examples of printing of the Song, Yuan and Ming dynasties. There are two notable examples of the Yuan dramas, *Pi pa ji* (Romance of the lute), 1610, and *Po yao ji* (The disused kiln), *c.*1573–1620, both printed from woodblocks with lively illustrations. The Taoist movement is represented by the *Yu shu jing*, an illustrated Sutra, 15th century, and the *Xing ming gui zhi*, a 'manual of inner cultivation', 17th century. The collection of maps, begun with the Morrison collection, contains a scroll map of the Yellow River, dated 1704 and manuscript maps of Peking and the Forbidden City, 18th–19th century.

One of the greatest printing enterprises in China was the first complete *tripitaka* or Buddhist canon, printed in its entirety in 5048 *juan* (sections or volumes) in Sichuan in 972–83. The department's earliest example is one *juan* from the edition published during the transition between the Song and Yuan dynasties, printed in 6362 *juan* between 1231 and 1322.

The many illustrated books in the collection contain examples of different techniques of illustration, such as the imperially commissioned manual of cotton cultivation and manufacture of 1808, both in printed woodblock form and 'rubbed' from engraved stone slabs. Another massive enterprise was the imperial encyclopaedia, *Gu jin tu shu ji cheng*, in 32 sections and 10,000 volumes, with woodblock illustrations and the text printed from movable copper types in 1728 in an edition of 64 copies. The Library's copy is the only complete example of the first edition outside China, and was purchased from an un-named 'Imperial Prince' by the 'book jackals' of Mr Mayers of the British Embassy in 1877. Imperial documents of this sort are visually striking, as are the album of the journeys of the Qianlong Emperor (1711–99) with beautiful paintings, or the illustrated inventory of court objects, related to Jiang Pu's *Huang chao li qu tu shi*, 2nd ed. 1766, with delicate woodcut illustrations. One quite exceptional item is the poems of the Kangxi Emperor on his summer resort at Chengde, illustrated with copper-engravings by the Italian Jesuit Matteo Ricci, 1711–12.

The 'export' albums for the European market are a familiar and colourful feature of Chinese art well represented in the collection, notably the collections of trades and occupations, a Hogarthian 'Rake's Progress' illustrating the awful effects of opium or the process of silk manufacture. Finally, there are some fine examples of that most characteristic of all Chinese arts, coloured woodblock printing, notably albums from the 'Ten Bamboo' studio *c.*1643 and the Mustard Seed garden painting manual, *Jie zi yuan hua zhuan*, *c.*1679–1701, and the finest picture manuscripts, such as *Yun tai xian rui* (keepsake from the cloud gallery), 1750.

The striking achievements of type-makers, block-cutters and book artists in Korea have long been overshadowed by the better-known productions of China and Japan. Nineteenth-century western scholarship failed to recognise the elegant, large-format editions of Chinese philosophical and historical texts which were added to the collections as Korean, and they assumed them to be Chinese or Japanese. A large number of fine illustrated works, including examples of virtuous conduct and edifying tales of rewards and retribution, were acquired in the late 19th and early 20th centuries.

Korea is known, above all, as the first society to perfect and develop movable-type printing. Although the invention of movable type originated in China in the 11th century, no pre-15th-century Chinese example has survived. It was in Korea in the 13th century that the invention took root and later flourished. The earliest examples pre-date Gutenberg's invention in the west, and the Library is fortunate to possess a volume set in *Kabinja* type, the 'Commentaries on the Spring and Autumn Annals', printed in 1434. Woodblock printing had arrived from China (whence Korea had hitherto imported books) in the 8th century: the catalogue (1248) of the edition of the *Tripitaka*, printed from 81,137 wood-blocks (which still survive) between 1236 and 1251, is in the collection, together with a fascicle of the *Tripitaka* text printed

Entertainments in Kyoto. One of a set of 50 paintings brought back from Japan by Engelbert Kaempfer in 1693. No date known (*c.*1661–72).
Add. MS 5252, f.37.

from blocks now conserved at Haein temple in Korea. The 'Jubilee of the Queen of Korea' of 1869 is a very handsome example of Yi dynasty ceremonial book painting and the vast 19th-century scroll map of Korea is a fine and unique example of its kind.

The first Japanese books ever seen in Europe were probably those the German physician Engelbert Kaempfer (1651–1716) brought back from Japan in 1693. Kaempfer is best known for his *History of Japan* which first popularised that country in the west. About 60 items were listed as sold to Sir Hans Sloane after Kaempfer's death and these are now in the British Library. All are printed materials except for a set of 50 colourful paintings by artists of the Tosa–Sumiyoshi school *c.*1661–72. Maps are also well represented, as a result of Kaempfer having made two return trips to Edo, accompanying the Dutch on their tribute-paying missions. Among the most celebrated has been the *Nagasaki ezu* of 1680, a hand-coloured woodcut map of Nagasaki. Recently, a route map in two rolls, mentioned in Kaempfer's *History of Japan*, has been discovered. It is one of the earliest route maps of Japan provisionally entitled *Tozai kairiku no zu* and it was printed around 1672. The acquisition, in 1868, of the collection of Dr Phillip Franz von Siebold who, a century after Kaempfer, was medical officer at Deshima, instantly enhanced the British Museum Japanese collection. The Siebold collection includes some 125 manuscripts, in addition to over 50 hand-drawn provincial maps. Printing and publishing in Japan developed relatively early which gave Von Siebold's manuscript collection a special significance. Some of the archival documents relate to contemporary political intrigues, laws, and the inquisition registers of native-born Christians; others reflect Von Siebold's scientific background and interest in technical matters.

Illuminated manuscripts of popular tales of medieval Japan, known as *Nara ehon* (Nara picture-books), have long been popular with western collectors because of their manifest charm and artistic merit. There are 25 such works in the British Library. The 16th-century *Ise monogatari zue* ('Tale of Ise in pictures'), the *Taishokkan*, late 16th century, and *Yuriwaka daijin*, early 17th century, are fine examples. They tell miraculous stories, with flowing calligraphy and fabulous pictures, embellished with gold and silver.

A more celebrated part of the Japanese collections is the more than 300 rare specimens of early printing acquired from Sir Ernest Satow (1843–1928), the British diplomat who became the doyen of Japanese bibliographers. Satow's career as a collector benefited from his close friendship with some discerning Japanese dealers and erudite bibliophiles and by the opportunities created by the Meiji Restoration. His first term of office in 1862–87 coincided with a turbulent era in which traditional Japanese art treasures became more readily available, as westernisation swept the country. The rare editions he amassed represent every phase in the Japanese achievement in book-making. They extend from the Buddhist monopoly in block-printing from the 12th to the 16th centuries, through the secularisation of production with the aid of movable type between the 1590s and the 1640s, to the beginning of commercial publishing in the 17th century.

Among the earliest items in the Satow collection is *Bonmókyō bosatsu shinjibon*, a basic Vinaya work on disciplinary rules which was first printed at the Hōryūji temple in Nara in 1220. This example of *Kasuga-ban* (Kasuga

Mother and child weaving in the countryside, with Mt. Fuji in the background. Print by Hokusai, from *Shunkyō-jō*, 'Album of Spring Amusement', Probably Edo, *c.*1798.
16099.c.87.

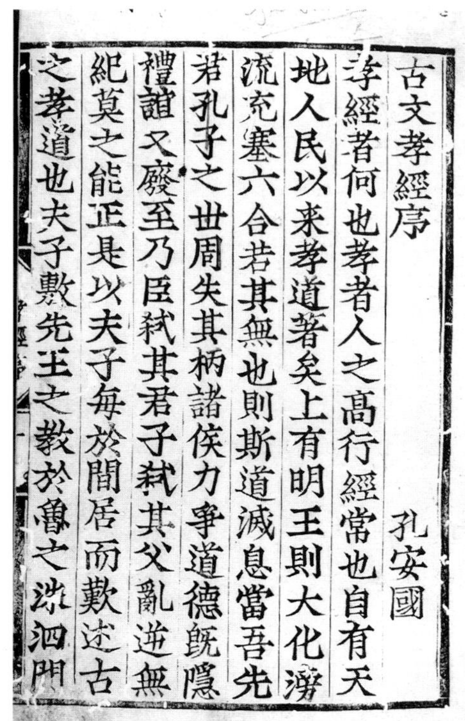
古文孝經序

孔安國

孝經者何也孝者人之高行經常也自有天地人民以来孝道著矣上有明王則大化滂流充塞六合若其無也則斯道滅息當吾先君孔子之世周失其柄諸侯力争道德既隱禮誼又廢至乃臣弑其君子弑其父亂逆無紀莫之能正是以夫子每於閒居而歎述古之孝道也夫子敷先王之教於魯之洙泗門

Opening page of the imperial edition of the Confucian 'Four Books', 1599.
15210 e.11.

NIFON NO COTOBA TO

Hiſtoria uo narai xiran to FOSSVRV FITO NO TAME-NI XEVA NI YAVA RAGVETA-RV FEIQE NO MONOGATARI.

IESVS NO COMPANHIA NO Collegio Amacuſa ni voite Superiores no go men-qio to xite core uo fan ni qizamu mono nari. Go xuxxe yori M. D. L. XXXXII.

Title-page of *Feiqe no monogatari*, printed by the Jesuit press in Amakusa, 1593.
Or.59.11.1.

imprints) is typical of fine Japanese Buddhist printing, noted for its quality of paper, glossy jet-black ink and skilful wood-block cutting. The *Shōsan jōdo busshōjukyō*, the principal sutra of the *jōdo* (pure land) sect, printed in 1280, is unique.

Movable-type printing, though a short-lived phase in the history of Japanese book culture, was of considerable significance, so much so that the number of such books in a library has become the yardstick by which the quality of its antiquarian holdings are judged. The British Library has over 70 examples in the Satow collection alone. They include the magnificent 1599 imperial edition of the Confucian 'Four Books', bound together with the 'Classic of Filial Piety' of the same date. The *Saga-bon* editions printed by the private Saga Press in 1608, are represented by a copy of *Ise monogatari*. This is one of the earliest of the classical literary works of Japanese authorship to have been printed and illustrated with woodcuts. In *Tsukihi no sōshi*, on the other hand, we see the beginning and development of popular fiction. The British Library is fortunate to have a unique copy of this work, printed in the early 17th century. *Feique no monogatari*, the historical epic *Heike monogatari*, printed in roman letters by the Jesuit Press in Amakusa in 1593, is another fine, unique example of Japanese movable-type printing. This was bound together with the first Japanese translation of Aesop's Fables and a collection of moral maxims, the *Kinkushū*.

Since Satow's time, the Japanese antiquarian collection has been further enriched by the acquisition of a unique set of eight *Hyakumantō darani* ('Million pagoda charms') printed between 764 and 770 by the command of the Empress Shōtoku. These are the earliest printed documents with authenticated dates to have survived. The earliest Japanese printed book in the British Library is *Jōyuishikiron jukki*, a Buddhist commentary printed towards the latter part of the Heian period, *c.*1170–80.

Early illustrated books with black-and-white woodcuts are well represented in the Kaempfer, Siebold and Satow collections. Indeed, from the mid-17th century onwards, virtually every newly published work carried some wood-block illustrations. Ihara Saikaku's *Kōshoku ichidai otoko* ('The Rake's Progress') heralded the golden age of illustrated popular novels. William Anderson provided the impetus for a comprehensive collection of illustrated albums and books printed from multi-coloured blocks. *Jinkō-ki*, a mathematical treatise produced in the Kanei era, 1624–43, is among the earliest to have made use of colour printing. More sophisticated experiments followed and where effected in private publications such as *Chichi no on*, a *haiku* anthology published in 1730 in memory of Ichikawa Danjurō I, the *kabuki* actor. Colour printing reached its first apogee in Suzuki Harunobu's celebrated *Ehon seirō bijin awase* of 1770, depicting courtesan beauties.

Some of the great works by artists of the *Ukiyo-e* school can be seen in the Library's excellent collection of *kyōka-bon*, anthologies of humorous poetry published in limited editions for club members or discriminating book lovers. Utamaro's contribution in *Otoko-dōka*, 1798 and Hokusai's in *Shunkyō-jō* of the same year are but two examples of superlative prints found in *kyōka-bon*. Similar versatility and artistic flair is demonstrated in the drawing albums: *Taigadō gafu*, 1803 and *Tokai-jo*, 1803. The former faithfully reproduces the evocative paintings of Ike no Taiga, master of the Chinese-influenced *Nanga* school. The latter, an exquisite *haiku* book, includes specially commissioned woodcuts by Saitō Shūho Nankei, Ippo, and other artists of the Maruyama-Shijō school which stressed abstract naturalism. These *kyōka-bon* and albums are rated very highly. Together with other illustrated books on a wide range of subjects, they offer a mine of information on Japanese society and culture.

The occidental mind and eye can form some idea of the variety and grandeur of all this material, but it cannot easily assess its importance. Importance is only measurable in relative terms: if, however, you were to search worldwide, including all the countries from which the British Library's oriental

Four of the set of eight *Hyakumantō darani* ('million pagoda charms'), 764–770, with a wooden pagoda in which the charms were originally issued. One of the million sets commissioned by the Empress Shotoku in thanksgiving for the suppression of a rebellion.
Or.81.c.31.

collections originally stem, you would find comparable treasures of local work; but you would not find enough in any single place to form a comparative view, either in terms of time or geographical spread. The importance of the collections can only be expressed in reverse, so to speak. If all the collections in the (western) manuscripts and printed books departments were totally destroyed, the loss to the world would be very great, and to Britain in particular: but, elsewhere in Britain, notably at the universities of Oxford and Cambridge, in France, where the Bibliothèque Royale, now Nationale, preceded the British Library, in the great libraries of Germany, Italy, Spain, Russia, and Europe generally and in America, particularly, whither have gone (ironically) many of the treasures of Britain, itself for so long the magnet for treasures from the rest of the world, from all these sources, and now from Japan too, it would be possible to recover not all that was missing but a fair imitation of it. But, if the oriental collections were to be destroyed, the loss to the world would be irreplaceable; the tangible evidence of much of the best of the literary and documentary culture of a large part of the globe, for considerable periods, would have been wiped out. Heaven forfend such a cataclysm: may future generations continue to enjoy the opportunity to appreciate all this, to grasp how one eastern culture grew from or was influenced by another, to see the major monuments of each, undisturbed. Unique though some of the individual items are, it is the totality of the collections that makes them so valuable to the rest of the world.

10

Maps and Music: the Printed and Manuscript Collections

GABRIEL NAUDÉ AND other early theorists on the correct furnishing of libraries laid down that no library was complete without a pair of globes, and adequate provision for maps and atlases, as the source of information about the surface of the world and its inhabitants, was equally essential. Appropriately, an example of the very large Coronelli celestial globe of 1693 ($3\frac{1}{2}$ feet in diameter) greets visitors in the vestibule of the present Map Library, and a pair of globes produced by George Adams *c.*1765 which once adorned the Library of George III, stand resplendent in the King's Library.

In the Map Library, and in the Department of Manuscripts, are concentrated the great mass of historic maps and atlases which have come to the Library over more than two centuries. All the original collections that came to the Library at the foundation of the British Museum were rich in cartographic material, notably the Cottonian Library. From the Old Royal Library came the copy of Christopher Saxton's *An Atlas of England and Wales*, engraved between 1574 and 1579 and published in the latter year. Christopher Saxton's other achievement, the great single map of England and Wales, published in 1583, of which only one other copy is known, is also in the Library. Shortly after, British cartographic skill was put to urgent practical purpose: two copies exist of Robert Adams's beautifully drawn manuscript plans showing the defences against the Spanish Armada erected along the Thames from Westminster to the Earl of Leicester's camp at Tilbury, one in the Map Library and the other, which has the route of the Queen's progress to the camp pricked on the vellum, in the Department of Manuscripts. But the real foundation of the present Map Library's collection is due to two men; George III and Richard Henry Major, its first keeper when it became an independent department in 1867. Many of the most important maps and atlases in royal possession had not passed with the Old Royal Library to the British Museum, since they were documents of immediate practical value. The great sea atlases of William Hack, made between 1682 and 1700, 'The Wagoner of the Great South Sea' (i.e., the west coast of America), the 'North Sea of America' (i.e. its east coast), and the Indian Ocean and Far East, were among these. There were even earlier maps, too. William Baffin's *The Empire of the Great Mogoll* (1619), the earliest English map of the Mughal territories, and Sir John Narborough's manuscript 'Draft of Magellan Straits', were also among them, as was the largest and grandest 'atlas' in the collection, the great collection of wall maps assembled by Johannes Klencke of Amsterdam for presentation to Charles II, and the contemporary (1664) 'Duke's Plan' of New York, the earliest English manuscript plan of the city. A copy of the Visscher panorama of London, *c.*1616, was also in the collection.

But, besides these early monuments of cartography and discovery, there were even more substantial contemporary documents. War had proved a great stimulus. The invasion of the Young Pretender in 1745 focused attention on Scotland, and one of the results was the great topographical survey of Scotland by William Roy (1720–90). This was undertaken for the Duke of Cumberland soon after the rebellion was over. Much of the material thus generated is in the Library. The original survey fell into two phases, that of Northern Scotland and the Highlands (1747–52) and of Southern Scotland (1752–55). A complete set of the fair drawings came to the Royal Library after Colonel Watson's death in 1761. At some date after 1763 it was lent or given by King George III to Colonel Roy (as he then was). This material was returned to the King in 1792, two years after Roy's death, when it joined the original first-phase drawings, which had passed to the King on the Duke of Cumberland's death in 1765.

The Duke's own draughtsman was Thomas Sandby (who gave the first warning of the '45). He and his more famous younger brother Paul Sandby, the first great English watercolour artist, both worked for Roy, Paul being responsible for the fine landscape drawings in phase one. Both brothers were

Opposite. The Klencke Atlas, a bound set of wall maps presented to Charles II, with Map Library curators. KAR.

Detail (much reduced) of a drawing from William Roy's survey of Scotland (1747–55) showing the area of the Firth of Cromarty.
Maps C.9.b.

Opposite, top. Page opening from William Hack's manuscript atlas of the South Sea of America, showing the original of Robinson Crusoe's island.
K.Mar. VIII.16.

Opposite, below. Nicolas of Cusa. Map of northern and central Europe. Eichstatt, 1491. One of six surviving examples.
Maps C.2.a.1.

employed in the Drawing Room of the Ordnance Office at the Tower of London, and Paul became drawing master at the Royal Military Academy at Woolwich, where military surveyors and draughtsmen were trained. These were the men, members of the Ordnance Office and Quartermaster General's Office, who charted the wars in America – the French and Indian wars and the American War of Independence – both of which made extensive demands on their talents. Two exceptional items are the birch-bark map made by Mrs Simcoe, wife of the Governor General of Upper Canada, after its establishment in 1791, and the 'Red-lined map', the 1775 edition of John Mitchell's *Map of the British and French Dominions in North America* first published in 1755, annotated with the demarcation lines of the possessions of the United States and its neighbours by Richard Oswald, British Commissioner at the Treaty of Paris in 1783, and presented by him to George III.

All this and much else, a total of some 50,000 maps, charts, views and drawings, the finest geographical collection of its day, was to come to the British Museum when the King's Library building was ready in 1828. Then there was a hitch. The Trustees learned that the King proposed to retain the maps and charts. They asked Robert Peel, the Home Secretary, to intercede with the King, suggesting that the maps (the Topographical Collection) should go to the Museum, while the charts (the Maritime Collection) should go to the Admiralty. This was done, and so matters remained until 1844, when the Lords Commissioners of the Admiralty offered to the Museum 'the Old Maps, Charts and Books which formerly belonged to his Majesty King George III'. The offer was accepted, although some 40 items were accidentally retained: restitution was made in 1952.

Richard Henry Major was born in Jersey and studied medicine under Abernethy before returning home to practise. In January 1844, a lifelong passion for cartography happily diverted him to the British Museum, whose collection of printed maps had just been catalogued by William Hughes, at the prompting of the newly founded Royal Geographical Society. He was put in charge of maps, and set about his task with great vigour, rearranging and reassembling the existing holdings, in particular the Ordnance Survey maps received by deposit since 1801. At the same time he took a leading part in the foundation of the Hakluyt Society in 1846, was its Secretary from 1849 to 1858, and edited 10 volumes for it, as well as publishing his own researches on the voyages of Prince Henry the Navigator and the Columbus letters. During this period the still unsuperseded *Catalogue of Manuscript Maps, Charts and Plans* was compiled by John Holmes and Frederic Madden.

Major's interest in the cartographic collections as a whole was acknowledged in 1867 by the establishment of the new Department of Maps, of which Major became the first keeper. Unfortunately, ill health forced him to retire in 1880; his successor, R.K. Douglas, was primarily an orientalist, and the collection languished. In 1892, when Douglas took charge of the new Department of Oriental Manuscripts and Printed Books (*see above*, p. 151), Maps became a sub-department of the Department of Printed Books, and the manuscript material (apart from the significant portion included in George III's Topographical Collection) was transferred to the Department of Manuscripts. This uneasy arrangement has existed ever since, with the collection divided between two departments (or three, if the notable topographical collections in the Department of Prints and Drawings of the British Museum are included). In 1914, during the tenure of A.J. (later Sir John) de Villiers, a worthy successor of Major, the Map Room (subsequently renamed the Map Library) was moved to its present quarters in the King Edward VII building.

Two significant acquisitions in Major's time were the chart collection of Admiral Lord Howe and the Japanese maps that came with the Philipp von Siebold collection. The individual acquisitions were as notable, including the Drake 'Broadside Map' by Jodocus Hondius (Amsterdam, *c.*1595) and the engraved map of north and central Europe, attributed to Cardinal Nicolas of

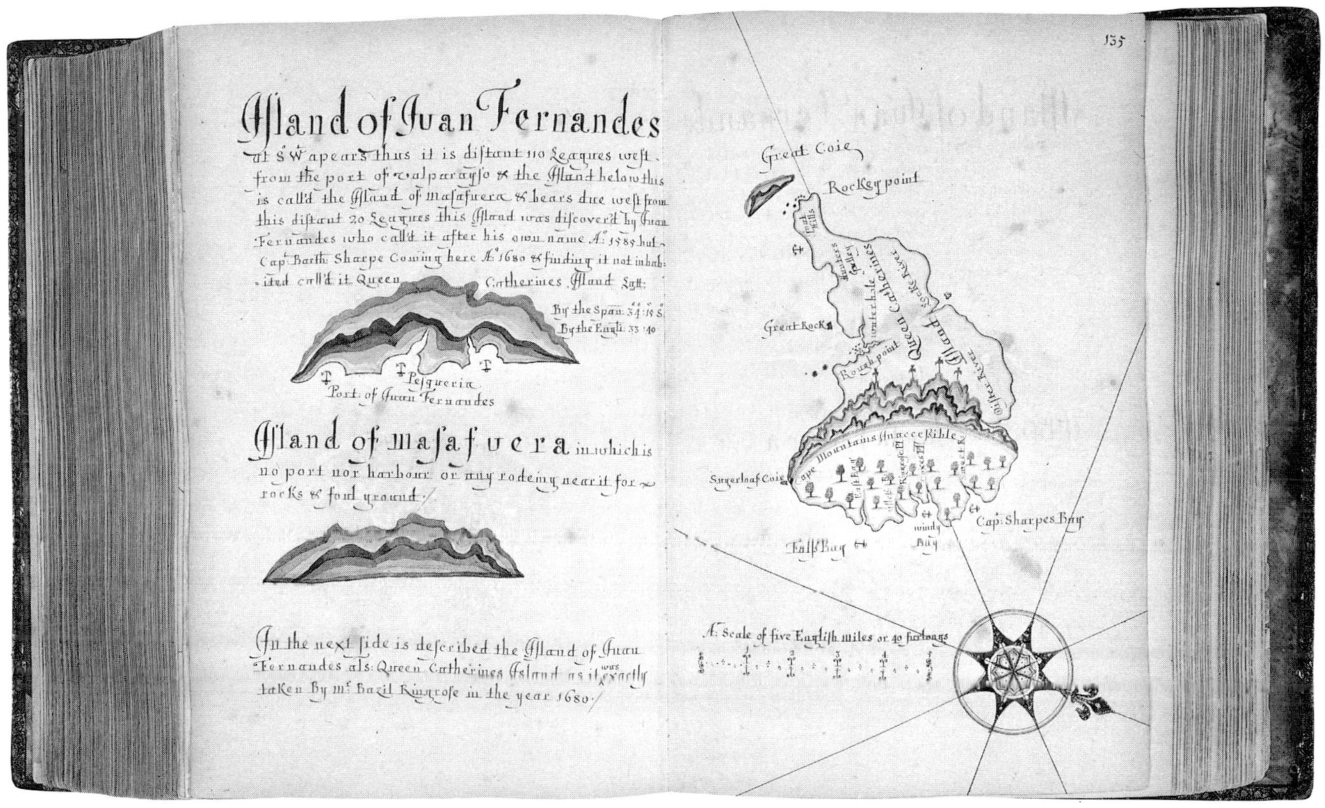

135
Island of Juan Fernandes
at S W apears thus it is distant 110 Leagues west from the port of Valparayso & the Island below this is call'd the Island of Masafuera & bears due west from this distant 20 Leagues this Island was discover'd by Juan Fernandes who call'd it after his own name Aº 1589 but Capt. Barth: Sharpe Coming here Aº 1680 & finding it not inhabited call'd it Queen Catherines Island Latt:
By the Span: 34: 15 S.
By the Engli: 33: 40
Pesqueria
Port of Juan Fernandes
Island of Masafuera in which is no port nor harbour or any rode any near it for rocks & foul ground
In the next side is described the Island of Juan Fernandes als: Queen Catherines Island as it was exactly taken By Mr Bazil Ringrose in the year 1680
Great Coie
Rockey point
Great Rock
Rough point
Queen Catherines
Island
Mountains Inaccessible
Sugerloaf Coie
Cap: Sharpes Bay
Falls Bay
windy Bay
A: Scale of five English miles or 40 furlongs

QVOD PICTA EST PARVA GERMANIA TOTA TABELLA: ET LATVS ITALIĘ GELIDAS QVOD PROSPICIT ALPES: SAVROMATVM QVE TRVCES POPVLI: GENTES QVE PROFVNDO VICINĘ ADRIACO: PELOPIS REGNVM QVE VETVSTI:
PANNONIOS ET FINDIT AGROS QVA FRIGIDVS HISTER: ATQVE LICAONIOS TERRARVM QVICQVID IN AXES VERGIT: ET EQVOREAS RHODANVS QVA VERBERAT VNDAS: ET MVLTĘ PVNCTIS VRBES VILLĘ QVE NOTATĘ:
GRACIA SIT CVSĘ NICOLAO: MVRICE QVONDAM QVI TYRIO CONFECTVS ERAT: SPLENDOR QVE SENATVS INGENS ROMANI: NVLLI EXPLORATA PRIORVM: ET LOCA QVI MODICO CELARI IVSSIT IN ERE.
EYSTAT ANNO SALVTIS 1491. XII. KALENDIS AVGVSTI PERFECTVM.
VICESIMVS · PARALELLVS
MARE OCEANVM GERMANIA
MARE SVEVICVM
DECIMVSNONVS PARALELLVS
DECIMVSOCTAVVS PARALELLVS
DECIMVSSEPTIMVS PARALELLVS
MARE PONTICVM SIVE PONTVS EVXINVS PARS
SEPTIMVM CLIMA
POLONIA MAGNA
SAXONIA
PRVSSIA
DACIA
SCANIA
HASSIA
VNGARIA
TRANSILVANIA
PARS MARE GALLICVM
MARE LIGVSTICVM
MARE TYRHENVM PARS

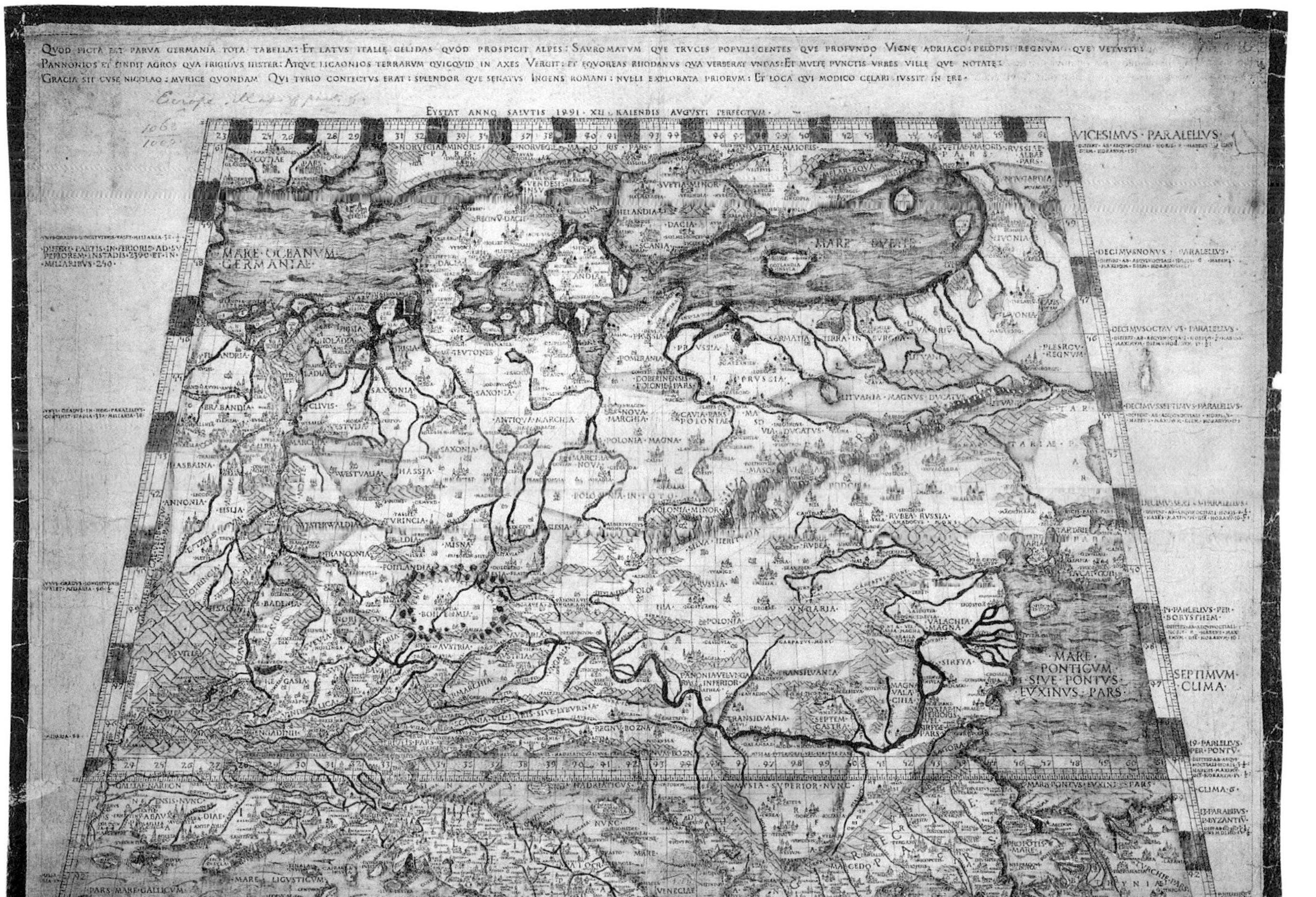

Cusa and dated 1491; only a few copies of either exist, while of Diego Gutierrez's Map of America (1562) only one other copy is known. The Beudeker Atlas, a unique collection of Dutch maps and prints gathered in 24 volumes by Christoffel Beudeker (1685–1756), was also acquired while Major was Keeper. The year of Major's retirement was marked by the purchase of the important collection of London plans made by Frederick Crace (1779–1859), architect and decorator; as commissioner of sewers he had discovered the value of old maps and plans, which he collected systematically for over 40 years.

Since then, the Map Library has been steadily augmented. In 1922, the Library acquired not only the unique copy of the 1506 World Map of Giovanni Matteo Contarini, the first printed map to show America but also the great eight-sheet world map (1564) of Abraham Ortelius, which joined Peter Laickstein and Christian Sgrooten's nine-sheet map of Palestine (1570), acquired in 1887. To these has recently been added the only known copy of the nine-sheet world map of Giacomo di Gastaldi, *c.*1561, as great a monument of Italian map-making as the Ortelius map is of that of the Low Countries. Other more recent acquisitions have numbered Philip Symonson's *A*

Christopher Saxton's map of England and Wales, 1583
Maps C.7.c.1.

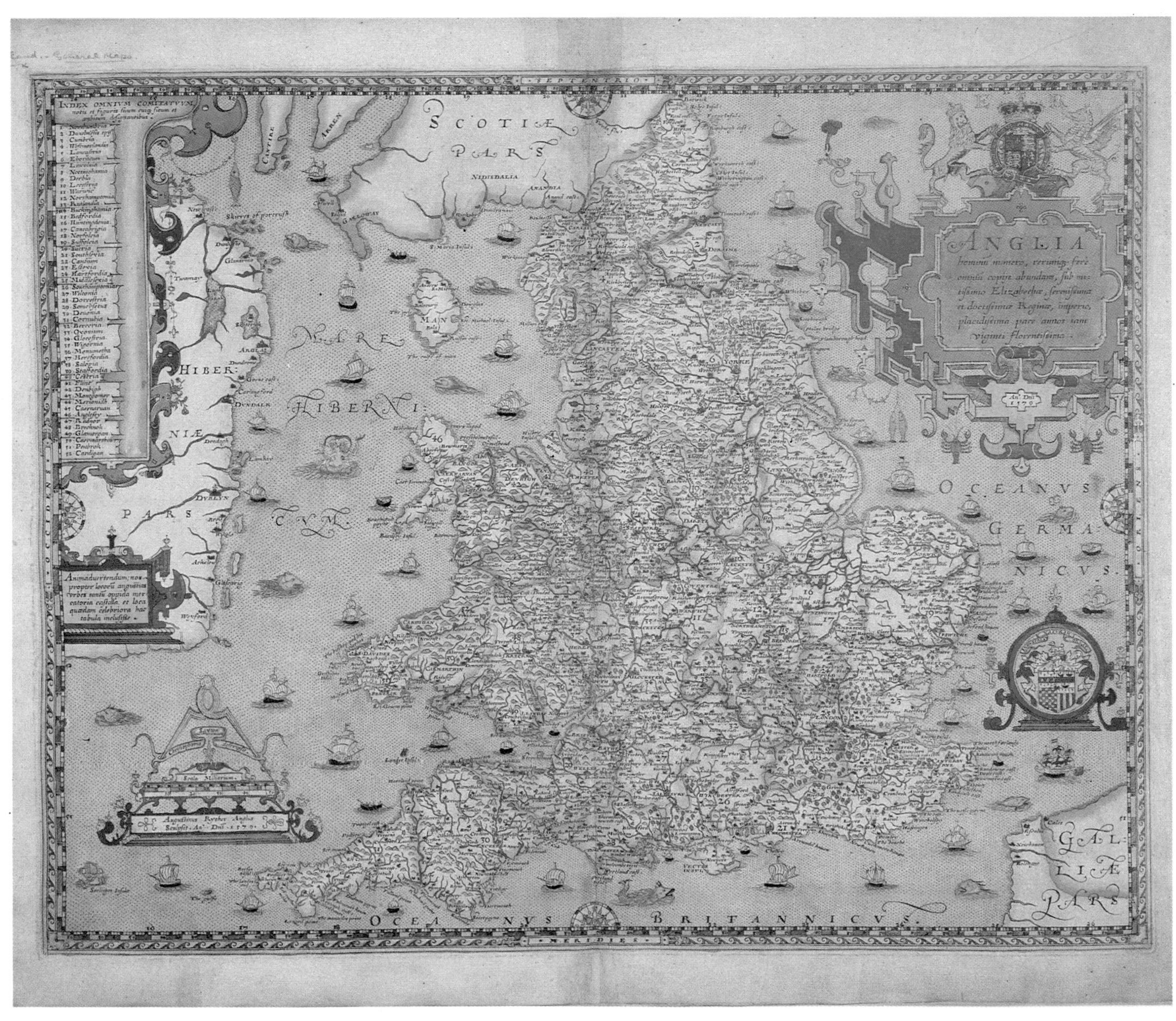

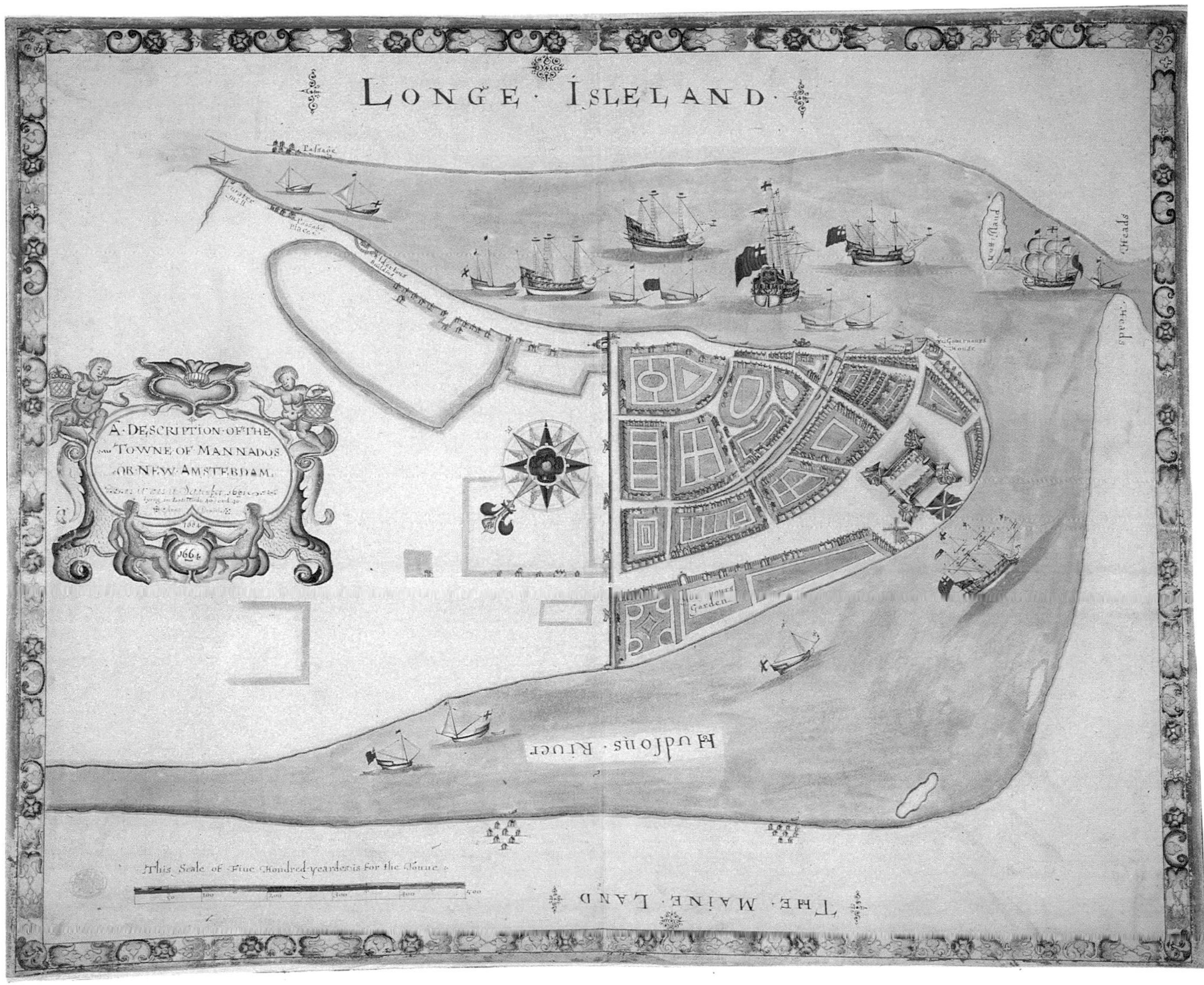

The 'Duke's Plan' of New York (then New Amsterdam). 1664.
K.Top.121.f.35.

new description of Kent (1596), the first separately published county map, the only known copy; three out of four sheets (all that survive) of John Speed's Battle Map of the British Isles (1603–4); the earliest known Chinese terrestrial globe, by Manuel Dias and Nicolò Longobardi (1623); and the first English lunar globe, by John Russell (1797). The Library has also recently acquired a set of the Polder Maps of Holland made by Floris Balthasarsz van Berckenrode between 1611 and 1616, a fine copy in contemporary colouring of one of the monuments of Dutch cartography.

The Map Library and the Department of Manuscripts cannot be considered separately, since they complement each other. The maps of India and the West Indies and the Hack charts in the Sloane collection fit in with those in King George III's Maritime Collection; if the royal copy of Saxton's Atlas is in the Map Library, among the Royal manuscripts is Lord Burghley's proof set, amplified with many manuscript maps, as vital to Elizabethan administration as 'Domesday Book' was to the Normans.

The earliest British cartography is found among the foundation collections. The famous Anglo-Saxon map with its precociously accurate rendering of the British Isles was acquired by Sir Robert Cotton, while his collection and the Old Royal Library both contain Matthew Paris's handsome maps from St Albans, the latter showing a pictorial itinerary from London to Rome with a view of London *c.*1255. The maps and topographical drawings that Cotton kept in the special 'Augustus' press are the richest collection of pre-1600 English maps and drawings in the world. Many of them come from the working papers of Henry VIII and Lord Burghley, whose interest was largely responsible for the technical improvement of topographical depiction in their lifetimes: the difference between the rendering of Edinburgh in 1544 by the King's surveyor Richard Lee (knighted at the siege) and Robert Adams's plan of Flushing in 1588 reflects the growth of mathematical expertise during the century. Royal patronage attracted spectacular foreign enterprises, such as the great atlas made in 1542 by the Scots-French cartographer Jean Rotz for Henry VIII, replete with new information about South America and the East Indies, including 'Java-la-Grande' (which can be interpreted as a reference to the early Portuguese discovery of Australia).

Each of the other early collections has its special treasures. The Harleian contains John Norden's 1607 survey of the Honour of Windsor, with its pictures of park and castle, and the Dieppe school world map of *c.*1547, known as the 'Dauphin', or Harleian, *mappemonde*; this was stolen by Edward Harley's butler and passed through several hands before it reached Sir Joseph Banks, who gave it to the Museum. The Lansdowne and Arundel collections each had its masterpiece; George III's first minister, Lord Shelburne, later first Marquis of Lansdowne, bought Lawrence Nowell's beautiful map of England of *c.*1564, the first modern map of the country, with the Burghley papers; it was retained by the family and only rejoined the rest of the collection in 1982. One of Lord Arundel's purchases on the Continent was the exceptionally fine late-15th century Flemish copy of Cristoforo Buondelmonte's *Isolario*, with its vivid depictions of Mediterranean ports.

Pressure from the Royal Geographical Society in the early 1840s produced not only the two catalogues but also some important accessions, notably from the Duke of Sussex sales, from which came the world map of Henricus Martellus *c.*1490, one of the first to show the southern tip of Africa. This map, or one like it, seems to have been consulted by Columbus and Cabot. In the last century, too, many charts by Captain Cook and watercolours illustrating his voyage were acquired (*see* below, p. 257), including those given or bequeathed by Banks. The Howe collection contains charts of great technical importance, particularly those by Alexander Dalrymple, first Hydrographer to the Navy. The Admiralty passed on other important historic material in addition to the King's Maritime Collection, notably the great atlas made in 1573 by Fernão Vaz Dourado, one of the monuments of the golden age of Portuguese cartography. It is dedicated to King Sebastian, and probably stayed in the Portuguese Royal Library until the great earthquake of 1755.

The Department of Manuscripts has the greatest collection of early maps of Spanish America outside Spain. Originally formed by Felipe Bauza (1764–1834), it contains maps of every size and scale, some early, but mainly from Bauza's lifetime; a notable example is the earliest surviving plan of Santa Fe, New Mexico produced by military engineers in 1766–67. Other remarkable acquisitions in the 19th century were an English psalter of *c.*1275 with a world map, Lord Nelson's map of Aboukir Bay drawn in 1803, the planisphere of Pierre Descelliers, 1550, and the atlas of maps and views of the frontier provinces of France made by French military engineers between 1604 and 1608.

Post-war additions have involved significant collections as well as individual items of note. In 1956, the Ordnance Surveyors' drawings (*c.*1784–1841) were presented to the Map Library by the Director General of the Ordnance Survey. These, with later additions, represent the greater part of the first systematic survey of England and Wales. The largest acquisition of recent times was the purchase of the sheet map collection of the Royal United Services Institution in 1968, divided between the Map Library and the Department of Manuscripts. The manuscript materials added considerably to the holdings of English maps of North America, mainly dating from the Seven

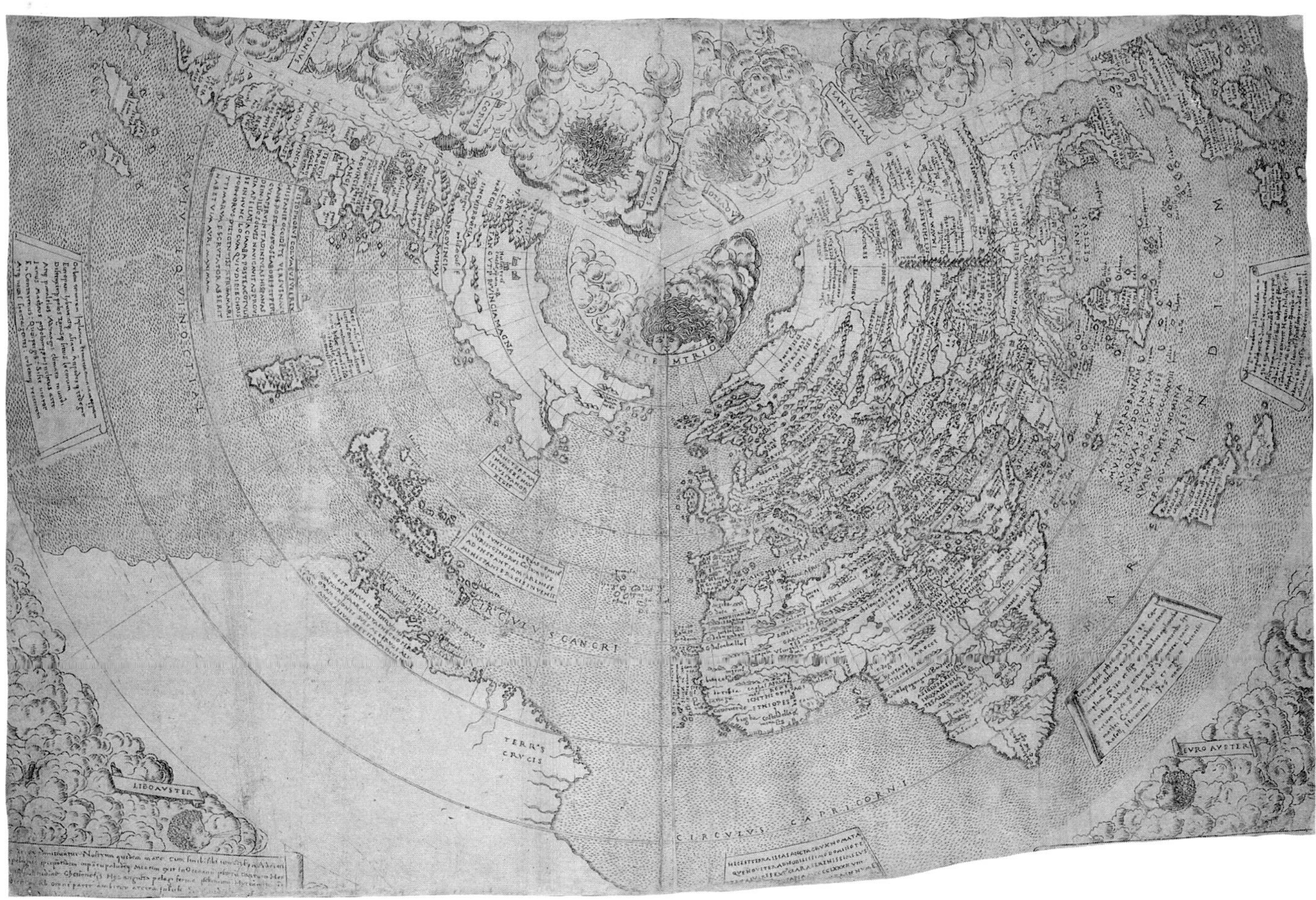

World map of G.M. Contarini. 1506. The unique example of the first map to show north America. Maps C.2.cc.4.

Years' War, and a collection of German maps of European battlefields, among them a splendid semi-pictorial map of the siege of Belgrade in 1717. One curiosity was an Indian birch bark map found at the watershed between the Ottawa River and Lake Huron in 1841. In 1968, a volume of estate maps of the Earl of Kildare's Irish lands, by John Rocque, author of the great 1746 printed map of London, was acquired, and among the Blenheim Papers was a printed map of the Tirol annotated by the Duke of Marlborough with alternative routes whereby an allied army under his command could be marched from north of the Alps into Italy. To this has since been added a manuscript map of the Blenheim campaign by the leading German cartographer Cyriak Blödner, who served on the campaign. William Lambarde's original map of the Beacons of Kent, 1585 and two estate maps by Christopher Saxton have augmented the English holdings, together with the vast collection (some 400 items) of plans from Althorp.

The position of the Music Library, like the Map Library, is complicated by the fact that, although the foundation collections contained remarkable works of music, manuscript and printed, no separate provision was made for them until, again, the early 1840s. Although the present Music Library, like the Map Library, is a collection of world renown, major material is still to be found in the General Library and Department of Manuscripts. All these resources combine to form source material for the musicologist of the highest importance.

The Old Royal Library, predictably, contains important relics of Henry VIII's taste for music. Among them are a collection of motets and a set of masses by Nicholas Ludford written for the King and Catherine of Aragon. To these were added in the 19th century a collection of songs, some composed or

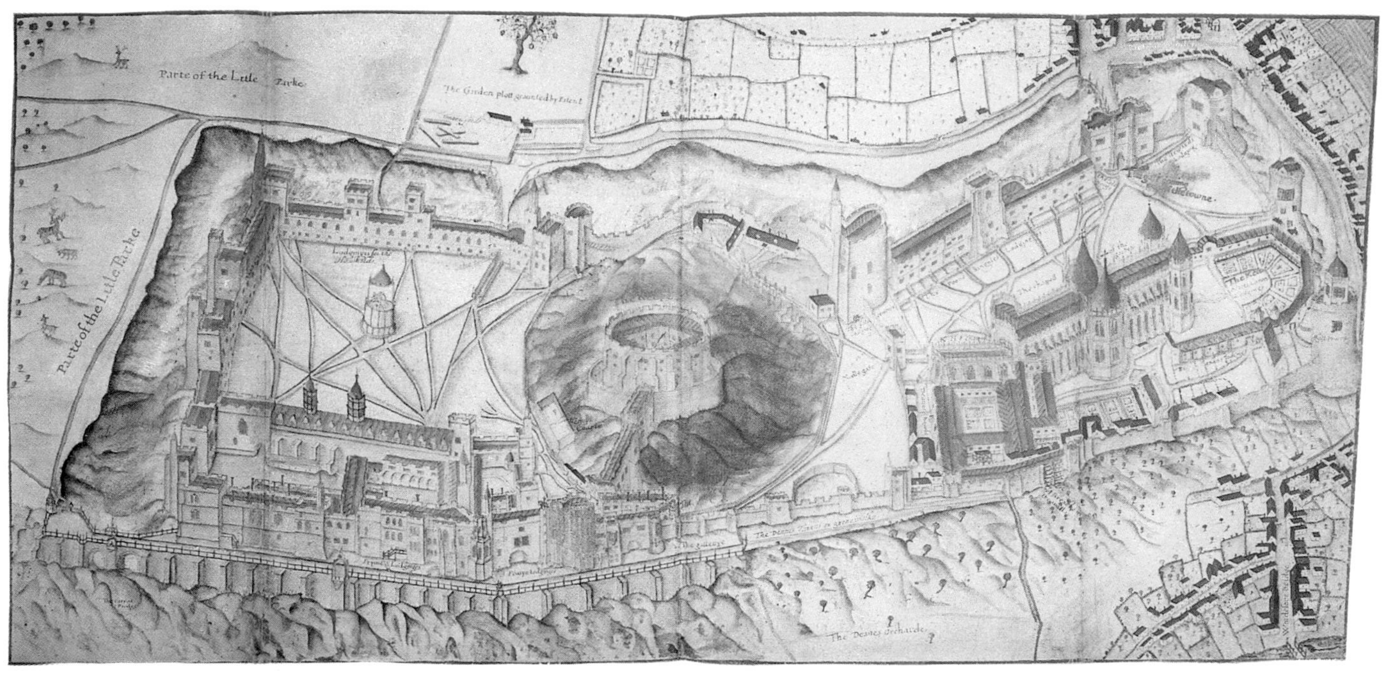

Bird's-eye view of Windsor Castle in John Norden's survey of the Honor of Windsor, 1607. Harley MS 3749, f.3.

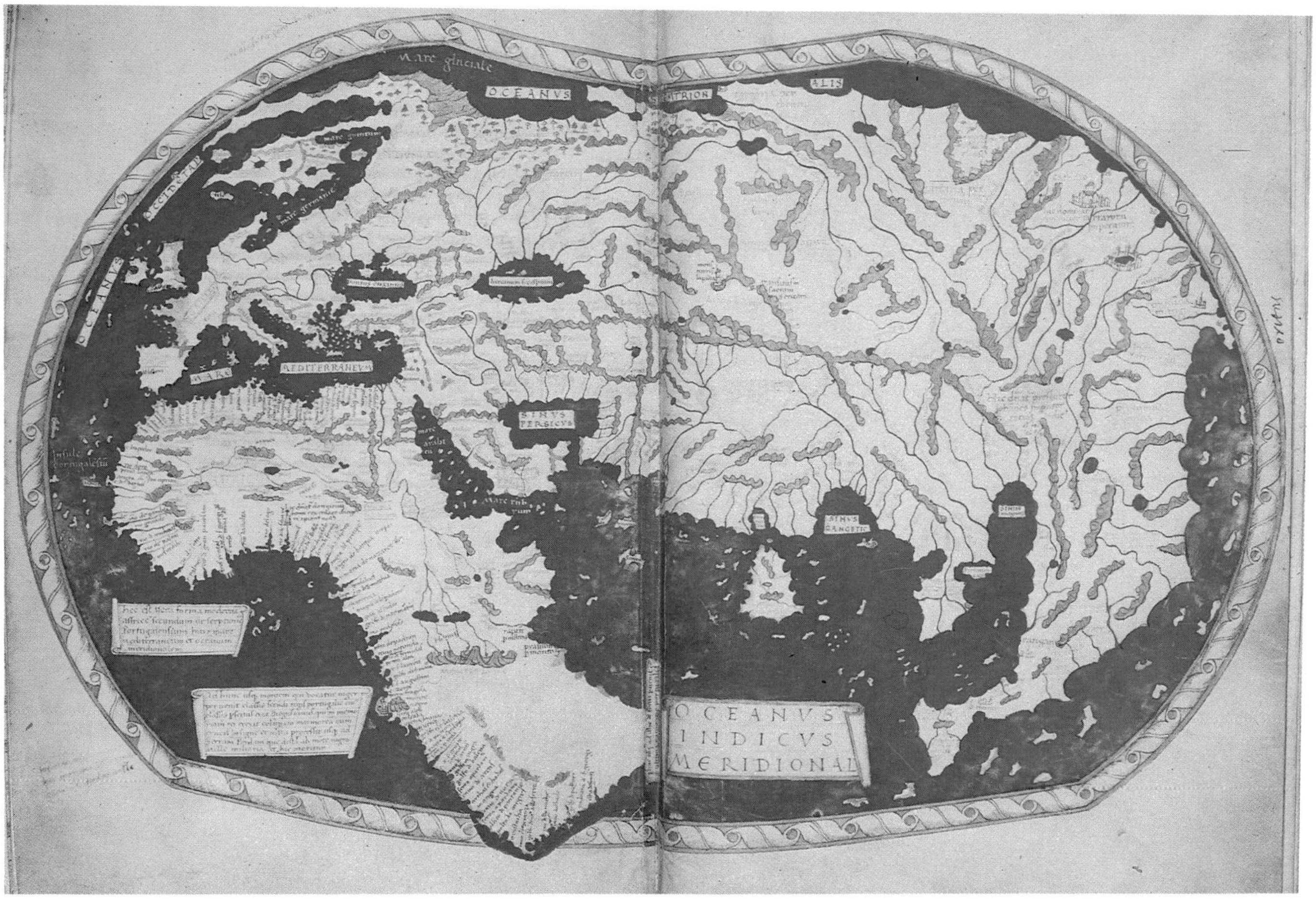

World map of H. Martellus, *c.*1490. Add. MS 15760, ff.68v–69.

Anglo-Saxon, World Map, *c.*1000 AD.
Cotton MS Tiberius B.V. Part 1.f.56*v*.

World map, from an English psalter, *c.*1275.
Add. MS 28681, f.9.

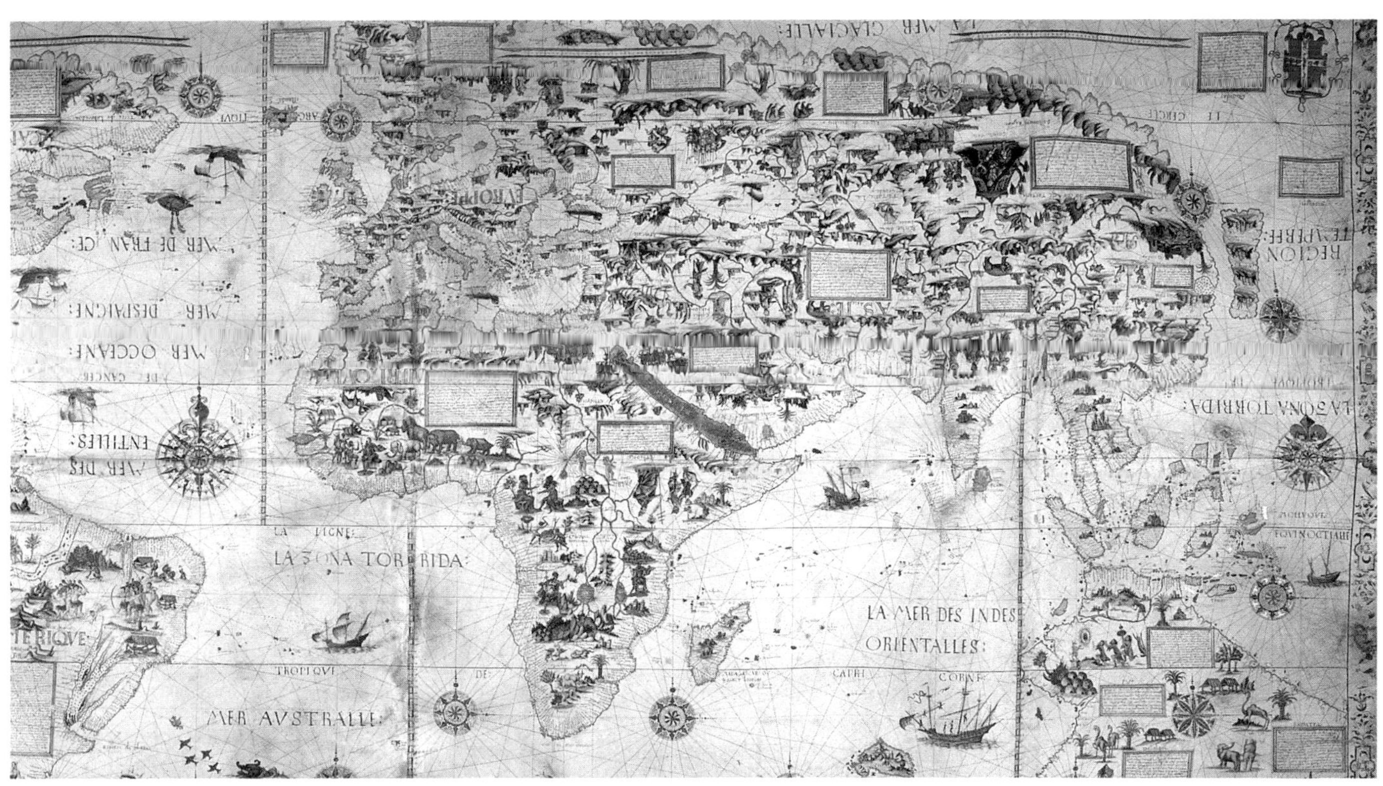

The planisphere of Pierre Desceliers, 1550. (Much reduced.)

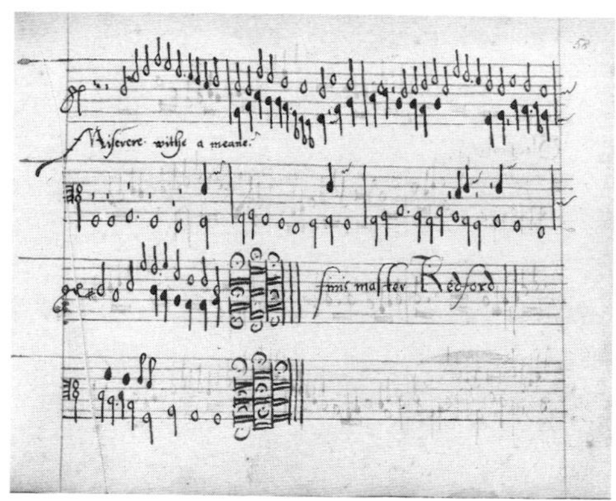

'Miserere' for organ by John Redford (died 1547), from the 'Mulliner Book'.
Add. MS 30513, f.58.

arranged by the King and the famous 'Mulliner Book' of contemporary keyboard music, both designed for royal use. Henry, Earl of Arundel, also had an exceptional interest in music, and printed scores of motets by Adrian Willaert, Tylman Susato, Jacob Arcadelt and Vincenzo Ruffo were in his library, besides manuscripts of the work of his household composer, a Fleming, Derick Gerarde; he also owned the collection of Josquin Desprez's masses printed at Fossombrone in 1516. John, Lord Lumley, added substantially to the collection, notably the works of William Byrd, who dedicated his *Liber secundus sacrarum cantionum* (1591) to him. The copy of Sir William Leighton's *Teares or lamentacions of a sorrowful soul* (1614) that belonged to Charles I as Prince of Wales reflects a later royal interest in music.

The Harleian collection contains the most famous of all English medieval music manuscripts, Harley MS 978, which not only includes the six-part round *Sumer is icumen in*, composed *c.*1250–70, but also the motet 'Ave mater gloriosa'; in addition, there is early 14th-century music, both sacred and secular. A later manuscript of great importance is the six-volume anthology entitled 'A collection of the most celebrated services used in the Church of England from the Reformation to the restauration of K. Charles II. Composed by the best masters' made by Thomas Tudway, Professor of Music at Cambridge, which ranged from Thomas Tallis, Byrd and Orlando Gibbons to Purcell and William Croft, with some by Tudway himself and his contemporary Maurice Greene. Unexpectedly, the collection also contains a contemporary score of Carissimi's motet 'Audite, sancti' in a group supplied by Humfrey Wanley himself.

Sir Hans Sloane was not much interested in music, although a miscellany in his collection written by Johann Stobaeus, Kapellmeister to the Elector of Brandenburg *c.*1640, contains lute music and German songs of the period. But the prestige of the newly-founded British Museum's collections soon attracted further donations. In June 1765, when Leopold Mozart visited the Museum with his children, he presented to it the printed scores of Wolfgang's sonatas K.10–15 and the autograph of his motet 'God is our refuge'. Count Algarotti gave his *Saggio sopra l'opera in musica* (1763) through Thomas Hollis, and in 1778 Sir John Hawkins gave some 50 works on musical theory, including two by Gafori, *Practica musicae* (1502) and *Divinum opus* (1508). From Charles Burney's music library, a number of works (of which unfortunately no list survives) was purchased for £253 in 1815.

But the neglect of any special interest in music, as in other branches of knowledge, was now awaking criticism from professionals. Above all, the lack of a catalogue was felt. Vincent Novello, composer, musical editor and founder of the firm that bears his name, wrote to the Trustees, setting out the shortcomings of the collection (augmented by his own gifts) from the musicologist's point of view in 1824, without success; nor did G.H. Rodwell, who in 1835 put in a memorial arguing the needs of young composers, do any better. Nevertheless, pressure grew on the Trustees, not only from outside, but from the energetic Panizzi, who eventually got permission in 1841 to prepare a catalogue on principles devised by himself. These principles have been used with modifications ever since, a remarkable tribute to the perspicacity of a man fully engaged with other problems and apparently quite unmusical. All that was needed was a cataloguer. For this the final impetus of a petition, signed by some 90 of the leading musicians of their day, organised by William Chappell, was required, and in November 1841 Thomas Oliphant was appointed.

At first all went well. Oliphant gathered the scattered material together, and diligently compiled the catalogue on Panizzi's rules, devising his own system of press-marking. By the end of 1846 he had dealt with 24,000 titles and catalogued the manuscript music as well. Substantial accessions had also been made. But at this point he fell foul of Panizzi. Oliphant liked to come and go as he pleased, provided the work was done; Panizzi insisted on regular

W.A. Mozart. Autograph of the motet 'God is our Refuge', presented to the British Museum by his father Leopold during the Mozarts' visit in 1765. K.10.a.17(3).

hours. On this Oliphant was obliged to resign. Panizzi's intransigence is regrettable, but Oliphant's cataloguing remained the basis for the collection for the next 60 years. During this time, Eugene Roy and Charles Evans maintained Oliphant's system and took advantage of an ever-expanding market; the catalogue of printed music was printed in 1884. In 1885, William Barclay Squire succeeded Evans.

To Squire belongs the credit for raising music from a minor to a major part of the Library's activities. His long tenure (he retired in 1920) saw the entire collection recatalogued, the level of acquisitions increased, the level of staffing improved; more, his own work, inside and outside the Museum, had made the collection known in the world as it never had been before. During the same time, too, Augustus Hughes-Hughes, working in the Department of Manuscripts, recatalogued the music there (1906–9). The summit of Squire's career was the transfer on loan to the Museum in 1911 of the great Royal Collection of Music, as important an acquisition as that of the Royal Maps almost a century earlier; this loan was converted into a gift by HM Queen Elizabeth II in 1957. Squire was succeeded by William Smith, and Smith in 1944 by Alec Hyatt King. In 1946 came the other great accession of the 20th century, the collection of Paul Hirsch, purchased for £120,000 in 1946, with the aid of special grants from the Treasury and the Pilgrim Trust. Hirsch's collection is the most substantial assemblage of printed music ever to be put together on historic principles. Rich in every period, it added notably to the previous wealth, especially in copies in original or fine condition.

The art of music printing came late to England, but the collection begins with copies, all unique, of the first three surviving pieces of English printed music, a fragment of the ballad 'Away mourning', *c.*1520 and the part song 'Tyme to pas' in the *Interlude of the four elements* *c.*1525, which are the first known examples of the use of movable type to print words and music at a single impression, an achievement to be credited to the lawyer-printer, John Rastell, brother-in-law of Sir Thomas More. With these is the bassus part of a set of 'Twenty songes', very well printed in 1530 by an as yet unidentified printer. The collection is rich in the sacred and secular printed music of the great Elizabethan composers, with all Byrd's masses (mainly bought by Squire in 1889), Thomas Weelkes and Orlando Gibbons, the *Cantiones*, 1575, with which Thomas Tallis and Byrd obtained a patent for 21 years to print music and music-paper, and *Parthenia or the maydenhead of the first musicke that*

'Tyme to pas', in the *Interlude of the four elements*. *c*.1525, one of the earliest English examples of music and words printed together in movable type.
C.39.b.17.Ev.

ever was printed for the virginalls (1612–13). Among later music, there is a wonderful collection of the work of the first great English music publisher John Playford, including several unique pieces; another book of which no other copy is known is *A choice collection of ayres for the harpsichord* (1700) by John Blow and others, including Jeremiah Clark, who contributed a little tune called 'The Prince of Denmark's March', better (if erroneously) known over the last 50 years as 'Purcell's Trumpet Voluntary'. The 18th century was a great era for the dance. Printed dances appeared in all forms, even on the backs of playing cards; a complete pack of cards in its original woven case is in the Hirsch collection.

The Copyright Acts secured an increasing amount of material in the 19th century, although an occasional rarity escaped, for example Elgar's *May Song*, with beautiful designs by Walter Crane, of which there was a limited edition of five copies on vellum, one of which was acquired later with the Hirsch collection. Of particular interest in showing the composer at work are a set of corrected proof sheets of music produced by Augener, the London music publishers, works by Delius, Ireland, Warlock, Frank Bridge and Butterworth, among others, including the German composer Max Reger. One of the great treasures of the 19th century is the vast collection of popular songs with handsome decorated and pictorial title pages, first engraved and then

'The Long and the Short of it' (1862), a pictorial song cover by Concanen and Lee. Coloured lithograph.
H.1772.e.(39).

Opposite. The 'Old Hall' manuscript, *c*.1410–15. The composer of this setting of the Gloria, 'Roy Henry', has been identified as King Henry IV or possibly the young King Henry V before he ascended the throne.
Add. MS 57950.f.12*v*.

Roy henry

chromolithographed by artists now largely forgotten, except perhaps Alfred Concanen (1835–86).

In Continental music, the 'Constance' Gradual of 1473, of which the Library has the only known complete copy, stands first. The major composers and collections are represented, beginning with superb polyphonic partbooks issued by Ottaviano Petrucci from 1501 on. In sacred music there is the great *Passionarium Toletanum* (Alcala, 1516), the first music book printed in America – Juan Navarro's *Liber in quo quattuor passiones Christi Domini continentur* (Mexico, 1605). One of the rarest of all is the copy, one of only two surviving, of the earliest book of keyboard music, Marco Antonio Cavazzoni's *Riecerchari, Motetti, Canzoni* (Venice, 1523), bought by Squire on 11 June 1897 for £75. There are some splendid dance books, notably Baltasar de Beaujoyeulx, *Balet comique de la royne* (Paris, 1582). Almost all the scarce lifetime editions of J.S. Bach are in the collections, including all four parts of the *Clavier übung* (1727–42), some with the composer's own manuscript corrections. Another beautiful French book is J.B. Laborde's *Choix de chansons* (1773), with full-page illustrations after J.M. Moreau-le-jeune. The unique first issue of Claude Joseph Rouget de Lisle's *Chant de guerre pour l'armée du Rhin* (Strasbourg, 1792), better known as 'The Marseillaise', is there, with the first illustrated edition, printed at Paris as a broadside in the same year. Among the romantic works of the earlier 19th century is the only known copy of Berlioz's first work, the song *Le dépit de la bergère*; among more contemporary rarities is the first edition of Norbert Schultze's *Lili Marleen*, the most famous song of the Second World War. An important source of interpretation is the set of Sir John Barbirolli's conducting scores.

There are also important music resources in the general library. Besides music in liturgical works, there are two remarkable collections of concert programmes, one made by Sir George Smart between 1810 and 1857, including the set of Philarmonic Society programmes, annotated by him, the other by Barclay Squire. Besides the early gifts of Sir John Hawkins and Count Algarotti there are some notable works on instruments, the first general work on the subject, Sebastian Virdung's *Musica getutscht* (1511) and the great organ book, François Bedos de Celles, *L'art du facteur des orgues* (1767–68); perhaps the best known book on instrumentation, Berlioz's *Grand traité d'instrumentation* (1843) escaped selection originally, but the author's own annotated copy is one of the treasures of the Hirsch collection.

Manuscript material is divided between the Music Library and the Department of Manuscripts. The Royal Music Library in the former contains two important sources of English virginal music, those made by Benjamin Cosyn (*c.*1620) and William Forster (*c.*1624); another is a set of fantasias by Charles I's musician, John Coprario. There is a substantial folio of Henry Purcell's fair copies of his own compositions, *c.*1690, which is complemented by a similar collection, including the famous *Chaconne*, *c.*1680–83, in the Department of Manuscripts. But the most famous of all is the collection of 97 volumes of Handel's autograph, preserved by his great admirer George II, including all his oratorios, among them *Messiah*, his operas and most of his other major compositions.

Paul Hirsch collected manuscripts of major works, such as 19th-century operas by Rossini, Bellini, Offenbach and others of which no printed score existed. He also acquired the only surviving manuscript copy, in a contemporary hand, of Gafori's *Theoriae musicae tractatus* (1480), the same work as the *Theoricum opus musice discipline*, the first printed work on musical theory, produced in the same year. He also had the autograph of Holst's famous carol *Lullay my liking* (1916).

The collection of manuscript music is one of the greatest in the world. Besides the early acquisitions, already noted, scarcely a year has passed since without important further accessions. In recent years, the collection of medieval English music has been strengthened by the most famous collection of

G.F. Handel, *Messiah*. 1742. Part of the 'Halleluiah Chorus' in the composer's autograph draft.
R.M. 20.f.2, f.103v.

early polyphonic music, the set of masses and motets written for the Chapel Royal of Henry IV called the 'Old Hall' manuscript. The wealth of 16th-century vocal music has been complemented by instrumental music, including important sources for the music of Byrd, whose rare autograph appears on a certificate dated 1581. Another even larger collection, made before 1645, includes autograph manuscripts by William Lawes, whose famous song-book is also in the collection. The partly autograph march by Matthew Lock 'for His Majesty's Sagbutts and Cornetts' is supposed to have been written for Charles II's progress through London on 22 April 1661. There is a vast collection of instrumental and vocal music by over 100 English and Italian composers, *c.*1600, related to the Fitzwilliam Virginal Book, and a full score of Tallis's 40-part *Spem in alium*, with an English text showing that this great motet was performed in 1610 at the investiture of Prince Henry as Prince of Wales, and again in 1616 for that of Prince Charles. Later vocal music includes 325 songs by Henry Lawes, brother of William and author of the music for Milton's *Comus*, and, besides the Purcell manuscripts mentioned earlier, there is the autograph of his *Yorkshire Feast Song*, *c.*1689.

Until very recently, the only original manuscript in the hand of J.S. Bach was that in the second book of *Das wohltemperirte Klavier*, the famous '48' preludes and fugues, bequeathed by Eliza, daughter of the composer Samuel Wesley (1766–1837), in 1896, although the department had long since owned the vocal parts of the *St Matthew Passion* used by Mendelssohn for the performance he gave in Berlin on 11 March 1829, which inaugurated the great Bach revival in Europe. Among several pieces in Mendelssohn's own beautiful musical hand are an organ fugue which he wrote for Vincent Novello, who gave it to the Museum, and a canon inscribed 'London, 7th Sept. 1837'. The copies of the 12 symphonies that Haydn wrote for the impresario Salomon, two autograph, at first on loan but recently acquired

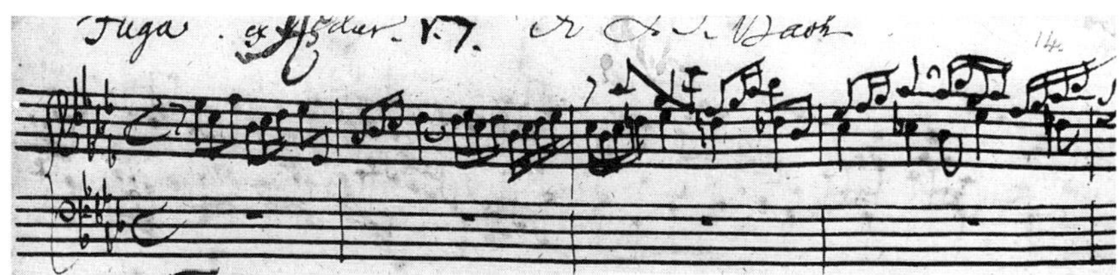

Detail from the beginning of the autograph of J.S. Bach's fugue in A flat major, from *Das Wohltemperirte Klavier*, Book II, 1740–42.
Add. MS 35021, f.14.

from the Royal Philharmonic Society, recall another important London visit, and a sadder occasion is commemorated by the score of Weber's *Oberon* used by the composer who conducted it at Covent Garden, probably for the première on 26 April 1826, and bequeathed by Sir George Smart, in whose house Weber died on 5 June 1826. The great collection of Italian music made by Guiseppe Selvaggi and presented by the Marquis of Northampton in 1843 contains notable works by Alessandro Scarlatti and Niccolò Porpora.

The Library's collection of Mozart autographs, recently significantly strengthened, was already rich, its chief pride the scores of his last ten string quartets, bequeathed in 1906 by Miss Harriet Chichele-Plowden. This, one of Barclay Squire's most important acquisitions (he had long known the testatrix) was imperilled when ill-judged publicity led the executors to sue for the bequest to be set aside, mercifully without success. From Julian Marshall came the Pastoral Symphony sketch-book by Beethoven and the complete autograph fair copy of the Violin Sonata *op.*30 no.3, while the copy of the 9th Symphony dedicated to the Philharmonic Society is on loan from the Society. The notable collection of Schubert autographs, in part given by Johann Ernst Perabo, in part acquired after his death in 1920 includes, among its more substantial pieces, the complete score of an early Mass by Schubert (in B minor, *op.*141, D.324).

Most of the major composers of the later 19th and 20th centuries are represented by autographs or important copies but in British music of the last hundred years the collection is unassailably the best. Beginning with the autograph full scores of *Patience* and *The Gondoliers*, it continues with 85 volumes of Elgar autographs, bequeathed by the composer's daughter, including the 'Enigma variations'. Thanks to Vaughan Williams's widow and other donors, the collection includes most of his work, his symphonies in sketch and complete score, the choral and other vocal works (among them *Linden Lea*), with his folk-song notebooks and *Job*. The third great pillar of the British 20th-century collection is an almost equally comprehensive set of works by Gustav Holst, acquired largely through the good offices of his daughter Imogen. Rutland Boughton, John Ireland, Sir Arnold Bax, Havergal Brian (most prolific of modern symphonists), Ethel Smyth and Sir Michael Tippett are represented in equal strength, while in 1976, after Benjamin Britten's death, the British Library was able to acquire some 30 of his scores in lieu of estate duty.

Besides the masterpieces of the great composers are the relics, no less important, of the popular music of the past. The London pleasure gardens at Ranelagh and Vauxhall were an important source of this, and the department is fortunate to possess several orchestral cantatas written for Vauxhall by James Hook, organist at the Gardens, in 1783, with a whole host of songs and catches, including some by the most famous of all early 19th-century English song writers, Charles Dibdin. A different form of popular music is recorded in the archives of the 'Wandering Minstrels', the amateur group who gave concerts, often for charity, between 1860 and 1890; here are to be found programmes, photographs, accounts, prints and drawings, badges and other mementos (including a sketch in Mozart's autograph); it presents a wonderfully vivid picture of musical life in a pre-recording age.

Maps and music, with manuscripts, form a triad in the history of the Library, each third of which joins on to, and is complemented by, the other. The scholarly elucidation of the material in each, as well as its acquisition, has been a permanent feature of their history for a century and a half, and the specialist catalogues have become as important to their users as the treasures they record. The enormous growth of interest in the history of discovery and of music in recent times has been fuelled, directly or indirectly, by the resources of the Map Library and the Music Library, with those of the Department of Manuscripts in both fields.

11

The India Office Library and Records

Ornamental letter of credence from the Prince Regent
to the Emperor of China, 19 January 1816.
Reproduced by kind permission of the Earl Amherst.
IOLR MSS Eur.F.140/43B.

THE EAST INDIA Company Records, which for 150 years had remained in essence the reports and accounts of a commercial concern, began in the second half of the 18th century (as we have seen in Chapter 5) to take a different course, which can be divided chronologically into three phases. The first, which starts with the creation of the Board of Control in 1784 and ends with the India Act in 1858, saw Britain's interest in India finally change from a commercial to a ruling role: it involved an increase and a substantial duplication in documentation. With the creation of the India Office in the second phase, which combined the functions of the Company's Court of Directors and the Board of Control, this duplication ceased. On the other hand, dualism in government continued: the Secretary of State for India in London and the Viceroy of India in Calcutta and later Delhi, had independent records, as well as their own copies of documents passing between them. 1947, the year of independence for India and Pakistan, initiated the third phase and with it a metamorphosis in the role of the Records. Since 1600 they had accrued as the archival deposition of the pursuit by Company, Board of Control and India Office of their commercial and political objectives. By the 20th century their importance for the academic study of the British connection with India was already being recognised, but their primary function, as the official memory of the organisation which created them, remained. Now, save for minor exceptions, fresh accruals ceased, and the need for official reference to the Records was slight. Instead the Records became, as the library had always been, chiefly a focus for historical study and scholarly research. The last 40 years have therefore seen a drawing together of the two legatees of the old India Office – its Library and its Records – as a single centre for Indian and related Asian studies offering resources which, thanks to this union of the printed word and the historical record, are of unrivalled depth and variety.

Inevitably, the later records of the East India Company are not as picturesque as the earlier. But its exceptional nature, part commercial, part governmental, and its contact with remote and exotic countries, produced some unique documents. Its own servants were often remarkable men in their own right. Charles Lamb, whose portrait is in the Library, was a clerk at East India House from 1792 to 1825, and his bond on taking up his post in the Accountant's Office is still preserved. James Mill and his more famous son John Stuart Mill, with Thomas Love Peacock in between, were successively Examiners of Correspondence from 1830 to 1858. Thus we find the author of *Headlong Hall* and *Nightmare Abbey* inditing a memorandum, dated 28 February 1831, on steam navigation on the River Ganges, while the draft of Political Department Despatch No. 12 of 1 April 1840 from the Court of Directors to the Government of India on the eastern frontiers of India was by the same hand that wrote *On Liberty*.

Another famous contemporary literary figure had a lasting influence on the role of Britain in India, although never in the Company's service. Thomas Babington Macaulay (1800–59) had an uncle and cousin in India; as a member of the Whig government he became a member of the Board of Control in 1832, and went to India as Legal Member of the Supreme Council of India in 1834, remaining until 1838. Macaulay was convinced that no good would come of too close an involvement with the native culture. Where Warren Hastings had administered justice through the local courts and Sir William Jones had urged the importance of familiarity with native languages and literature, Macaulay was convinced that a superior intellect needed no such training. In the conflict between the 'Anglicists' and the 'Orientalists', Macaulay, as President of the Committee of Public Instruction, cast a decisive vote for the former.

It was a decision with far-reaching consequences: immediately, it brought about the closure of the Company's College at Fort William and a decline in the study of Arabic, Persian and Sanskrit; the detachment of the governors

Death and burial of Napoleon, the entry in the Parish Register of St Helena, 9 May 1821.
IOLR N/6/2, f.211.

Photograph of Lady Canning 'going out to sketch', *c.*1861.
IOLR MSS Eur.D.661, f.12.

from the governed ultimately detached the empire. (We are still suffering from Macaulay's belief in the absolute priority of competitive examination over experience in the field.) The India Office Library was itself, perhaps, fortunate to survive. Extant there is not the autograph which is lost, but one of the few surviving contemporary official copies of Macaulay's famous minute on Indian Education to Lord William Bentinck, then Governor-General, and issued as India Public Proceedings No. 15 of 7 March 1835.

Besides the Company's own proceedings, a vast amount of documentation of all kinds has reached the India Office Library and Records: here is a coloured map of Salsette Island sent to the Chairman of the East India Company in 1819 by Lt.-Col. C.B. Burr; there a collection of 1500 drawings made by Colin Mackenzie and his draftsmen of the landscapes, peoples and antiquities of India and Java. There is the parish register of St Helena, recording on 9 May 1821 the death of 'Napoleon Buonaparte, late Emperor of France; he died on the 5th instant, at the old House at Longwood and was interred on Mr Richard Torbett's Estate'.

Some of the more exotic documents seem to owe their preservation to curiosity rather than archival obligation. Among these are the original 'letter of credence' of the Prince Regent to the Emperor of China introducing Lord Amherst's embassy, dated 9 January 1816, which nicely blends the best British calligraphy with an engaging if somewhat hopeful *chinoiserie*. Equally exotic is the similar letter from Louis Philippe to Ranjit Singh, dated 27 October 1835, empowering General Jean François Allard as French Agent, clearly prepared by a hand not unfamiliar with the *murasala* of Indian diplomacy and contained in a magnificent embroidered bag. Another *trouvaille* is the copy of the proclamation by the Queen in Council, dated Allahabad, 1 November 1858, announcing the transference of the Government of India from Company to the Crown, which ultimately reached the India Office Library through the hands of a bookseller.

As a picture of the British in India, the India Office Library and Records collections are unmatched. Sometimes it is, literally, a picture. Fanny Eden's Journal, kept during her memorable journey with her brother Lord Auckland, Governor-General 1836–42, is illustrated with her own more than competent watercolour drawings. Her sister Emily published an account of the same journey, *Up the country*, in 1866. An album of photographs of the Canning family show Earl Canning (Governor-General, 1856–62) reading the papers of Sir Charles Metcalfe, who in 1809 had negotiated a peaceful adjustment of relations with Ranjit Singh, the ruler of the Punjab, and also Lady Canning on an elephant, captioned 'going out to sketch'.

Sometimes the picture is no less vivid because expressed in words: there is the telegram to Lt.-Col. H.B. Edwardes, Commissioner at Peshawar, announcing that the mutineers had reached Delhi, or Florence Nightingale writing to Sir William Wedderburn about the General Election of 1885 and affairs in India, or the young Winston Churchill congratulating Lord Curzon, the Viceroy, on his stand against the Commander-in-Chief, Lord Kitchener, in 1905. Sometimes, too, the picture is graphic in both senses, as in the ornamental address of welcome from the citizens of Delhi to Lord and Lady Hardinge on their official entry in 1912 to mark its establishment as the new capital of the Indian Empire. 'Anglo-Indian' families returned to India, generation after generation: here is Lord Amherst, Governor-General of Bengal, writing to the Hon. Mountstuart Elphinstone, Governor of Bombay (and notable historian of India), to announce the end of the first Burmese war in 1826, and there the delightful illustrated journals of young Jeffrey Amherst, Captain in the Rifle Brigade, 1867–73.

Nearer in time, the documentation is no less vivid. Here is Eric Blair (George Orwell) applying to take the examination for the Indian Police in 1922; his success resulted in *Burmese Days*. On the one hand Mahatma Gandhi writes to the Secretary of State for India from prison, where he had not expected to find

Right. View of the hills near Coonoor, by Lady Canning, 1858.
IOLR WD 4188.

Below right. 'Thugs fixing the attention of a traveller upon something mysterious in the clouds that he may be strangled unawares'. Illustration from the Journal of Fanny Eden, January 1838.
IOLR MSS Eur.C.130, f.74.

himself 'so soon', while on the other Lord Willingdon complains irritably to the Governor of Bengal, Sir John Anderson, in 1932 – 'That little devil Gandhi is as clever as a barrel load of monkeys'. A separate Instrument of Abdication is required in 1936 to inform Edward VIII's subjects in India that he is no longer their King-Emperor; and in the middle of the war Churchill begs Attlee to stop any new political initiative in India. Finally, Lord Mountbatten paints his own vigorous picture of the last days of the Raj in his weekly newsletter to the King, the Prime Minister, the Secretary of State and the India and Burma Committee of the Cabinet. It is the very stuff of history.

During the same two centuries, the Library grew in company with the Records, maintaining an interest 'in all the languages of Asia; but particularly in the Persian, Arabic, and Sanskrita' that its founding father Sir Charles Wilkins (*see* Chapter 5) had prescribed, and adding manuscripts and printed books to supplement the records. It was also a museum until 1879 when, due to lack of space, its collections were divided between the South Kensington (now Victoria & Albert) Museum, the British Museum and other institutions. Indeed, the first accession recorded in the *Day Book* of the Library is not a book but 'Three Elephant Heads, with several detached parts intended to illustrate the natural history of those Animals, so far as it relates to their curious mode of Dentition'. To the general public it was better known as the home of the 'Babylonian Stone', received from the Company's Resident in Baghdad in 1801, one of the earliest cuneiform inscriptions to arrive in Britain (now in the British Museum), and of 'Tippoo's Tiger', the celebrated automaton of a tiger savaging a British Officer, whose shrieks and growls used to disturb readers in the Library, now on exhibition in the Victoria & Albert Museum. The Library still retains something of its character in the collection of paintings and drawings, furniture and sculpture: a portrait of Stringer Lawrence painted in 1760 by Sir Joshua Reynolds, the seat of the Chairman of the East India Company, upholstered in red velvet embroidered with the Company's coat of arms, *c.*1730, and the fine bust of Henry Colebrooke (1820) commissioned by the Company from Francis Chantrey in order to celebrate his munificent gift of manuscripts. All these recall the surroundings amongst which Wilkins built up the memorials of India and Britain's impact upon it.

Address of welcome to the Viceroy and Vicereine Lord and Lady Hardinge, on their official entry into Delhi, 23 December 1912. Reproduced by kind permission of the Hon. Julian Hardinge.
IOLR MSS Eur.E.389/5.

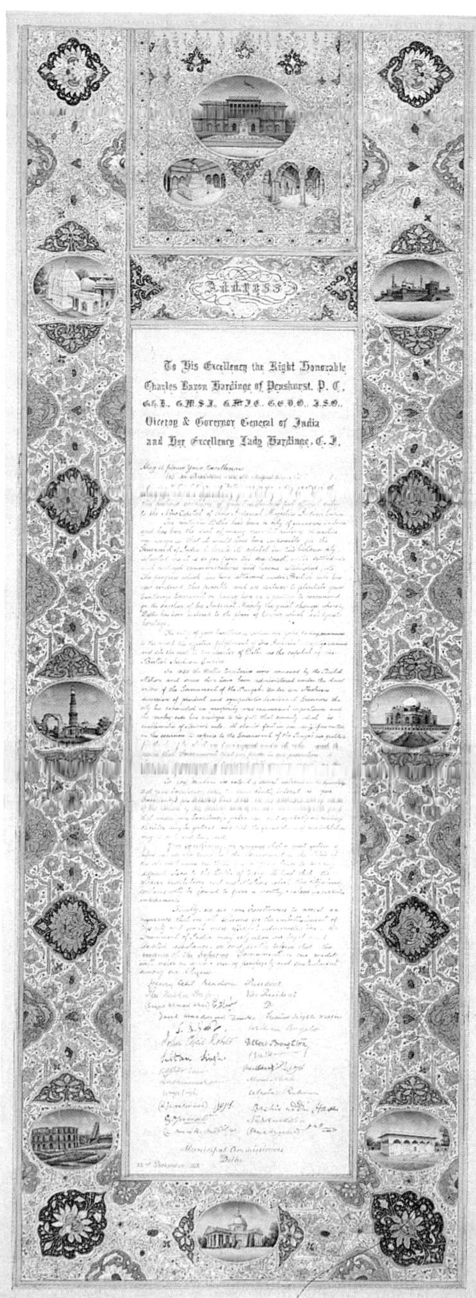

After Wilkins's death in 1836, and some little deliberation, Horace Hayman Wilson was appointed to succeed him. Wilson was in many ways a second edition of Wilkins. Born in 1786, he too went to Calcutta as a young man. Like Wilkins also he had been inspired by the example of Sir William Jones and had learned first Urdu and then Sanskrit. He had come out as an assistant surgeon, but his knowledge of metallurgy led to his immediate appointment in 1808 as an assistant in the Calcutta Mint which brought him into contact with John Leyden, also a surgeon and a linguist, whom he succeeded as assay-master in 1816. Like Wilkins's printing, this gave him a practical bent, and when he returned to England in 1832 as the first Boden Professor of Sanskrit at Oxford, he too turned his attention to printing. In 1819 he had published his *Sanskrit–English Dictionary*, which remained the standard work for many years. In 1836 he was the ideal successor to Wilkins. He was responsible for the cataloguing of the collection and, in 1845, the first printed catalogue. His reputation fortified and augmented the Library in the difficult years of the Company's decline and the transfer of its authority (and with it the Library and Records) to the Crown.

In 1860 Wilson died. Neither of the next two Librarians held the post long, but in 1869, two years after the Library moved to the newly-built India Office building in Whitehall, Reinhold Rost, another universal linguist, was appointed. He had come to England in 1847, and remained Librarian till 1893. He was the first Librarian to benefit from the (Indian) Act of 1867 which effectively made the India Office Library a copyright deposit library for Indian books. The consequent influx proved overwhelming and 10 years later Rost had to propose that only a selection – made at the Librarian's discretion – of the copyright material should be transmitted to the Library. The selection was nevertheless to include all works of importance published in India, whether in English or in any oriental language; and that is still the aim today, even though the books must now be purchased. Books published outside India always had to be purchased and the principles governing the scope of such acquisitions were also considered in 1877 by the Library Committee which reported that 'the main object is to obtain a complete collection of works relating to the East, and more especially to India, and the countries adjoining it'. Subsequent reviews have introduced a greater degree of selectivity (certain subject areas such as science and technology and modern law are now the responsibility of other departments of the British Library) but the basic objective enunciated in 1877 still remains the Library's goal.

In the mean time, the India Office Records, after a long period of quiescence, punctuated chiefly by the destruction of documents between 1858 and 1860 (*see* above, p. 78), and a further reduction made in 1867 preparatory to the move to the new India Office building, were placed under the control of the Statistics and Commerce Department in 1874. The unbound records were examined and Dr (later Sir George) Birdwood arranged and roughly catalogued the 17th-century documents from which the well-known Factory series was later largely formed. Birdwood's *Report on the old records of the India Office* (printed for official use in 1879, published with additions in 1891) gave an enthusiastic account of these neglected materials and led indirectly to a further reorganisation in 1884 when the Records were placed under a new Registry and Records Department headed by a 'Registrar and Superintendent of the Records'.

The first holder of this post was F.C. Danvers who was succeeded in 1898 by Mr (later Sir Arthur) Wollaston. In 1907 he in turn was succeeded by William (later Sir William) Foster who had worked in the department throughout the reigns of his two predecessors, and for whom, on his retirement in 1923, the ancient post of Historiographer was revived which he held until 1927. It was with the work of these three men that the modern history of the India Office Records really begins. Their essential achievement was to initiate the opening up of the old pre-1858 archives to academic research. The records were sorted and arranged, and press lists were compiled on sound archival principles. The work has continued ever since and now of course covers the records right down to 1947 as well as those of earlier vintage. The publication of important documentary series was also initiated, for example the *Letters received by the East India Company from its servants in the East* 1602–17, six volumes (1896–1902), *The English Factories in India* 1618–69, 13 volumes (1906–27), and Foster's own *Guide to the India Office Records 1600–1858* (1919). This tradition of publication has also continued, two recent notable examples being the 12-volume series on *The Transfer of Power in India* (1970–83) and its companion on *Burma: The Struggle for Independence*, 2 volumes (1983–84).

In 1954, after Independence, S.C. Sutton, then Librarian of the India Office Library, became Keeper of the Records, and the two *fonds* were gradually united, the process being completed by the appointment of the Librarian and Keeper as first Director of the India Office Library and Records in 1971, following their move in 1967 from the old India Office building to their present site at Orbit House in Blackfriars Road. Finally in 1982 custody of the India Office Library and Records was transferred from the Foreign and Commonwealth Office to the British Library – perhaps the greatest single accession of treasures, at any rate in terms of volume, ever received.

This, then, is the present repository of the conjoined Library and Records, the twin progeny of the administrative and intellectual apparatus of the old East India Company and its successor, the India Office.

The first major acquisition to be received by the newly-established Library in 1801 was the private papers of Robert Orme, the Company's Historiographer (*see* Chapter 5) comprising the documentary material which he had collected to write his great history. This donation marked the beginning of the 'European Manuscripts' – the section of the Library responsible for the acquisition of private papers, or historical documents in private hands. The Orme collection was followed between 1822 and 1833 by the various collections of Colonel Colin Mackenzie, Surveyor General of India 1815–21, whose papers provide a rich source of materials of all kinds on Java, the Dutch East Indies and South India. These 'foundation collections' have been enriched by others throughout the 19th and 20th centuries: the papers of Warren Hastings's great enemy Sir Philip Francis, with whom he fought a duel; and of the founder of Singapore Sir Stamford Raffles; the diaries and correspondence of men such as George Bogle, Charles Masson or William Moorcroft who were among the first to explore the remote territories of central Asia bordering India's frontiers; the collections of great scholars such as H.H. Wilson, B.H. Hodgson and C.P. Brown; the political and private papers of statesmen, soldiers, politicians and administrators, for example Clive; the two Lawrence brothers, Henry and John; Disraeli's appointee as Viceroy and promoter of the 'forward policy' in Afghanistan, Lord Lytton; the archetypal pro-consul Lord Curzon; or the Strachey and Macnabb families, both of which produced

Top left. Mahatma Gandhi to the Secretary of State for India Sir Samuel Hoare, 15 January 1932.
IOLR MSS Eur.E.240/16, f.4.

Top right. The Viceroy Lord Willingdon to the Governor of Bengal Sir John Anderson, 18 September 1932.
IOLR MSS Eur.F.207/7.

Bottom left. The final Personal Report of the last Viceroy of India Lord Mountbatten, 16 August 1947.
IOLR L/PO/6/123, f.245.

Bottom right. Message from the Delhi Telegraph Office sent on the outbreak of the Indian Mutiny, 11 May 1857.
IOLR MSS Eur.E.211/4A, f.2.

Dear Sir Samuel,

I had not expected to write to you, at any rate, not quite so soon from prison.

I had promised to let you know before I took any serious step. But the events came upon me with such a sudden rush that there was no time or choice left for me. I have no doubt you have seen the telegrams exchanged between the Viceroy & me. I tried my best to keep up cooperation but failed in my opinion, through no fault of my own. I cannot help feeling that the Viceroy was wholly in the wrong in refusing to see me except on impossible conditions. I have just written a personal letter to Lord Willingdon urging him to reconsider his position.

4

MSS Eur F 207/7

a. 24/9

THE RETREAT.
MASHOBRA.

18. 9. 32

My dear Anderson

I am writing to ask y. opinion of one Sarma, late editor of the 'Bengalee' & who I believe about to start a weekly political journal. He seems to be dreaming of some honour such as a Knighthood, but I don't want to do anything without asking you & anyhow I don't feel sure I could do anything for him this time. He seems to have stuck loyally to Govt. without much recognition & has been much abused by his Hindu friends in consequence. Will you give me y. views on this point.

That little devil Gandhi is as clever as a barrel load of monkeys. You have seen his letters & that of the P.M. Well his latest is that he won't leave prison & that if we put him in a house outside with any restrictions, he will break all our orders at once. So we

TOP SECRET
AND PERSONAL.

VICEROY'S PERSONAL REPORT NO. 17.
DATED 16TH AUGUST, 1947.

This last week of British rule in India has been the most hectic of any. We have been working longer hours and under more trying conditions, and with crises of differing magnitudes arising every day, and sometimes two or three times a day. The problem of the States continued to occupy most of my time, particularly of those Rulers who have kept changing their mind up to the last moment, whether to accede to India, to Pakistan, or to neither. I paid my farewell visit to Karachi, and took part in unbelievable scenes on the day of the transfer of power in Delhi. The issue which has created the greatest and most serious crisis to date has been the awards of the Boundary Commissions, a summary of which is given in Appendix I.

2. I had always anticipated that the awards could not possibly be popular with either party, and that both would probably accuse the Chairman of the Boundary Commissions of being biased against them. I have therefore taken the greatest pains not to get mixed up in the deliberations of the Commissions in any way. In fact, though I have repeatedly been asked both to interpret the Boundary Commissions' terms of reference and to put forward to them certain points of view (for example on behalf of the Sikh Princes), I have resolutely refused to do this. I have firmly kept out of the whole business but I am afraid that there is still a large section of public opinion in this country which is firmly convinced that I will settle the matter finally. For this reason I made my position as regards the Boundary awards absolutely clear in my address to the India Constituent Assembly (Appendix II).

3. I feel it necessary to put on record a brief review of the history of the Boundary Commissions, for the crisis that has been caused is in my opinion the most serious we have ever had to meet, and might have undone all the work of the past four months - so bitter have been the feelings.

4. On 10th June, Nehru wrote agreeing to the proposal that each Commission should consist of an independent chairman and four other persons of whom two would be nominated by the Congress and two by the Muslim League. This proposal was agreed to by Jinnah.

Sir,

I beg to forward for your information the said intelligence just recd. from the Delhi Telegraph Office —

"We must leave office all the Bungalows are being burnt down by the Sepoys from Meerut, they came in this morning. We are off. Mr C Todd (assistant in Charge of the Delhi Office) is dead I think, he went out this morning and has not yet returned, we hear that nine Europeans are killed."

The above message I think was sent by one of the Assts of the Tel: Office 2

The seat of the Chairman of the Court of Directors of the East India Company, subsequently that of the Secretary of State for India. Made *c.*1730.
IOLR Hardy 8.

Indian civil servants or soldiers for generation after generation.

To this succession of officials a growing number of collections of non-officials and voluntary associations have been added, like the letters of Theodore Beck, first Principal of what is now the Aligarh Muslim University, or the papers of the Indian Tea Association; and the papers of Indians who settled in Britain like the pioneer woman lawyer Cornelia Sorabji, or the novelist Sudhīndra Nātha Ghose.

The list could be continued endlessly: and it is still growing, for British people are still writing their memoirs, still going to India, and still offering their letters and papers to the European Manuscripts Section. Though small in comparison with the official archives, the private papers not only complement them at many points but also include areas such as the social life of the British in India and the work of non-officials not covered by the official archives. The close relationship between the private papers and the official archives was recognised in 1975 by the transfer of the European Manuscripts from the Library to the Records.

Turning to the Oriental Manuscripts it is only proper to begin by noting Henry Colebrooke's great donation of Sanskrit manuscripts received in 1819 – 'without doubt the finest and most precious benefaction which the Library has ever received from any individual', in Professor Arberry's words. Another great accession came almost a century later with the spectacular finds of Sir Aurel Stein (*see* above, p. 162). Of these, the India Office Library received most of those in Tibetan, Khotanese and Kuchean, and 80 per cent of the Sanskrit manuscripts; those in Chinese, Turki, Uygur and Sogdian as well as the other 20 per cent of the Sanskrit, including all the Prakrit documents in Kharosthi script, going to the Department of Oriental Manuscripts and Printed Books, then part of the British Museum. Among these are the 64 7th-century palm leaves of a *Prajñāpāramitā* from Dunhuang, the *Vinayapiṭaka* (Rules of monks) in Tocharian (written in Gupta script) from Kucha in Xinjiang province, 5th–6th century, and the *Aparimitāyuḥ* (Incantation of the Sutra of Eternal Life) in Khotanese, 9th–10th century, a text which with a contemporary *Prajñāpāramitasūtrā* provided the means of deciphering the then unknown language. Both are illuminated with delicate little drawings of the Buddha within a roundel. There is also a ritual scroll of *dharanis* and *Sūtras*, which opens with a headpiece of geese standing on lotuses with lotus buds in

Opposite. Umar rescues Gulnar by throwing her kidnappers into the sea, from the *Khāwarnāma* (Epic of the Caliph Ali), an 18th century Deccani manuscript.
IOLR I.O. 834, f.343.

Headpiece with geese, from a ritual Khotanese and Sanskrit scroll in Gupta script, AD 943.
IOLR Ch.c.001.

عمر امیه
کلنار را غرقی بندد
عمر مردم در آب انداخته

their beaks, which clearly derives from late classical or Byzantine headpieces; the text is in Khotanese, in Gupta script and datable as 943.

Of the classic later manuscripts there is a particularly fine Jain *Kalpasūtra* by Bhadrabahu, dated 1427, and a very decorative section of a mid-17th-century Mewar *Rāmāyaṇa (Sundarakāṇḍa)*, of which other parts are in the Department of Oriental Manuscripts and Printed Books. The *Bhāgavatapurana* scroll, written in minuscule Devanagari in 1792, with 48 miniatures, accompanies a manuscript of the same given to Warren Hastings by Sir Robert Chambers, Chief Justice of Bengal 1789–99. A delightful example of the close association of the Company's officers with the pandits is the *Lalitavistara* (the early life of the Buddha) written by Pandit Amritananda at Patan for Captain W.D. Knox in 1803; its cover shows Knox, in uniform, depicted as an avatar of Buddha. This manuscript was part of Colebrooke's donation.

The Islamic manuscripts begin with a fragment of the Qur'ān in Kufic script, 9th–10th century, once ascribed to the third Caliph 'Uthman (died 665), and certainly once in the libraries of Timur and Akbar, presented by Sir Henry Rawlinson. The oldest dated Persian manuscript is a Qur'ān commentary (*Tafsīr al-Qur'ān*), in fine *naskh*, of 1129. Other remarkable Persian manuscripts are the *Ni'matnāma* (Book of recipes) of Nasir al-Din Shah of Mandu, written and illustrated at Malwa *c.*1495–1505. This is the key-document in the discovery and classification of the mixed Indian and Persian painting styles of medieval India. Another unique text is the *Sindbādnāma* (Tales of Sinbad) with interesting miniatures in the Persianate style practised at Golconda. Among the Mughal manuscripts is the *Laylā va Majnūn* written in 1558 with miniatures in the court style added *c.*1605–10. One Urdu manuscript, interesting as an example of Deccani book production, is a sumptuous *Khāwarnāma* (Epic of the Caliph Ali), an 18th-century copy of the original written for Khadijah, wife of Sultan Muhammad 'Adil Shah of Bijapur in 1649, with illustrations on almost every page. This came to the library with the collection of Richard Johnson, and it is well that it did so. The last pathetic remnant of the library of the Adil Shahs that remained at Bijapur was discovered in the 1840s in the last stages of decay and brought to the Library in 1851.

Another sad remnant of a still greater library is the Delhi collection, acquired after the Mutiny. The once magnificent collection of the Mughal Emperors, which numbered 24,000 manuscripts in the 17th century, was already being dispersed in the 18th century: what came to the Library in 1858 is a fragment, with none of the great masterpieces of calligraphy, illumination and binding it once possessed. It does, however, contain a damaged copy, reputedly in his own hand, of the poems of Sultan Valad, son of the great Jalal al-Din Rumi, which also bears the autograph of Dara Shukoh, son of Shah Jahan. A happier memory of the end of Mughals is the *Kābīnnāmah* (marriage certificate), dated AH 1256 (AD 1840), of Bahadur Shah II, the last Mughal ruler, a wonderfully ornate example of late Persian calligraphy.

The chief monument of Richard Johnson's collection (*see* above, p. 85) is the 'Johnson Albums', 67 in number, containing over 1000 miniatures, many of outstanding quality. The most famous is the 'Squirrels in a plane tree' attributed to Abul Hasan Nadir al-Zaman, *c.*1610, perhaps the Emperor Jahangir's finest painter. There are many fine miniatures of the 18th century in the collection including one by Muhammad Afzal, 1740. Johnson was fascinated by *Rāgamālā* albums, miniatures illustrating the 36 modes of Indian music, and perhaps the finest of the many such sets in his collection is that from Hyderabad, *c.*1760, with its romantically nocturnal scenes. Another 1000 fine miniatures have been added since the accession of the Johnson collection, including the beautiful album made for Dara Shukoh to give to his cousin Nadira Banu Begum, whom he married in 1633.

The impact of British taste on Indian art can be seen in the 'Company

Leaf from a Kufic fragment of the *Qur'ān*, 9th–10th century. Personal stamps on this page indicate that it once belonged to the Mughal Emperors Timur and Akbar.
IOLR Loth 5, f.181.

drawings' produced by Indian artists for European patrons. Here the Library's collection is unparalleled. Thus William Fraser, one of the Company's civil servants, took a Mughal artist, probably Ghulam Ali Khan, with him on a tour in the Punjab, simply to depict what he saw in the villages he passed through. Sir David Ochterlony, twice Resident in Delhi, lived in Indian style and was thus depicted *c.*1820. Other fine examples are the set of drawings of the Mughal monuments of Agra and Delhi by artists such as Latif and the sets of drawings of the people, buildings, and modes of transport of Calcutta by artists such as Shaikh Muhammad Amir. The two styles, East and West, merged in the work patronised by Raja Serfoji of Tanjore (ruled 1798–1839).

Another subject of common interest was the depiction of natural history. Chief among the Library's treasures in this respect is the Wellesley collection of 2660 drawings collected when the Marquis Wellesley was Governor-General (1798–1805), many of them sent to him in Calcutta from all over India and Australasia. This includes what is almost certainly the earliest depiction of the Australian koala bear painted by J.W. Lewin. Serfoji was a notable collector here too: an album contains all his hawks and animals from his menagerie depicted by Indian artists as well as his own notes in a rather quaint English. The style of these drawings is not very different from that of skilful English draughtsmen such as Lieutenant (later General) Ezekiel Barton (born 1781). The Company was itself a notable patron of the publication of this sort of work, assisting Nathaniel Wallich, the Superintendent of its Botanic Garden at Calcutta, to publish his *Plantae Asiaticae rariores* (1830–32) and subscribing for no less than 40 copies of John Gould's *The Birds of Asia* (1850–83).

There are over 15,000 drawings by British artists in the collection, both by professionals and amateurs. One of the largest series of drawings of India, 429 in all, was made by Thomas Daniell (1749–1840) and his nephew William Daniell (1769–1837), during a seven years' stay (1786–93); the tinted aquatint engravings based on them, *Oriental Scenery* (1795–1807), gave people in Europe a clearer understanding of the architecture, archaeology and landscape of India. William Hodges spent some years in India (1780–83), and the Library has among its oil paintings his view of Benares painted for Warren Hastings. John Gantz was employed as a Surveyor by the Company from 1800, and may himself have been the architect of 'Bentinck's Buildings', a range of offices built at Madras while Lord William Bentinck was Governor, 1803–07. Axel Haig's magnificent drawing of F.W. Stevens's

Sita rejects Ravana's advances, miniature from a fragmentary copy of Book V of the *Rāmāyana*. Udaipur, *c.*1655.
IOLR I.O. 3621, f.3r.

Above. Wooden cover to a manuscript of the *Lalitavistara* (the early life of the Buddha), showing the patron of the manuscript, Captain W.D. Knox. From Patan (Nepal), 1803.
IOLR I.O. 688.

Right. Squirrels in a plane tree, by Abul Hasan, Mughal, *c.*1610.
IOLR Johnson Album 1, no.30.

The Chinese Emperor Qianlong, by William Alexander, *c.*1793.
IOLR WD 959 (93).

Bombay Railway Station, exhibited at the Royal Academy in 1880, is a monument to the great Victorian architecture of India.

William Alexander went as official draughtsman with Lord Macartney's embassy to China in 1793, and the three volumes of his drawings record not only the reception of the Embassy but also a wide variety of views of life in China at the time. Henry Salt, who had trained with Farington and Hopper, departed in 1802 with Lord Valentia on his eastern tour, before becoming British Consul-General in Egypt, where he took part in the archaeological discoveries there. The Library has some of his drawings made while in India as well as most of the worked-up drawings ready for the engravers of his *Twenty four views in St Helena, the Cape, India, Ceylon, the Red Sea, Abyssinia and Egypt*, published London 1809.

Portrait and landscape painters, too, came to India, profiting by the new wealth of the 'nabobs', and sometimes painting the native rulers as well. Zoffany is the most famous of these, but other painters who went to India and whose work is in the collections include Thomas Daniell, Arthur William Devis, Thomas Hickey, Robert Home, Francesco Renal, James Wales and William Hodges. Zoffany's portrait of Hasan Reza Khan, the Nawab of Oudh's chief minister, (illustrated on p. 204) is a fine example of his work. Other portraits were painted in England after the sitter's return, such as Romney's Warren Hastings painted in 1796. Chinnery was employed in India, before he went on to Macao and Hong Kong, and there are a number of his lively sketches of animals and village life.

Apart from the professionals, about half the drawings in the collection are by amateur artists, soldiers, Company officials, and their wives, many of them very talented, who passed the often tedious time in India in sketching and painting. Many of the most skilful in the early 19th century had taken lessons from Chinnery, who was a gifted teacher – Sir Charles D'Oyly, John and Harriet Elliot, the children of the Governor-General Lord Minto, and Lady Sarah Elizabeth Amherst, the daughter of another Governor-General. Others, such as Alexander Allan, Robert Colebrooke, George Atkinson, and Robert Grindlay were sufficiently talented to have their work engraved and published. Yet others sketched entirely for their own amusement, like the various members of the gifted Prinsep family. James Prinsep was employed as an Assay Master, but is famed as the decipherer of the hitherto unreadable Kharosthi and Brahmi scripts. His brother William was a merchant in Calcutta and another brother, Thomas, a surveyor. Some of the great characters of pre-Mutiny India were artists, like Hyder Young Hearsey, an Anglo-Indian who accompanied Webb in 1808 to discover the source of the Ganges and Moorcroft in 1812 to Tibet to discover the source of the Sutlej and Indus.

All this material, and the many other drawings in the collection, both by professionals and amateurs, are immensely important for the light they shed on India during the British period, before the advent of photography.

The vast collection of photographs, about 200,000, covering the period 1856 to 1947, is a wonderful resource for visual documentation of British life in India and India's landscape, monuments and people. Perhaps the most important part of the collection are the 30,000 photographs of the monuments of India taken between 1858 and 1920 which are the basis of the Archaeological Survey of India's own collections. Many of these early photographs are also visual delights, such as Captain Lyon's view of the drawing-room of the Judge at Madura in a 17th-century Indian house. Early photographs of the British in India are poignant reminders of the fragility of their lives, such as Ahmed Ali Khan's albums of society in Lucknow in 1856 just before the Mutiny, as well as other views taken just after the Mutiny in Delhi, Lucknow and Cawnpore by pioneers of Indian photography such as John Murray, Principal of the Agra Medical School 1853–57, and Captain Robert Tytler and his wife Harriet. The most famous of the Indian pioneers is Samuel Bourne, who worked in India from 1862 to 1870. He made three separate

Opposite. A feast being prepared for the Sultan of Mandu, from the *Ni'matnāma* (book of recipes), Mandu, *c.*1495–1505.
IOLR EThé 2775, f.11.

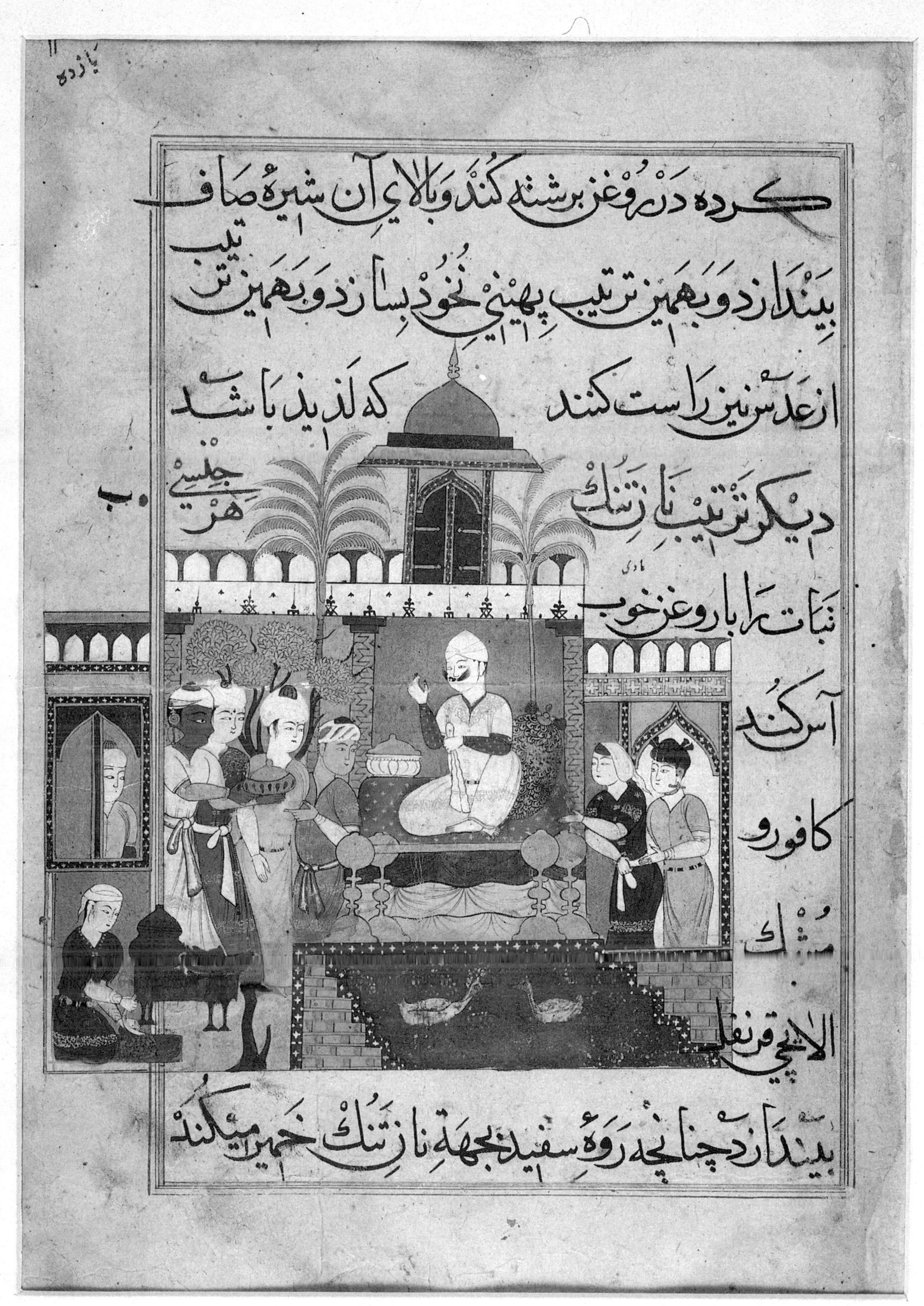
یازده ۱۱

کرده در روغن برشته کند و بالای آن شیرهٔ صاف
بیندازد و بهمین ترتیب پهینی نخود بسازد و بهمین ترتیب
از عدس نیز راست کنند که لذید باشد
دیگر ترتیب نان تنک هر جلیبی
نبات را با روغن خوب
آس کند
کافور و
مشک
الاچی قرنفل
بیندازد چنانچه روه سفید بجهة نان تنک خمیر میکند

11

Right. A prince in Persian costume, by Muhammad Khan, from the Dara Shikoh Album, 1633–34.
IOLR Add. Or. 3129, f.2.1v.

Below. 'Rani Jindan's Book', a selection of hymns from the *Adi Granth*, prepared for the wife of Maharaja Ranjit Singh, written in Gurmukhi in white ink on a black ground, 1828–30.
IOLR MSS Panj. D.4. ff. 1–2.

Above. Sir David Ochterlony at a nautch in his house, Delhi, *c*.1820.
IOLR Add. Or.2.

Left. Koala bears, by J.W. Lewin, *c*.1800–05.
OILR NHD 33, f.40.

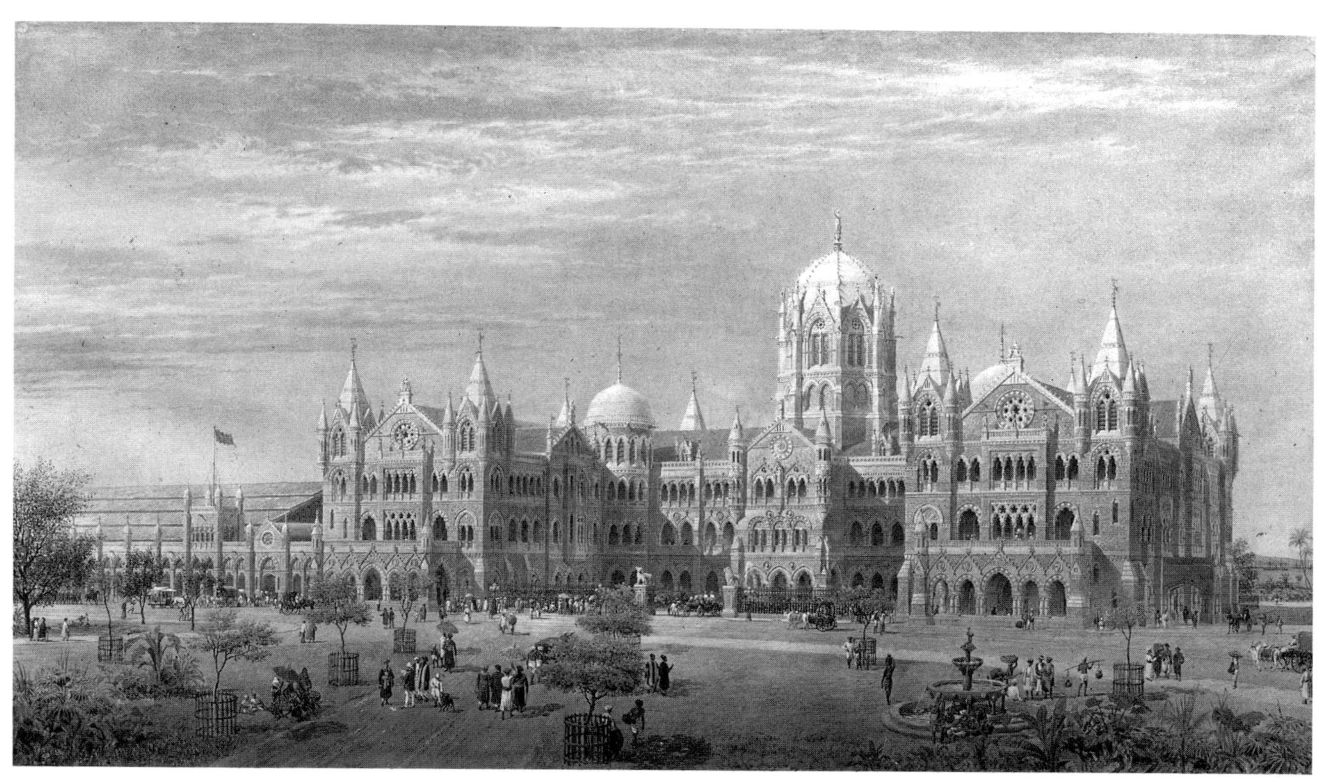

Opposite, above. Victoria Railway Terminus, Bombay, by Axel Haig, 1878.
IOLR WD 2443.

Opposite, below. Picket officers at the Alambagh, Lucknow, during the Indian Mutiny, by Patrick Fitzgerald, 1858.
IOLR Photo 591 (7).

Right. Lake at Naini Tal, by Samuel Bourne, *c*1865.
IOLR Photo 782 (88).

expeditions to the still largely unexplored Himalayas to take photographs, along with an enormous baggage train to carry his essential equipment. Other pioneers such as Saché, Beato, Robertson and Tripe are also well represented.

After photography became a well-established and routine process, it was used as part of the official record as much as the written word; during the high noon of the empire in India, it records a world now vanished for ever, of a leisured British society in club and sports-field, and of an imperial pomp surrounding the Viceroy greater even than in London. The Curzon collection of photograph albums perhaps records this latter aspect best, including the Dèlhi Durbar of 1903 and a large number of presentation albums commemorating visits to the various princes of India.

Besides these pictorial and manuscript documents of the British in India, there is the vast mass of printed books in the Library. Some of these have already been mentioned, but among treasures of this part of the collection are João Tavares de Véllez Guerreiro, *Jornada que Senhor Antonio de Albuquerque Coelho . . . fes de Goa* (Macao, 1718), the diary of the adventures of the Portuguese Governor of Macao *en route* to his post from Goa, printed from woodblocks in the Chinese style but in roman letters; *Nature's self-printing: a series of useful and ornamental plants of the South Indian flora . . . Mangalore: botanautographed and published by J. Hunziker, Basel Mission Press, 1862*, a marvellous example of 'nature printing', by which leaves and flowers, inked first or tinted afterwards, were actually used as printing material; and *Collection of specimens and illustrations of the textile manufactures of India*, (1873–80), with over 1000 specimens of the textiles themselves, made up from exhibits sent to the 1867 International Exhibition at Paris.

The India Office Library is also the repository of Indian periodicals. Besides the 18th-century magazines already mentioned, it contains what is often the most complete file extant of the early vernacular newspapers. One recent acquisition is a set of 31 issues of *Nūr-i Maghribī*, 16 August 1856 to 12 April 1857, an Urdu weekly published in Delhi, of particular interest since it covers the period up to the Mutiny. The *Cartoons from the Hindi Punch* of Bombay give a vivid picture of the first years of the 20th century in which the first stirrings of nationalism can be seen.

Above. Hasan Reza Khan, minister to the Nawab Vizier of Oudh, by Johan Zoffany, 1784.
IOLR F.108.

Opposite, above. A view of Benares, by William Hodges, 1781.
IOLR F.94.

Opposite, below. View of the Benares ghats, by James Prinsep, 1825.
IOLR WD 4164.

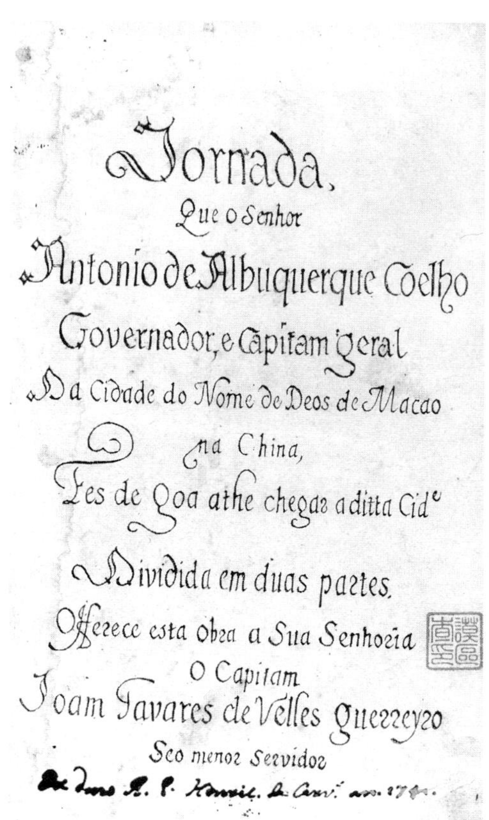

Jornada,
Que o Senhor
Antonio de Albuquerque Coelho
Governador, e Capitam Geral
Da Cidade do Nome de Deos de Macao
na China,
Fes de Goa athe chegar a ditta Cid.e
Dividida em duas partes.
Offerece esta Obra a Sua Senhoria
O Capitam
Joam Tavares de Velles Guerreyro
Seo menor Servidor

The *Jornada* of Antonio de Albuquerque Coelho, Governor of Macao, printed from woodblocks in the Chinese style, but in Roman letters, Macao 1718. IOLR V 23579.

Other collections are as rich in the 'classic' oriental languages, Arabic, Persian, Sanskrit, but the India Office Library is uniquely strong (thanks in great part to Johnson and Colebrooke) in manuscripts in modern Indian languages. One of the earliest acquisitions was a copy of the famous Hindi epic *Padumāvatī* by Malik Muhammad Jayasi, relating the story of Padmini, wife of Raja Ratan Sen, and the sack of Chitor by Ala al Din, written in Devanagari at Mirzapur, in the 18th century. From Johnson's collection comes the *Rāmacaritamānasa*, Tulsi Das's Hindi version of the *Rāmāyaṇa*, copied 1760–65, and there is a fine illuminated *Bhāgavatapurāṇa*, translated into Hindi and written in Nastaliq in 1777–82. Among the monuments of Sikh culture in the Punjab is a copy in Gurmukhi of *Janamsākhī*, the life of the first Guru Nanak (1469–1539), with illustrations; 'Rani Jindan's Book', a collection of the principal hymns from the *Ādi Granth* made for a wife of Maharaja Ranjit Singh of the Punjab, elegantly written in white letters on black, 1828–30; and the most famous of all the Punjabi manuscripts in the Library, another collection of *Sākhīs* of Guru Nanak, *Valāit-vālī Janamsākhī*, written in archaic Gurmukhi script in the 17th century, given by H.T. Colebrooke.

The languages of South India have contributed their own remarkable documents to the collection. The palm-leaf manuscript of the *Kèraḷa-vartamānam* in Malayalam, though written in 1792, preserves an account of the Portuguese arrival in Malabar in 1497. There are three specimens of *Kaḍatas*, long pieces of cloth impregnated with a mixture of ground tamarind seeds and charcoal powder which toughens the cloth and provides a black surface, on which texts in Kannada are written in white with a soap-stone pencil. In Tamil, there is the author's autograph manuscript of *Tēmpāvaṇi*, an epic poem on the life of Joseph, husband of Mary, the mother of Jesus Christ, written in 1726 by Costanzo Giuseppe Beschi, an Italian missionary in South India from 1700 to 1742, who learned to write in Tamil with as great a fluency as Bartholomaeus Ziegenbalg (*see* above, page 150). Most exotic of all are two grants by members of the Zamorin ruling family of Calicut of commercial privileges to the Dutch East India Company. The terms of each grant are incised in Malayalam on long thin strips of metal: the earlier, dated 1691, is on gold, the other, dated 1710, on silver. These extraordinary objects came into English possession later in the 18th century and were presented to the Library in 1840.

Finally, mention should be made of the South East Asia collections, principally from Burma. The fact that Burma was ruled by the British as part of their Indian Empire means that the India Office Library and Records became the repository not only for official archives but also for manuscripts (including some from the Mandalay Palace Library), photographs, maps and drawings relating to Burma. Many are of special historical interest, such as a folding book (*parabaik*) with detailed illustrations of objects in daily use at the palace, and an album of drawings and paintings presented by Lord Wynford in 1849, which includes pictures of Burmese ministers and processions.

The India Office Library and Records are very far from static. The Records, although essentially an historical rather than an active archive, have nevertheless a growth point in the European Manuscripts Section which continues to receive about 100 new accessions each year ranging from sizable collections of private papers to individually significant historical documents. The acquisitions of the Library, with its responsibility to keep abreast of publications on India and South Asia produced world-wide, are naturally on a far larger scale and currently run at about 5000 volumes a year. In addition, pictorial and photographic material continues to be acquired. With a new popular interest in all aspects of the 'Raj' on the one hand, and the continuing scholarly attention devoted to Indological and Asian studies on the other, the collections are increasingly in demand, a demand which finds its own treasures in the diversity of material preserved at Orbit House. Now approaching the bicentenary of its foundation, the India Office Library and Records, created to serve the diverse needs of the East India Company and then of the British Empire, has become an important element of the British Library, finding a modern role as the specialist collection and reference source for India and South Asia – where, although no longer part of an empire, a fifth of all the people in the world live.

Treaty between the Zamorin of the Kirakke Kovilakam and the Dutch East India Company, 10 November 1691, recorded in Malayalam on a strip of gold $1\frac{3}{4}$ inches by 80 inches.
IOLR MSS Mal. 12.

12 Bookbindings, Newspapers, Stamps

THE COLLECTING OF examples of bookbinding, as objects of historical or artistic interest, properly began with the accession of the Cracherode collection in 1799 (*see* above, p. 70). But the older collections had already provided many specimens whose importance has been recognised then or later: Sloane's collection had included the earliest English embroidered bookbinding, on Anne Felbrigge's Psalter (above, p. 20). The largest number came with the Old Royal Library, the repository of both manuscript and printed books in bindings made for members of the royal family or acquired by them. Some are among the masterpieces of major binders or workshops, and important documents of the history of the craft: others, notably the fabric bindings, are unique witnesses to the skill of unknown artists and craftsmen.

Two royal bindings made for Henry VIII were mentioned earlier (*see* p. 30): another, the copy of Sir Thomas Elyot's *Image of Governance* (1541), is bound by the 'Greenwich Binder' for presentation to the King in white deerskin with the initials 'H.R.', and motto 'Dieu et mon droit', and the further legend painted on the gauffered edges of the leaves 'Rex in aeternum vive'. The presentation manuscript of the commentary on the Emperor Charles V's campaign against the French addressed to Henry VIII by Anthonius de Musica of Antwerp (1544) is bound by the 'Medallion Binder' (so called from the medallions of Plato and Dido that he used) with the legend 'Vero defensori fidei', and the dedication copy of Martin de Brion's description of the Holy Land is in red velvet, embroidered and decorated with seed pearls. Another embroidered binding of purple velvet covers Queen Catharine Parr's copy of Petrarch (1544).

Opposite. Paris mosaic binding of *c.*1640, on Chacon, *Historia Belli Dacici*, Rome, 1616.
C.14.c.12.

Below. H. Evans. Lower cover on a Bible, London 1657.
C.108.n.7.

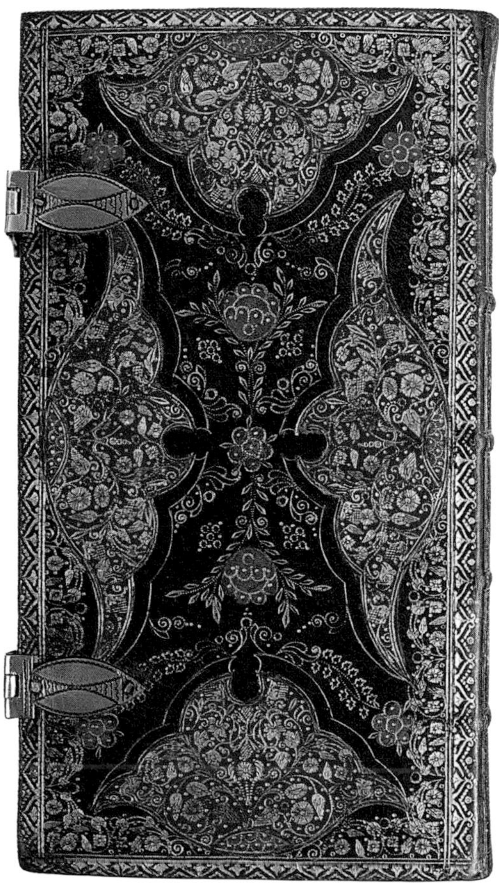

Some relics of Edward VI's precocious reading are in remarkable bindings, notably the 'backless' binding, the spine disguised as the edges which would then have faced outwards on the shelf, with the royal arms and initials 'E.R.' and the date '1552', on Pietro Bembo's *Historia Veneta* (1551). The presentation manuscript of William Thomas's translation of the Venetian Giosafat Barbaro's travels in the Crimea and Persia presented to Edward VI is in an elaborate interlaced binding. Queen Elizabeth's books include two fine examples of the work of the great emigré French binder, Jean de Planche, one in black morocco on Nicolay, *Navigations et pérégrinations orientales* (1568), the other Archbishop Parker's presentation copy of *Flores Historiarum* (1570) in brown calf, both onlaid with white leather; the latter had strayed from the Royal Library, and returned with the Cracherode bequest. The Queen's textile bindings include another Parker presentation, his *De antiquitate Britannicae ecclesiae* (1572) in green velvet embroidered with a deer-park scene, and the little crimson velvet binding with enamelled gold clasps and corners on *Meditationes Christianae* (1570), which came with the King's Library in 1823. Three other remarkable 16th-century English bindings came with the Old Royal Library, a polychrome binding in the style of Grolier's made in Paris for Thomas Wotton on Cicero *Les questions Tusculanes* (1543), another with the bear and ragged staff badge of Elizabeth's favourite Robert Dudley, Earl of Leicester, on Plato *Convivium* (1543), and the inlaid binding on the Bible (1544) with the white horse and oak-spray device of Henry Fitzalan, Earl of Arundel.

One extraordinary survival from the Jacobean court is the travelling library of Sir Julius Caesar, 44 little volumes in similarly gilt limp vellum bindings, shelved in a box made in the form of a large turkey leather-bound folio, the inner side of whose front board provides a decorative catalogue of the books that face it. Among James I's books is a copy of André Thevet's *Les vrais pourtraits et vies des hommes illustres* (1584) in handsome dark green morocco. Henry Prince of Wales's bindings have already been mentioned: many still survive in the Library, of which an exceptional example is on Julius Ferretti *De re et disciplina militari* (1575); the normal bindings are still striking, and before the silver of the ostrich feathers oxidised, the effect must have been brilliant.

The New Testament, London 1625, and *The Whole Booke of Davids Psalmes*, London 1635. Canvas embroidered with coloured silks.
C.46.a.19.

The Whole Booke of Psalmes, London 1643. White satin embroidered binding with portrait of Charles I.
C.17.a.25.

The reign of Charles II coincided with the first great flowering of the art of bookbinding in England, in which the Royal bookbinder, Samuel Mearne, had a central part. Mearne's own bindings range in elaboration from the comparatively plain brown turkey leather bindings of the Hebrew books, returned in 1759 by the generosity of Solomon da Costa, of which the *Mishnah Abhoth* (1566) is an example, to the exceptionally grand service books bound in red turkey, elaborately worked, with decorated edges, 'for the King's Own Use' in his private chapel. These include the *Book of Common Prayer* of 1669 and 1681; both these books were retained in 1757 and came with the King's Library in 1823, clear evidence of George III's early bibliophilic taste. Others were the dedication copy of Loggan's *Oxonia illustrata* (1675) in red turkey and the Bible (1674) in blue, both bound by the binder who may have been William Nott, 'the famous book-binder' according to that famous diarist, Samuel Pepys.

Royal taste at the turn of the century is exemplified by the dedication copy of Bates's *Works* (1700) bound for William III by Richard Balley in characteristically original style, and by George I's *Book of Common Prayer* (1715). The unusual work of James Edwards of Halifax, in which a painted design was covered with transparent vellum, can be seen in Queen Charlotte's *Book of Common Prayer* (1760), while George III's own taste is exemplified in the splendid blue morocco binding, by his own bindery, on his 42-line Bible, and in the new rococo style, of which Baumgarten's binding on Beattie's *Essay on Truth* (1774) is a fine example. The new neo-classical style is prefigured by the grandest of all George III's contemporary bindings, the presentation copy of Robert Adam's *Ruins of the Palace at Spalatro* (1764), which Adam himself designed.

These examples of royal patronage are only a cross-section, if one of peculiar interest and artistic merit, of the vast number of historically important bindings that came to the Library incidentally, rather than as specimens of the bookbinder's art. The first major accession of bookbindings, collected on a systematic basis to illustrate the progress of binding, came with the bequest of Felix Slade in 1868. Slade is now chiefly remembered as the man whose bequests established the Slade School of Art and the two professorial chairs of art at Oxford and Cambridge. He also bequeathed his notable collection of glass, and a major part of his prints and bookbindings, which he had put together over 50 years, to the British Museum. Among the treasures that thus came to the Library were a notable medieval binding, a German gospel book of *c.*1200 in a later 13th-century binding of leather over wooden boards with panels of Limoges enamel-work. Among those on printed books were the most beautiful binding for Apollonio Filareto, with his device of an eagle soaring over rocky sea, on a Ptolemy printed at Lyon in 1541, and a fine Venetian binding with sunk panels in oriental style, Piccolomini *Della institutione morale* (1560). There were two splendid French bindings, Paulus Aemilius *De rebus gestis Francorum* (1555), and the Cedrenus (1566); a fine polychrome German binding with the arms of the Emperor Maximilian II painted on the gauffered edges, on *Der Stat Nürnberg verneute Reformation* (1566); and the dedication copy of Bishop Joseph Hall's *Contemplations on the Old Testament* (1626) bound in olive turkey with the arms of Charles I. There were also four French 18th-century 'mosaique' bindings of the first quality, notably the floral binding by Padeloup on *Heures nouvelles* (1749), and an elaborate German tortoise-shell binding, inlaid with silver and mother of pearl, on Arndt *Paradiessgärtlein* (1722).

This collection, joined to the Museum's hereditary riches and the Cracherode and Grenville collections, proved the impetus for the serious study of bookbinding, in which the catalogues of H.B. Wheatley, W.Y. Fletcher and W.H.J. Weale have an important place. Here, the whole history of the subject is exemplified, beginning with the earliest, the Coptic bindings of stamped leather over papyrus paste-boards. The St Cuthbert Gospel (on loan) is in a

Gold-tooled binding by T.J. Cobden-Sanderson, 1888, on P.B. Shelley, *The Revolt of Islam*, London, 1818.
C.68.i.10.

P.L. Martin. Modern French binding on Suarès, *Hélène chez Archimède*, Paris, 1955.
C.108.eee.18.

scarcely later western binding, made in Northumbria in the time of St Cuthbert, at the turn of the 7th to 8th centuries.

The earliest surviving (if substantially reconstructed) jewelled binding is on a 10th–11th century German gospel book, with its gilt central figure of Christ; a similar but later (14th-century) binding adorns a 9th-century gospel book. The most beautiful of these is the Psalter of Queen Melissenda, daughter of Baldwin, King of Jerusalem (1118–31), and wife of Foulques, King of Jerusalem (1131–44), with its two fine contemporary Byzantine ivory panels. Later Byzantine metal-work is found on a 10th-century Greek gospel book.

The tradition of leather bookbinding in the west continues in the second half of the 12th century, from which period dates the fine romanesque binding on the glossed text of the Wisdom of Solomon. Other later medieval bindings include the fine presentation binding of Thomas Ebendorffer's 'History of the German Empire' for the Emperor Frederick III (*c.*1450), two remarkable examples of *cuir giselé* work on the Petrus Comestor (dated 1451) and the Feibusch Haggadah, and the fine early Italian gilt binding on a late 15th-century pontifical.

The 16th century saw the art of bookbinding reach a peak of decorative art, notably in the fine Italian and French bindings of the mid-century. These appealed particularly to Cracherode and Grenville, and so (besides those already mentioned) the Library now owns the Celsus (1497), a magnificent plaquette binding, the Martial (1501), the Wittekind (1532) and Theodoret (1552), all from Grolier's collection. Other splendid Parisian bindings of the period include two, both *c.*1555, on Lucian (1522) by Wotton's Binder C and by Claude de Picques on Bernal *Don Christalian de Espana* (1545), from the Cracherode and Grenville collections. Among the notable later continental examples, the Parisian mosaic binding of *c.*1640 on Chacon *Historia belli Dacici* (1616) from the King's Library, and the magnificent missal bound by the great 17th-century Dutch binder Albert Magnus, are outstanding.

All these books were in the Library before the arrival of Howard Nixon in 1936, Deputy Keeper in the Department of Printed Books, who over 30 years gave not only the British Museum's collection, but the whole history of bookbinding, a new foundation. The acquisitions that he made, notably from Major Abbey's collection, stand comparison – no mean achievement – with the books that they joined. There were two remarkable Grolier bindings, the first in a style unrepresented hitherto in the collection, on A. Krantz *Wandalia* (1519) and, from Chatsworth, Marlianus *Urbis Romae topographia* (1544). Even more remarkable were two of the finest examples of contemporary Parisian binding, the Caesar (1543) bound for Mahieu to a design of astonishing subtlety and restraint from the Holkham Library, and the Bible (1540) of Sir Thomas Cornwallis, Treasurer of Calais, which is one of the masterpieces of Claude de Picques.

In the 17th century, the exquisite *Delices de l'Esprit* (1661) bound for Louis XIV's Queen Marie Thérèse parallels a binding in the Slade bequest, but it was the English School to which Nixon principally contributed, not only by the acquisition of books but in the scholarly work that reestablished Mearne's work and distinguished it from that of his competitors. This was commemorated in the notable exhibition 'English Restoration Bookbindings' in 1974, which was the summation and monument of Nixon's work in this field. Amongst the remarkable bindings that he acquired were the magnificent Mearne Bible (1659) bound for Nathaniel, Lord Crewe; another Bible (1657) bound by Henry Evans, to join two other specimens of his work, one in Sloane's collection, the other bequeathed by Speaker Onslow in 1768; yet another (1638), the masterpiece of John Fletcher, acquired from the Chatsworth Library; a binding by Roger Bartlett on the first volume of Comber's *A Companion to the Temple* (1684) and one of Richard Balley's 'backless' bindings. A copy of Aesop's *Fables* with Francis Barlow's illustrations, by the

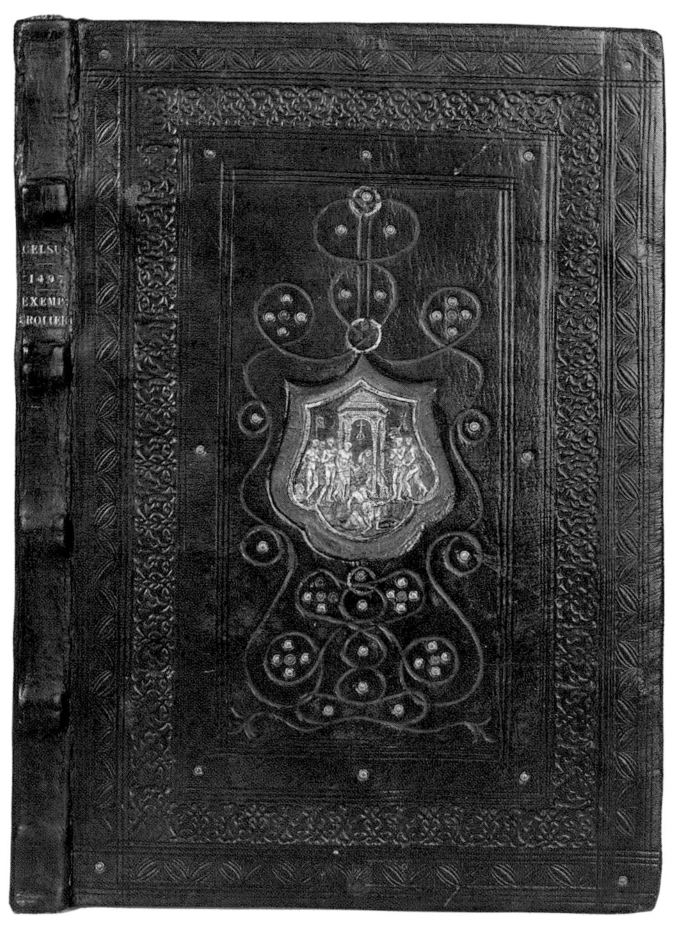

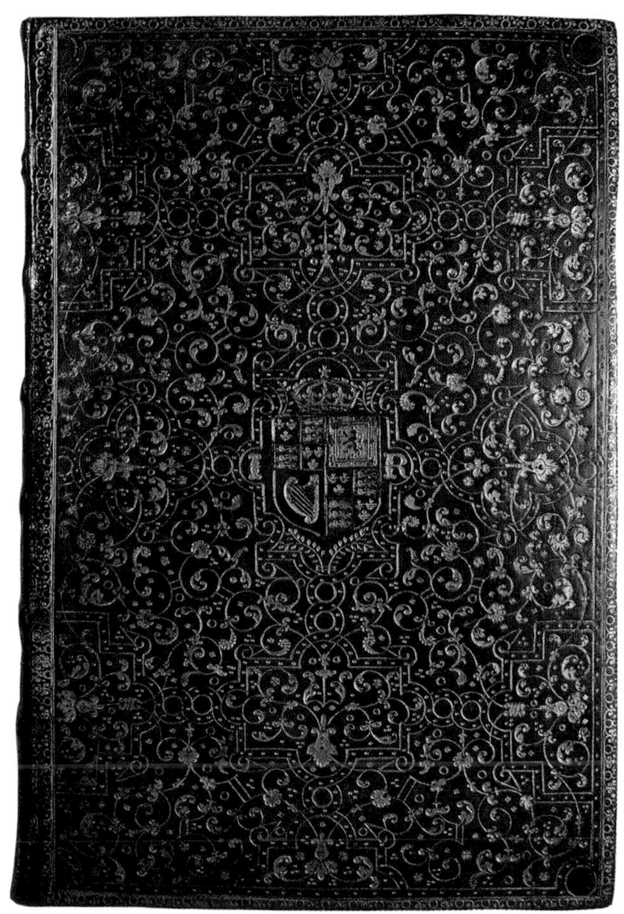

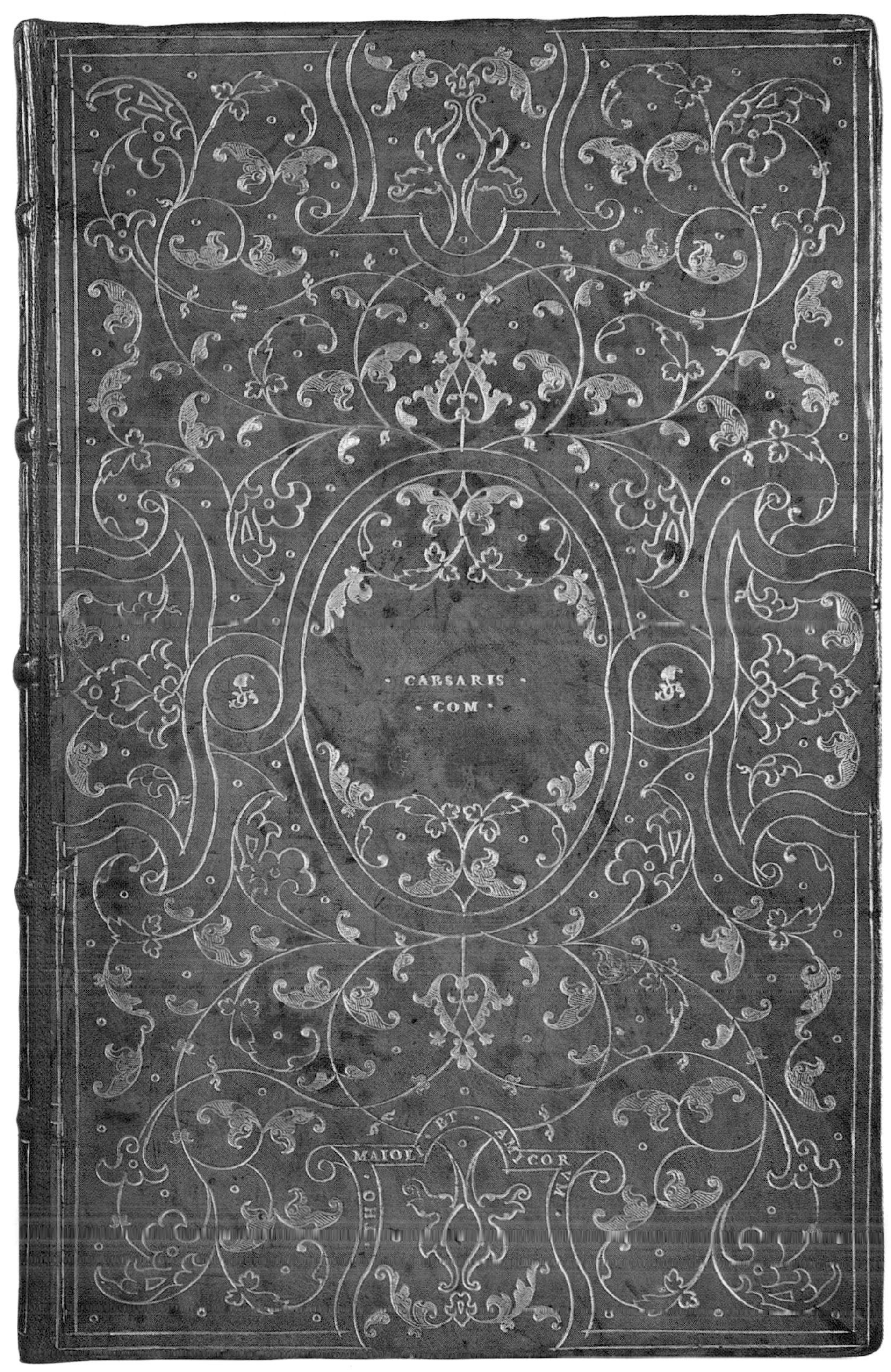

Above. Binding for Mahieu on Caesar, *Commentarii*, Paris, 1543.
C.132.h.49.

Opposite, top left. Grolier plaquette binding on Celsus, *De medicina libri*, Venice 1497.
G.9026.

Opposite, top right. Backless binding by R. Balley on *Book of Common Prayer*, London, 1668.
C.108.d.35.

Opposite, below left. Binding for Queen Marie Thérèse, Paris 1661, on J. Desmarests de St. Sorlin, *Delices de l'Esprit*, 1661.
C.132.i.62.

Opposite, below right. Binding for James I on Thevet, *Pourtraits*, 1584.
C.22.f.4.

1607.

A true report of certaine wonderfull ouerflowings of Waters, now lately in Summerset-shire, Norfolke, and other places of England: destroying many thousands of men, women, and children, ouerthrowing and bearing downe whole townes and villages, and drowning infinite numbers of sheepe and other Cattle.

[illegible] at London by W. I. for E[illegible]ard White and are to be solde at the signe of the [illegible] North [illegible] of [illegible]

An early newsbook, 1607.

binder who bound several copies of that splendid book, one of which, in blue turkey, belonged to Cracherode, was now joined by the dedication copy to the Earl of Devonshire in red turkey, also from Chatsworth. One final acquisition demands mention, the copy of James 'Athenian' Stuart and Nicholas Revett's *Antiquities of Athens* (1762), in a presentation binding designed by Stuart himself, a masterpiece of neo-classic design to set beside Adam's *Ruins of Spalatro* in the King's Library.

But of all Nixon's acquisitions the most remarkable was the gift of the Henry Davis Collection of bookbindings, 'the finest formed in this century', all the more welcome since collector and expert had worked together, complementing and not duplicating the Library's existing collection. Thus, the signed Monnier floral mosaic binding on Cicero *De amicitia* (1749) challenges comparison with Slade's Padeloup example, and the books bound for Thomas Wotton, Robert Dudley and Mahieu (a fine Pausanias (1551) in the same style as Slade's Cedrenus) fit in with existing acquisitions. The London *dos-à-dos* binding on the *Nouveau Testament* and *Psaumes* (1564–65) in calf with sunk blue velvet panels goes with the red velvet embroidered *dos-à-dos* binding on the same texts (1633). There is a Parisian romanesque binding on a glossed gospel book, *c.*1200, to set beside the Museum's existing specimen.

In particular, the Restoration bindings add still further to the Library's great riches, notably another fine Mearne Bible (1659) and a fine signed binding by Alexander Cleeve on a 1663 Bible. There are several 15th-century English bindings, otherwise rare in the Library, including a 13th-century Bible bound *c.*1470 by the Canterbury Binder and an example of the work of the Scales Binder.

The Continental bindings number a restrained but elegant gilt binding for Cardinal Olivero Carafa on the dedication manuscript of P. Balbi *Epistola ad Theodosium*, before 1479, another for Apollonio Filareto, the presentation binding by Lucas Weischner on the dedication copy to Rudolph II of E. Reusner, *Opus genealogicum catholicum* (1592), a splendid Viennese 18th-century binding tooled in silver and gold on an album of Amandus Schickmayer, Abbot of Lambach, *c.*1750, and a fine late 15th-century Spanish *mudéjar* binding on a manuscript Toledo breviary. There is even a fine late 14th-century blind-tooled Egyptian Qur'an binding with gold paint to set beside a similar binding in the Department of Oriental Manuscripts and Printed Books.

But besides these historic treasures, Nixon inaugurated the collection of bindings by contemporary binders. Now, in addition to buying works already bound, the Library commissions work from the binders of today. There are examples by the great contemporary French binders, Pierre Legrain (Colette, *Vagabonde*, 1927), Paul Bonet (Suarès, *Cirque*, 1933) and P.L. Martin (Suarès, *Hélène chez Archimède*, 1955). Recent work by English binders includes Lou Smith's on Gogol, *The overcoat* (1975), Jeff Clements's on John Sparrow, *Lapidaria Septima* (1975), and a fine example of one of the senior and most respected of modern binders, the late Sydney M. Cockerell's on Britten, *Death in Venice* (1979), to a design by Joan Tebbutt.

One of the first and most important events in the history of the Library in the 20th century was the decision (for which statutory authority was acquired by Act of Parliament in 1902) to store newspapers away from the main Museum site. Newspapers had been a growing problem throughout the previous century. Initially, the complications of the Stamp Act had delayed their receipt; copyright deposit had been hard to enforce; and the growing bulk and number of papers had aggravated the ever-present problem of storage space. The integrity of the collections was threatened by a Parliamentary Bill, mercifully not passed, authorising the transfer of provincial newspapers to local authorities. The first building, for storage only, was erected at Colindale in 1906; it has been enlarged several times since, and, with the construction of a reading room, it was renamed the Newspaper Library in 1932. Originally,

Detail from the front page of *The Ipswich Journal*, 15 April–22 April 1721.

THE Ipſwich Journal, OR, *Weekly-Mercury:*

The South Eaſt Proſpect of Ipſwich.

With the Freſheſt Advices Foreign and Domeſtick.

the provincial newspapers only were stored at Colindale, but in 1932 the London papers from 1801, except for the last years of those in the Burney Collection, acquired in 1818 (see p. 93), were moved to Colindale, which is now the major repository in Britain.

The Library's collections thus run from the first newsletter of 1513 to today's papers. Its holdings of 17th-century papers, notably those in the Thomason Tracts and Burney's considerable retrospective acquisitions, are the largest in the world. They include the earliest examples of newsbooks – *A true report of certaine wonderful overflowings of waters* (1607) has a picture that anticipates today's television reports of floods – and the Corantos, such as *Corante, or newes from Italy, Germaine, Hungarie, Poland, Bohemia and France* (1621), based on the Holy Roman Empire's newsletter system, the ancestor of today's news agencies. Ichabod Dawks, who had the modern newspaper proprietor's eye for his public, caught it with a folio sheet set in a special type devised to imitate the hand-written (and therefore more up-to-date) newsletter. The provincial press which grew fast in the 18th century, emphasised its local appeal with pictures of the town in which it was issued (for example, the *Ipswich Journal*, 1721). Pictures, such as that of Robert Owen's new model town at Lanark, might appear even in *The Times*, but great events, Trafalgar or Waterloo, were generally announced in sober words, although Queen Victoria's coronation brought a special gold-printed issue of *The Sun* (28 June 1838).

Advertisement in *The Gentlewoman*, Christmas number 1899.

The 19th century saw a great increase in the demand for pictures, and the *Illustrated London News*, using hand-engraved wood-blocks, achieved miracles of speedy transfer of sketches on the spot into pictorial news, notably during the Crimean War. Advertising, which went with news from early on, also needed special effects and colour printing came to revolutionise weekly journals. *The Gentlewoman* was the first to make a regular feature of this, and the new needs of the feminist movement found other, more vigorous, outlets (for example, *The Suffragette* no. 1, 1912). Colour printing came to effect an equal revolution in children's reading.

All these, once printed in thousands, are now to be found in the Newspaper Library; all too often the copy there is the only one, or one of very few, to survive. Others, however, were rare from the outset. The earliest issues of *Pravda*, printed in 1917 before the October Revolution, are rare in the

The  Sun.

WITH WHICH THE "TRUE SUN" IS NOW INCORPORATED.

No. 14,289. LONDON, THURSDAY EVENING, JUNE 28, 1838. PRICE

God Save

Victoria R

THE CORONATION.

Mr. Thompson, in his work on 'The Processions and Ceremonies observed in the Coronation of the Kings and Queens of England,' gives the following account of

King Edward's Chair.

"This chair (commonly called St. Edward's chair) is an ancient seat of solid, hard wood, with back and sides of the same, variously painted, in which the kings of Scotland were in former periods constantly crowned; but, having been brought out of the kingdom by King Edward I., in the year 1296, after he had totally overcome John Baliol king of Scots, it has ever since remained in the abbey of Westminster, and has been the royal chair in which the succeeding kings and queens of this realm have been inaugurated. It is in height 6 ft. 7 in., in breadth at the bottom, 38 in., and in depth 24 in.; from the seat to the bottom is 25 in., the breadth of the seat within the sides is 28 in., and the depth 18 in. At 9 inches from the ground is a board, supported at the four corners by as many lions. Between the seat and this board is enclosed a stone, commonly called Jacob's, or the Fatal Marble Stone, which is an oblong, of about 22 in. in length, 13 in. broad, and 11 in. deep; of a steel colour, mixed with some veins of red. History relates that it is the stone whereon the patriarch Jacob laid his head in the plain of Luz. It is also added that it was brought to Brigantia, in the kingdom of Gallicia in Spain, in which place Gathol king of Scots, sat on it as his throne. Thence it was conveyed into Ireland by Simon Brach, who was king of Scots, about 700 years before Christ's time; from thence into Scotland by king Fergus, about 370 years afterwards; and, in the year 850, it was placed in the abbey of Scone, in the sheriffdom of Perth, by King Kenneth, who caused it to be enclosed in this wooden chair, and a phophetical verse to be engraved, of which the following is a translation:—

'Should fate not fail, where'er this stone is found
The Scots shall monarchs of that realm be crown'd.'

"This is the more remakable by its having been fulfilled in the person of King James I., grandfather to the Princess Sophia, electress dowager of Hanover, grandmother to King George II., who was grandfather to his late Majesty, George III. This antique regal chair, having (together with the golden sceptre and crown of Scotland) been solemnly offered by King Edward I. to St. Edward the Confessor, in the year 1297 (from whence it derives the appellation of St. Edward's chair), has ever since been kept in the chapel called by his name; with a tablet affixed to it, whereon several Latin verses are written, in the old English character. The ornaments of this chair consist of crockets and fret-work, richly gilt. It has a cushion, covered with the same materials. The stone maintains its usual place under the seat of the chair, but is hid from observation by the fringe which surrounds it."

The Regalia.

These are—St. Edward's Staff—the Spurs—the Sceptre with the Cross—the Pointed Sword of Temporal Justice—the Sword of Mercy—the Sword of State—the Sceptre with the Dove—the Orb—St. Edward's Crown—the Patina, the Chalice, and the Bible.

St. Edward's Staff, in length four feet eleven inches and a half, is a sceptre of gold, having a foot of steel about four inches and a quarter in length, with a mound and cross at the top; the ornaments are also of gold, and the diameter is upwards of three-quarters of an inch.

The Spurs, called the great golden Spurs, are elaborately wrought; they have no rowels, but end in an ornamented point.

The Sceptre with the Cross, or Sceptre Royal, is likewise of gold, the handle plain, and the upper part wreathed; it is in length two feet nine inches and a quarter, and is of the same thickness as the former. The point at the lower part is enriched with rubies, emeralds, and small diamonds; and the space of five inches and a half in length, above the handle, is elegantly embellished with similar precious stones. The top rises into a fleur-de-lis, with six leaves, of which three are upright, and the other three are hanging down, all enriched with precious stones; out of the fleur-de-lis issues a mound made of an amethyst, set round with table-diamonds, and upon the mound a cross, wholly covered with precious stones, and a large table-diamond in the centre.

The Sword of Justice of the Temporality, or Third Sword, is sharp-pointed; the length of the handle is four inches, the pommel an inch and three-quarters, and the cross seven inches and a half; the scabbard in all respects is like the two former.

Curtoma, or the Pointless Sword, representing the Sword of Mercy, is the principal in dignity of three swords which are borne naked before the kings at the coronation. It is a broad bright sword, of which the length of the blade is thirty-two inches, the breadth almost two inches, the handle, which is covered with fine gold wire is four inches long, and the pommel an inch and three-quarters, which, with the cross, is plain steel gilt, the length of the cross is almost eight inches. The scabbard belonging to it is covered with a rich brocaded cloth of tissue, with gilt ornaments.

The sword of state, which is a large two-handed sword, having a splendid scabbard of crimson velvet, decorated with gold plates of the royal badges, in order as follow:—Up at the point is the orb or mound, then the royal crest of a lion standing on an imperial crown; lower down are a portcullis, harp, thistle, fleur-de-lis, and rose; near the hilt is the portcullis repeated; next are the royal arms and supporters; and, lastly, the harp, thistle, &c., occur over again. The other side of the scabbard is exactly the same. The handle and pommel of the sword are embossed with similar devices in silver gilt; and the cross is formed of the royal supporters, the lion and unicorn, having a rose within a laurel between them on one side, and a fleur-de-lis, encircled in the same manner, on the other.

The king's sceptre with the dove is a sceptre of gold, in length three feet seven inches, three inches in circumference at the handle, and two inches and a quarter round the top. The pommel is decorated with a circle or fillet of table-diamonds, and in several places with precious stones of all sorts, and the mound at the top is embellished with a band or fillet of rose-diamonds. Upon the mount is a small Jerusalem cross, wherein is fixed a dove with wings expanded, as the emblem of mercy.

The orb, mound, or globe, is a ball of gold of six inches diameter, encompassed with a band of the same, embellished with roses of diamonds encircling other precious stones, and edged about with pearl. On the top is a very large amethyst, of a violet or purple colour, near an inch and a half in height, of an oval form, and which, being encompassed with four silver wires, becomes the pedestal of a splendid cross of gold of three inches and a quarter in height and three inches in breadth, set very close with diamonds, having, in the middle, a sapphire on one side, and an emerald on the other. It is also embellished with four large pearls in the angles of the cross, near the centre, and three more at the ends of it. The whole height of the orb and cross is eleven inches.

The first and principal diadem, denominated St. Edward's Crown, with which his Majesty is invested, is so called in commemoration of the ancient one, which was kept in Westminster Abbey till the beginning of the great rebellion, when, with the rest of the regalia, it was sacrilegiously carried away. It is a very rich imperial crown, embellished with pearls and precious stones of various kinds, as diamonds, rubies, emeralds, and sapphires, with a mound of gold on the top of it, encircled with a band of the same, embellished also with precious stones; and upon the mound a cross of gold decorated in a similar manner, having three very large oval pearls, one at the top of the cross, and two others pendant at the sides of it. This crown is composed, as all those of England are, of four crosses and as many fleur-de-lis upon a rim or circle of gold, all embellished with precious stones, from the tops of which crosses arise four circular bars or arches, which meet at the top, and at the intersection is the pedestal whereon is fixed the mound. The cap within the crown is of purple velvet lined with white taffeta and turned up with ermine, thickly powdered in three rows.

The Ampulla and Anointing Spoon.

The ampulla, which contains the holy oil, is in the form of an eagle, with the wings expanded, standing on a pedestal, all of pure gold, finely chased. The head unscrews at the middle of the neck for the convenience of putting in the oil, and, the vessel being entirely hollow, it is poured out into the spoon through the point of the beak. The weight of the whole is nearly eight or ten ounces, and the cavity of the body is capable of containing about six ounces. The anointing spoon is likewise of pure gold, with four pearls set in the broadest part of handle; the bowl of the spoon is finely chased both within and without, and, by its extreme thinness, appears to be very ancient.

THE CORONATION DAY.

All hail, Queen Victoria! all hail to this day,
So teeming with promise—we welcome it here!
As the bright stream of glory pursues its glad way,
And the blessing of thousands ascends in that cheer!

But if thousands on thousands are happy before thee,
Saluting thy favours, and catching thy smiles;
Oh! think of the millions of hearts that adore thee—
For this day is a JUBILEE over the isles!

Not alone o'er the isles—but Hindostan afar
Doth *our* jubilee spread—in the West, the poor slave,
As he prays for thy mercy, "fair Liberty's star!
"Be the Queen of the FREE, as the Queen of the brave."

Let the African joy, for his freedom is nigh;
Our Queen would not reign but o'er happy and free:
Let that thunder attest it—yon banner on high—
The Banner of Glory o'er land and o'er sea!

Bear witness, ye Nations! the homage we pay,
The pride that we feel, and the love we declare;
For the Queen of our hearts is, on this happy day,
Not alone of the brave—but THE Queen of the Fair!

Nor can chivalry boast, in the rolls of renown,
A scene such as THIS—for old Time stands apart,
While the Crown of her PEOPLE VICTORIA puts on,
All radiant with beauty—and pure as her heart!

Then fill up a bumper to honour THE QUEEN!
Our hands and our hearts in devotion we give;
And our children, while weeping with joy o'er this scene,
Shall pray, GOD bless VICTORIA! and long may she live.

SKETCH OF HER MAJESTY.

Her most gracious Majesty is the only daughter of the duke of Kent, the fourth son of George III., and of the duchess of Kent, the sister of Leopold, king of the Belgians. She was born on the 24th of May, 1819, and had reached the age (eighteen) required by the law, before she could assume the reins of government, in the month previous to her accession to the throne on the death of William the Reformer, on June 20th, 1837. On the present memorable day her Majesty was crowned, and now reigns over an affectionate and trusting people by all possible legal titles.

Till her accession to the throne her Majesty led a retired life under the care of her mother, who, giving up her native land; devoted herself most assiduously to the education of her child, in order to make her Majesty worthy of the high station to which she was born.

During the short time her Majesty has reigned she has well responded to the "tender and enlightened mother," under whose care, her Majesty said, "I have learned from my infancy to respect and love the constitution of my native country." On her first memorable appearance before the Council on the day of her accession, "stepping from the privacy of domestic life to the discharge of her high functions," she so demeaned herself as to cause general approbation. "She inspired," said Sir Robert Peel, "a confident expectation that she was destined to a reign of happiness for her people and of glory to herself." "There is something," he added, "which art cannot make nor lessons teach, and can only be suggested by a high and generous nature." Her Majesty has completely realised the hopes with which her careful education and her demeanour on her accession to the throne inspired all her subjects.

Her Majesty has always willingly met her people, and on both occasions she opened and closed the Parliament in person. One of the most memorable events since her accession was the great festival given to her by the City of London in November last year, which her Majesty honoured with her presence.

All who have had occasion to approach her Majesty speak with delight of her condescension and affability, and no deserving object of the royal bounty ever applied to her Majesty in vain.

Of her Majesty's personal appearance we need not speak, as the splendid portrait above gives more information at a glance than we could convey in a column. We may observe, however, that her Majesty is not tall, though she is graceful in her movements.

Her Majesty is said to be a good musician, and to be well versed in modern languages as well as in those sciences, such as botany, which are suitable for an an accomplished lady. She has shown herself, since her accession to the throne, a generous patron of the theatres and the fine arts, and has already done much to restore them in England to the splendour of the Elizabethan age. Men of science have not been overlooked, and England promises to be as celebrated under her reign for the peaceful arts as ever it was for warlike deeds under the most renowned of her predecessors.

Her reign has been already distinguished by the establishment of a regular communication by steam with the United States, and the rapid improvements now continually made in the arts, of which our journal this day presents one splendid specimen, betoken an unprecedented progress in civilization. For her Majesty's reign to be glorious for herself and happy for her people, her political measures must correspond with the extraordinary movement now impelled on society. Following a monarch who acquired a deservedly high reputation as a reformer, her task, and the task of her statesmen, it must be admitted, is not easy. But those who see in all things the directing hand of Providence will probably look on the graces of a female reign as likely to temper most advantageously the character of the monarchy, which, in this age of the world and with the present temper of mankind, might be exposed to much risk were either a heartless debauchée or a wilful tyrant to be on the throne.

Opposite. The Sun, 28 June 1838. Special issue printed in gold, to commemorate Queen Victoria's coronation.

Right. The Mafeking Mail, 'Special siege slip . . . issued daily, shells permitting'. 10 February 1900 ('121st day of siege').

THE MAFEKING MAIL

SPECIAL SIEGE SLIP.

ISSUED DAILY, SHELLS PERMITTING.   TERMS: ONE SHILLING PER WEEK, PAYABLE IN ADVANCE.

No. 70   Saturday, February 10th, 1900.   121st Day of Siege.

The Mafeking Mail.

SATURDAY, 10TH FEBRUARY, 1900.

LADYSMITH RELIEVED ?

Although there is no definite information to hand about Ladysmith, one may adopt, with feelings of confidence, the assumption that its relief has already been effected. We think on or about Wednesday, the 24th January. Space will not permit of giving the various pegs upon which to hang that belief, but Buller's advance on the 17th, the report of fighting at Spions Kop, on the 22nd and 23rd, the statement made in the paper of the 26th as to fighting having taken place 30 or 40 miles North of Ladysmith, the particular viciousness of the Boers here on the 27th to 31st. The London wire of the 2nd February telling of the upward bound on the Stock Market, all suggest that there is good news for us somewhere on the road.

With deep regret we record the death of Mr. James Dall, Town Councillor. All Mafeking will join in heartfelt condolence with his family in this their hour of sorrow and bereavement, and none will withhold tribute to the sterling integrity, the intense devotion as husband and father, and the worth of our late townsman.

POSTPONEMENT.

We are desired by Mr. Feltham, who is acting as Secretary to the Bachelor Officers Dance Committee, to state that as a tribute of respect to the family and friends of the late Mr. Dall, the dance announced for this evening will be postponed till to-morrow.

AUCTION SALE.

The undersigned, duly instructed, will sell by Public Auction, on

Sunday Next,

At 10-30 a.m.

A quantity of Ladies and Mens Boots and Shoes, Mens Underwear, Trousers, Jackets, Shirts,

And many other articles too numerous to mention.

Also a lot of New and Second hand Novels.

In addition to the above a lot of

GOOD SECOND HAND CLOTHING

ABSOLUTELY NO RESERVE !

Don't fail to receive Bargains.

Aldred & Ross,

Auctioneers & Sworn Appraisers.

With the sanction of the Col. Commanding

CYCLE SPORTS

will be held at the

RECREATION GROUND,

— ON —

Sunday, February 11th,

Commencing at 2-30 p.m.

Lady Sarah Wilson has kindly consented to distribute the prizes, which comprise: *Watches; a Clock; a most handsome hand-painted "Watteau" Fan; Silver Glove Buttons; Candlestick Mirror; Silver mounted Pipes; Amber Cigarette Holders; Cigarette Cases, &c.*

Referee: H. H. Major Goold-Adams.
Judges: Major Godley; Capt. Cowan. Inspector Marsh.
Handicappers: Lieut. Colonel Walford; Inspector Browne.
Starter: C. G. H. Bell, Esq., C.C. & R.M.
Clerk of Course / *Lap Scorer*: To be appointed on the Ground.

The Totalisator

Will be upon the Grounds.

Under charge of Sergt. Major Merry.

PROGRAMME:

	Start.
1. One Mile Siege Championship	2-40
2. Team Race of One Mile ... Four members of: The Prot. Regiment, the B.S.A. Police, the Cape Police, the Bechuanaland Rifles, and the Town Guard.	3-0
3. Half Mile Bicycle Race in Fancy Costume. *One prize for Winner, and one prize for best Fancy Dress.*	3-20
4. Half Mile Ladies Race ...	3-40
5. Three Lap Race ... ... *Walk a lap. Ride a lap. Run a lap.*	4-0
6. One Mile Bicycle Handicap *POST ENTRIES.*	4-40

Bicycles will be provided for those who have not their own. Lots being drawn for them.

The distribution of Prizes will take place directly after the last race.

By the kind permission of Capt. Cowan the Band of the Bechuanaland Rifles will play during the intervals.

Book Early for the

Concert,

Plan rapidly filling up.

Only a few Reserved Seats left.

ALDRED & ROSS, Market Square.

GRAND SIEGE CONCERT

UNDER THE PATRONAGE OF

Colonel R. S. S. Baden-Powell and Officers of the Garrison,

AT THE

MASONIC HALL,

February 11th, 1900,

TO CELEBRATE

THE 18TH SUNDAY OF THE SIEGE.

Commencing at 5-30 p.m.

Proceeds to be given to the Sports and Prizes Funds.

PROGRAMME:

PART I.

1. Cape Police, D. H., Khaki Band
2. Song ... "Anchored," Mr. Campbell
3. Pianoforte Recital, Signor Paderewski.
4. Song, "At the Ferry," Miss Friend
5. Mandoline Solo, "Mary" Waltz, Pte. J. P. Murray
6. Song, "Beauty's Eyes," Mr. Bulleid
7. Siege Song ... Pte. E. W. Coxwell "If it wasn't for the Maxim in between,"

Interval of 5 Minutes.

PART II.

1. Piccolo Solo ... Mr. Westland
2. Leger de main ... Mr. F. J. Jacobs
3. Song, "Sunshine above," Capt. Ryan, D.A.A.G.,B.
4. Recitation, "Bill Tinka," Lieut. C. X. McKenna.
5. Siege Sketch ... Gentleman Joe
6. Song, "The Outpost," Mr. Campbell
7. Comic Song ... Pte. E. W. Coxwell

God Save the Queen.

Owing to time no encores will be allowed.

HURRAH !!

Here is something Good.

F. FIRTH

Has still some hundreds of

Pianoforte Pieces and Songs

AT 4 COPIES FOR 1s.

ACCORDEONS

At 16s., 17s. 6d., 20s., 30s., 32s. 6d.

MAFEKING MUSIC DEPOT.

Printed and published by Townshend & Son, Market Square, Mafeking Editor and Manager: G. N. H. Whales.

extreme, and the *Mafeking Mail*, for obvious reasons while the Siege was on, was restricted by the shortage of raw material; wrapping paper was substituted for non-existent white paper. Few copies of the German forged issue of the *Evening Standard*, dropped from the air on 17 February 1940, reached their target.

Rarities apart, the real treasure of the Newspaper Library is its bulk. Nowhere else can the vast mass of topical information and diversion that once occupied the daily or weekly attention of millions of British people be studied in its entirety. The serried ranks of bound volumes, if sadly diminished when part of the Library was hit by bombs in 1940 (the only known set of the 18th century *Pue's Irish Intelligence* was lost), remain as an invaluable mirror of the concerns and preoccupations of the past and present. It is no less valuable as an electronic age finds more immediate, but fugitive, substitutes for printed news.

The Newspaper Library at Colindale after being hit by enemy bombs, 1940.

Stamps, like newspapers, are originally common and become rare through the accidents of time. To this is added the special accident of error – mistakes in engraving or printing, usually identified before many of the 'errors' ever come to be issued. Unlike newspapers, however, stamps were collected from early on: the Philatelic Society, now the Royal Philatelic Society, London, founded in 1869, formed a focus for an occupation already established 29 years after the 'Penny Black' became the world's first postage stamp. This movement might have passed the British Museum by if it had not been for one man, who did for stamps what Burney did for newspapers, Thomas Keay Tapling.

Tapling was born in 1855, and began collecting stamps before he was ten. At Harrow and Cambridge he continued, and a year after he graduated in 1880 he became Vice-President of the Philatelic Society, of which he had already been a member for ten years. In the following year he succeeded to the management of his father's carpet factory. He stood for Parliament and was elected in 1886. In 1891 he died of pleurisy, aged only 36, bequeathing his entire collection to the Museum on condition that it should never be sold or broken up and should be arranged and mounted following the system that he had initiated but had not lived to complete.

Reporting the bequest to the Trustees in October, Richard Garnett, then Keeper of Printed Books, wrote:

> Extraordinary as it must appear, it is unquestionable that never since the bequest of the Grenville Library has the Library of the British Museum received a benefaction remotely approaching the pecuniary value of this collection of stamps. This value cannot be estimated at less than £50,000. A sheet of Hawaiian stamps alone would sell for £600. There is probably no object in the world, bank notes and other promissory notes excepted, where value is so curiously out of proportion to the original cost of the material, or to the labour or artistic skill employed in its production, as a rare postage stamp. Whether this will always be the case is an interesting subject for speculation.

Thomas Keay Tapling.

Time has done nothing to reverse Garnett's verdict, and the foundation thus laid has grown by subsequent acquisition till it now forms a collection virtually complete in all issues of adhesive postage stamps from 1840 to 1889, and rich in many areas since. (See illustrations, p. 220.)

When Tapling was at Harrow he was offered the Canada 12*d.* black for £2 which he was obliged to refuse (and never found another) since he could not afford it. If he missed another opportunity, history does not record it. He was wealthy enough to indulge his taste to the full, and he did. His complete Heligoland set (1867–79) was bought on a yachting trip there, and when he went with the G.F. Vernon cricket tour to India in 1890 he bought Indian stamps, including a pair of 1854 four annas 'inverted head' on a cover. He also exchanged stamps, acquiring the Mauritius 'Post Office' Two-pence Blue thus; the Mauritius Penny Red, on a complete envelope used to send out

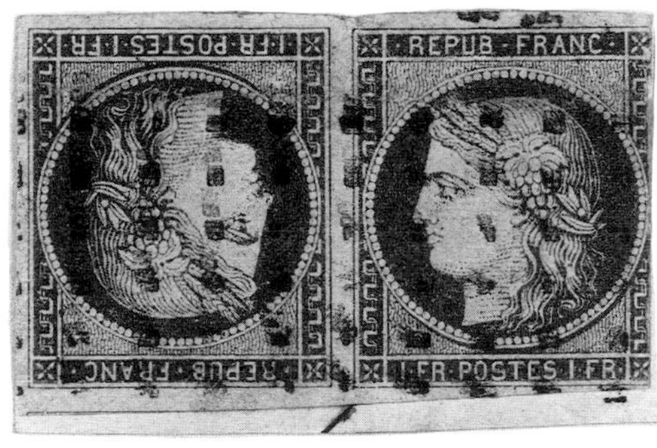

France. 1849 1 franc 'tête-bêche'.

invitations to a ball at Government House in 1847, he bought for £75. He also bought complete collections, notably the W.E. Image collections in 1881 for £3000, and in 1887 that of the brothers Caillebotte for £5000. He was in advance of his time in studying the systematic issue of stamps, reconstructing whole sheets of the New South Wales 'Sydney Views' from a huge parcel of stamps sent by an Australian cousin; and in collecting cancelled stamps and whole covers as well as unused stamps.

Among the rarities thus acquired were the Hawaian 'Missionaries' referred to by Garnett, the 1850–51 British Guiana 'Cotton Reel' 2 cents, the 'woodblock' errors of the 1*d* and 4*d* Cape of Good Hope triangular stamps, the 1851 Canada 12*d* Black and the 1854 Western Australia 4*d* Blue 'inverted frame'. The European stamps included a whole range of France 1849 'tête-bêche' varieties, a complete set of Moldavia 1858 'Bulls' and the Sweden 1872–77 vermillion inscribed 'Tretio' (thirty) instead of 'Tjugo' (twenty). From further afield came the fine range of 1843 Brazil 'Bulls-eye', the Uruguay 1858 180 centesimos green 'tête-bêche' pair and the steamship 'Lady MacLeod' Trinidad local issue of 1847. Finally, from Great Britain itself came an unused example of the Penny Red from the notoriously rare plate no.77, and a whole range of essays, including the design of Prince Albert by Henry Archer (1850), proofs and imprimatur sheets, as well as the Mulready covers that preceded the first stamps.

To these treasures have now been added many others. From 1891 till his death in 1938, Tapling's friend Sir Edward Bacon supervised the collection, generously adding to it stamps which filled its few gaps, notably the Barbados one shilling blue error of colour of 1861–70. The Crown Agents have added stamps, mainly British colonial and post-colonial issues and essays, commissioned by them. Mrs Augustine Fitzgerald's airmail collection was given in 1947, including the first transatlantic mail covers, Newfoundland, 1919, proofs of Franklin D. Roosevelt's design for US airmail stamps (1934), with the President's autograph inscription, and other historic pioneer airmail flights. Special stamps, revenue, railway, National Savings and Insurance stamps have come from the issuing authorities and other sources.

No account of the philatelic collections would be complete without mention of the Crawford collection of philatelic literature, formed by James Ludovic, 26th Earl of Crawford, the founder of scientific philately, who inspired George V when Prince of Wales to begin collecting stamps and thus inaugurated the great Royal Collection. Like Tapling, he began by buying a collection, that of John Kerr Tiffany of St Louis, who had been collecting post office manuals and official forms and guides, as well as strictly philatelic books and magazines and dealers' catalogues, from as early as 1870. Lord Crawford augmented it substantially, and bequeathed it to the Museum on his death in 1913. Up to that date it is virtually complete.

Bookbindings, newspapers and stamps, so different from each other, share the common quality of requiring a special expertise in their curators. In each field, the Library's collection is unapproachable elsewhere. The treasures of each amplify specialist study and will do so for generations to come.

Above. Great Britain. Two 1840 'VR' 1d blacks with experimental cancellations (never used). The handwriting is that of Rowland Hill.

Left. Great Britain 1858–79. 1d. Plate 77. (Enlarged.)

Right. Pigeon Post. Souvenir 'identical specimen' of microfilm carried out by pigeons during the siege of Paris 1870–71.

Above. 1934–36 Air Special Delivery stamp. Designed, and here annotated by, Franklin D. Roosevelt, then US President.

13

Printed Books and Manuscripts in the 20th Century

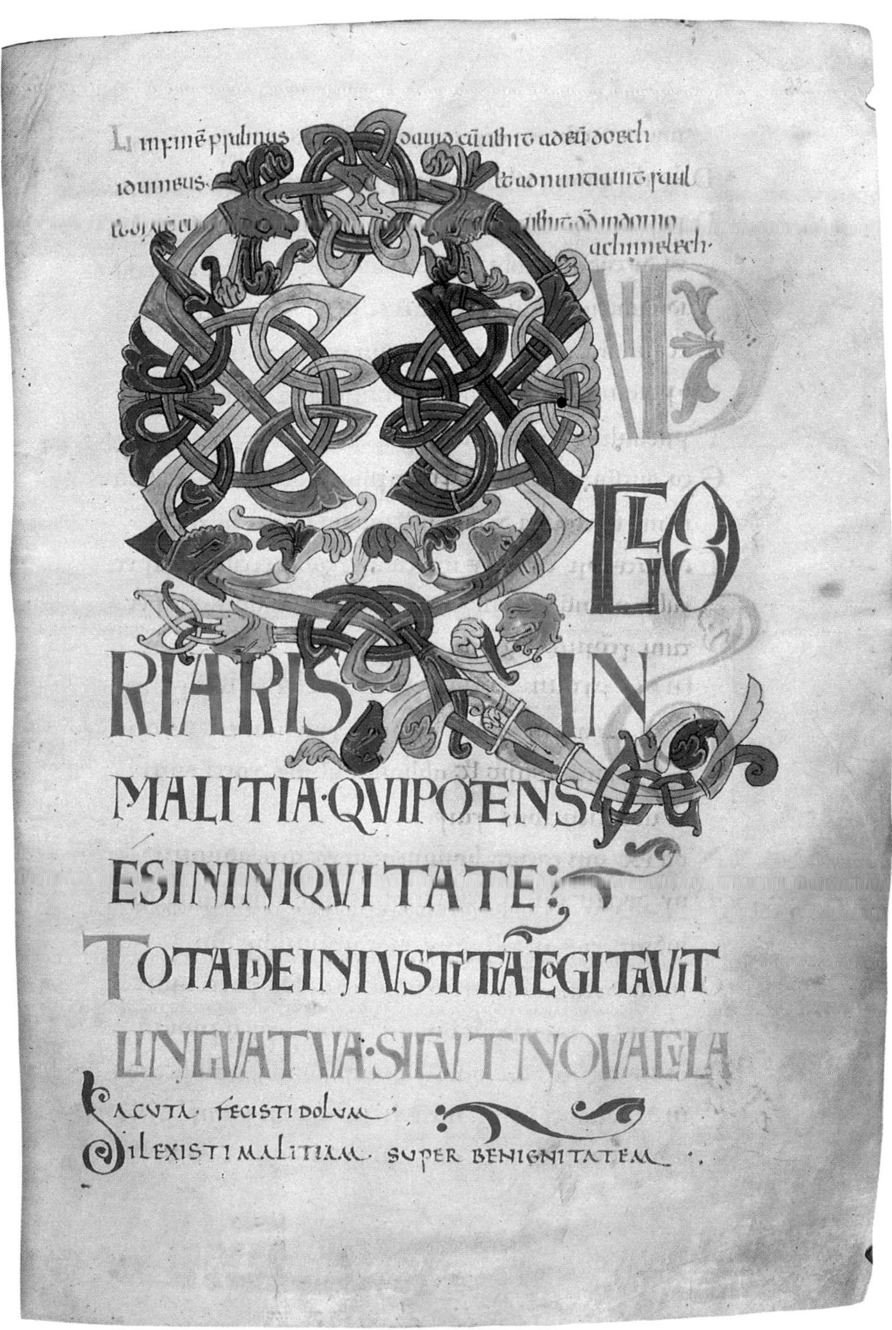

Page from the Bosworth Psalter. Anglo-Saxon, 10th century.
Add. MS 37517, f.33.

THE PRODIGIOUS INCREASE in every part of the collection in the second half of the 19th century had, so far as retrospective acquisition was concerned, a marked effect on the Library's mission. Wholesale purchase, in the knowledge that little or none would be duplicate material, changed to a cautious but informed policy of filling gaps. In no area was this better maintained than in the Library's collection of 15th-century books. Incunabular scholarship was given its foundation in the publications and correspondence of J.W. Holtrop, Royal Librarian at The Hague, and Henry Bradshaw, University Librarian at Cambridge, from the 1850s onwards. This was not lost on their colleagues at the British Museum, and acquisitions were steadily made to amplify the riches of the earlier collections.

In 1893 Robert Proctor joined the staff from Oxford, where he had put a seemingly innate gift for identifying early printing by its types to good use at the Bodleian. In 1903 he went for a solitary walking tour in the Tyrol, set off to cross a pass after fresh snow, and was never seen again. In that brief decade, working long and late after his normal duty was done, he had gathered together all the incunables in the collection (except those in the King's and Grenville libraries), and arranged them chronologically by countries, towns and presses, starting with the first press, the arrangement now universally known as 'Proctor Order'. Between 1897 and 1903 he printed at his own expense the *Index of early books printed in the British Museum*, which formed the basis of the great *Catalogue of books printed in the XVth century now in the British Museum* (1908–), begun by A.W. Pollard and Victor Scholderer, and continued since by their successors.

Among the books acquired in accordance with this new pattern were the Paris Boccaccio *Ruine des nobles hommes et femmes* (1483/4), bought in 1900, with the illustrations whose blocks subsequently passed with Richard Pynson to England, to be used in John Lydgate's translation of the same work, *The fall of princes* (1494). The second illustrated Italian Bible came to join the first, acquired in 1897, with the *Disputationes super theoria planetarum* (1474) of the astronomer Regiomontanus, the only book that he printed at his press in Nuremberg. The only known copy of the first London edition of the *Doctrinale* of Alexander de Villa Dei, printed by Pynson in 1492, was bought, while the single-sheet advertisement of the books in Low-German mostly printed at Lübeck, offered for sale by an itinerant bookseller, *c.* 1495, a fascinating document of the early book trade, was presented by the University of Uppsala, where two copies of it had been found, used as binder's waste. From the sale of the collection of George Dunn, whose premature death in 1912 deprived the Museum of a bequest which would have added signally to the incunable collection, came several important books, among them the *editio princeps* of the classical commentary of Servius on Virgil, printed at Florence in 1472.

The First World War brought its anxieties, notably the threat of occupation of the Museum premises by government departments, but no actual losses. Between the wars, the unsettled economic conditions brought more books to the market, notably from Germany. The Second World War, with the all too real threat of aerial bombardment, caused the evacuation of many treasures, notably the incunable and manuscript collections, to the National Library of Wales at Aberystwyth. Those that remained did not escape unharmed. The bomb which penetrated the roof of the King's Library mercifully did little damage, but the South-West Quadrant was partially destroyed, with the loss of 150,000 books, including irreplaceable examples of 16th-century Greek printing, and a major part of the Bunyan collection. Replacement became a major preoccupation when the war was over, absorbing most of the Library acquisition funds. The sale of Sir Leicester Harmsworth's library in 1947 enabled the Museum to replace all but five of the pre-1800 Bunyan editions that it had lost, and an anonymous benefactor paid for these and all the other purchases made at the sale.

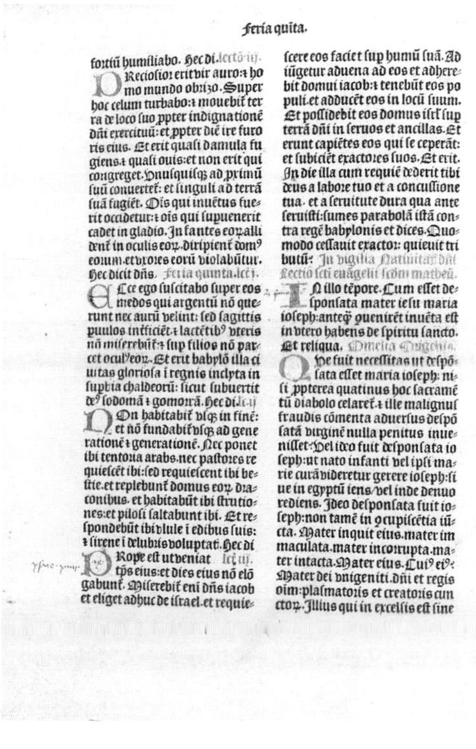

After the war, some diminution in the flow of books might have been expected as the supplies first released at the beginning of the 19th century began to run out, but, just as successive Settled Lands Acts had brought major inherited libraries to the market at the end of the 19th century, so now marked increases in the rate of Estate Duty had the same effect. More important books became available, either through 'in lieu' arrangements between owners and the Treasury, or in the market-place, where the Library's ability to contend with competition from abroad was strengthened by ever more stringent export licensing arrangements.

Two major libraries from which important books thus came to the Library were the Earl of Leicester's at Holkham (1951) and the Duke of Devonshire's at Chatsworth (1958). From the first came the block-book *Biblia pauperum* (*c*.1465) and the 1459 Psalter, a different issue from George III's copy, both earlier in the collection of the Liverpool connoisseur William Roscoe. From Holkham also came the only perfect copy of Wynkyn de Worde's Bonaventure, *Speculum vitae Christi* (1494), two illuminated books – the second De Spira edition of Virgil (1471), with wood-cut border, and the splendid *Missale Virdunense* (Verdun Missal), in this copy adapted to Roman use, probably to be dated 1491, in spite of the printed date '1481' – a Caxton, John Russell's *Propositio ad Carolum ducem Burgundiae* (*c*.1477) and the Plato *Epistolae* (1472) from the first Paris press.

Two other books from the same press, making a notable trio, came from Chatsworth, the Sallust (1471) and Terence (1472). The first edition of the *Silvae* of Statius (Rome, 1475), as well as third and second editions of Juvenal (Rome, *c*.1471) and Strabo (Rome, 1473) added to the early editions of the classics, while the *Fior di virtù* (1471), the third edition of the *Roman de la Rose* (Lyons, *c*.1487) and Caxton's translation of Raoul Lefèvre's *History of Jason*, printed at Antwerp in 1492 with woodcuts in contemporary colouring, represented modern languages; the French translation of Orosius *Historiae adversus paganos* (1491) was in a remarkable binding by Claude de Picques.

Besides these treasures from great private libraries, the Library could also boast another unique Caxton, the *Legenda ad usum Sarum*, printed for Caxton in Paris in 1488, discovered in 1956 by Mr Paul Morgan at St Mary's Church, Warwick, and bought in 1957.

Legenda ad usum Sarum, printed for Caxton in Paris, 1488.
IB 40010, C.2v.

One of the great strengths of the Library, due to the accumulation of great collections upon which it is based, is the number of rare and important books in duplicate (and sometimes more – there are no less than eight copies of the Aldine Theocritus of 1495). This gives a rare opportunity of seeing the variations, some obvious, some more subtle, which are always to be found in different copies of the same book – and not all of which are due to the printer. Incunables, unlike most printed books since, were sometimes illuminated like the manuscripts they resemble. As such, they are apt to escape the attention of students of illumination. There are some fine examples among the Library's earliest incunables, notably one of the four copies of the Fust and Schoeffer Bible of 1462 and both copies of the Mainz Cicero *De officiis* of 1465, decorated with naturalistic foliage. The magnificent Venetian *trompe-l'oeil* style of the last third of the 15th century is found in two editions of Pliny, De Spira's of 1469 and Jenson's of 1472. French illumination is well exemplified by the Verdun Missal, mentioned above, while simple but elegant pen-work initials, imitated in the 1457 and 1459 Psalters and common in northern Europe, are found, for example, in Johannes Nider, *Preceptorium divinae legis* (Cologne, *c*.1472, *c*.1474). There was, too, a distinctively English style, of which the 42-line Bible leaf from Sloane's collection is an example.

Styles of illumination, however, cannot be simply divided nationally: of the first book printed at Venice by Nicolas Jenson in 1470 – Eusebius, *De praeparatione evangelica* – the King's Library copy is decorated in the 'new' classical *trompe-l'oeil* style, while another, received in 1986 (the Clifford Rattey Gift), has rich illumination, more medieval in style. At the same time, illumination

The *Missale Virdunense*. Probably 1491.
IB 39305, f.1.

Missale scdm usum Romane ecclesie
Dnica prima aduēt⁹. Ad missā. Introit⁹.
Ad te leuaui
animam meam deus
meus in te cōfido non
erubescam. neq3 irride
ant me inimici mei. et
enim uniuersi qui te expectant nō
cōfūdētur. ps. Vias tuas dn̄e demōstra
michi: et semitas tuas edoce me Collecta
Excita domine quesumus po-
tentiam tuā et ueni. ut ab im
minentibus peccatorum nostrorū
periculis: te mereamur protegente
eripi: te liberāte saluari. Qui uiuis
et regnas cum deo patre in unitate
spiritus sancti deus. Per omnia.
Lectio epistole beati pauli apostoli.
Ad romanos. xiii.

can join books together, as well as distinguish them. There was a shop in London that specialised in decorating William de Machlinia's books, and the Library's three copies of Thomas Littleton's *Tenores novelli*, *c*.1481–83, from the Old Royal Library, King's Library and Grenville Library, all demonstrate the homogeneity, as well as vitality, of its work.

There is, in short, no such thing as a duplicate of a printed book. This lesson has been reinforced over and over again by the unfortunate experience of the 'duplicate sales' between 1769 and 1832. Multiple editions of the same book can be as informative as multiple copies. Most surviving incunables are large books. Little books are rare, not because fewer were printed but because they are more vulnerable to the ravages of use and time. There is, thus, a special value and interest in such diminutive books as the *Soliloquia Augustini*, printed at Cologne *c*.1475, the only known copy, and the beautiful little *Officium B.V.M.* printed by Jenson at Venice in 1474. These survivals demonstrate the versatility and variety of the early press.

By way of conclusion, it is proper to commemorate the last great benefaction of 15th-century books the Library has received, from the Broxbourne Library (*see* p. 262).

Ad Sanctissimũ Papam Nicolaum quintum Georgii trapezuntii in traductione Eusebii praefatio :-

VSEBIVM Pamphili de euangelica præparatione latinum ex græco beatissime pater iussu tuo effeci. Nam quom eum uirum tum eloquẽtia: tũ multaꝝ rerum peritia: et ĩgenii mirabili flumine ex his quæ iam traducta sunt præstantissimum sanctitas tua iu/dicet: atq; ideo quæcũq; apud græcos ipsius opera extẽt latina facere istituerit: euangelicã præpationẽ quæ in urbe forte reperta est: primum aggressi tra/duximus. Quo quidem in libro quasi quodam in speculo uariam atq; multiplicem doctrinã illius uiri licet admirari. Cuncta enim quæ ante ipsũ facta fuentaq; fuerunt quæ tamen græce scripta tũc inueniretur: multo certius atque distinctius ipsis etiam auctoribus qui scripserunt percepisse mihi uidetur. Ita quom constet nihil fere præclarum unq̃ gestum fuisse quod illis temporibus græce scriptum non extaret: nihil in rebus magnis naturaq; abditis quod a philosophis non esset expli/catum: omnia ille tum memoriæ tenacitate: tũ mẽtis pcepit acumine: ac ut apes solent singulis insidere floribus: indeq; quod ad rem suam conducit colligere: nõ aliter ille undiq; certiora uerisimilioraue deligẽs mirabilem sibi atq; inauditũ scientiæ cumulum confecit: multiplices uariasq; philosophorum sectas nõ ignorauit: infinitos pene gentium omnium religionis errores tenuit: orbis terrarum historiam serie sua dispositam solus cognouit & cæteris tradidit. Nam quom non esset nescius gestaꝝ rerum historiam titubare sãctissime pater nisi distincta tẽporibus pateat: Quippe quom natura tẽporis faciat ut quæ ĩ tẽpore fuerunt nisi quando fuerũt scias: nec fuisse qdem ,ppter confusionem uideantur: eo ingenio: studio: industria huic incubuit rei: ut omnium scriptorum peritiam in unum congestam facile supauerit: distinctiusq; cuncta ipsis suis ut diximus cognouerit auctoribus. Conferendo enim inter se singulos: ueritatem quæ ab omnibus simul emergebat: nec ab ullo exprimebatur: consecutus est. Quæ omnia ab aliis quæ scripsit & ab hoc opere perspicere licet. Quod ille ideo suscepit: quoniam quom apud gentiũ præclaros philosophia uiros nobilissimus esset: ac priscã paternamq; deorũ religionem catholicæ ueritatis amore cõtempserit: partim accusãtibus suum propositum respondere: partim nostra pro uiribus suis uoluit cõfirmare. Itaq; ĩ duas uniuersum partis negotium partitus est: quarum primam quæ nunc traducta nobis est: qua illis

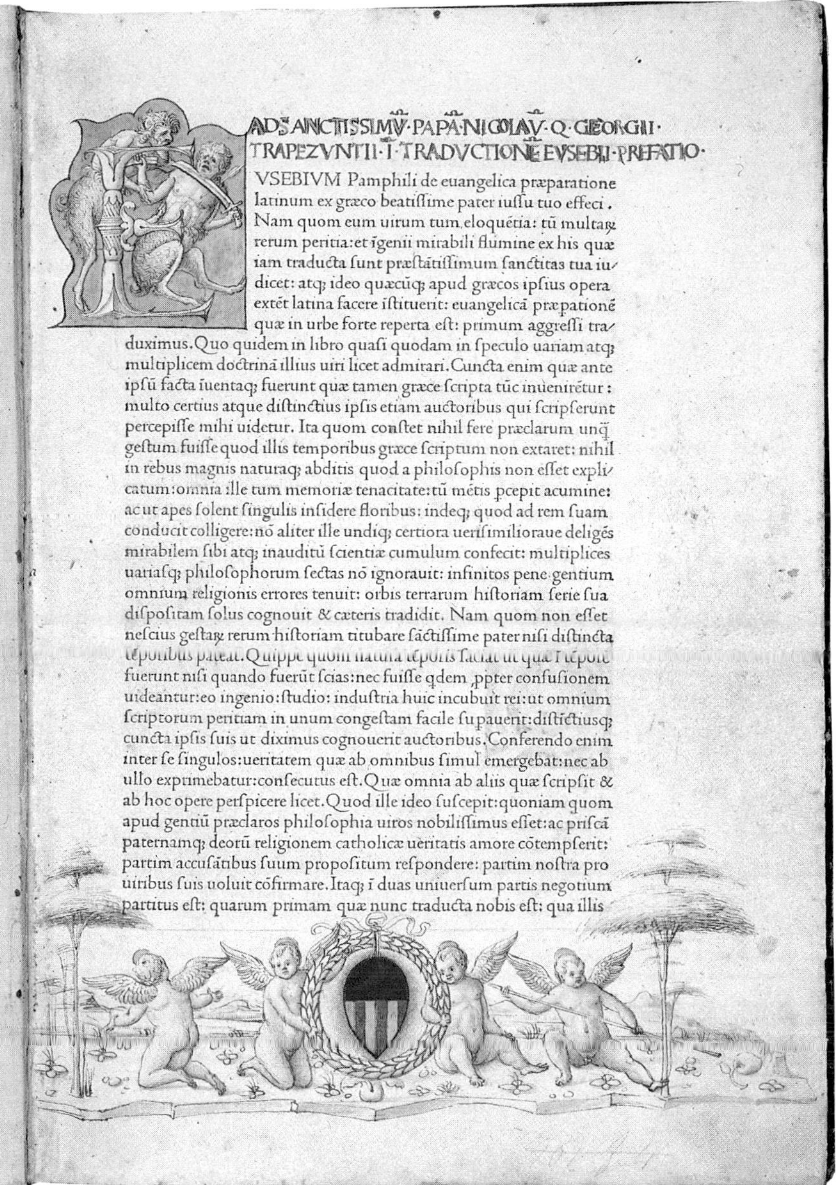

AD SANCTISSIMV̄ PAPĀ NICOLAV̄ Q. GEORGII TRAPEZVNTII I TRADVCTIONĒ EVSEBII PREFATIO.

VSEBIVM Pamphili de euangelica præparatione latinum ex græco beatissime pater iussu tuo effeci. Nam quom eum uirum tum eloquẽtia: tũ multaꝝ rerum peritia: et ĩgenii mirabili flumine ex his quæ iam traducta sunt præstãtissimum sanctitas tua iu/dicet: atq; ideo quæcũq; apud græcos ipsius opera extẽt latina facere istituerit: euangelicã præpationẽ quæ in urbe forte reperta est: primum aggressi tra/duximus. Quo quidem in libro quasi quodam in speculo uariam atq; multiplicem doctrinã illius uiri licet admirari. Cuncta enim quæ ante ipsũ facta fuentaq; fuerunt quæ tamen græce scripta tũc inuenirẽtur: multo certius atque distinctius ipsis etiam auctoribus qui scripserunt percepisse mihi uidetur. Ita quom constet nihil fere præclarum unq̃ gestum fuisse quod illis temporibus græce scriptum non extaret: nihil in rebus magnis naturaq; abditis quod a philosophis non esset expli/catum: omnia ille tum memoriæ tenacitate: tũ mẽtis pcepit acumine: ac ut apes solent singulis insidere floribus: indeq; quod ad rem suam conducit colligere: nõ aliter ille undiq; certiora uerisimilioraue deligẽs mirabilem sibi atq; inauditũ scientiæ cumulum confecit: multiplices uariasq; philosophorum sectas nõ ignorauit: infinitos pene gentium omnium religionis errores tenuit: orbis terrarum historiam serie sua dispositam solus cognouit & cæteris tradidit. Nam quom non esset nescius gestaꝝ rerum historiam titubare sãctissime pater nisi distincta tẽporibus pateat. Quippe quom natura tẽporis faciat ut quæ ĩ tẽpore fuerunt nisi quando fuerũt scias: nec fuisse qdem ,ppter confusionem uideantur: eo ingenio: studio: industria huic incubuit rei: ut omnium scriptorum peritiam in unum congestam facile supauerit: distinctiusq; cuncta ipsis suis ut diximus cognouerit auctoribus. Conferendo enim inter se singulos: ueritatem quæ ab omnibus simul emergebat: nec ab ullo exprimebatur: consecutus est. Quæ omnia ab aliis quæ scripsit & ab hoc opere perspicere licet. Quod ille ideo suscepit: quoniam quom apud gentiũ præclaros philosophia uiros nobilissimus esset: ac priscã paternamq; deorũ religionem catholicæ ueritatis amore cõtempserit: partim accusãtibus suum propositum respondere: partim nostra pro uiribus suis uoluit cõfirmare. Itaq; ĩ duas uniuersum partis negotium partitus est: quarum primam quæ nunc traducta nobis est: qua illis

Right. Eusebius, *De praeparatione evangelia*, printed by Jenson, Venice 1470, with *trompe l'oeil* decoration.
C.14.c.2. f.1.

Above. Another copy from the same edition, with a different style of decoration.
IB 19612a. f.1.

The Official Publications Library is a treasure of a different kind. Established as the State Paper Room in 1932, its antecedents lie in the collection of printed state papers from all over the world which was one of Panizzi's great goals. Its achievement (largely by exchange with other countries) has given the Library immense resources of official enactments, reports and statistics, invaluable to historians, economists, demographers and sociologists. Its principal treasures can only be recorded in bulk, such as the unbroken sequence of Parliamentary Papers. Some individual items stand out, however; for example, one of the earliest printed royal proclamations (1514), the first statute printed by William de Machlinia (1 Richard III, 1489), the illuminated copy, printed by Wynkyn de Worde, of 11 Henry VII, and the first treaty (Brétigny) headed 'The promise of matrimonie' (De Machlinia, 1483?). Other historic documents include the charge against Charles I (1649), Cromwell's constitution (1653) and the 1689 *Declaration of Rights*.

These are only a few examples of the wealth that has stemmed from Panizzi's energetic initiative. His equal determination to encompass the world's literature has had the same effect in other branches of the printed collections. The literature of the Slavonic countries and Eastern Europe figured only rarely in the early collections. It is now thoroughly covered. The

Dys puchlein hat gemacht vnnd erfarn Mayster Clement von Gracz von allen paden dye von natur hayss sint

Jn yeist zu mercken das register dyß puchleins jn ainer gemayn von denen so jn die wiltpad ziehen wellen ꝛc.

a

Woodcut of a bathing scene, in the unique copy of a Czech incunable, Hans Folz, *Von den heissen Bädern*, Brno, 1495.
IA 51720.

earliest Church Slavonic books now include the Acts and Epistles in White Russian, printed by Frantsisk Skaryna at Wilno in 1525, the *Azbuka* (Primer) printed by Ivan Fedorov at Lvov in 1574, one of two known copies, two copies of Fedorov's Ostrog Bible of 1581, one previously owned by Ivan the Terrible, and one of the most outstanding Moscow imprints of the 17th century, the first Moscow Slavonic Bible of 1663. The Glagolitic *Mirakuli*, printed at Senj in 1508, is the only complete copy surviving. The Rumanian collections include the Gospels in Church Slavonic printed at Tîrgovişte in 1512, Simeon's *In contra Eresiilor*, printed in Greek and finely bound at Jassy in 1683, as well as Varlaam's *Cheia înţelesului*, the first book printed in Rumanian in Bucharest in 1678. The Library's collections also include the first book printed in Bulgarian in the Cyrillic script, Stanislavov's *Abagar*, printed in Rome in 1651.

Printing came early to what is now Czechoslovakia, and among the Library's Czech incunables is the unique tract on the hot springs printed at Brno (1495), with its lively woodcut. A fine sequence of bibles is crowned by the great *Biblj Česká* (1579–93), printed in six volumes by the secret press of the Czech Brethren. From the same press came the finely printed hymnal *Písně duchownj Evangelistské* (1564), with hand-coloured woodcuts. The important printer Melantrich is represented by Mattioli's 'Herbal', written in Prague, published in Czech as *Herbarz* (1562), with its fine woodcut illustrations. There is also the great *Kozmograffia Czeská* (1554), Dubravius's *Historiae* (1552), Tovačovsky's *Knjiha hadanj* (1539), Harant's travelogue *Putowanj* (1608), and the early law code *Zřízenj zemská* (1530). Science is represented by J. Kepler's important *Astronomia nova* (1609) and F. Noël's *Observationes mathematicae* (1710).

Among the great baroque illustrated books printed at Prague are Althann's *Imago principum Bohemiae* (1673), Balbinus's *Epitome* (1677), Hammerschmidt's *Prodromus gloriae Pragenae* (1723), and Ramhofský's *Trogj popsánj* (1743). Modern literary first editions include K. Čapek's *RUR* (1920), *Věc Makropulos* (1922) and *Krakatit* (1924), the Nobel Prize winner J. Seifert's *Na vlnách TSF* (1925) and others. One special treasure is the unique copy of the Latin verses of Elizabeth Jane Weston (1582–1612), an infant prodigy admired by Scaliger, Heinsius and all scholarly Europe, involuntarily exiled by the death of her improvident father in Prague, where *Parthenicon* was printed in 1606; the Library's copy is augmented with a leaf of verses in her own beautiful hand.

Work by the early Polish printers is well represented in the collection. Some of the most notable books are the first editions of *Zwierzyniec* and *Zwierciadło* (Cracow, 1562 and 1568 respectively) by M. Rej, the 'Father of Polish Literature', and the only known perfect copy of the earliest *Hortus sanitatis* in Polish, *O ziołach i o mocy ich* by S. Falimirz (Cracow, 1534). There is a large collection of the early Polish bibles including the great 'Radziwiłł Bible' (Brześć Litewski, 1563) and the very rare Socinian New Testament (Cracow, 1577). Among important 17th-century first editions are S. Klonowic's *Victoria deorum* (Raków, 1600?), J. Długosz's *Historia Polonica* (Dobromil, 1611) and K. Dorohostajski's *Hippica* (Cracow, 1603). Notable literary first editions include I. Krasicki's *Mikołaja Doświadczyńskiego przypadki* and *Pan podstoli* (Warsaw, 1776 and 1778 respectively). Scholarly literature of the period is represented by astronomical works of J. Hevelius among which are *Selenographia, Machina coelestis* and *Firmamentum Sobiescianum* (Gdańsk, 1647, 1673–79 and 1690 respectively).

Among the first editions of the modern classics are found *Ksiegi narodu* by A. Mickiewicz, with a dedication in his hand (Paris, 1832), *Pan Tadeusz* (Paris, 1834), *Balladyna* by J. Słowacki (Paris, 1839) and *Promethidion* by C.K. Norwid (Paris, 1851). First editions of works by Nobel Prize for Literature winners are represented by the much-translated *Quo vadis* by H. Sienkiewicz (Warsaw, 1896) and many works by C. Miłosz from *Ocalenie* (Warsaw, 1945)

Title-page of Fedorov's Bible, Ostrog, 1581. This copy was once owned by Ivan the Terrible.
B.12203.

This Bibell in the Sclauonian tonge, had owt of the emperors libran. Jer. Horsey. 1581

Библіа сирѣчь книгы

ветхаго и новаго завѣ

та, по языку словенску.

Ѿ еврейска, въ еллинскій языкъ, седмию десятъ и двѣма, ...дрыми преводники. прежде воплощенія Гда Бга и Спса нашего Іс Ха, т҃ и лѣта, нажеланіемъ повелѣніе Птоломеа Филадельфа цр҃я египетска. преведенаго зводу съ тщаніемъ, и прилѣжаніемъ елико мощно, помощію Бжіею послѣдоваса, и исправиса. в лѣто, по воплощеніи Гда Бга и Спса нашего Іс Ха.

҂АФ ПА.

Hic liber qui est Sacra Biblia fuit extractus ex Bibliotheca Magni Ducis Moscoviae. Anno 1582 estque scriptus idiomate Sclavonica.

and *Zniewolony umysł* (Paris, 1953) onwards.

The collection of contemporary clandestine publications from Poland includes some translations of English authors. The most numerous among them are various editions of George Orwell's works, the most spectacular of which is *Folwark zwierzęcy (Animal Farm)* in hard covers and with colour plates by J. Lebenstein, published in Cracow in 1985.

The most spectacular Polish manuscripts in the Library are two Royal prayer-books in Latin. The more modest one was made in Cracow in 1491 by Jan Złotkowski for King Alexander of Poland before his accession. The other was made in 1524 for King Sigismund I (1506–48); it includes very fine illumination and full page miniatures, some of which were painted by Stanisław Samostrzelnik.

Poland also produced the first book in Hungarian, the Pauline Epistles printed at Cracow in 1533. The great Hungarian history, János Thuróczi's

Lithograph by Goncharova, 'Angels and Aeroplanes', from her portfolio entitled *War*, 1914.
Folder 35, Litho 10.

Chronica Hungarorum, was printed earlier, in Latin. The Library's copy of the second edition (Augsburg, 1488) is printed on vellum, with the woodcuts in contemporary colouring. The collection includes as well the famous Bible printed in Amsterdam by Nicholas Kis, who engraved the punches for his own types, used all over Europe, *Szent Biblia... magyar nyelvre fordittatott* (1685). Scientific literature is well represented with the first edition of Antal Mártonfi's *Initia Astronomica speculae Bathyanianae Albensis in Transilvania* (Albae, Caroline, 1798). The renaissance of modern Hungarian literature is marked by György Bessenyei's *Ágis tragédiája* (Betsben, 1772). Of the 19th-century romantic novelist Mór Jókai's prolific output the Library possesses the complete autograph of *A gazdag szegények*, 1889. A recent acquisition pays tribute to Endre Ady, the greatest Hungarian poet of the 20th century; the 25 first editions of his works, uniformly bound, are a remarkable addition to the collections.

Of material in the Baltic languages, early examples are the very rare *Postilla* by Jonas Bretkūnas (Königsberg, 1591), and the fragment of the Bible translated into Lithuanian by S.B. Chilinskis, whose printing in London (1660?) was never completed. The first Latvian and Estonian Bibles are also in the Library.

Printing in Russian – rather than Church Slavonic – Cyrillic characters began only in the 18th century, with the reforms of Peter the Great. This also marked the beginnings of modern Russian literature, with the titanic figure of Lomonosov whose polymathic gifts are represented in his *Drevniaia rossiiskaia istoriia* (1766), *Petr Velikii* (1761) and *Oratio de origine lucis* (1756), among others. His grammar, *Rossiiskaia grammatika* (1755) and *Kratkoe rukovodstvo k krasnorechiiu* (better known as *Ritorika*) (1748) codified for the first time the contemporary Russian lanugage. The works of other 18th-century authors such as the Emin brothers, Kheraskov, Sumarokov and Trediakovsky, many of whom have not been reprinted since the 19th century, are well represented. Many first editions of the works of the major 19th-century authors are in the collection, among them Pushkin's *Evgenii Onegin* (1833) and *Boris Godunov* (1831), the first part of Gogol's *Mertvye dushi*, originally entitled *Pokhozhdeniia Chichikova*, (1842) and his *Revizor* (1836); Dostoevsky's *Prestuplenie i nakazanie (Crime and Punishment)* (1867), *Idiot* (1874), and *Besy* (1873), and Tolstoy's *Voina i mir* (*War and Peace*) (1868).

The collection is particularly rich in documents covering the political ferment in Russia and emigration at the end of the 19th century. The *Polnyi tekst protokolov 2-ogo ocherednogo s"ezda RSDRP* (Geneva, 1903) records the proceedings of the Congress of the Social Democratic Party in 1903 that saw the split between the Bolsheviks under Lenin and the Mensheviks led by Martov. Among early editions of the works of the leaders of the Revolution, the Library has Lenin's *Za 12 let* (1908), presented to the Library by the author, his *Chto delat'?* (1902), and many pamphlets published by émigrés abroad and clandestinely in Russia.

One of the Library's most recently acquired treasures is the substantial collection of Russian futurist books which mirror, in words and graphically, the social explosion. Kruchenykh's *Pomada* (1913), illustrated by Larionov, and *Igra v adu* (1912), written jointly with Khlebnikov, illustrated by Goncharova, and Mayakovsky's *Dlya golosa* (1923), 'constructed' by El Lissitsky, and *Pro eto* (1923), with Constructivist montages by Rodchenko, are among the books which have brought about a graphic revolution, as well as reflecting that in Russia.

Another unexpected link with the Revolution is to be found in the pressmark 'Voynich'. W.M. Voynich was a bookseller of great ability, who offered the Library, in 1906, 158 books, all hitherto unknown. They were bought and given to the Library by Lord Strathcona and Mountroyal, the Hon. Walter Rothschild, and others. Little did they know that all Voynich's profits went to finance the revolutionaries, or that his English-born wife, Ethel Boole,

Opposite, above. Christ descends into Hell. From Albrecht Dürer's *Passio*, 1511.
7.f.3(2).

Opposite, below. Engraving of a stage set from *Il Pomo d'oro*, Vienna 1668.
640.L.19.

Concretosq; pio crines barbamq; cruore
Ingratæ moriens plebi monstrabat ab alta
Arbore.& ingenti mortem clamore ciebat.
Cuius ad interitum cœpere elementa moueri.
Sol gemuit.nigroq; caput velauit amictu:
Contremuit tellus.tumuit mare.palluit aer
Et collisa graui sonuerunt marmora planctu.
Hæc fuit atra dies & lamentabile tempus
Cum subito media tenebris in luce subortis
Lumen in horribilem fugit sine nubibus vmbram.
Sic est parta salus homini.longæuaq; primæ
Cum gemitu & lachrymis deleta iniuria culpæ est.
Hierony Dulcis amica veni Iesumq; auersa vocantem
Aspice.& ardenti amplectar te pectore charam.
Dulcis amor.quo sola fugis?nam tuta per altas
Transieris nunq̄ sine me caliginis vmbras.
Ille.anima.ille tuus heu nunc agnosce creator
Ille ego sum flagrans.& viuo saucius igni
Quem noua flamma.tuæ.quem cura salutis adurit.
Huc celeres huc flecte gradus hoc aspice lignum
Quo super infixus.ne iam damnata subires
Crudeles pœnas.ego te miseranda redemi.
Expecto.ac nimio dilectæ accensus amore
Brachia aperta dedi.frontem quoq; ad oscula flexi.

CHRISTVS DESCENDIT AD INFEROS.

Chelido. ¶ Tum deus infernis reuocauit sedibus vmbras
Baptista Insontes vmbras patrum.quos longa sub alto.
Carcere clauserunt obscuri vincula circi.
Non vada.non furiæ.non ferrea claustra vetabant
Chelido. Authoremq; suum sequitur gens libera Christum

venantium.
Laqueus contritus eſt, & nos liberati ſumus.
Adiutorium noſtrum in nomine domini, qui fecit cælum & terram.
Gloria patri, & filio, & ſpiritui ſancto.
Sicut erat in principio, & nunc, & ſemper, & in ſecula ſeculorum. Amen. Pſalmus.
QVi cõfidunt in domino ſicut mons Si-ón: non cõmouebitur in æternum qui habitat in Hieruſalem.
Montes in circumitu eius, & dominus in circumitu populi ſui: ex hoc nunc & vſque in ſeculum.
Quia non relinquet dominus virgam peccatorum ſuper ſortem iuſtorum: vt non extendant iuſti ad iniquitatem manus ſuas.
Benefac domine bonis & rectis corde.
Declinantes autem in obligationes adducet dominus cum operãtibus iniquitatem: pax ſuper Iſrael.
Gloria patri, & filio, & ſpiritui ſancto.
Sicut erat in principio, & nunc, & ſemper, & in ſecula ſeculorũ. Amen. añ. In odorem vnguentorum tuorum currimus, adoleſcentulæ dilexerunt te nimis. Capitulum.
ET radicaui in populo honorificato, & in partes dei mei hæreditas illius, & in plenitudine ſanctorum detentio mea. ℟. Deo gratias. ℣. Benedicta tu in mulieribus. ℟. Et benedictus fructus vẽtris tui. Kyrie eleiſõn. Chriſte eleiſon. Kyrie eleiſon. ℣. Domine exaudi orationem meam. ℟. Et clamor meus ad te veniat. Oratio.

F.iiij.

Page from Geoffroy Tory's Books of Hours, 1525, once owned by King Henry VIII.
C.27.k.15.

was the author of *The Gadfly*, classic novel of the cause, which still sells by the million in the Soviet Union.

German literature is reflected in all its forms in a depth unequalled outside Germany. This was not always so. Compared with the romance languages, the original collections were deficient in German, and it was not until the bookseller Adolphus Asher, given full rein by Panizzi (whom he loyally supported at the Royal Commission), set to work, that it grew to its present comprehensive state. True, George II owned the Dürer *Passio* (1511) and Banks added the metallurgical classic Ercker, *Beschreibung allerfürnemsten mineralischen Ertzt* (1574), but the great Luther collection, including *Das newe Testament Deutzsch* (1522) came later. There are the first edition of Georg Rollenhagen's satire *Froschmeuseler* (1595), the *Buch von der deutschen Poeterey* (1624) of Martin Opitz, 'the father of German poetry', the first dictionary containing German, *Vocabularius ex quo* (2nd edition, 1469), an unique Speyer edition of a litany for the dead in the Peasants' War, *Eynn schones Lied wie es mit den Baüren ergangen ist* (1526), and a collection of 125 pieces of verse, mainly by Simon Dach (1638–59), bought with many other items of great rarity at the Maltzahn sale in 1885.

From Vienna came the delightful libretto of Francesco Sbarra's masque for the wedding of Leopold I, *Il pomo d'oro* (1668), with handsome engravings of the stage sets. Besides the first editions of Kant's works is the fifth of *Critik der reinen Vernunft* (1799), with Hegel's *Wissenschaft der Logik* (1812–16), both annotated by Coleridge. As well as the first editions of all main works of both Goethe and Schiller, including Goethe's first separate publication in German *Neue Lieder* (1770), and *Das römische Carneval* (1789), one of an edition of 250 copies with coloured plates after J.G. Schütz, there is Schiller, *Das Eleusische Fest* (1816), 'London: gedruckt mit Bensley & Sohn's Schriften', on the new perfecting press of Friedrich König and Andreas Bauer (installed at *The Times*), with commendatory verses by them on the German invention of printing and the benefits of British technology, a dedication copy from König. With Marx's *Das Kapital* there is also Engels's *Die Lage der arbeitenden Klasse in England* (1845). Besides the first edition, there is the suppressed French translation of *Mein Kampf* (1934). Thomas Mann's *Der Tod in Venedig* is no. 13 of the Hyperion Verlag edition of 100 (1912) which preceded the first trade edition. A recent acquisition is the powerful *Kreuzigung* (1920) of Lothar Schreyer, printed from wood-blocks and hand-coloured.

Sir Joseph Banks gave the Library an early start in the literature of Scandinavia, notably Icelandic, to which was added in 1913 the Psalms, printed at Holar in 1589, in a fine contemporary binding. Banks's admiration for Linnaeus secured for the Library his *Öländska och Gothländska resa* (1745), the second (Stockholm) edition of the *Systema naturae* (1740) – the first, printed at Leyden in 1735, was only recently acquired – and he annotated the *Flora suecica* (1745). Banks too obtained the masterpiece of Swedish topography, Dahlberg's *Suecia antiqua et hodierna* (1661–1715), with its handsome engraved plates. *Dat Gotlandsche Waterrecht* (Copenhagen, Godfred af Ghemen, 1505), the first separate printed maritime code, is interesting since its implications are international: it anticipates the 17th-century controversy of Grotius and Selden. Banks missed this (it is very rare), but not the first Danish history, Saxo Grammaticus, *Gesta Danorum* (1514), or Pontoppidan's *Den Danske Atlas* (1763–81). The works of Tycho Brahe were mostly added later, *De mundi aetherei recentioribus phaenomenis* (1588) and *Astronomiae instaurata* (1598) being presentation copies, the latter with the woodcuts coloured. George III had the great Danish architectural book, Thirah's *Den Danske Vitruvius* (1746–49). The first collected edition of Hans Christian Andersen's *Eventyr* (1850) has Vilhelm Pedersen's illustrations. The Norwegian books include Pontoppidan's *Glossarium Norvagicum* (1749), the first work on the Norwegian language to be printed in Norway.

The cultural dominance of France supplied all Europe with fine books for

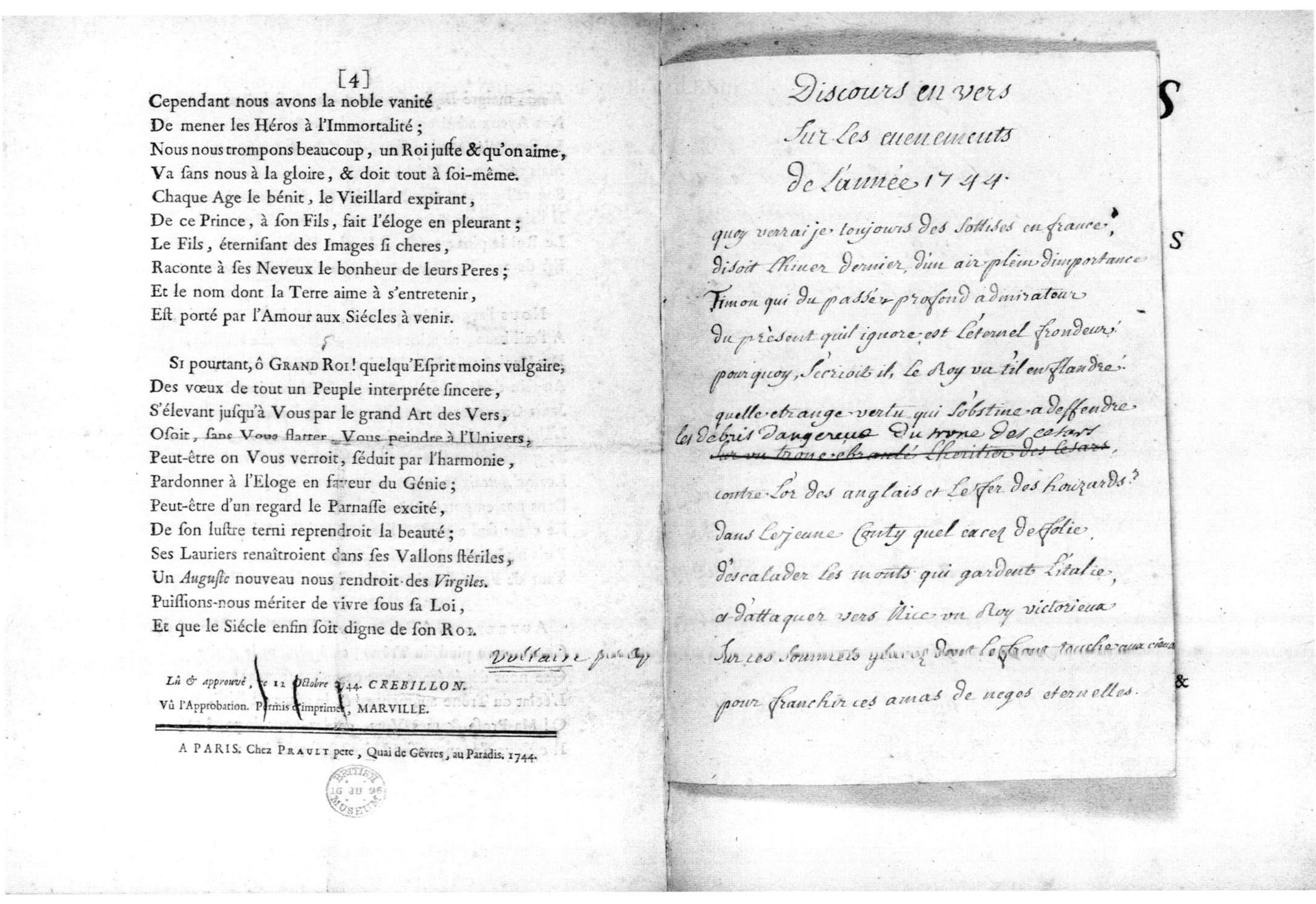
[4]

Cependant nous avons la noble vanité
De mener les Héros à l'Immortalité ;
Nous nous trompons beaucoup, un Roi juste & qu'on aime,
Va sans nous à la gloire, & doit tout à soi-même.
Chaque Age le bénit, le Vieillard expirant,
De ce Prince, à son Fils, fait l'éloge en pleurant ;
Le Fils, éternisant des Images si cheres,
Raconte à ses Neveux le bonheur de leurs Peres ;
Et le nom dont la Terre aime à s'entretenir,
Est porté par l'Amour aux Siécles à venir.

Si pourtant, ô Grand Roi ! quelqu'Esprit moins vulgaire,
Des vœux de tout un Peuple interpréte sincere,
S'élevant jusqu'à Vous par le grand Art des Vers,
Osoit, sans Vous flatter, Vous peindre à l'Univers,
Peut-être on Vous verroit, séduit par l'harmonie,
Pardonner à l'Eloge en faveur du Génie ;
Peut-être d'un regard le Parnasse excité,
De son lustre terni reprendroit la beauté ;
Ses Lauriers renaîtroient dans ses Vallons stériles,
Un *Auguste* nouveau nous rendroit des *Virgiles*.
Puissions-nous mériter de vivre sous sa Loi,
Et que le Siécle enfin soit digne de son Roi.

Lû & approuvé, ce 11 Octobre 1744. CREBILLON.
Vû l'Approbation. Permis d'imprimer, MARVILLE.

A PARIS. Chez Prault pere, Quai de Gêvres, au Paradis. 1744.

Discours en vers
sur les evenements
de l'année 1744.

quoy verrai je toujours des sottises en france,
disoit l'hiver dernier, d'un air plein d'importance
Timon qui du passé profond admirateur
du présent qu'il ignore est l'eternel frondeur.
pourquoy, s'ecrioit il, le Roy va t'il en flandre
quelle etrange vertu qui s'obstine a deffendre
les débris dangereux du trone des cesars
contre l'or des anglais et le fer des houzards?
dans le jeune Conty quel exces de folie
d'escalader les monts qui gardent l'italie,
et d'attaquer vers Nice un Roy victorieux
sur ces sommets glacés dont le front touche aux cieux
pour franchir ces amas de neges eternelles.

Voltaire, *Discours en vers sur les événements de l'année 1744*. Proof copy with the original manuscript interleaved.
C.60.n.8.

three centuries, and many of them have already been mentioned. Among the early treasures are the first book printed in Chambery, Maurice de Sully's *Exposition des Evangiles* (1484) with its fine woodcuts, bought in 1919, Villon, *Le grant testament, et le petit* (Paris, 1489), the oldest dated edition, the illuminated *Le rommant de la rose* (?1496) and the first illustrated Gaston Phébus, *Des deduiz de la chasse* (?1510). French printing at its best is exemplified in Geoffroy Tory's two books of hours, of 1525 (Henry VIII's copy), and 1527, and the earlier issue of the *Oeuvres* of Louise Labé, printed at Lyon by Jean de Tournes and dated 1555, which came to join Grenville's of 1556.

One of the most influential books of the 16th century, Calvin's *Christianae religionis institutio*, is there in its first edition (1536), by no means common, as is Ronsard's very rare first work, *Epithalame d'Antoine de Bourbon* (1549), and the first edition of Montaigne's *Essais* (1580).

One 17th-century French book of great rarity is the Virgil, *Traductieou de l'Eneido*, a translation into Narbonnais dialect printed at Béziers in 1682. Besides this, there is the first complete Molière (1666), while George II's Molière (1734) is one of Boucher's earliest graphic works. Sloane's admirer Voltaire is represented by the original manuscript, proofs and final text of *Discours en vers sur les événements de 1744*. Of the great illustrated books of the 18th century, one of the last, La Fontaine's *Contes et nouvelles* (1795), illustrated by Fragonard, is also one of the rarest, since it was overtaken by the Revolution, which turned printers to other tasks, such as Marat's *L'ami du peuple*, not to mention the tracts accumulated by Croker. One unusual souvenir of the First Empire is Comte Roederer's *Oeuvres* in eight volumes (1853–59), the very rare account of Napoleon's conversation. Among more modern works are Verlaine's *Poèmes saturniens* (1866), a presentation copy, some fine *livres de peintre*, among them Reverdy, *Une aventure méthodique*

Above. Illustration by Fragonard in La Fontaine, *Contes et nouvelles*, 1795.
C.97.g.13 (vol.1), p.87r.

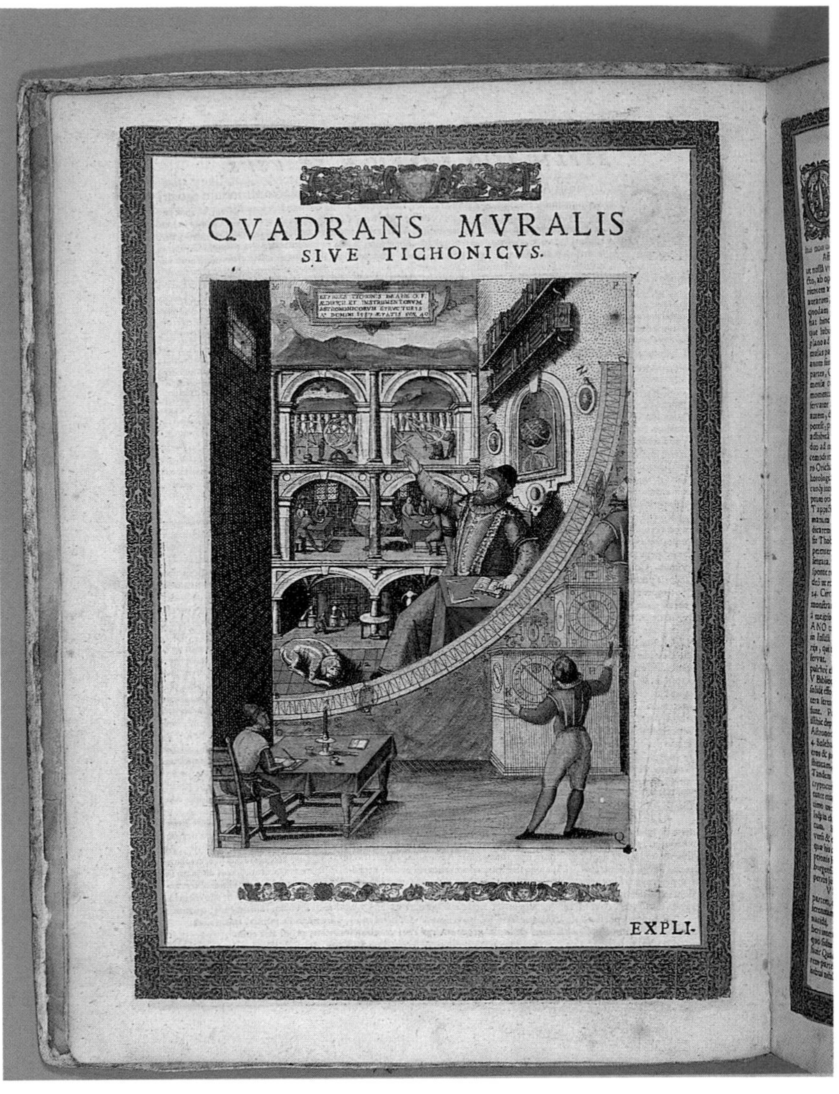

Coloured woodcut in Tycho Brahe, *Astronomiae instaurata*, 1598.
C.45.h.3.A4v.

(1949) with illustrations by Braque, and Michel de Saint Pierre, *Les côtes normandes* (1961) with Dufy's illustrations.

In 1900 the Museum received the bequest of H.S. Ashbee, rich in 18th-century books, with notable collections of Fielding and Sterne and a vastly augmented set of Nichols's *Literary Anecdotes*, and notable accessions to the Private Case, the repository of obscene and libellous books not normally available to the public. Its chief pride, however, was the Cervantes collection, altogether 8764 editions of 15,299 volumes. Now to add to Grenville's first edition of *Don Quixote* came a host of others, Ibarra's magnificent edition of 1780, later joined by the extraordinary edition printed in Barcelona in 1909 on cork. Other Spanish treasures are the first edition of the *Grammatica* of the Spanish humanist Antonio de Lebrixa, printed at Logroño in 1510 and the first novel in any romance language, apart from the French Arthurian romances, the *Libellus de amico et amato* of Ramon Lull, the 13th-century philosopher and mystic, printed at Alcalá in 1517. There is also the first edition of the first book of Juan de Yciar, the great Spanish writing master, one of two recorded copies, *Cosa nueva: este es el estilo de escrivir cartas mesageras* (1547). From Portugal there is the historian Resende's rare *História da antiguidade da cidade Evora* (1553), the first Portuguese book on hawking, Ferreira, *Arte da caça de altaneria* (1616), and the first edition of Camões's famous epic,

Os Lusíadas (Lisbon, 1572); Garcia da Orte, *Colóquios dos simples* (Goa, 1563) contains a dedicatory poem addressed to Camões.

One of the most influential books to issue from the press in the 15th century was the *De imitatione Christi* of Thomas à Kempis (*c.*1472), the first of a succession of editions which make a separate section in the Library, given by Edward Waterton. Perhaps no other book, printed at more or less the same time as it was written, has been so often reprinted, in the original Latin or translated into a host of other languages. Unexpectedly, the first edition was printed at Augsburg, not in the Low Countries, where it was not printed until the 1480s.

It was, however, in the Low Countries that three other books, equally famous, were printed in the 1480s. Thierry Martin, printer at Antwerp and Louvain, was not the most distinguished printer of the early 16th century, but he it was who printed the first edition of three of the great classics to be issued there, Erasmus's *Moriae encomium* (the first acknowledged edition, 1512), *Enchiridion militis Christiani* (1515), and More's *Utopia* (1516). Printing in the Low Countries always served an international market, and Goltzius's fine *Antiquissima... Anglorum regum origo* (1586) was firmly

Libellus vere aureus nec
MINVS SALVTARIS QVAM FESTIuus de optimo reip. statu, deque noua Insula Vtopia authore clarissimo viro Thoma Moro inclytæ ciuitatis Londinensis ciue & vicecomite cura M. Petri Aegidii Antuerpiẽsis, & arte Theodorici Martini Alustensis, Typographi almæ Louaniensium Academiæ nunc primum accuratissime editus.

Bequeathed by Thos Tyrwhitt Esqr. 1786.

Cum gratia & priuilegio.

Above. Title-page of the first edition of More's *Utopia*, printed by Thierry Martin, 1516 (bequeathed by Thomas Tyrwhitt in 1786).

Right. Pride and humility. From an illustrated emblem book, *Amoris divini et humani effectus*, 1626.

Above. Title-page of Petrarch's *Rime*, Florence, 1822.
C.29.c.13.

Below. Title-page of Angel Day's *Daphnis and Chloe*, 1587.
Huth 37.

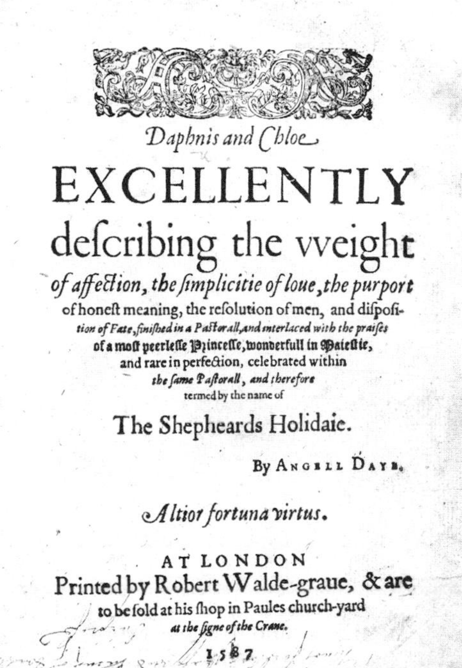
Daphnis and Chloe

EXCELLENTLY

describing the weight

of affection, the simplicitie of loue, the purport of honest meaning, the resolution of men, and disposition of Fate, finished in a Pastorall, and interlaced with the praises of a most peerlesse Princesse, wonderfull in Maiestie, and rare in perfection, celebrated within the same Pastorall, and therefore termed by the name of

The Shepheards Holidaie.

By Angell Daye.

Altior fortuna virtus.

AT LONDON

Printed by Robert Walde-graue, & are to be sold at his shop in Paules church-yard at the signe of the Crane.

1587.

directed across the English Channel. Emblem books, such as *Amoris divini et humani effectus* (1626), picture books such as Crispin de Passe's *Hortus Floridus* (1614), and atlases, such as those of Ortelius and Blaeu, had an international market, as did Hugo Grotius's *Mare liberum* (1609), and the works of the great Dutch writing master and engraver Jan Van den Velde.

Literature in the vernacular, however, also found a market, from Dirck Coornhert's *Wercken* (1630), to Hendrik Conscience, who gave the Museum Library his *De Leeuw van Vlaenderen* in 1848. The Library has a fine collection, too, of the books clandestinely printed during the last war, notably *De Nederlanden: door Folk van Holland* (1943) with its fine woodcut illustrations.

Italian books have always been a prime influence in the impact of European literature on British culture. From the days of Sir Thomas Hoby and John Florio, Italian has intertwined with English in a strand of which the collections of Consul Smith and Thomas Grenville are part. But even here, gaps remained to be filled. Ariosto's *Satire* (1537), with notes in Aretino's hand, came later, and Grenville's *Rime* of Tasso has been joined by the 1581 Parma *Gerusalemme liberata*, with corrections in the hand of Aldo Manuzio (Aldus Manutius), to whom (according to an old note) Tasso dictated them from his cell. Very recently, *Il re Torrismondo* (Ferrara, 1587) has been added to the collection, with the signature of the Elizabethan poet Francis Davidson.

Of all the later wealth too great and too diverse even to be sampled, one aspect only must suffice, the Anglo-Italian links in the collections. Here, for example, is the Italian translation of Gray's 'Elegy', *Elegia inglese del signor Tommaso Gray sopra un cimitero di campagna*, translated by the Abate M. Cesarotti (Padua, 1782) with Gray's own corrections, and Lippi, *Il Malmantile racquistato* (1748), heavily annotated by Johnson's friend Joseph Baretti. With the 19th century comes the beautiful illuminated copy, one of two on vellum, of Petrarch's *Rime*, printed in 1822 for the Florentine firm of Molini, who supplied generations of English visitors with books. Here too is Ugo Foscolo, whose most famous *Dei sepolcri* (1807) was only acquired in 1957; it is odd that neither of his English friends, Grenville or Panizzi, acquired a copy. Panizzi did not miss Leopardi, whose *Annotazioni* (1823) and *Operette morali* (1827) were early acquired, and also the rare early *Canzoni* (1818). Panizzi gave Grenville a unique vellum copy of his *Bibliographical Notices* (1831) on Boiardo and Ariosto, and the Library also has his attack on the sentence of the Modena court that caused his exile (1823), with the imprint 'Madrid' (really Lugano). Panizzi's sufferings awoke the sympathy of a great modern poet, Giosuè Carducci, who published an account of them in 1897; his own famous *Inno a Satana* was bought new in 1869. Cavour's *Discorso . . . sul progetto di legge* (1858), given by him to Gladstone and by Gladstone to the Library, reflects another of Panizzi's friendships. The most recent link is Giovanni Mardersteig's warm friendship for the Library. The greatest printer of the 20th century and Italian by adoption, he printed for the Library special copies of his editions – masterpieces of his art – of Bodoni's *Manuale tipografico* (1968), Bembo's *De Aetna* (1969) and Terence's *Andria* (1971). The Library also has Salvatore Quasimodo's translations of the *Iliad* and *Odyssey*, illustrated by De Chirico and Manzu (1976–77).

The tale of English books acquired in the 20th century is the most impressive of all, and like the rest it is a mixture of great collections acquired and single gaps filled. Henry Huth (1815–78) was one of the greatest 19th-century collectors, and his collection, increased by his son Alfred (1850–1910), was rich in rare English books. The younger Huth left 50 books, both manuscript and printed, to the Museum, and the rest were sold between 1911 and 1920. Among the English books thus acquired were a fine copy (replacing a bad one) of Caxton's *Dicts and sayings of the philosophers* (1477), the unique copies of Angel Day's *Daphnis and Chloe* (1587), Munday's *Banquet of Daintie Conceits* (1588), and *A marvellous history, intitled, beware the cat* (1584) by William Baldwin, author of the famous *Mirror for Magistrates*

Above. Engraved title-page of the Winter Queen's copy of Ralegh's *History of the World*, 1614.
C.38.i.10.

Below. Plate from Raynalde, *The byrth of mankynde*, 1545.
C.54.b.4.

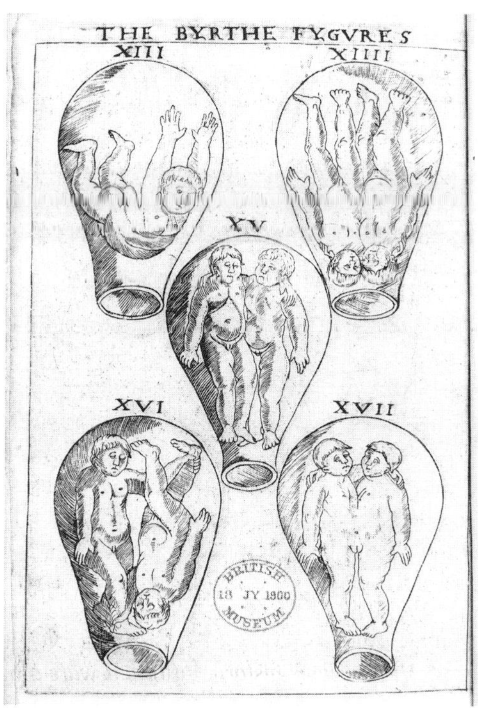

and the unique *Historie of Sir Bevis of South Hampton* printed in 1630 at Aberdeen by Edward Raban. There were several other early English books, notably by Nicholas Breton, almost as rare, besides a block book *Ars memorandi c.*1470. In the sales that followed, and even more so in the Britwell Court sales (1916–27), the Museum was hampered by lack of funds and the competition of Henry E. Huntington, whose resources seemed almost limitless, but among the books acquired were Harrington, *The Commendations of Matrimony* (1528) and Hanson, *Time is a Turne Coate* (1604), an account of James I's entry to London, both unique, as well as Wynkyn de Worde's *Four leaves of truelove* (*c.*1530), unique until the Britwell Court sales (as so often) revealed another, and Harman's *Caveat or warening for commen cursetors* (1567), a vivid picture of the life of the Elizabethan tramp.

The Library is still looking for David Garrick's copy of Gerard Langbaine's *An account of the English dramatick poets* (1691), in which he marked the sources from which he acquired his collection, but it has several important annotated copies of the work, notably that of William Oldys, the 18th-century literary bibliographer. Other remarkable association copies now in the collections include the copy of Ralegh's *History of the World* (1614) that belonged to Elizabeth, the 'Winter Queen', daughter of James I, Lord Burghley's Aretino and *Orlando furioso* (1591) and the copy of Jonson's *Volpone* (1607) that he gave to the great translator, John Florio. Jonson's copy of Montaigne's *Essais* (1603) is also in the Library, and another copy of the same edition bears the signature 'William Shakespeare'.

Among fine engraved books are Raynalde, *The byrth of mankynde* (1545), the first illustrated obstetric book, and the pictorial account of Sir Philip Sidney's funeral by Thomas Lant. Besides the classic *Herball* of John Gerard, there is the unique copy of the first edition of his *Catalogus arborum* (1596), the list of plants in his garden at Holborn. All the works of John Skelton, the first prolific English poet in print, are rare, and *A ballade of the Scottysshe kynge* (1513) is unique, as is the first edition of Heywood's famous play *A woman kilde with kindness* (1607). Besides the several copies of the *Compleat Angler* (Banks's as well as Thomason's) is Izaak Walton's *Book of Common Prayer* (1639), with family records in his hand.

From the later 17th century comes the unique copy of Andrew Marvell's *Miscellaneous poems* (1681) with the suppressed poems in praise of Oliver Cromwell, and two remarkable early children's books: Festus Corin *The Childes first tutor* (1664) was found behind a wall in a butcher's shop in Hampshire in 1985, where it had fallen the day it was bought, to judge by its mint condition; it was followed shortly after by 'S.T.' *The childs book* (1662), also unique. Both these make a remarkable addition to the Library's best known early children's book, the first edition of *Little Goody Two Shoes* (1765).

The long-continuing reciprocation of the interest that Samuel Johnson took in the Library has borne much fruit. Here, for example, is the Bible given him by his friend, the printer Alexander Strahan, the copy of Isaac Watts's *Logick* (1745) marked up by Johnson for the *Dictionary*, and with it George III's copy of the *Dictionary* (1755) itself, besides Edmund Burke's. One copy of volume one (only) of the third edition (1765) has Johnson's own corrections, while there are the proofs of two sheets of the life of Dryden in the *Lives of the Poets*, also corrected by Johnson. Of Goldsmith, the Library has the *Life of Richard Nash* (1762) annotated by the author. Pope's multifarious works include two presentation copies of the *Works* (1717), an odd volume two, corrected by the author, of the 1736 *Works*, and the suppressed edition, with the libel on the Duchess of Buckingham, of *Epistles to several persons*. There, too, is the Strawberry Hill copy of Walpole's *Castle of Otranto* (1765), Burns's *Ayrshire Garland* (1789), Mary Wollstonecraft's *Vindication of the Rights of Women* (1792), marked by her for a new edition, and the only known copy of William Godwin's novel *Damon and Delia* (1784). Two copies of Gibbon's *Decline and Fall of the Roman Empire* bear his corrections. Finally, there is a copy

Ben Jonson, *Volpone*, 1607, with Jonson's autograph dedication 'to his loving Father, and worthy Friend, John Florio'.
C.12.e.17.

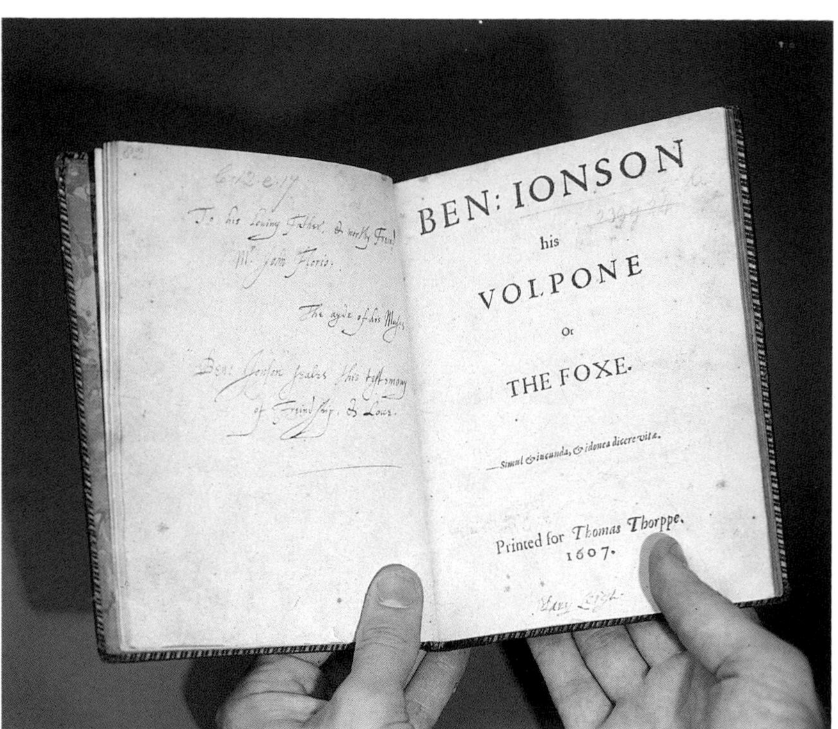

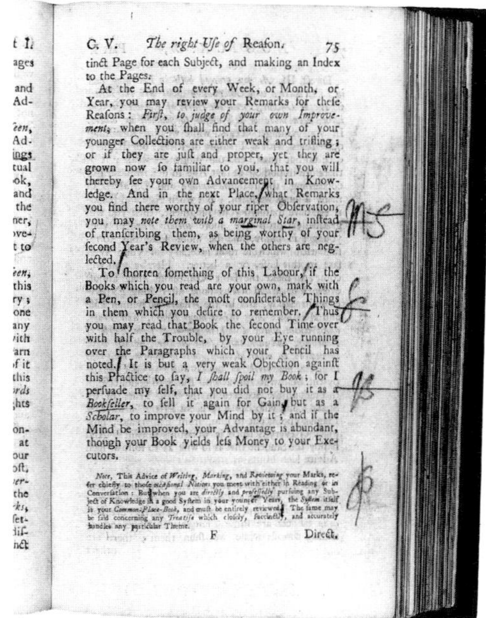
C. V. *The right Uſe of* Reaſon. 75

tinct Page for each Subject, and making an Index to the Pages.

At the End of every Week, or Month, or Year, you may review your Remarks for theſe Reaſons: *Firſt, to judge of your own Improvement*, when you ſhall find that many of your younger Collections are either weak and trifling; or if they are juſt and proper, yet they are grown now ſo familiar to you, that you will thereby ſee your own Advancement in Knowledge. And in the next Place, what Remarks you find there worthy of your riper Obſervation, you may *note them with a marginal Star*, inſtead of tranſcribing them, as being worthy of your ſecond Year's Review, when the others are neglected.

To ſhorten ſomething of this Labour, if the Books which you read are your own, mark with a Pen, or Pencil, the moſt conſiderable Things in them which you deſire to remember. Thus you may read that Book the ſecond Time over with half the Trouble, by your Eye running over the Paragraphs which your Pencil has noted. It is but a very weak Objection againſt this Practice to ſay, *I ſhall ſpoil my Book*; for I perſuade my ſelf, that you did not buy it as a *Bookſeller*, to ſell it again for Gain, but as a *Scholar*, to improve your Mind by it; and if the Mind be improved, your Advantage is abundant, though your Book yields leſs Money to your Executors.

Note, This Advice of *Writing*, *Marking*, and *Reviewing* your Marks, refer chiefly to thoſe *occaſional Notions* you meet with either in Reading or in Converſation: But when you are *directly* and *profeſſedly* purſuing any Subject of Knowledge in a good Syſtem in your younger Years, the *Syſtem* itſelf is your *Common-Place-Book*, and muſt be entirely reviewed. The ſame may be ſaid concerning any *Treatiſe* which cloſely, ſuccinctly, and accurately handles any particular Theme.

F Direct.

Isaac Watts, *Logick*, 1745, marked up by Samuel Johnson in preparing his *Dictionary*.
C.28.g.9, p.75.

of the rarest of all the great poems of the 18th century, Christopher Smart's *A Song to David* (1763).

A curious link connects Pope with the Romantic poets in the Library's collections. There is a set of Pope's *Iliad* (1720) in the Department of Manuscripts, there because Pope gave it to Gilbert White, whose portrait and notes it bears; White was author of *The natural history of Selborne* (1789), a copy of which belonged to Southey, and was covered by him in a piece of old dress-material, the style that led him jokingly to refer to his 'Cottonian Library'.

This is a cheerful beginning to the later English literature in the collections, to offset the more sombre mark of the accession in 1937–38 of the Ashley Library, formed by Thomas James Wise (1859–1937), and sold to the British Museum after his death. This is no place to dwell on his thefts of leaves from the Museum copies of early plays, save to mark the recent return of the last residue, nor on his forgeries, save the most notorious, the 'Reading' *Sonnets* of Elizabeth Barrett Browning ('1840'). It is better to remember his collection's treasures: remarkable in items of the 17th century, with Webster's *The white divel* (1612); rich in the 18th century – of the Library's 11 copies of the seven different editions or issues of Pope's *Dunciad* (1728), eight are in the Ashley Library; and incomparable in its coverage of the 19th century. Wise's holdings of the Lakeland poets are the best in the world (although Southey's unique copy of *Lyrical Ballads* (1798–1800) came independently). His copy of Browning's *Bells and Pomegranates* (1841–46) was given by the poet to Carlyle. He had the suppressed first edition of Byron's *Fugitive pieces* (1806), the copy of *Whims and oddities* (1826) that Hood gave to Coleridge, Coventry Patmore's privately circulated *Odes* (1868), and, among the virtually complete collection of Swinburne and Tennyson, the first issue of Swinburne's *Poems and ballads* (1866) and the unique copy of Tennyson's *The birth of Arthur* (1868). His long acquaintance with W.M. Rossetti brought him an equally strong collection of his brother Dante Gabriel's works, including every form of the privately printed *Poems* (1869–70) from the manuscripts exhumed from the grave of Rossetti's wife, Lizzie Siddall.

The ever-growing interest in William Blake has always been reflected in the Library's collections, together with those in the Department of Prints and

Drawings in the British Museum. The Library is notably strong in Blake's texts, with two copies of *Poetical Sketches* (1783), one bought in 1890 (and perhaps Samuel Palmer's copy), and the other, once Blake's patron Thomas Butts's, in the Ashley Library. A remarkable single volume contains *Visions of the Daughters of Albion* (1793), *America* (1793) and the *Song of Los* (1795), bound together, and there is an uncoloured copy of *Songs of Innocence and Experience* (1794); a copy of Joshua Reynolds's *Works* (1798) is disapprovingly annotated by Blake.

The Department of Manuscripts has maintained the same interest in Blake. The manuscript of *Tiriel* was bought, and the *The Four Zoas* was an anonymous gift in 1913. The greatest of all Blake manuscripts, the Rossetti MS, so-called after D.G. Rossetti who discovered it in 1847, came in 1957 by the hand of the great Blake scholar, Geoffrey Keynes, and through the generosity of Mrs Emerson, daughter of the collector W.A. White of New York. This collection continues to grow; in 1986 the newly discovered illuminated poem 'The Phoenix to Mrs Butts' was acquired.

Blake is only one of many authors whose manuscripts have been acquired in the last 80 years. Two notable early acquisitions were Milton's Commonplace Book and the autograph of Massinger's *Believe as you list*, later joined by the long-lost *Vanities and toys of youth* of the Elizabethan Sir Arthur Gorges. The remarkable poems of Robert Sidney, Earl of Leicester, are a recent acquisition. Gabriel Harvey's heavily annotated Chaucer is another important source of Elizabethan literature. Locke's famous tract *On Education* was acquired, and, by the gift of Geoffrey Keynes, Gibbon's library catalogue. The strong holdings of Keats were supplemented with *Hyperion*, soon after Southey's *The Curse of Kehama* was acquired, with important manuscripts of Coleridge and Peacock.

Of the great 19th-century novelists, two chapters of *Persuasion* have been joined by Jane Austen's letters, one given by John Pierpont Morgan, and also her early 'History of England'. The manuscripts of all George Eliot's novels have been joined by the notable bequest of the publisher George Smith, which provided the manuscripts of Charlotte Bronte's *Jane Eyre*, *Shirley* and *Villette*, Emily Bronte's 'Gondal Poems', Browning's *The Ring and the Book* and his wife's *Sonnets from the Portuguese*. The autograph of *Nicholas Nickleby* and part

Portrait of Gilbert White, in a copy of Pope's *Iliad*.
Add. MS 38877, f.1.

THE
HISTORY
OF
Little Goody Two-Shoes;
Otherwise called
Mrs. Margery Two-Shoes.
WITH
The Means by which she acquired her Learning and Wisdom, and in consequence thereof her Estate; set forth at large for the Benefit of those,

Who from a State of Rags and Care,
And having Shoes but half a Pair;
Their Fortune and their Fame would fix,
And gallop in a Coach and Six.

See the Original Manuscript in the *Vatican* at *Rome*, and the Cuts by *Michael Angelo*. Illustrated with the Comments of our great modern Critics.

LONDON:
Printed for J. Newbery, at the *Bible* and *Sun* in St. *Paul's Church-yard*, 1765.
[Price *Six-Pence*.]

Title-page of *The History of Little Goody Two-Shoes*, 1765.
C.180.a.3.

William Blake. Page from his notebook, the 'Rossetti Manuscript'.
Add. MS 49460.

of *Pickwick Papers*, with Dickens's letters to his wife, Trollope's autobiography, Carlyle's *Past and Present*, and Thackeray's papers complete an important sequence.

It was perhaps remarkable that Robert Ross's gift of Oscar Wilde's manuscripts should be greeted, in 1909, as a major acquisition. Charles Fairfax Murray donated William Morris's poetical manuscripts, and Morris's calligraphic *Rubaiyat*, illuminated by Burne-Jones and himself was given by Lady Burne-Jones. These have since been joined by the complete residue of manuscripts and papers, bequeathed by Morris's daughter, May. To these Sydney Cockerell added a mass of printed material connected with the Kelmscott Press. John Galsworthy presented all but one of the 'Forsyte' manuscripts in 1929–30, and the bulk of Kipling's manuscripts, including *Kim* and *The Jungle Book* (with the author's original illustrations) came by his gift and the bequest of Mrs Kipling. The poems of Edward Thomas, Isaac Rosenberg, and Wilfred Owen were also acquired, while T.J. Wise's Ashley Library contributed the vast collection of manuscripts acquired with his books.

The major archives of political and other figures have also been significantly increased. Nelson's battle plan for Trafalgar has been added to already important holdings. The papers of William Windham have joined those of the Prime Ministers Lord Liverpool, Peel, and others. Dwarfing both these is the vast mass of Gladstone's papers. Other important figures whose archives came were those of Bishop Berkeley and Florence Nightingale, with her annotated copies of the Parliamentary Reports on hospitals. The manuscript of the famous Greville Diary was acquired in 1924, and the first of the 'Lord Chamberlain's Plays', the copies of every play submitted to the Lord Chamberlain's office for censorship between 1824 and 1851 was transferred to the British Museum library in 1932, followed at intervals by further batches of plays up to 1968. Four important business archives, which throw much light on the transmission of text into print, are the papers of Richard Bentley & Son and Macmillan & Co, publishers, and of the Chiswick Press and William Strahan, printers.

Among the earlier manuscripts, the oldest and by any standards the most important was the Codex Sinaiticus, discovered by Tischendorf in the monastery of St Katherine on Mount Sinai in 1846 and presented to the Tsar. It was purchased in 1934 from the Soviet Government for £100,000, raised by public subscription (which brought vast masses of visitors to the Museum) and a government grant. Another acquisition that recalled the manuscript collecting forays to Mount Athos and the Near East in the 1840s was the bequest by Robert Curzon's daughter, Lady Zouche, in 1917 of his collection, with its exceptionally diverse Greek manuscripts, the Gospels of the Bulgarian Tsar John Alexander and the 'Comnenos' Gospel-Book.

Two important English acquisitions were the Bede on Isaiah written at Tours in Alcuin's time in two hands, one French, the other insular, from the Ashburnham sale in 1901, and the leaves, rescued from wrapping later account books, from a magnificent early 8th-century Bible written at Jarrow-Wearmouth, once the twin of the famous 'Codex Amiatinus'. Three important manuscripts were acquired at the Chester Beatty sale, all of which had earlier been in the Phillipps collection, the 8th-century Augustine and Jerome from the North Italian abbey of Nonantola, a 10th-century Gregory the Great, and a collection written in the 13th century at Dore Abbey, important since it was a copy of one of the Cotton manuscripts ruined in 1731. Among later manuscripts were the Rievaulx Missal, purchased with one of the earliest grants from the Friends of the National Libraries, who have nobly supported the Library's acquisitions ever since.

There have been some notable additions to the heraldic manuscripts – the Jenyns Ordinary, the Parliament Roll of 1515, Fenn's Book of Badges (late 15th century), the vast collections of John Writhe, Garter King of Arms, and his son and successor, Sir Thomas Wriothesley; and the English version of the

Charlotte Bronte, *Jane Eyre*. Part of the autograph fair copy sent to the publishers in August 1847.
Add. MS 43475, f.237.

The Codex Sinaiticus. Greek Bible, 4th century. (Detail.)
Add. MS 43725, f.260.

most vivid of 15th-century armorial rolls, the Rous Roll. These lead on naturally to the most spectacular accessions, the illuminated manuscripts.

The century began with the bequest by Sir Thomas Brooke of the 9th-century Lothair Psalter, and the acquisition of the 10th-century Anglo-Saxon Bosworth Psalter, once Archbishop Cranmer's, and of a single leaf of the Hours of Etienne Chevalier (of which the major part is at Chantilly), the only example in the collection of the work of Jean Fouquet. With the Huth bequest came a number of fine French and English manuscripts, notably a Book of Hours from Valenciennes by Simon Marmion. In 1918, Henry Yates Thompson celebrated his 80th birthday by presenting the great 14th-century East Anglian St Omer Psalter, and from his much-lamented sale came the little illuminated copy of Bede's *Life of St Cuthbert*, Durham, *c.*1200, and the *Tesoro* of Brunetto Latini. The year 1929 was an *annus mirabilis* which saw the acquisition, from the Lulworth Castle Library, of the Luttrell Psalter, the most picturesque of all 14th-century manuscripts, and the Bedford Hours and Psalter, one of the major monuments of early 15th-century English illumination. The total cost was £64,500, made possible through a generous loan from John Pierpont Morgan backed again by subscription, organised by the Trustees, the Government and the National Art Collections Fund.

Another notable acquisition was the second volume of a fine 13th-century French Bible, given by Mrs Yates Thompson in memory of her husband which now rejoined the first volume in the Harleian collection. The Belluno Herbal joined the two early Egerton herbals already in the Library. In 1931 the fine 13th-century Abingdon Apocalypse was bought, to be followed by the Evesham Psalter, also 13th-century. The acquisition of the Psalter presented in memory of M.R. James, who did so much for the study of English medieval art and manuscripts, was particularly satisfying, since its firmly northern English provenance linked it with the Egerton Genesis (*see* p. 129). The Bohun Psalter added further new evidence of the influence of Italian art on English 14th-century manuscripts, while the acquisition of more fragments to add to those of Hanrott made possible the reconstruction by Margaret Rickert of the great early 15th-century 'Carmelite Missal'.

Greatest of all accessions of illuminated manuscripts was the bequest of the residue, 46, of the Yates Thompson collection by Mrs Yates Thompson in 1941. Henry Yates Thompson (1838–1928) set himself to acquire only the finest illuminated manuscripts. He limited himself to 100 examples, and ruthlessly discarded earlier acquisitions if later offered better. Threatened with blindness, he dispersed part of his collection in 1917–19, but retained some of the best. These included the Hours of Jean de Dunois, among the finest work executed in Paris in the second quarter of the 15th century and related to the Bedford Hours, and the Breviary of Verdun made in 1302 for Renaud de Bar, who also commissioned the Metz Pontifical. Among the English manuscripts, the Taymouth Hours, 14th century, lavishly illustrated in the 'East Anglian' style, is outstanding. The Hours of Yolande of Flanders, although damaged by damp, is a remarkable example of the work of Jean Pucelle, and the Sainte-Chapelle Epistolar resembles it. The three finest Italian manuscripts were the Dante written for Alfonso, King of Aragon and Naples, with 85 miniatures, those of the 'Paradiso' by the Sienese artist Giovanni di Paolo; the Ghislieri Hours written by Pierantonio Sallando, and with a miniature by Perugino; and the Hours of Dionora, Duchess of Urbino. Willem Vrelant painted two miniatures in a Flemish Book of Hours. Yates Thompson's was, beyond any doubt, the choicest collection of illuminated manuscripts ever made, and the part that came to the Library was a major augmentation of its resources.

The collection of manuscripts, like that of printed books, benefited from the enforced disposal of books from Holkham Hall in 1951. Thence came the Cicero written at Tours and the Schuttern Abbey Gospels, both 9th century, the 12th-century *Agrimensores Romani* and the remarkable Psalter in Greek

Beatus page from the St Omer Psalter. English, 14th century.
Add. MS 39810, f.7.

Opposite, above. Rubaiyat of Omar Khayyam, illuminated by William Morris with contributions by Edward Burne-Jones.
Add. MS 37832, ff.11v–12.

Opposite, below. A man sowing. Marginal decoration in the Luttrell Psalter. English, 14th century.
Add. MS 42130, f.170v.

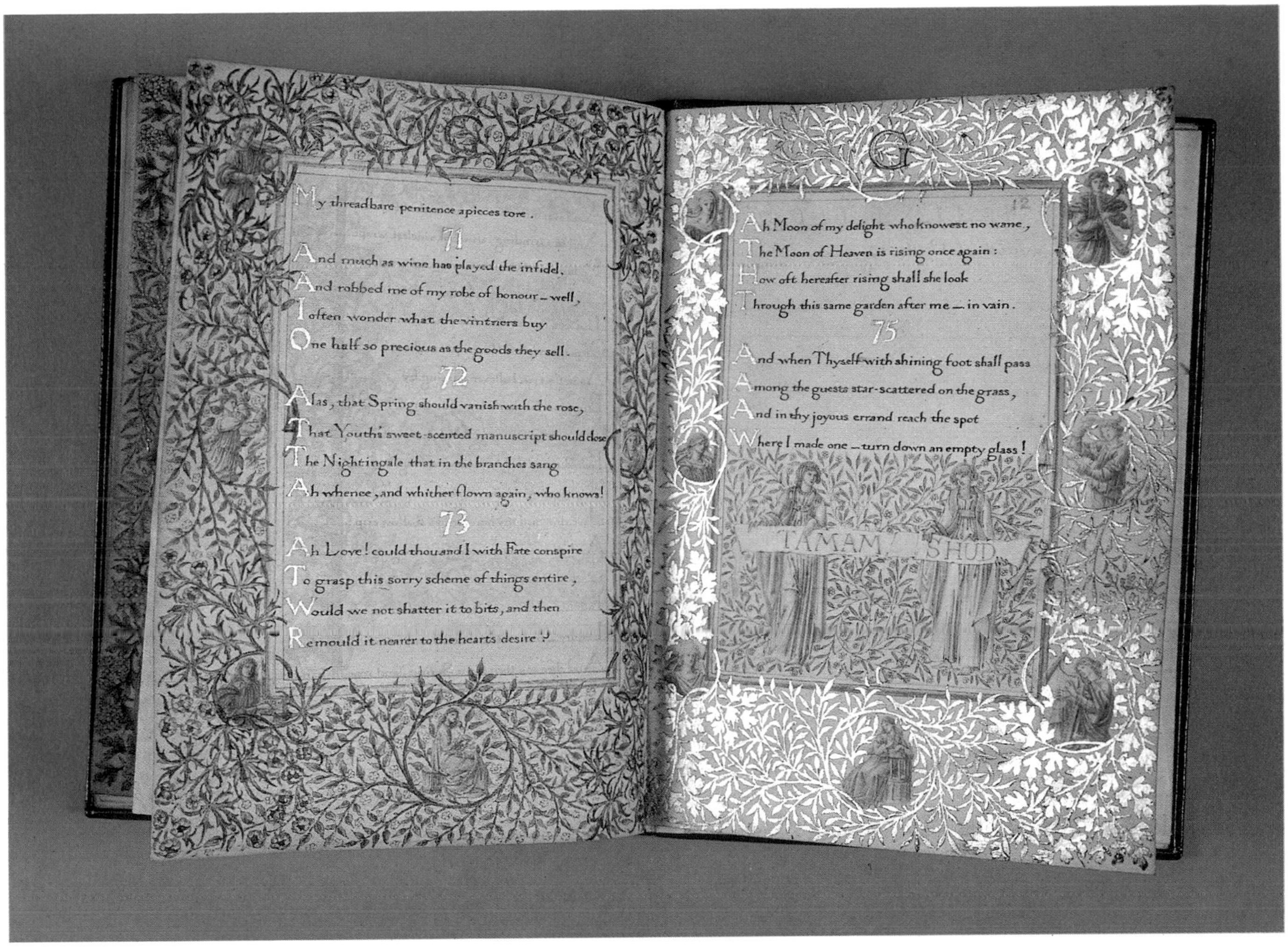
My threadbare penitence apieces tore.
71
And much as wine has played the infidel,
And robbed me of my robe of honour – well,
I often wonder what the vintners buy
One half so precious as the goods they sell.
72
Alas, that Spring should vanish with the rose,
That Youth's sweet-scented manuscript should close!
The Nightingale that in the branches sang
Ah whence, and whither flown again, who knows!
73
Ah Love! could thou and I with Fate conspire
To grasp this sorry scheme of things entire,
Would we not shatter it to bits, and then
Remould it nearer to the hearts desire!
G
Ah Moon of my delight who knowest no wane,
The Moon of Heaven is rising once again:
How oft hereafter rising shall she look
Through this same garden after me – in vain.
75
And when Thyself with shining foot shall pass
Among the guests star-scattered on the grass,
And in thy joyous errand reach the spot
Where I made one – turn down an empty glass!
TAMAM SHUD

Quoniam deus magnus domi
nus : & rex magnus super omnes
deos.

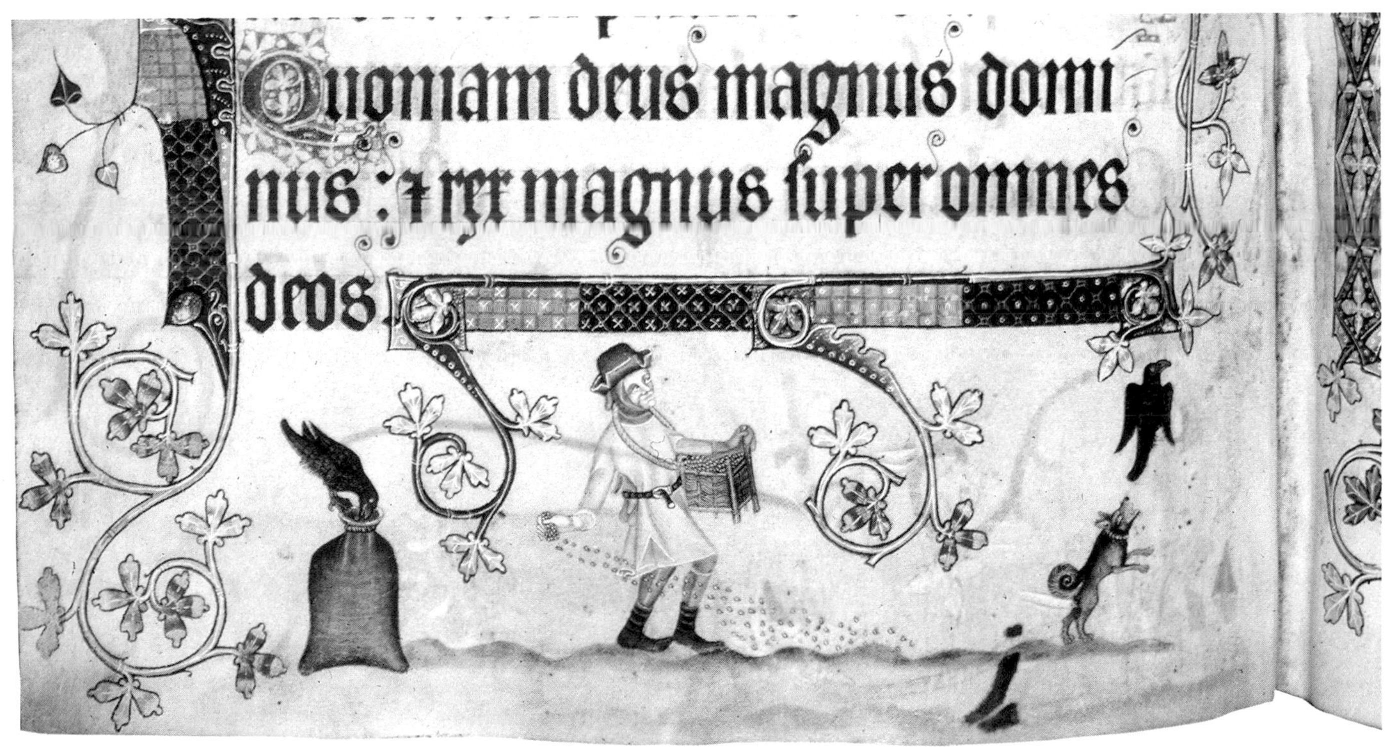

S.T. Coleridge, autograph manuscript of 'Kubla Khan'. It differs in several respects from the version published in 1816.
Add. MS 50847, f.1v.

and Latin, *c.*1215–25, the Bible Picture Book, *c.*1327–35, the Bible of Anti-pope Clement VII, and one of the manuscripts of the extraordinary humanist antiquary Felice Feliciano. Other notable acquisitions were the Salvin Hours, given by Sir Chester Beatty, the early 13th-century treatise on painting, *Pictor in carmine*, given by J.W. Hely-Hutchinson, and the 10th-century Anglo-Saxon Orosius from Helmingham Hall (illustrated, p. 267).

Thanks to the Pilgrim Trust, a vast collection of S.T. Coleridge's papers, notebooks, poetical drafts and correspondence was acquired, also in 1951, together with a large number of books annotated by Coleridge to amplify the considerable number already acquired, to which was added in 1961 the original draft, of 'Kubla Khan'. Joyce's *Finnegan's Wake* has joined the collection of literary manuscripts. Further papers on the trial of Mary Queen of Scots came among the rich collections of Robert Beale, clerk to the council of Elizabeth I, a prime source for Elizabethan history. G.M. Trevelyan gave correspondence of Charles James Fox, collected by his father, Fox's biographer. Wilson's Antarctic diary was followed by the sequence of Captain Scott's diaries.

Another major acquisition of medieval manuscripts came with the dispersal of the Dyson-Perrins Collection in 1956–60. As long ago as 1919, C.W. Dyson-Perrins had given the Museum a copy of Sannazaro's *Arcadia* (1502) in its original 'paper-back' binding with a woodcut design on it. Early printed Italian illustrated books and medieval manuscripts engaged his collecting enthusiasm. He bequeathed to the Museum the 14th-century Gorleston Psalter, one of the great 'East Anglian' manuscripts, and his executers arranged for another eight manuscripts, including the De Brailes Hours, the Prayer Book of Arnulf of Milan, 10th–11th century, and the early 15th-century Hours which later belonged to Elizabeth, Henry VII's Queen, to be sold to the Museum before the rest were auctioned. Chief of these acquisitions was the great Oscott Psalter, a magnificent example of English work at the second half of the 13th century; soon after, in 1968, Mrs Perrins bequeathed the Hastings Hours, a major example of late 15th-century Flemish illumination for an English patron. Shortly before this, from Chatsworth, came the great illuminated Anglo-Saxon book, the Benedictional of St Aethelwold.

The great charter collections of the Museum's foundation, the Cotton, Harley, Royal and Sloane Charters, have been continually augmented. To the magnificent Campbell, Topham, Wolley, Lansdowne and Stowe collections, acquired at various times between 1804 and 1883, have been added the long and still growing series of Additional Charters, now more than 76,000 in number, and the Egerton Charters, bought (like the Egerton Manuscripts) with the income from the Bridgewater Fund. Accessions to these series in recent years include not only vast family archives such as the Shrewsbury-Talbot deeds and the Thoresby Park (Pierrepont) charters, but also many important individual charters; for example, the superb charter of Waleran Fitz Ranulf granting land in Suffolk and London to St Stephen's Abbey, Caen, 1072–76, attested with the autograph crosses of William the Conqueror and Queen Matilda; and the sentence of excommunication against violators of Magna Carta pronounced in Westminster Hall in 1253 by the Archbishop of Canterbury and 13 bishops, in the presence of King Henry III and the nobility. A more recently acquired charter is a document whose presence in these

A charter of Waleran FitzRanulf. Detail showing the crosses made by William the Conqueror, his wife Matilda, and other nobles, signifying approval of the grant. 1072 1076.
Add. Charter 75503.

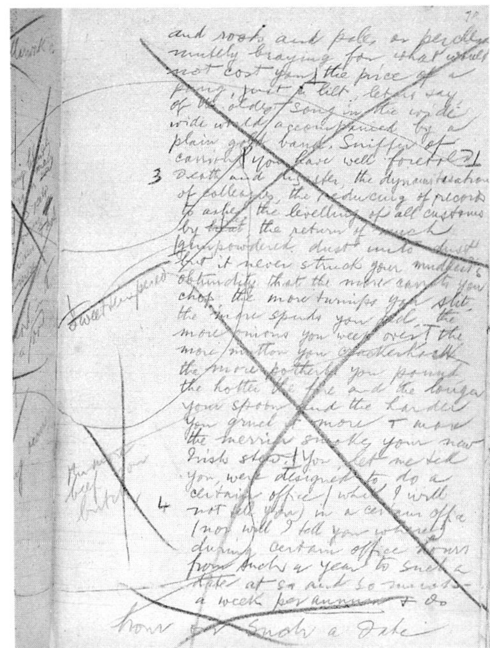

Draft of James Joyce's *Finnegan's Wake* (published 1939).
Add. MS 47471B, f.70.

incomparable collections is particularly fitting: the will of Sir Robert Cotton, 1631, by which he established a trust for the preservation of the library which was destined to become, in the words of Sir Frederic Madden, 'the most valuable present ever given to the Nation'.

Among the post-incunabular printed books from Chatsworth was an extraordinary volume of 12 pieces all printed by Wynkyn de Worde, ranging in date from Lydgate's *The Chorle and the byrde* (*c.*1495) to the two Boccaccio tales translated by William Walter (1532), once in the Farmer and Roxburghe collections, and the only known copies of Breton's *Wits Private Wealth* (1607) and Barnes's *Parthenophil and Perthenophe* (1593). The Holkham purchase, too, contained two remarkable collective volumes, one with Marot's *L'enfer* and 15 other French tracts, by Ronsard, Etienne Pasquier and others (1532–89), the other containing 35 tracts in English on the French Civil War (1589–92), many unique.

Other remarkable printed acquisitions are Robert Bridges's *Testament of Beauty*, as first printed in a few copies for the author to revise (1927–29), Augustin Heckle's delightful *The Lady's Drawing Book* (1753), a manual of flower painting, Sassoon's *Morning glory* (1916), number seven of an edition of 11, given to Sydney Cockerell, the first edition of Cleland's *Memoirs of a woman of pleasure* (1749) and Wilde's presentation copy to Lord Alfred Douglas of *Salome* (1894). Coleridge's books have been followed by a selection from the library of Walter Savage Landor, and a complete set of the pieces printed by Kipling with his own hands. The copy of Marcus Vigerius, *Decachordon Christianum*, printed by Soncino at Fano in 1507 on vellum, with the author's presentation inscription to Henry VII, in which he apologises for not having it bound (it is in fact in a handsome contemporary London binding by 'L.V.L'), was retrieved in 1954, thus rejoining the Old Royal Library, whence it had escaped centuries before.

These are some of the major single acquisitions of the last 80 years. It remains to notice three remarkable sources of material, unlike any other that have entered the collection.

Photography has provided some notable treasures in the last 150 years, accidentally at first – Daguerre's *Historique et description des procédés du daguerreotype* (1839) arrived with a consignment of contemporary French books – but latterly with increasing appreciation of their importance. The arrival of Fox Talbot's *The pencil of nature* (1844) was a landmark, but one anticipated by the acquisition of the *Art Union* for June 1846, with its pioneering calotype frontispiece. Hill and Adamson's *One hundred calotype sketches* (1848) was only acquired in 1953, but the Library was a natural recipient of one of the 130 presentation copies of the official catalogue of the Great Exhibition (1851) with 154 calotype illustrations, each bound in red morocco by Rivière with the gilt monogram of Queen Victoria and Prince Albert. Blanquart-Evrard's *Album photographique* (1851–53) was a pioneering attempt at photographic publication.

The monuments of Egypt provided ideal conditions, as well as subject-matter, for photography, and the works of Maxine du Camp, Felix Teynard, and the notably aesthetic photographs of Captain Sir William Abney, *Thebes and its five greater temples* (1876) attest it. Francis Frith's *Egypt and Palestine* (1858–59) was another early example, and Frith also turned his talents to the illustration of local topography, in Wright & Jones's *Memorials of Cambridge* (1860), and – a by-product of the first work mentioned – *The Holy Bible* (1862). Frith's firm lasted for a century and there were other successful commercial photographers, such as Philip Delamotte and Joseph Cundall, whose *Photographic tour among the abbeys of Yorkshire* (1856) was an early success. Patrick Barry's *Dockyard economy* (1863) was the first to grasp the aesthetic power of industrial scenes, and the possibilities of photography as a stimulus to social consciousness. Julia Cameron's *Alfred Lord Tennyson and his*

Giovanni di Paolo, miniature from a manuscript of Dante's *Divine Comedy*. Sienese, 15th century.
Yates Thompson 36, f.149.

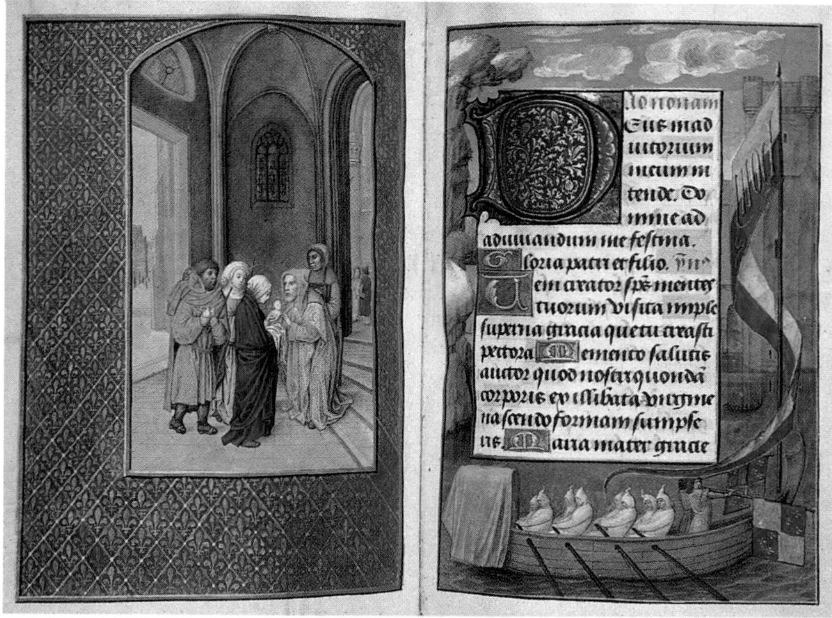

The Hastings Hours. Left: the Presentation in the Temple. Right: a royal barge. Flemish, before 1483.
Add. MS 54782, ff.125*v*–126.

Opposite. The Nativity, from the Benedictional of St Aethelwold. Anglo-Saxon, 10th century.
Add. MS 49598, f.15*v*.

A 'psychic photograph' from the Barlow albums.
CUP.407.a.1.

friends (1893) is a more famous later treasure, as (in a different way) are the remarkable photographs of Shackleton's *Aurora australis* (1907), printed in the Antarctic and bound in the Expedition's packing cases. But the strangest of all the Library's photographic treasures is the Barlow collection of psychic photographs, made at the turn of the century at the height of popular interest in the investigation of psychic phenomena. It remains an astonishing document of the movement, not to say the extraordinary events depicted.

The Evanion collection of ephemera was formed by Henry Evans Evanion, a moderately successful 19th-century conjuror and ventriloquist. Evanion was born Henry Evans in Kennington, South London, most likely in 1832. He was attracted to conjuring as a boy, and had already begun his professional career by the time he was 17. During his early years he travelled extensively throughout Great Britain, adopting his stage name as his legal surname, possibly in the 1860s. Evanion continued to undertake performances into the last year of his life, but the heyday of his career was in the 1860s and 1870s. He began to appear before eminent persons such as Earl Winterton, the Bishop of Winchester and even the Royal Family, and had several lengthy runs at the Crystal Palace, Sydenham. Evanion's interest in collecting seemed to have started early in his life. Much of his earliest material, concerning conjuring, may have come from his father and grandfather, but he himself also meticulously preserved copies of bills of his own performances. He also, early in his professional life, began reading in the British

Advertising handbill. An item of late 19th-century ephemera from the Evanion Collection.

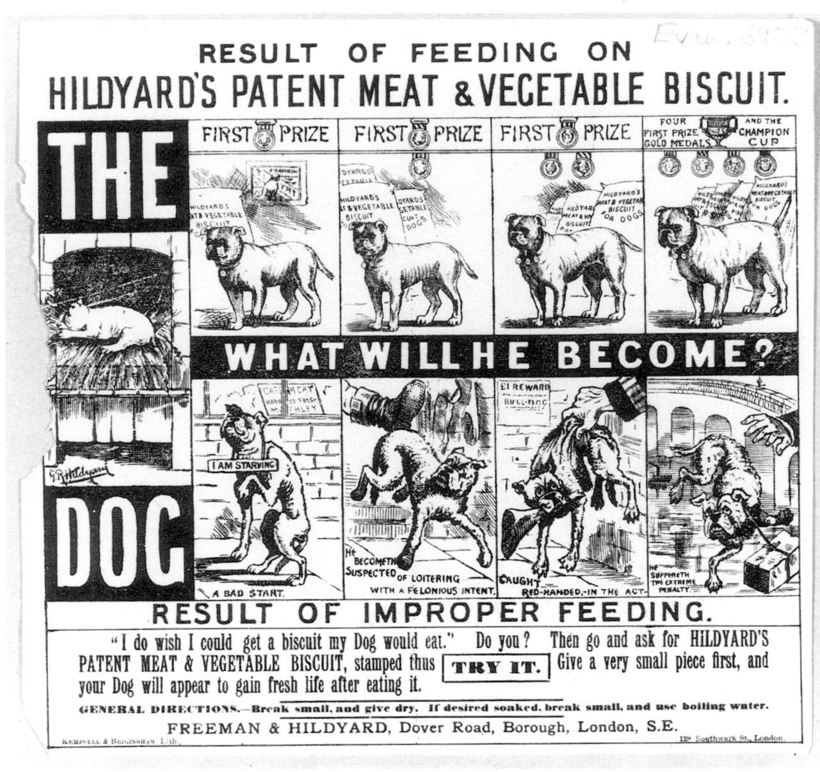

Museum to follow up his interest, and in 1895 sold what must have been the main part of his collection to the Museum, after corresponding with Richard Garnett on the subject. That part of Evanion's collection which is in the British Library consists not only of ephemera from the 19th-century entertainment world, but also of manufacturing ephemera, in about equal proportions. Much of the material is delightful, and all of it evocative. Hundreds of handbills and posters advertise circuses, menageries, pleasure gardens, conjuring, ventriloquism, impersonation, choirs, and the various panoramas and dioramas which were the historical predecessors of film. The manufacturing ephemera cover all aspects of Victorian domestic and social life, mainly from the 1870s onwards. There is a wealth of types of advertising material – bills, prospectuses, trade cards (some, for example, with cloth samples attached) and calendars. In the collection are also such miscellaneous items as Christmas cards and racing fixture cards. It forms a lively panorama of an aspect of both printing and social life rarely represented in libraries.

Bennet Woodcroft.

The other major collection, which became part of the British Museum Library with the National Library of Science and Invention in 1966, was the Patent Office Library. The Patent Office and its library were the creation of another remarkable Victorian, Bennet Woodcroft (1803–79). Born in Lancashire, the son of a textile manufacturer, he learned weaving at an early age and also studied chemistry under John Dalton at Manchester. A partner in his father's firm by 1829, he showed his inventive genius in a series of patents both for textiles and propellers for marine propulsion, and in 1843 added the roles of consulting engineering and patent agent to his business. He moved to London and became professor of machinery at University College. The Patent Law Amendment Act (1852) called for a Superintendent of Specifications, which he became until 1864, when he was appointed Clerk to the Commissioners of Patents, with sole charge of the Patent Office. To him belongs the credit for the entire system of registering patents. In five years he printed and published all the specifications, 14,359 in all, from 1617 to 1852, with subject abridgements which were widely circulated. He founded the Patent

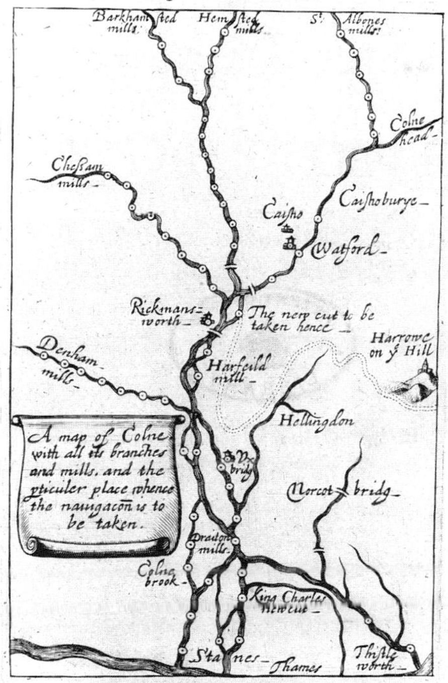

The Colne River, From Forde's *A design for bringing a navigable river from Rickmansworth* . . ., 1641. 1651/789(1).

James Watt and Matthew Boulton, *Directions for erecting and working the newly-invented steam engine*. c.1780. Plate showing plan and cross-section of the engine piston.
SRIS LF 16(2), pl.XI.

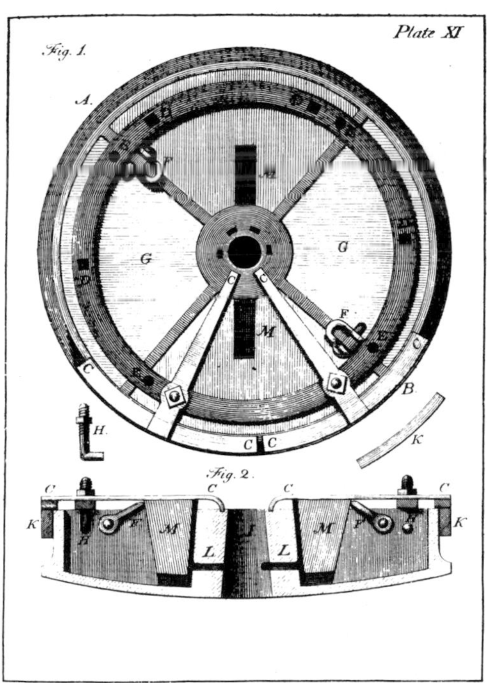

Office Library in 1855 and made it the best technical library in the country, and the Patent Office Museum, for which he rescued the first marine engine ever made, Symington's.

Woodcroft's library was very much the creation of these avocations and interests. He was interested in every kind of innovation and mechanism, ancient (he edited the *Pneumatics* of Hero of Alexandria) or modern, and expected other inventors to be so. He believed that technical information should be open to all, and the delightful reading room at the Patent Office embodies his belief in open access. History has unfortunately repeated itself and the integrity of the library has been broken since 1973, by the incorporation of all the pre-1800 and some later material in the main collection at Bloomsbury, but, though divided, the individuality of Woodcroft's collection remains.

Besides theoretical mechanics and the practical details of machinery, the pre-1800 collection is remarkable for the sheer variety of topics covered. Canals, comets, tar-water, chimneys (as designed by Robert Adam, Benjamin Franklin or Count Rumford), earthquakes, hydrostatics, sea-bathing, scurvy, mining, metallurgy, aerostatic machines, inoculation and potash, all figure among the books and pamphlets that stretch back to the 16th century. Thus are preserved the bound volume of 77 broadsides advertising patent medicines of the 18th century, the unique copy of Sir Edward Forde's *A design for bringing a navigable river from Rickmansworth in Hertfordshire to St Gyles in the Fields* (1641) which would have passed through the site of the new British Library building, Benjamin Franklin's *Observations on the causes and cure of smoky chimneys* (Philadelphia, 1798), and J. Fitch's *The original steamboat supported* (Philadelphia, 1788), a pro-Fulton controversial tract. There too are James Watt's scheme for a Forth-Clyde canal, with supporting manuscript documents together with his *Directions for erecting and working the newly-invented steam engine* (c1780); *The air-balloon: or, a treatise on the aerostatic globe, lately invented by the celebrated M. Mongolfier of Paris* (1783); and *A plan for improvement of the fishery in the River Thames* (1787). The infant prodigy Quin Mackenzie's *A method to multiply and divide any number of figures by a like or a less number . . . invented by Quin Mackenzie-Quin . . . at the eighth year of his age* (1750) is there; and from the same source comes Antoine-Joseph Loriot's *A practical essay, on a cement, and artificial stone* (St Jago de la Vega, 1775), one of the first books printed in Port-of-Spain, Trinidad.

Nor was Woodcroft's acquisitive interest purely historical. In the Library still is a copy of the very rare Sadi Carnot, *Réflexions sur la puissance motrice du feu* (Paris, 1824), the seminal work on thermodynamics, and with it Fourier's classic *Théorie analytique de la chaleur* (Paris, 1822). Gaspard Félix Tournachon, better known as Nadar, patented in 1858 the art of aerial photography, the ancestor of today's LANDSAT satellite survey, now based in the Map Library, which also acquired from the Patent Office Library the remarkable chart of the Mediterranean (1666) by John Burston, still – unusually mounted on its folding wooden base for use on board ship. Woodcroft too inaugurated the system of exchange, akin to Panizzi's for state papers, that resulted in the collection of all specifications of all the major and most of the minor patent-issuing countries. The need for international patent protection led to the Wright Brothers' registering in Britain (no.6732 of 19 March 1904) the aeroplane in which they made the first mechanically powered flight.

These and many other documents of great importance in the history of science and technology are now linked with older collections that encompass also Tartagli's *Nova Scientia* (1537), the primary treatise on ballistics, in the Old Royal Library, Benjamin Franklin's *Experiments and observations in electricity, made at Philadelphia in America* (1751), bound in the first British Museum series of pamphlets, Sir Joseph Banks's copy of Lavoisier's *Traité élémentaire de chimie* (1784), and Woodcroft's teacher, John Dalton's *A new system of*

Late 19th-century advertisement for performances in London by the famous conjurors Maskelyne and Cooke. From the Evanion Collection.

chemical philosophy, 1808–27. There are also the Copyright Deposit copies of Faraday's *Experimental researches in electricity* (1839–45), and Darwin's *On the origin of species*, 1859, the very rare Semmelweiss *Die Aetiologie* (1861), the tract on an outbreak of puerperal fever in Vienna that inaugurated the whole science of immunology, bought for the Museum by Asher, and the classic papers by Clerk Maxwell, Planck, Einstein and Rutherford on electromagnetics, quantum theory, relativity and atomic physics, all preserved in learned journals.

In all this, little has been said of the staff who have made the Library what it is in the 20th century. If it is invidious to distinguish recent names, it is also because an organisation now two centuries old develops its own traditions that are greater than those who work within them. But it would not be proper to end any account of the Library in the 20th century without giving the credit due to the men who made it great in this century: Sir Frederick Kenyon, Director and Principal Librarian (1909–31), A.W. Pollard, Assistant Keeper and Keeper of Printed Books (1909–24), Sir Henry Thomas, Deputy Keeper and Keeper of Printed Books (1924–48), Cecil Oldman, the same (1943–59), Sir Idris Bell and Eric Millar, Keepers of Manuscripts (1929–47) and Sir Frank Francis, Secretary, Keeper of Printed Books and Principal Librarian and Director (1946–68). These were the men who saw the Library through two world wars and produced the foundation on which the British Library was to be built.

14

America and the Spread of English Overseas

Fold-out map in Capt. Thomas James's *Voyage*, 1633, recording his search for a north-west passage.

IN 1979, AT THE generous inspiration of Viscount Eccles and Mr Arthur A. Houghton, the American Trust for the British Library was founded. This event set the seal on a special relationship which long preceded the foundation of the British Library, and even the British Museum. British interest in America, stretching back to the 16th century, is evinced by the number of books about it. British book-collectors from Henry Fitzalan, Earl of Arundel, to George III, and most of all Thomas Grenville, laid the foundation of knowledge about the 'new-found land' and its history. The great American historians of the 19th century, William Hickling Prescott, Jared Sparks, John Lothrop Motley, came to lean on the Library's resources, but in this respect, as in so much else, it was Panizzi who transformed an accidental interest into a deliberate policy.

It was, however, chance that provided the means by which he did it. In 1845, a young man from Vermont 'drifted in', as he later wrote, with a letter of introduction from Jared Sparks, who had come to Britain earlier to search for the source-material of American history. It was a stroke of genius on Panizzi's part to realise that Henry Stevens (1819–86), on his many transatlantic journeys in search of early Americana in Britain for John Carter Brown and James Lenox, could be persuaded to reverse the process. His instructions were 'to sweep America for us as you have done London for America': Stevens tackled the task with energy and gusto, but the credit he gave 'to the broad chest and broader mind of Panizzi'. Both were energetic, neither afraid to speak his mind, but as Stevens wrote in his memoir in 1884, 'No two men ever worked together in more harmony or less friction'.

Stevens was Panizzi's first and most successful agent in obtaining official publications. He persuaded the United States Government to present all its official publications to the British Museum. 'I hope you will be able to find room for them for they are very numerous', he wrote, and added 'I have now little doubt that I shall prevail upon all the States to imitate this liberality of the General Government'. In this he was at least partly successful. By 1847, Stevens and Panizzi were firm friends: Stevens, with characteristic energy, rounded up influential support for Panizzi during the Royal Commission of 1847–50, persuading Professor George Sumner and Charles Jewett, Librarian of the Smithsonian Institute, to write testimonials. 'I do not hesitate to declare', wrote Sumner, 'that in none of the large libraries of Europe have I found the readers in the public room enjoying so great facilities as do those of the British Museum'. It was an opinion shared by an even greater number of his countrymen. In 1852 Panizzi and Stevens went together to Oxford, Bangor and Dublin, as part of the campaign to enforce legal deposit that made Panizzi so unpopular with other members of the book-trade.

Woodcut in the 'Columbus Letter' printed at Basel in 1493.
G.6663.

There were, in 1843, by Stevens's account, no more than 1000 American books in the Library. In 1858 he was able to claim that the collection had grown to 30,000 volumes, more than double the size of any then existing in the United States. In 1865, the year of Panizzi's retirement, it had grown to 50,000, and in 1873 numbered between 70,000 and 75,000, 'a total of American Books ... far surpassing that of any other library in Europe or America'. The pride that Stevens and Panizzi took in this collection was reciprocated. 'It is becoming a matter of pride with many Americans to be well represented in the Museum Catalogue', Stevens wrote. 'Indeed the British Museum Catalogue is becoming a sort of *Campo Santo*, where all good American authors desire to be buried. No minor catalogue, not even the best in America, seems to satisfy them in this respect'.

The collection that earned these encomiums was indeed remarkable. If originally short of North American imprints, as Stevens had guessed, it was by no means deficient in those of Spanish America, or books about America printed in Europe, no new areas of book collecting interest even in 1845. Some of these have been mentioned already in earlier chapters, but it will do no harm to signal some others which are among the treasures, not only of the

Title-page to *Of the newe landes*. . ., Antwerp, *c.*1520.
G.7106.

Woodcut in the 'Columbus Letter' in G. Dati's translation.
IA 27798.

Library, but of the history of Americana, the idea and ideal of America that has grown up in the European mind. Amerigo Vespucci's *Mundus novus* (Paris, ?1504) is, perhaps, its first expression, although the point is not lost in R.Fernández de Santaella's edition of the travels of Marco Polo, adapted to take note of the new discoveries (Seville, 1503).

The primary document is the letter that Columbus wrote while still at sea announcing the discovery of new lands in the west. This document achieved a remarkable circulation in print: the earliest known edition is in Spanish, datable after 4 March 1493; nine Latin editions and one German followed, with five of Giuliano Dati's Italian verse paraphrase and a final Spanish edition in 1497. Of these, the Library possesses seven, including the unique Basel edition of 1493 and one of the Dati versions, printed at Florence, also unique. Only the New York Public Library and the John Carter Brown Library at Providence, have more. In later English translations the Library's holdings are unsurpassed: it has the first printed account in English, *Of the newe landes and of ye people founde by the messengers of the kynge of portyngale named Emanuel*, printed by 'John of Doesborowe' at Antwerp (*c.*1520), and the first mention of the discovery printed in England in John Rastell's *A new interlude and a mery of the nature of the .iiij. elements* (*c.*1520). An earlier voyage is recalled by Jónsson's *Gronlandia edur Grænlandz saga* (Skallholt, 1688) with its portrait of Erik the Red.

The later voyages are also covered in unique strength. There is the only known copy of the first account of Pizarro's voyage, Davila's *Conquista del paese del mar occeano*, printed probably in Florence in 1525. Cortés's letter, with his own map of the lake and city of Mexico, *Praeclara Ferdinandi narratio* (Nuremberg, 1524), and both the earlier accounts of the conquest of Peru, the anonymous *La conquista del Peru* (April, 1534), and Pizarro's secretary, Francisco Xeres's *Verdadera relacion de la conquista del Peru* (July, 1534). There,

ARTE DE GRAMMATICA DA LINGOA mais vſada na coſta do Braſil.

Feyta pelo padre Ioſeph de Anchieta da Cõpanhia de IESV.

IHS

Com licença do Ordinario & do Prepoſito geral da Companhia de IESV.
Em Coimbra per Antonio de Mariz. 1595.

Robert Southey.

The firſte Chapiter,

wherein the Argument of the Booke is Contayned.

IT was my fortune (good Reader) not many dayes paſt, to meete with a right honeſt and diſcrete Gentleman, who accompanied that valiāt & worthy Knight Sir *Humfry Gilbert*, in this laſt iourney for the Weſterne diſcoueries. And is owner and Captaine of the onelie Veſſell which is as yet returned from thence: Maiſter Edward Hay

By him I did vnderſtande, that Sir *Humfrey* departed the coaſte of *Englande* the eleuenth of Iune laſt paſt, with fiue ſayle of Shippes from *Caushenbay* neere *Plimmouth*, wherof one of the beſt forſooke his companie, the thirtenth day of the ſame moneth, and returned into *England*.

The other foure (through the aſſiſtaunce of almightye GOD) did arriue at Saint *Iohns* Hauen, in *Newfounde Lande*, the thyrd of Auguſt laſt. Vpon whoſe arriuall all the Maiſters and cheefe Mariners of the Engliſh Flete, which were in the ſayd Hauen before, endeuouring to fraughte themſelues with Fyſh, repayred vnto Sir *Humfrey*, whom he made acquainted with the effect of his cōmiſſion: which being doone, he promiſed to intreate them and their goods well and honourably as dyd become her maieſties Lieftennaunt. They did all welcome him in the beſt ſorte that they coulde, and ſhewed him and his, all ſuch courteſies as that place coulde affoorde or yeelde.

Sir Humfrey Gilbert did arriue at S. Iohns hauen in Newfounde Land, the 3. of Auguſt. Anno.Do. 1583.

B.j. Then

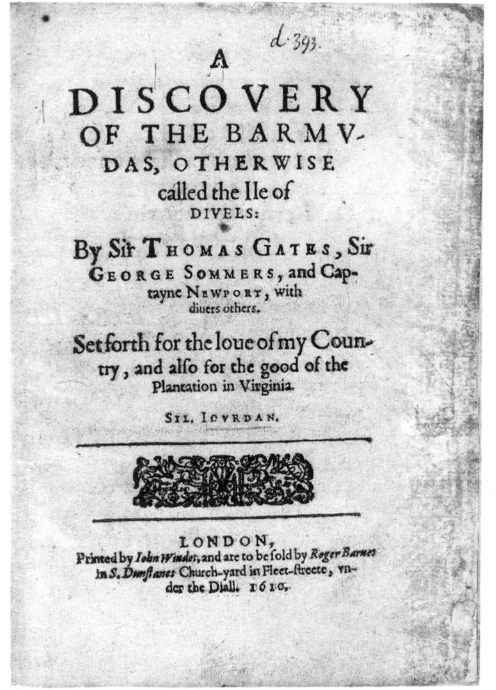

d.393.

A DISCOVERY OF THE BARMVDAS, OTHERWISE called the Ile of DIVELS:

By Sir THOMAS GATES, Sir GEORGE SOMMERS, and Captayne NEWPORT, with diuers others.

Set forth for the loue of my Country, and alſo for the good of the Plantation in Virginia.

SIL. IOVRDAN.

LONDON,
Printed by *Iohn Windet*, and are to be ſold by *Roger Barnes* in *S. Dunſtanes* Church-yard in Fleet-ſtreete, vnder the Diall. 1610.

Top right. First page of Peckham's *True Reporte*, 1583, giving an account of Sir Humfrey Gilbert's voyage of discovery that year.
C.32.c.12.

Top left. Title-page to J. de Anchieta, *Arte de Grammatica da lingoa . . . do Brasil*, Coimbra 1595. Once Robert Southey's copy.
C.33.c.38.

Above. Title-page to Jourdain, *Discovery of the Barmudas*, London 1610, one source for Shakespeare's *The Tempest*.
C.32.c.2.

too, is the first complete book printed in Mexico to survive, Zumarraga, *Doctrina breve* (1543); from Peru, the *Doctrina Christiana*, printed at Lima, 'Ciudad de los Reyes' (1534), and the first vernacular books, Alonso de Molina, *Confessionario breve* (Mexico, 1565) and the *Tercera catechismo* (Lima, 1534). The copy of Anchieta *Arte da grammatica da lingoa do Brasil* (Coimbra, 1595) was one of two surviving copies in the public library of Bahia, and was given by the last viceroy to Robert Southey when he was writing his *History of Brazil*. There is also the first work in the Paraguayan language by a native, Nicolas Yapuguay's *Explicacion de el catechismo en lengua Guarani*, (Santa Maria la Mayor, now in Brazil, 1724).

The first book about New France, and Jacques Cartier's voyage to the source of the St Lawrence is the *Brief recit . . . de la navigation faicte en ysles de Canada, Hochelage & Saguenay* (Paris, 1545), while Ribaut, *The whole and true discoverye of Terra Florida* (1563) is the earliest account of the first settlement, by Huguenots, in what is now the USA (at Parris Island, North Carolina). Le Challeux, *Discours de l'historie de la Floride* (1566) records their second attempt, in Florida, as it is today. *A true declaration of the troublesom voyadge of M. John Haukins* (1569) recalls England's first challenge to Spain in the West. Sir Humfrey Gilbert's *Discourse of a new passage to Cataia* (1576) anticipates his famous voyage, while Peckham's *True reporte* (1583) is of the voyage itself. Thomas Hariot's *Briefe and true report of the new found land of Virginia* (1588) records Ralegh's first British Colony.

Silvester Jourdain's *Discovery of the Barmudas, otherwise called the Ile of Divels*

(1610) was due to an accident, but it was the source of Shakespeare's *The Tempest* and (indirectly) of Marvell's 'Bermudas', most magical of all expressions of the early colonists' hopes. Robert Rich's *Newes from Virginia. The lost flocke triumphant* (1610) is the rarest of the Virginia Company's promotional tracts; it came to the Library with the Huth bequest (*see* p. 234). Christopher Levett's *Voyage into New England begun in 1623* (1624), from Holkham, is unique. *A relation or journall . . . of the English plantation settled at Plimoth* (1622) records the first colony in New England. The unique copy of *A true state of the case between the heires and assignes of Sir William Courten . . . and planters in the island of Barbados* (*c.*1674) recalls the first settlement there, and also the man who set Sloane collecting.

The Library has no copy of *The whole booke of psalmes*, the 'Bay Psalm Book' (1640), although it has the second edition of 1647. The broadside *The capitall lawes of New England* (1643) is there, as well as William Wood's *New Englands Prospect* (1634), the first proper account of Massachusetts, all the different editions of Eliot's Indian Bible, and William Hubbard's *Narrative of the troubles with the Indians* (1677), which includes the earliest map of the colonies.

All this was not lost on the sovereigns whose acts precipitated colonisation. Besides the standard atlases (Ortelius, *Theatrum orbis terrarum*, London, 1606, is in the publisher's presentation binding for James I) and accounts of voyages, James I had Sir Richard Hawkins's *Observations . . . in his voiage into the south sea* (1622), and Charles I received the dedication of Captain Thomas James's North-West Passage *Voyage* (1633), as well as Captain John Smith's

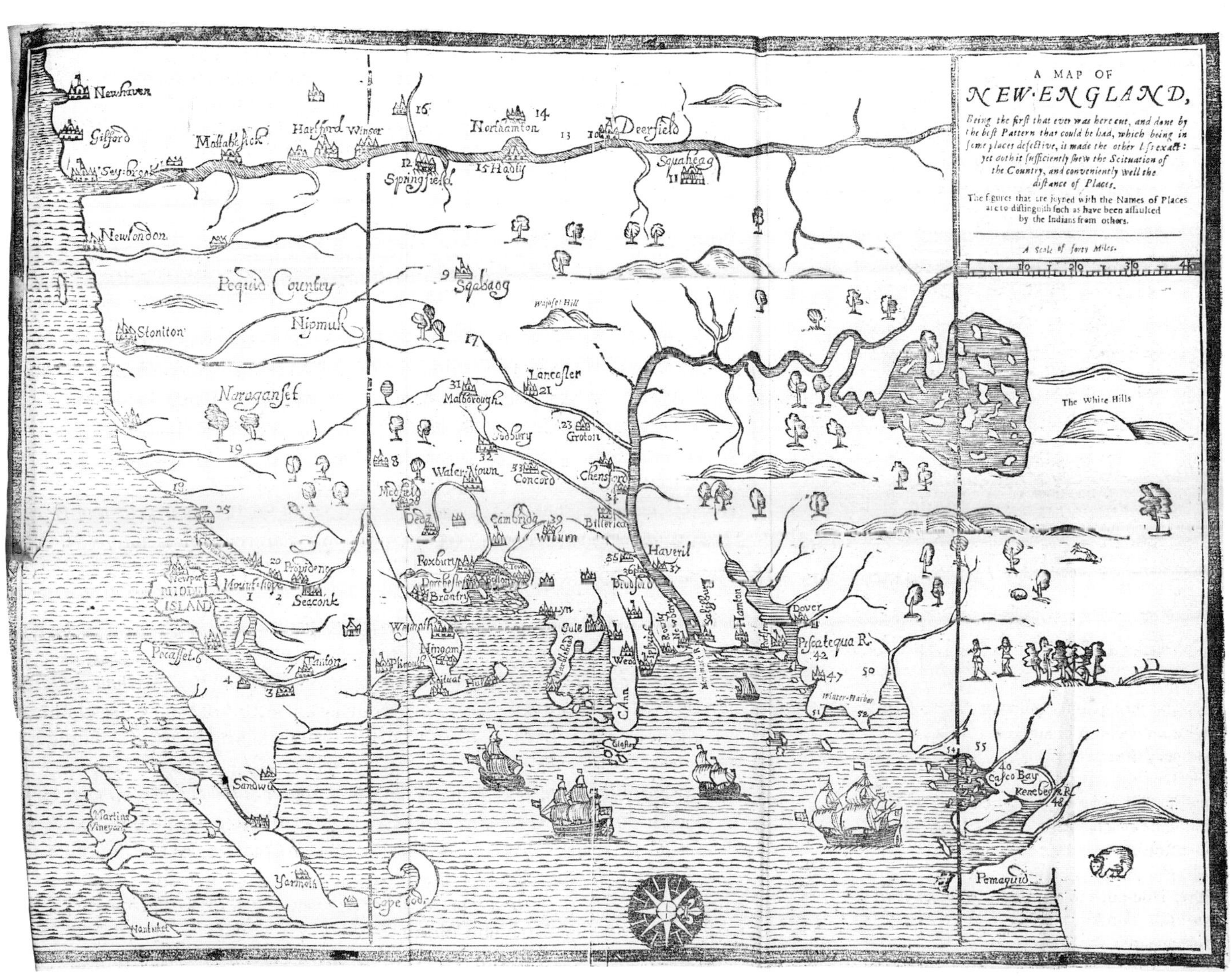

Map of New England, 'being the first that ever was here cut', from William Hubbard's *Narrative of the troubles with the Indians*, 1677.
G.7146, opp.p.132.

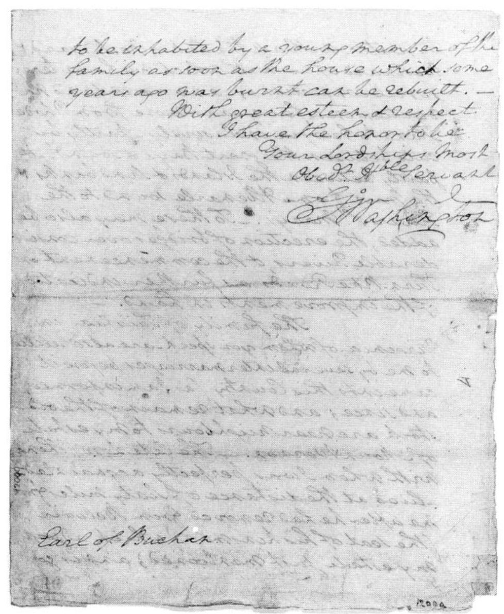
to be inhabited by a young member of the family as soon as the house which some years ago was burnt can be rebuilt. — With great esteem & respect I have the honor to be Your Lordships Most Obed. Servant
G. Washington

Earl of Buchan

Letter from George Washington to the Earl of Buchan, 1793.
Add. MS 12099, f.30*v*.

24

Chapter II.

They were indeed a curious looking party that assembled on the bank — the birds with draggled feathers, the animals with their fur clinging close to them — all dripping wet, cross, and uncomfortable. The first question of course was, how to get dry: they had a consultation about this, and Alice hardly felt at all surprised at finding herself talking familiarly with the birds, as if she had known them all her life. Indeed, she had quite a long argument with the Lory, who at last turned sulky, and would only say "I am older than you, and must know best," and this Alice would not admit without knowing how old the Lory was, and as the Lory positively refused to tell its age, there was nothing more to be said.

Page from the autograph manuscript of Lewis Carroll's *Alice's Adventures under Ground*, illustrated and written between 1862 and 1863 for Alice Liddell (the original Alice).
Add. MS 46700, f.13*v*.

Generall historie of Virginia (1626). A much rarer book, Sir Robert Gordon of Lochinvar's *Encouragements for... New Galloway* (Edinburgh, 1625) was passed on to Charles I by the dedicatee, William Alexander, Earl of Stirling. Prince Henry, rather unexpectedly, had a copy of Lescarbot's *Histoire de la nouvelle Frahce* (1611). Another important association is represented by the copy of Richard Hakluyt's *Divers voyages touching the discoverie of America* (1582) given by the author to Sir Philip Sidney.

The Swedish colony in Delaware is commemorated by the translation of Luther's catechism into the native language by J. Campanius, *Lutheri catechismus öfwersatt på American-Virginiske språket* (Stockholm, 1696), with its map of 'Nova Suecia'. The Map Library holds the first marine atlas published in America, Cyprian Southack's *New England Coasting Pilot* (?1723–24). The Huth sale provided the Quaker George Fox's *Gospel family order, being a short discourse concerning the ordering of families both of Whites, Blacks and Indians* (1676). In 1917 the Society for the Propagation of the Gospel, whose missionary work was so important in 18th-century America, gave the Museum Library 79 books from Bishop White Kennet's collection (the first ever made) on the spread of Christianity in America, and it has since acquired one of the two surviving copies of the SPG's original Royal Charter (1701). Treasures of more recent date include Jeremy Bentham's annotated copy of Alexander Hamilton's *The Federalist* (1802), Poe's *Tamerlane* (1827), Whitman's *Leaves of Grass* (1855) and the first issue of *Drum Taps* (1865), and *Outcroppings* (1866), the earliest anthology of Californian verse. A.W. Pollard's friendship with the American printer Bruce Rogers resulted in the acquisition in 1921 of all the books printed at the Riverside Press under Rogers's direction. The American stamps, too, in the Tapling collection are outstanding, including remarkable sets of the early Postmasters' stamps, the local issues of the Confederate States, and a specimen of the stamp imposed by the Stamp Act of 1765 (the 'Boston Tea Party Stamp').

A library which, besides all these printed treasures, can also boast possession of a long letter from George Washington to the sympathetic Earl of Buchan, written in 1793, setting out the policy of the United States, 'to be little heard of in the great world of politics' and sending 'the Plan of a new City situated about the centre of the Union of these States', the city that now bears his name, and many other original documents of American history, cannot but attract many American readers and friends, whose gratitude has been generously expressed. An American benefactor, Mrs Emerson, gave the Rossetti manuscript of Blake; another, Zenas Crane, bequeathed a set of autograph letters of all the presidents of the United States from Washington to Woodrow Wilson; yet another, Mrs E.P. Merivale, gave the autograph manuscript of Nathaniel Hawthorne's *The Marble Faun*, written during his stay in England in 1855. The 'American Testimonial Manuscript', a collection of Middle English verse, purchased by subscription and given by the 'Teachers of English in American Universities and Colleges' in 1920 commemorates the bonds that link British and American literary scholarship. Most affecting of all these tributes is the original manuscript of *Alice in Wonderland*, entitled *Alice's Adventures under Ground* and illustrated by Lewis Carroll himself, which was purchased by American subscribers in 1948 and presented in recognition of Great Britain's efforts during the Second World War.

The greatest American benefactor this century was John Pierpont Morgan, whose generosity to the Library stretched over more than 20 years. In 1908 he presented the finely printed *Catalogue of Early Printed Books* in his own collection and the first volume of Edward S. Curtis's magnificent photographic record of *The North American Indian* (1907), continuing the series of 20 volumes in all to its completion in 1930. When his own collection became a public institution in 1924, its publications too were donated. Finally, when the Lulworth Castle manuscripts came on the market in 1929, he not only withdrew his own competition but wrote urging the Museum to 'go ahead

Buffalo Bill's
WILD WEST
COURIER
And International Horticultural Exhibition Gazette.

JOHN M. BURKE, Editor. CARTER COUTURIER, Publisher.] EARL'S COURT, LONDON, SATURDAY, MAY 7th, 1892. [DAILY ISSUE, 100,000.

[LATEST EXTRA.]
RETURN OF THE VETERANS.
THE
JUBILEE FAVOURITES OF '87.
BUFFALO BILL'S
(COL. W. F. CODY)
WILD WEST
CAMPS AT EARL'S COURT, '92,
EN ROUTE HOME,
TO GIVE
A POSITIVE FAREWELL,
AFTER A TRIUMPHANT
FIVE YEARS' CAMPAIGN
ON TWO CONTINENTS.
THE
OLD TIME ETHNOLOGICAL STUDY,
IN CONJUNCTION WITH THE
INTERNATIONAL
HORTICULTURAL EXHIBITION.
THE RUGGED FRONTIER CAMP,
COMBINED WITH
A MODERN PARADISE OF ROSES.

On Saturday afternoon, May 7th, the Arena and Camp Grounds at Earl's Court, and its connecting buildings, renovated, re-decorated—the adjoining Gardens, Main Buildings embellished and planted with the Flowers of the World, arranged in the most artistic manner of the Botanist's skill—will be opened by the International Horticultural Exhibition Company and Buffalo Bill's (Col. W. F. Cody) Wild West, as the Mecca of the Citizens of the Metropolis for the summer of '92. The instructive character, the entertaining novelty, and the remarkable success of the Wild West in '87—Jubilee Year—is such recent indelible history of enterprise, in presenting a truly natural exhibition, as to be familiar to all. Suffice it to say that this is the same Original Organisation, under the same Chieftainship, Col. W. F. Cody and Mr. Nate Salsbery, as a guarantee of its merit, magnitude, and completeness in detail, as upon the former occasion, and to impress the fact that this is POSITIVELY THE LAST TIME this aggregation of Western American Characters will appear in Europe, being a POSITIVE FAREWELL presentation of this interesting page of passing history. Every department will be, if possible, more complete, and as many of the old favourites as the fates have preserved from joining "the great majority" will be in the saddle. The Indians will be from the various Tribes of the great Sioux Nation—which nation, since the former visit here, has figured in the sanguinary uprising of the winter of '91. Reference to this affair and the phase occupied by this combination is possibly covered by the following Editorial Extract from *Le Journal Alsatin*, Strasburg, April 22nd, 1891, from which place Col. Cody and his men hastened at the first news of the impending frontier war: "On the Wild West's first visit every promise was fulfilled, every expectation justified, when there suddenly came an unexpected test of many of the claims made for the originality, truthfulness, and *bona fide* character—that many thought savored of romance—in the shape of an uprising and bloody war, precipitated through many causes by "Sitting Bull," "Kicking Bear," "Short Bull," and other Chiefs of the Sioux Nation. Anxiously the amusement world looked to see the result of this most critical and crucial position. Then came the authenticated Press accounts that immediately on landing, they with their band of Indians had proceeded without delay to seat of hostilities and taken arms on the side of the government, and that Col. Cody, without the loss of a day, had accepted the perilous mission of going alone to meet the celebrated Chief, "Sitting Bull," at the request of the General Commanding, Nelson A. Miles. His mission, on the day of its almost successful fulfilment, was countermanded by political intrigue, resulting in the killing of "Sitting Bull" and others, and the kindling of the flames of war. The daily journals exploited the facts, and the closing of the campaign after the battles of Wounded Knee (Pine Ridge), The Mission, and Wolf Creek, in a more peaceful manner than was at one time predicted, brought government acknowledgment to these sturdy people, and resulted in the vindication of the Wild West as the greatest natural exhibition of the kind in history, and in the triumphant return of Buffalo Bill to Strasburg with a larger troupe, and among the Indians the great "Short Bull," "Kicking Bear," "Lone Bull," and twenty-three of the principal military hostages held by the army in Fort Sheridan, besides sixty others, many of them warriors of the greatest celebrity and all participants two months ago of the last page in the blood-stained history of the white and Indian races in America. Such an unexpected endorsement before the world must place Col. Cody and his exhibition as an object of *strongly increased interest* to the lovers of the realistic, which is more combined in this organisation than anything yet presented to the student, the artist, and historian."

"Col. Cody has done his part in bringing America and England nearer together."—Editorial, London *Times*, November 1st, 1887.

COLONEL W. F. CODY—"BUFFALO BILL."
"Be sure you're right, then go ahead."—*Davy Crockett.*

FROM GEN. "PHIL" SHERIDAN'S AUTOBIOGRAPHY.

(Since the last visit to London, the Memoirs of this celebrated Cavalry Chieftain of the U. S. Army have been given to the public).

General SHERIDAN refers to his meeting "BUFFALO BILL." "He undertakes a dangerous task," chapter xii, p. 281—289, in his autobiography, published in 1888. The world-renowned cavalry commander maintained continuous friendly relations with this old scout, even to social correspondence, friendly assistance, and recognition in his present enterprise up to the year of his death. After relating his conception of the *first winter campaign* against Indians on the then uninhabited and bleak plains, in the winter of [illegible], he says, "The difficulties and hardships to be encountered had led several experienced officers of the army and some frontiersmen like old Jim Bridger, the famous scout and guide of earlier days, to discourage the project. Bridger even went so far as to come out from St. Louis to discourage the attempt. I decided to go in person, bent on showing the Indians that they were not secure from punishment because of inclement weather [illegible] which they had hitherto relied with much assurance. We started, and the very first night a blizzard struck us and carried away our tents. The gale was so violent that they could not be put up again; the rain and snow drenched us to the skin. Shivering from *wet and cold I took refuge under a wagon*, and there spent such a miserable night that, when morning came, the gloomy predictions of old man Bridger and others rose up before me with greatly increased force. The difficulties were now fully realized, the blinding snow, mixed with sleet, the piercing wind, thermometer below *zero*—with green bushes only for fuel—occasioning intense suffering. Our numbers and companionship alone prevented us from being lost or perishing, a fate that stared in the face the frontiersmen, guides and scouts on their solitary missions.

"An important matter had been to secure competent guides for the different columns of troops, for, as I have said, the section of *country to be operated in was comparatively unknown.*

"In those days the railroad town of Hays City was filled with so-called 'Indian Scouts,' whose common boast was of having slain scores of redskins, but the real scout—that is, a guide and trailer knowing the habits of the Indians—was very scarce, and it was hard to find anybody familiar with the country south of the Arkansas, where the campaign was to be made. Still, about the various military posts there was some good material to select from, and we managed to employ several men, who, from their experience on

Front page of *Buffalo Bill's Wild West Courier*, 7 May 1892, distributed free at the Earl's Court, London, Wild West show.

and buy the Luttrell Psalter' at the auction then planned, and offering to lend the money interest-free for a year, extending this to cover the Bedford Hours and Psalter as well. In the event, the first was bought for £31,500 by private treaty, the second at auction for £33,000, and the subscription repaid the loan within the year.

Stevens's 'sweep' continued after his death: besides official documents and all major books and periodicals, it brought in ephemera, such as J. de Tivoli's *Guide to the Falls of Niagara with a splendid lithographic view by A. Vaudricort from a daguerreotype by F. Langenheim* (New York, 1846), the first pictorial guide to the Niagara Falls; an issue of the Vicksburg *Daily Citizen* of 1863, printed on the back of wallpaper, for want of newsprint during the Civil War; and the issue of *Buffalo Bill's Wild West Courier and International Horticultural Exhibition Gazette*, distributed free at the Wild West Show at Earl's Court on 7 May 1892. But by then the drastic cut in the Treasury Grant, which reduced the funds available for acquisition by 40 per cent by 1897, had had a serious effect on the Library's ability to maintain its comprehensive acquisition of American material. Not until 1950 was it possible to restore the level; in the intervening years many gaps were left to fill.

This fact lay behind the decision to form the American Trust for the British Library, as well as the opportunity it offered to American donors to make

The first pictorial guide to the Niagara Falls, J. de Tivoli's *Guide to the Falls of Niagara*, New York, 1846. 792.g.35, between pp.12–13.

tax-exempt gifts. This initiative has received a warm welcome in the United States, and substantial support from American corporations and individuals, as well as foundations, both in America and Britain, and has already made it possible first to survey the American holdings in order to identify the most serious deficiencies, and then to supply the books, in original copies, as and when available, or by commissioning microfilm copies of rare or out-of-print works. The Andrew W. Mellon Foundation, for example, has made a grant specifically to finance the microfilming of the 6000 volumes still missing in 1979 of American publications lost in the Second World War. So far, more than 2 million dollars have been raised, and the material now flowing in a steady stream to London includes books and periodicals, literary and historical, on the social sciences, medicine, technology, architecture, and church history. American libraries, notably the Library Company of Philadelphia, have parted with duplicate material. Individual bequests have included the Ansel and Virginia Adams Collection of 230 scarce and unusual publications from the Roxburghe Club of San Franscisco, presented in 1984 by Mrs Adams, widow of the renowned photographer who was a charter member of the club. Special subject areas, such as American Judaica, hardly represented before, are now covered. Files of important newspapers have been acquired, and the National Archives have supplied copies of important diplomatic and military papers.

The American Trust for the British Library thus provides a focus for a much wider body of interest, the mutual and reciprocal benefit that Britain and America have derived from each other's institutions and the records of them that each has preserved. The earnest care that George III and his predecessors gave to the formation of a representative collection of source material on the 'new-found land' has been repaid a hundred-fold on both sides of the Atlantic.

If America, inevitably, takes the largest place in the Library's collection of books in English printed outside the British Isles, it is no less substantial, and sometimes more complete, in its holdings of material from the other former

Young woman of Tahiti, by John Webber, 1777. Webber was official artist on Captain Cook's Third Voyage, 1776–1777.
Add. MS 15513, f.17.

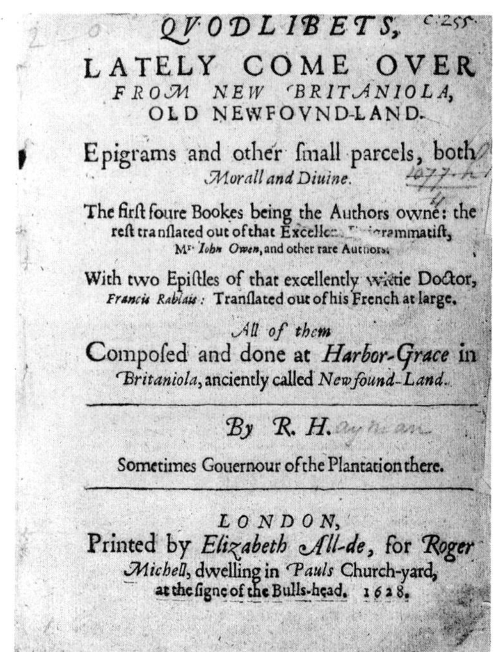

QVODLIBETS,
LATELY COME OVER
FROM NEW BRITANIOLA,
OLD NEWFOVNDLAND.
Epigrams and other ſmall parcels, both
Morall and Diuine.
The firſt foure Bookes being the Authors owne: the reſt tranſlated out of that Excelle[illegible]grammatiſt, Mr. Iohn Owen, and other rare Authors:
With two Epiſtles of that excellently wittie Doctor, Francis Rablais: Tranſlated out of his French at large.
All of them
Compoſed and done at Harbor-Grace in Britaniola, anciently called Newfound-Land.
By R. H.
Sometimes Gouernour of the Plantation there.
LONDON,
Printed by Elizabeth All-de, for Roger Michell, dwelling in Pauls Church-yard, at the ſigne of the Bulls-head. 1628.

Title-page to Robert Hayman's *Quodlibets, lately come over from New Britaniola, Old Newfoundland*. London, 1628.
C.34.f.15.

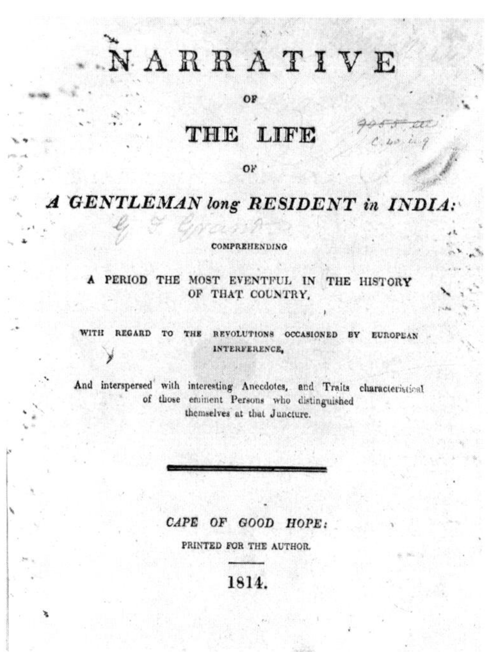

NARRATIVE
OF
THE LIFE
OF
A GENTLEMAN long RESIDENT in INDIA:
COMPREHENDING
A PERIOD THE MOST EVENTFUL IN THE HISTORY OF THAT COUNTRY,
WITH REGARD TO THE REVOLUTIONS OCCASIONED BY EUROPEAN INTERFERENCE,
And interspersed with interesting Anecdotes, and Traits characteristical of those eminent Persons who distinguished themselves at that Juncture.
CAPE OF GOOD HOPE:
PRINTED FOR THE AUTHOR.
1814.

Title-page to G.F. Grand's *Narrative of the life of a gentleman*..., Cape of Good Hope, 1814.
C.40.i.9.

colonies and dependencies. The bicentenary of the arrival of the first colonial voyage to Australia at Botany Bay in January 1788 put a special focus on the holdings of Australiana. Here, beginning with Sir Joseph Banks's first voyage with James Cook in the *Endeavour* in 1768–71, the Library can command matchless resources. 'The Charts, Plans, Views and Drawings in the years 1768, 1769 and 1770 by Lieutenant James Cook; all executed in Indian ink (thought then to be by the hand of Lieutenant Cook himself') were acquired early in the 19th century, and Banks's bequest added further sketches and views. In the early 1840s, the main set of drawings by the professional artists Sidney Parkinson, A. Buchan and J.F. Miller on the first voyage, the charts made on the second voyage on the *Resolution*, William Hodges's fine large drawings and John Webber's finished drawings of the third voyage were added, followed by Webber's sketches, all transferred from the Admiralty, while Cook's last journal was purchased in 1870.

Even more important, however, was the sequence of log-books, covering a substantial part of the voyage of the *Endeavour* and the first voyage of the *Resolution*, between 5 November 1768 and 28 July 1775, together with Cook's text for the published version of the second voyage, all acquired in 1870–71, besides further drawings and charts. Altogether, these provide an incomparable record in words and pictures of Cook's major discoveries, the disproving of the existence of a great Antarctic continent, the charting of the Pacific islands, and the survey of the coast of Australia, which gave Botany Bay and New South Wales their names. To set beside these, the Library has the copy of De Bougainville's *Voyage au tour du monde* (1771) with the map on which Cook traced his route in 1768–71, and Banks's copies of all Cook's many published works.

The history of Australia, from the first colony that stemmed from Cook's voyages, has its treasures too. The copy of the first governor, Arthur Phillip's *The Voyage of Governor Phillip to Botany Bay* (1789) is in an original – in every sense of the word – binding of kangaroo skin. The exotic fauna of the new continent, as shown, for example, in the lyre bird plate in Collins's *Account of the English colony in New South Wales* (1798–1802), so captivated European readers that the coloured plates of John Lewin's *Birds of New Holland* (1808) were engraved and coloured on the spot, though the text was printed in England. The first book printed in Australia was the prosaic *General Standing Orders* (Sydney, 1802), though more interest is today attached to *First fruits of Australian poetry* (Sydney, 1819), the first book of poetry printed there, by Barron Field, Chief Justice of New South Wales and friend of Charles Lamb, who reviewed it in the *Examiner* on 16 January 1820. Another relic of the early press in Australia is the chap-book *Michael Howe, the last and worst of the bush rangers* (Hobart, 1818).

Early printing for and in New Zealand was dominated by missionary fascination with the Maori and their language. Lee and Kendall's *Grammar... of the language of New Zealand* (1820) was printed in London, but the Pauline epistles in Maori, *Ko nga puka puka* was printed at the Church Missionary Press at Paihia in 1835. The career of the great colonial governor, Sir George Grey, later Prime Minister of New Zealand, is aptly recalled by the annotated copy of his *Vocabulary of the aboriginal language of Western Australia* (Perth, 1839). The manuscript of *Erewhon*, given to the Library by Samuel Butler's executor, Henry Festing Jones, and the enchanting pictorial verses of E.E.M. Montgomery's *The Land of the Moa* testify to the idealism aroused by the land and its people.

After the documents of its discovery, the next major monument of Canadian literature is Robert Hayman's *Quodlibets, lately come over from New Britaniola* (1628), which can reasonably be claimed as the first book of original English verse written in North America; it also contains the first English translation of any work by Rabelais. Frances Brooke's *The History of Emily Montague* (1769) is, equally, the first English novel written (though not

Pictorial verses in E.E.M. Montgomery's *Land of the Moa*, Wanzanui, New Zealand.
1509/1919.

A typical example of Nigerian market literature of the 1950s.
× 0909/588 (131)

printed) in North America. Two other unusual books emanate from Canada in the 18th century, the *Ritual du diocèse de Quebec* printed at Paris in 1703, one of the very few copies that survived shipwreck *en route*, and La Brosse *Nithira iriniui* (Quebec, 1767), a prayer-book in the language of the Montagnais Indians.

The first book in English, on what was now known to be the continent of Africa, was *A Description of the contrey of Aphrique* (1554), translated from the French by William Prat. Richard Jobson's *The golden trade: or, a discovery of the river Gambia* (1623) is the first book in English on the main attraction of the West Coast. As in America and Australia, the exotic fauna of Africa attracted the interest of natural historians, and Le Vaillant's *Histoire naturelle des oiseaux d'Afrique* (1799–1802), with its 300 coloured plates, is one of the classic colour-plate books. G.F. Grand's *Narrative of the life of a gentleman* (Cape of Good Hope, 1814) is supposed to be the first literary text printed in English in South Africa: in 1987 Wole Soyinka won the Nobel Prize for Literature (the Library has his *Three Plays*, 1963).

It is a far cry from these, and the intervening tradition, to the little books published, mainly in English, at Onitsha and elsewhere in Nigeria, and printed for the most part on presses discarded by newspapers and government printers. The publishing business operating from book-sheds or market-stalls has its own remarkably efficient system of circulating books by pedlars or mail-order, recalling the 18th-century chap-book market or the 'colonial libraries' of the 19th century. The titles, romances, political pamphlets, manuals of courtship or business correspondence, defy description. They may be far removed from Caxton, but they are the liveliest proof that English is not a dead language, nor printing a dying craft.

Epilogue

THE GREAT EXPANSION of the Library over the last century and a half has brought it many treasures: but with every year the problem of finding space for new acquisitions has become more acute. Smirke's original quadrangle at the British Museum has been expanded internally and externally, notably with the King Edward VII Building. The monumental classical façade, whose steps have so long been the entry to the treasures of the library for its visitors, gives an illusory impression of changeless stability. Plans for substantial expansion, themselves changing as predictions of growth change, have been entertained for many years. The Holford Plan of 1951 was the first full-scale attempt to solve the problem. It was an imaginative scheme involving the redevelopment of the site south of the British Museum. But decision was deferred by successive governments: what proved to be the last chance was declined in 1967, prompting Lord Radcliffe, then Chairman of the Trustees of the British Museum, to such Parliamentary oratory on its behalf as had not been heard since the days of Speaker Onslow.

At the same time, the complex and growing need for a national library brought about the appointment by Patrick Gordon Walker, then Minister of Education, of a committee to examine the matter under the chairmanship of Frederick Dainton, later Lord Dainton, who was to succeed Lord Eccles as Chairman of the British Library. This was the name bestowed on the organisation recommended by the Dainton Committee, which brought together the government-financed libraries and information agencies, the Library of the British Museum (thus detached administratively though not physically from its traditional base), the National Central Library (the nucleus of the public inter-library loan system), the national reference and lending libraries in the field of science and technology and the British National Bibliography. The British Library was thus formally established by Act of Parliament in 1973. One of its earliest tasks was to find a new site for this combined wealth of library resources, and in 1975 the British Library Board, its governing body, accepted the Government's proposal that a new building for its Reference Division should be erected on the Somers Town site, next to St Pancras Station.

All these complex moves had taken place against a background of growing concern about the preservation of the nation's literary heritage. Some of the factors have already been mentioned: competition from abroad, quiescent during the Depression and the Second World War; increases in the rate of Estate Duty, which forced private owners into the market; and the general rise of prices, following increased public interest, of old artefacts of all sorts. All these provided the Library with new opportunities for major acquisitions, but at prices hitherto far beyond its acquisition budget. The mechanisms of export licence control and the acceptance of material of national importance in lieu of Estate Duty (now Capital Transfer Tax) eased this problem, while involving the Library's staff in complex new obligations. Many of the treasures already mentioned came to the Library in these circumstances. The principal competition it had to face, from foreign academic institutions, chiefly in America, has been mitigated by the personal links that have grown up between the Library and its staff and individual members of institutions abroad, facilitated by the growth of travel and communications.

It is significant, then, that the first major treasure acquired by the British Library, the Old Hall Manuscript (illustrated above, p. 181), was bought in the open market, at Sotheby's, by the Library's agent, Bernard Quaritch, for £68,000. It was a high price, requiring special subvention from the Government, but one achieved without competition from abroad, where potential buyers were deterred by the virtual certainty that an export licence would be refused.

But despite these complexities, new treasures have continued to pour in. In the year after the Old Hall Manuscript, two important literary manuscripts

Opposite. Beatus page from the Rutland Psalter. English, mid-13th century.
Add. MS 62925, f.8v.

Psalmus
EATVS:VIR:QVI:NON:HABIIT

Artist's impression of the new British Library building, scheduled to open in 1993.

were acquired, the poems of Robert Sidney and of Henry King, Bishop of Chichester, as well as Sir Edward Coke's copy, corrected in his own hand, of his treatise on ecclesiastical jurisdiction. Meanwhile the Music Library acquired the autograph score of Stravinsky's 'Capriccio' and Thomas Attwood's manuscript of musical extracts, with corrections in the hand of Mozart.

The year of the Caxton quincentenary, 1976, was made memorable for the British Library by the purchase, from Winchester College, of the unique manuscript of Malory's *Morte d'Arthur*. Its importance was amplified by the discovery by Dr Lotte Hellinga of traces of ink offset from types used by Caxton on its leaves, evidence that the manuscript was used, and largely followed for the first edition (1485) of the great English epic. For the first time, the minutiae of the historic study of typography became headline news. The Library celebrated the Caxton quincentenary with a memorable exhibition: in the same year it also mounted a large-scale Qur'ān exhibition to coincide with the 'World of Islam' festival.

In the following year, the Library was augmented by three major collections, by gift, bequest and loan. The Broxbourne collection of early printed books, formed by Albert Ehrman, was perhaps the last that will ever be put together with that catholic view of the growth of printing that inspired earlier contributors to the Library's collection – the Harleys, Consul Smith, George III, Cracherode, Grenville. The collector's son, John Ehrman, now gave 20 books, among them Jacob Twinger, *Martymiany*, Prague 1488, the first Czech incunable acquired since 1885, all filling significant gaps in the Library's collection; Mr Ehrman also enabled the Library to purchase other books before the residue of the collection was sold. The Henry Davis Gift, which was formally transferred to the Library on the collector's death, was a bequest of an importance to the study of bookbinding equal, in the Library's history, to that of the Slade Bequest, over a century earlier. The third great addition was provided by the Scrope Davies find – the trunk full of papers, including important Byron and Shelley manuscripts, discovered at Barclay's Bank, Pall Mall, whence it was transferred to the Library on loan.

In 1977–78, the library of John Evelyn (1620–1706), virtuoso and diarist, was, despite attempts to preserve it (in which the Library participated), dispersed. Encouraged by gifts from outside bodies and individuals, the Library was able to rescue most of the books annotated and used by Evelyn, many in the handsome bindings that he commissioned for them: the 270 books thus preserved represent an important nucleus of one of the great 17th-century English libraries, as well as evidence of Evelyn's own diverse intellectual interests. In January 1978, the Minister for the Arts allocated to the British Library, in lieu of Estate Duty, the Blenheim Papers, comprising chiefly the papers of the 1st Duke and Duchess of Marlborough and their son-in-law the 3rd Earl of Sunderland, a political and social archive of incomparable importance. The Department of Manuscripts also acquired the manuscripts of Jane Austen's *Volume the Second* and George Bernard Shaw's *Heartbreak House*, the latter a notable addition to extensive holdings of one of the most famous users of the Library, whose bequest in 1950 of one-third of the royalties on his works has been transformed by the success of *My Fair Lady*.

The sale of the collection of Arthur Houghton in 1979–80 provided the Library with the chance to acquire a number of early English books so rare as to have escaped the collection hitherto. These include John Raynolds's *Dolarnys primerose* (1606), with its soliloquy on the skull, based on Hamlet's; the fine folio Bible (1629), bound by one of the foremost contemporary French bookbinders for George Thomason, the bookseller and collector of the Thomason tracts, was bought in 1982, and in the same year Dr Esmond de Beer presented a group of over 100 European travel books and guides from the early 16th to the mid-18th century. Two remarkable ephemeral pieces, recently acquired, are the only known copies of John Taylor the water poet's *The first part of the discourse held between the felt-hat, the beaver, French hood and black-bagge* (1639) and *A true and perfect description of the strange and wonderful she-elephant, sent from the Indies, which arrived at London, August 1 1683*.

The oriental collections have benefited from the dispersal of the Sassoon collection, receiving eight major Hebrew manuscripts, among them a 14th-century Spanish copy of Maimonides, *Moreh Nevukhim*, and acquiring others in the sale-room. Two remarkable Persian manuscripts came from the Marquess of Bute's collection, a 15th-century copy of the *Divan* of Hafiz with Mughal miniatures of scenes from daily life added *c.*1605 and *Hidayat arrami*, an illustrated treatise on archery composed for Husayn Shah, Sultan of Bengal, and copied in 1722. Some notable Arabic Mamluk manuscripts from the Levant, including a complete Qur'ān in a contemporary binding, have been acquired. The Dubosc collection has provided five early examples of Chinese wood-block printing. In Sanskrit, two fine Nepali tantric texts, both on black paper with vignettes of Buddhist deities, one dated 1185, have been acquired, with a notable Pali palm-leaf manuscript cover, the inner side illuminated, also 12th-century.

Two notable Armenian books have been acquired, the Breviary of King Leo II (*c.*1274) and (also from the Bute collection) the Gospels, written and illuminated at the Church of St George the General in Constantinople in 1695. A Samaritan scroll, 11th–12th century, a royal manuscript of the *Hitopadesa*, made at Uniara in 1761, a Japanese manuscript of the *Kanji-bon* chapter of the Lotus Sutra, illuminated in gold and silver and written in gold on purple dyed paper – all these have added notably to the variety and excellence of the oriental collections.

At the same time, the story has not been one of unqualified success. An immense amount of work, and not inconsiderable funds, specially raised, could not prevent two major treasures, the 13th-century World History of Rashid Al-Din, the earliest major Persian illuminated manuscript in the world, and the 'Codex Leicester', the only one of Leonardo da Vinci's

Above. Plate from Heideloff, *The Gallery of Fashion* (1774–1802)
C.106.K.16. Fig. 55.

Opposite, above. Opening from Mozart's thematic catalogue, his *Verseichnüss . . . aller meine werke . . .* Mozart entered details of his compositions from 1784 until his death in 1791.
Zweig MS 63, ff.28v.–29.

Opposite, below. Laurence Nowell's 'General description of England and Ireland', *c.*1564, is the first modern map of Britain. Nowell (shown at bottom left) was commissioned by William Cecil, later Lord Burghley, to produce the map, and Burghley was said to have always carried it with him.
Add. MS 62540.

OC. HIBERNICVS
OC. GERMANICVS
Mare Hibernicum

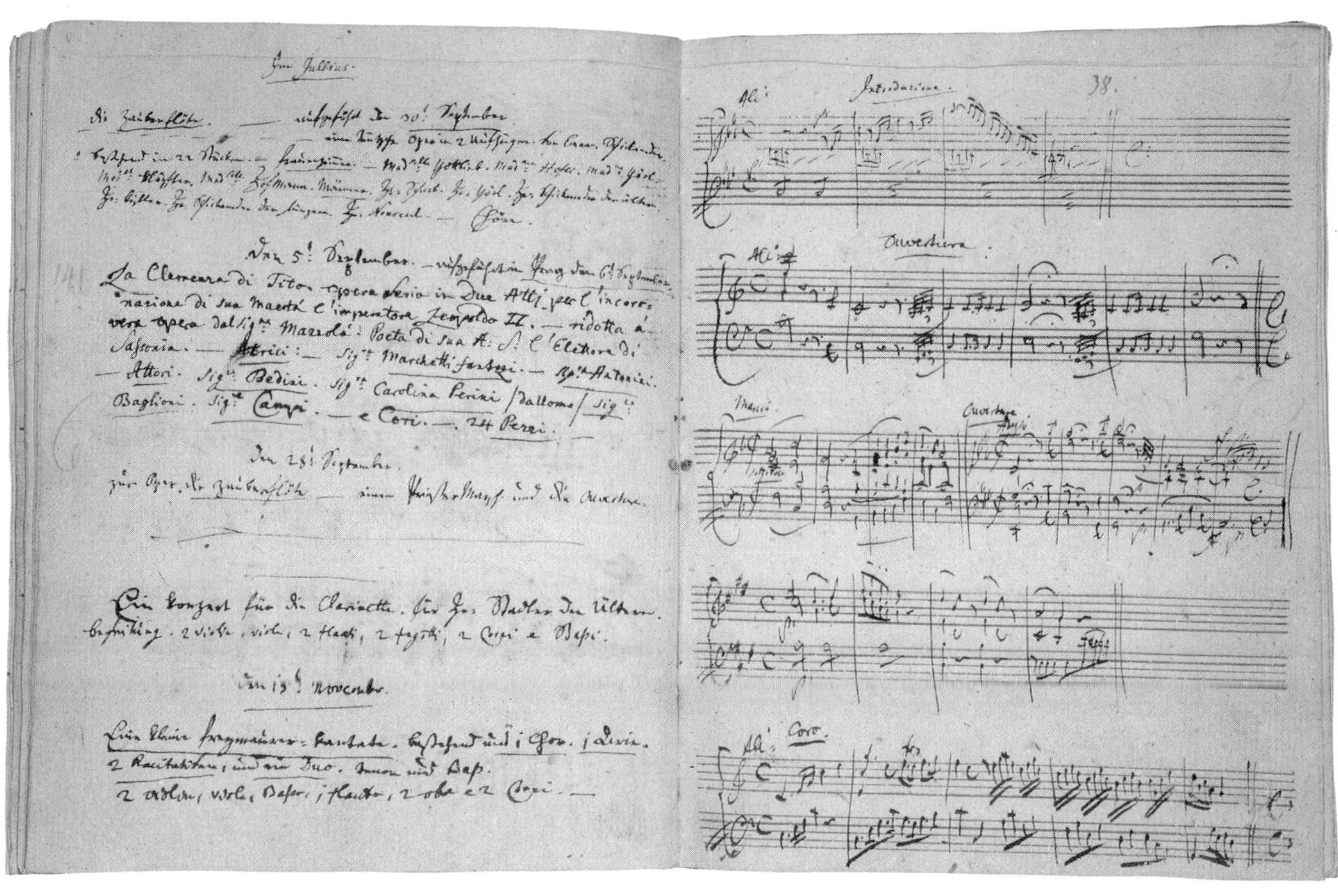

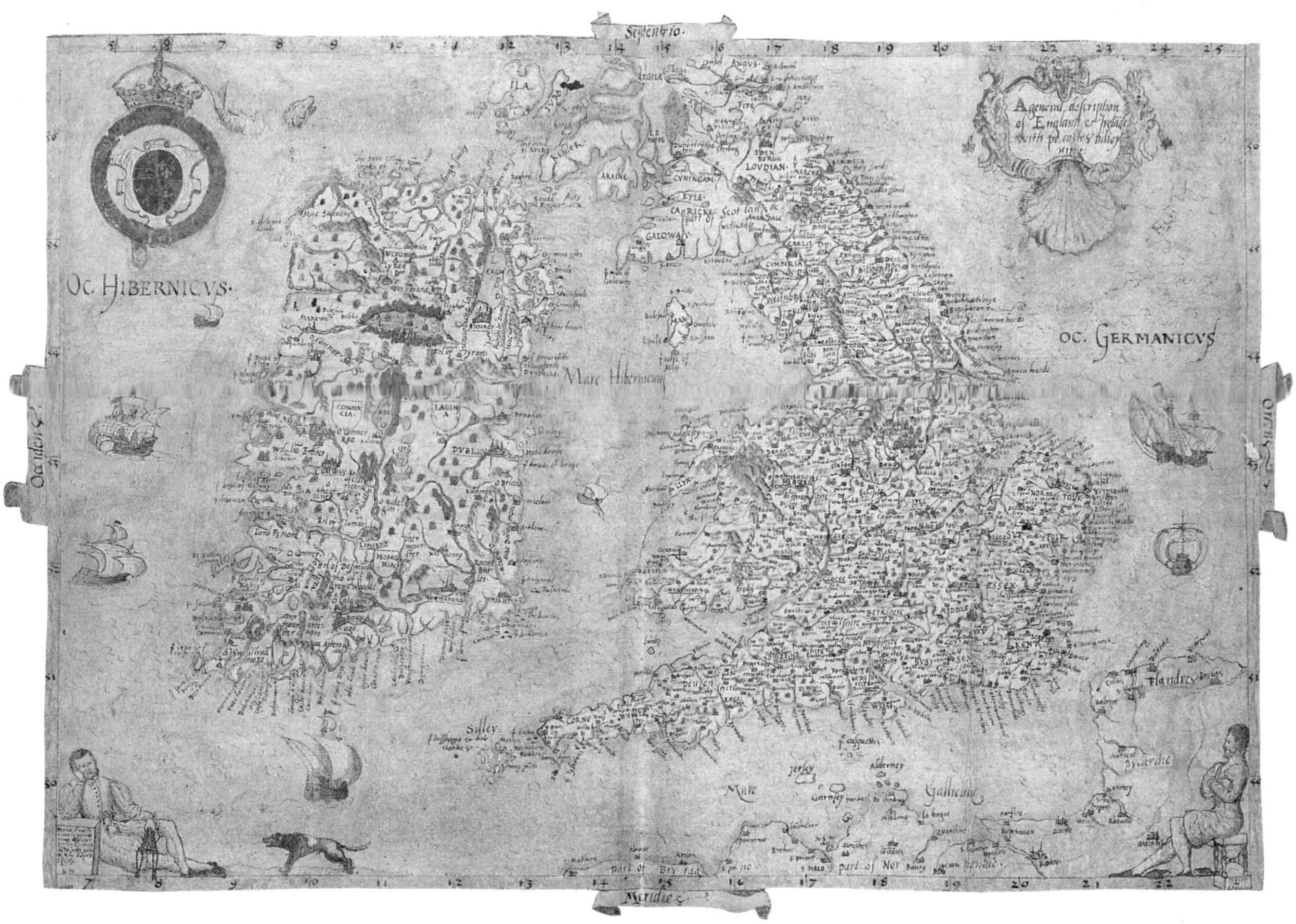

'The Cat who walked by himself', Rudyard Kipling's own illustration to his *Just So Stories*.
Add. MS 59840, ff.178.

illustrated notebooks in private hands, from leaving Britain, where they had been for many years. The National Collection of Contemporary Writers, an archive created by the funds provided in 1962 by the Pilgrim Trust and administered by the Arts Council, was brought to an untimely end in 1974. These setbacks are a sad diminution of the British literary heritage, as well as the Library's collections.

On the other hand, the recovery of a copy of Heideloff's *The Gallery of Fashion* (1794–1802), the most splendid of English costume books, to replace the copy destroyed during the Second World War, is a triumph. So too is the rescue of the unique manuscript of Thomas Traherne's *Commentaries of Heaven* from the burning rubbish-dump in Lancashire to which it had been consigned in 1967. It was acquired by the Library in 1984. The acquisition of the autograph manuscript of the *Just So Stories*, with the originals of the author's own wonderful illustrations, bequeathed by Kipling's daughter, of the original of Sassoon's *Memoirs of a Fox-hunting Man*, bought back from America in 1982, and of the *Book of Margery Kempe* – these are triumphs too. The arrival of two of the greatest English medieval manuscripts remaining in private hands – the Rutland Psalter, by purchase, and the Sherborne Missal, deposited on loan – enriches collections already rich. The Nowell-Burghley Atlas, *c.*1564–70, the joint work of Laurence Nowell and William Cecil, Lord Burghley, John Russell's lunar globe of 1787, and the copper plate for part of a wall map of England and Wales by Christopher Saxton, *c.*1580, are all new-found monuments of British cartography.

Besides these individual treasures, there have been acquisitions great in size as well as value. The 'Lord Chamberlain's Plays', copies of every play submitted for censorship by the Lord Chamberlain's office (up until 1968), has brought a prodigious increase to the Library's dramatic resources, while the archive of the Spencer family and others from Althorp complements the Blenheim archive. As we have seen in Chapters 5 and 11, the Government's decision to transfer the India Office Library and Records from the Foreign and Commonwealth Office to the British Library on 1 April 1982 added treasures on an even larger scale. It brought together two traditions in the maintenance of the national literary heritage which have run parallel without overlapping for almost two centuries. A year later, in 1983, the National Sound Archive, picturesque as well as sonorous, added a new diversity to the Library's collections (illustrated, p. 268).

But the greatest treasure among recent acquisitions is both a major collection in itself, as well as a set of individual items, every one of which is a treasure in its own right. On 9 May 1986, the Trustees of the Collection of Stefan Zweig, the Austrian poet, novelist and biographer, presented to the British Library their entire charge, part of which was already on loan to the Library. Of the 203 pieces, 131 were music manuscripts, 67 literary and political manuscripts and five printed books and music. They had been collected with a taste, acumen and sense of occasion hardly ever equalled. To those who know Zweig's work, his collection is the best possible portrait of the man; to those unfamiliar with it, this will be a monument to be remembered if ever work or author should be forgotten.

The full autograph score of a Bach cantata and two other pieces partly in his hand and part in his copyist's, notable pieces by Beethoven (not only scores but his diary for 1792–94), Brahms, Chopin, Debussy, Haydn (the full score of the Symphony no.97), Mahler and Strauss, are only a few of its musical treasures, which are dominated by the collections of Mozart (18 pieces, including full scores of the concerto for horn, K.447, and violin and piano, K.377, as well as letters, his thematic catalogue, and his marriage contract) and Wagner (27 pieces, of almost equal importance). The other manuscripts include important pieces of Goethe, Heine and Hölderlin, Nietzsche and Rilke (the last a present from the author), a play by Lope de Vega, part of Tolstoy's novella *The Kreutzer Sonata*, the proofs of Balzac's *Une*

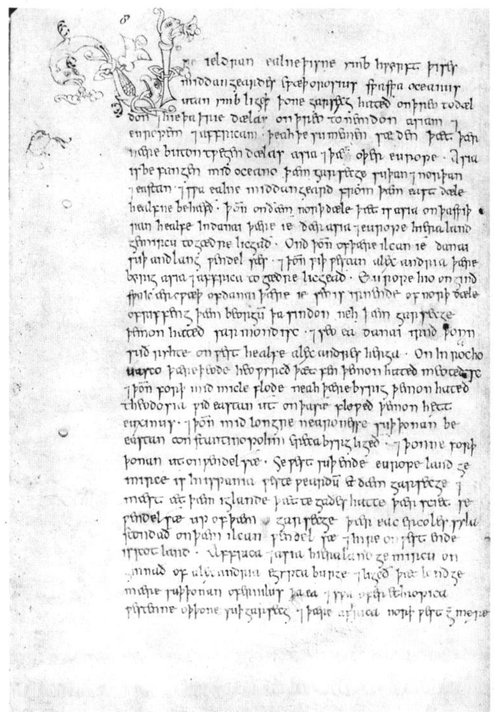

The Norse captain Ohthere's gift of a walrus ivory to King Alfred, recorded in a 10th-century copy of Orosius.
Add. MS 47967, f.5v.

Overleaf. Treasures of the National Sound Archive.

ténébreuse affaire, important poems by Baudelaire, Verlaine and Leopardi, part of Keats's corrected draft of 'I stood tiptoe upon a little hill', Shelley's sonnet on Byron, and – appropriately – Pope's poem 'To the Earl of Oxford upon a piece of News'. There is a substantial collection of Rimbaud's poems alongside the first edition of *Une saison en enfer*; the other printed books consist of the first editions of *Don Quixote* and Holbein's *Dance of Death*, and two collections of Schubert songs.

A collection that can command loyalties and affections that cross the boundaries of languages and continents – as does Zweig's, as does the British Library's – carries with it the duty of communication. A light under a bushel illuminates nothing. For the last 20 years, the Library has mounted a regular series of exhibitions in addition to its permanent displays, related to current events, acquisitions, centenaries, and so on. Some of them have already been mentioned; these and others have revealed new treasures in the Library to a host of visitors, while learned and vividly illustrated catalogues have made them yet more widely familiar. The Silver Jubilee exhibition in 1977 and the Drake Quatercentenary, the centenary of George Eliot, and the wonderful exhibition that commemorated the 1500th anniversary of the birth of St Benedict and the work of the Benedictine order, enlarged this sphere of the Library's activities.

The work of the Friends of the National Libraries, the Art of the Book in India, Japanese popular literature, 'The World Backwards' (based on the Library's remarkable holdings of Russian futurist books), Virgil and Karl Marx, all have been the basis of exhibitions and catalogues. Remarkable exhibitions of material from the library have gone to America, revealing its treasures of Renaissance book-painting or the history of Ralegh's first ill-fated colony in Virginia. 'The English Provincial Printer' has opened a window nearer home, the result of the important lead taken by the Library in recataloguing its 18th-century English holdings. 'The Mirror of the World' demonstrated the strength of its cartographic collections.

One of the most recent of these exhibitions (shared with the British Museum) was 'The Golden Age of Anglo-Saxon Art', which brought together the great library treasures of Oxford, Cambridge and elsewhere in England with those from further afield, such as the two great treasures from the Bibliothèque Municipale at Rouen, the Benedictional of Archbishop Robert and the Missal of Robert of Jumièges, as well as the Boulogne Gospels. The exhibition was visited by Her Majesty Queen Elizabeth II, thus envincing that royal interest in the bibliothecal treasures of Britain which has benefited the British Museum, and now the British Library, so much for more than two centuries. But it is a tradition which we can see stretching far further back, past the time of Queen Elizabeth I and Sir Robert Cotton, when the concept of a national library first took form, to the 9th and 10th centuries, when King Alfred translated Bede and Boethius, St Gregory and Orosius – the fine 10th-century copy of Orosius that came to the Library from Helmingham Hall records the Norse captain Ohthere's gift of a walrus ivory to Alfred, the subject of a famous poem by Kipling; when, too, during the reign of Aethelstan, the treasures with which we began our account came into being or to England. It is a tradition that stretches back over 1000 years of mischance and victory, of great losses offset by great gains. Now, as the British Library looks forward to a new life in a new building, may another millennium build on that foundation, with as many treasures and a more peaceful growth.

PHILIPS
SANYO
stereo
CONTEMPORARY LITERATURE ON TAPE
GRACE NICHOLS & SAMUEL SELVON
Konzertante
BAROCKMUSIK
Bach · Händel · Scarlatti
BOOSEY and HAWKES
RCA VICTOR
"HIS MASTER'S VOICE"
The Hallmark of Q
SYMPHON
DAT
R90
R120
METAL POWDER
JVC
CLOSER TO THE MUSICAL TRUTH

Index

Further Reading

1. General histories and biographies

ARUNDELL ESDAILE
The British Museum Library: a short history and survey (London, 1946).

EDWARD MILLER
That Noble Cabinet: A History of the British Museum (London, 1973).

J. MORDAUNT CROOK
The British Museum (London, 1972).

E. EDWARDS
Lives of the Founders of the British Museum (London, 1870).

EDWARD MILLER
Prince of Librarians. The Life and Times of Antonio Panizzi of the British Museum (Reissued, London, 1988).

G.R. DE BEER
Sir Hans Sloane and the British Museum (London, 1953).

ERIC ST J. BROOKS
Sir Hans Sloane: the great collector and his circle (London, 1954).

HAROLD B. CARTER
Sir Joseph Banks 1743–1820 (London, 1987)

ROGER LONSDALE
Dr Charles Burney: a literary biography (Reissued, Oxford, 1987).

HELEN R. SMITH
David Garrick, 1717–1779: a brief account (London, 1979).

KEVIN SHARPE
Sir Robert Cotton 1586–1631: History and Politics in Early Modern England (Oxford, 1979).

The Diary of Humfrey Wanley, edited by C.E. and R.C. Wright (London, 1966).

A.J. ARBERRY
The India Office Library: A historical sketch (Reprinted, London, 1967).

2. Aspects of the history of the collections

The Library of Sir Simonds D'Ewes, edited by A.G. Watson (London, 1966).

T.A. BIRRELL
The Library of John Morris: the reconstruction of a 17th century collection (London, 1976).

T.A. BIRRELL
English monarchs and their books: from Henry VII to Charles II (London, 1987).

C.E. WRIGHT
Fontes Harleiani (London, 1972).

The Lumley Library: the catalogue of 1609, edited by Sears Jayne and Francis R. Johnson (London, 1965).

A. HYATT KING
Printed Music in the British Museum (London, 1979).

A. HYATT KING
A Mozart Legacy. Aspects of the British Library Collections (London, 1984).

GEORGE M. KARHL and DOROTHY ANDERSON
The Garrick Collection of Old English Plays (London, 1982).

A.H. CHAPLIN
GK. 150 years of the General Catalogue of Printed Books of the British Museum. (Aldershot, 1987).

3. Exhibition catalogues

Recent catalogues include:

The Golden Age of Anglo-Saxon Art 966–1066, edited by Janet Backhouse, D.H. Turner and Leslie Webster (London, 1984).

Buddhism, edited by W.Zwalf (London, 1985).

Renaissance Painting in Manuscript: treasures from the British Library, edited by Thomas Kren (New York and London, 1983).

4. Illustrated introductions to the collections

The British Library. The Reference Division Collections (Reprinted, London, 1986).

JANET BACKHOUSE
Book of Hours (London, 1985).

FRANCES WOOD
Chinese Illustration (London, 1985).

DAVID GOLDSTEIN
Hebrew Manuscript Painting (London, 1985).

JOHN WESTMANCOAT
Newspapers (London, 1985).

HILTON KELLIHER and SALLY BROWN
English Literary Manuscripts (London, 1986).

JOHN BARR
Illustrated Children's Books (London, 1986).

J.P. LOSTY
Indian Book Painting (London, 1986).

MIRJAM FOOT
Pictorial Bookbinding (London, 1986).

ARTHUR SEARLE
Music Manuscripts (London, 1987).

ANN PAYNE
Views of the Past: Topographical drawings in the British Library (London, 1987).

R.F. SCHOOLLEY-WEST
Stamps (London, 1987).

ANDREW PRESCOTT
English Historical Documents (London, 1988).

YU-YING BROWN
Japanese Book Illustration (London, 1988).

MORNA DANIELS
Victorian Book Illustration (London, 1988).

5 Other illustrated books

P.R. HARRIS
The Reading Room (Reprinted, London, 1986).

RAY DESMOND
Wonders of Creation. Natural History Drawings in the British Library (London, 1986).

JANET BACKHOUSE
The Lindisfarne Gospels (Oxford, 1979).

NORAH TITLEY
Persian Miniature Painting and its influence on the art of the Turkey and India. The British Library Collections (London, 1983).

G.R.C. DAVIS
Magna Carta (Revised edition, London 1985).

6 Department Guides

M.A.E. NICKSON
The British Library: Guide to the catalogues and indexes of the Department of Manuscripts (2nd edition, London, 1982).

J.H. GOODACRE and A.P. PRITCHARD
Guide to the Department of Oriental Manuscripts and Printed Books (London, 1977).

S.C. SUTTON
A Guide to the India Office Library, with a note on the India Office Records (2nd edition, London, 1971).

MARTIN MOIR
General Guide to the India Office Records (London, 1988).